Getting Paid For Exports

Getting Paid
For Exports

A Guide To More Profitable Management Of Export Credit And Finance

Burt Edwards F.I.C.M., F.I.Ex.

Gower

First published in 1980 by Shaws Linton Publications Ltd.

Reprinted 1983, 1984 by Gower Publishing Company Ltd.

Second edition published 1990 by
Gower Publishing Company Limited
Gower House
Croft Road
Aldershot
Hants GU11 3HR
England

Gower Publishing Company
Old Post Road
Brookfield
Vermont 05036
USA

British Library Cataloguing in Publication Data
Edwards, Burt
   Getting paid for exports: a guide to more profitable
   management of export credit and finance. – 2nd ed.
   1. Great Britain. Exports. Financing
   I. Title
   382'.6'0941

ISBN 0566 02740 2

Printed in Great Britain by
Dotesios Printers Ltd, Trowbridge, Wiltshire

Contents

Illustrations

Checklists

Foreword

'Business involves taking risks; good management tries to shorten the odds'
– G.H. Sharman

At last, British industry has woken up to the fact that exporting is not just a good idea for overcoming a slump in the home market, not a quick solution to surplus domestic stocks, but is a special form of trading that needs special expertise and planning over a very wide range of topics and techniques. That awakening has also brought the realization that the export trade contains risks and costs which do not exist in the domestic market, not least the effect on expected profit of waiting to be paid. The keystone of this quite superb manual is profitability and the author shows how expert management of Export Debtor exposure can prevent the erosion of planned returns on the capital invested in credit.

All too often we see a division, almost a rivalry, between the Sales and Credit functions, when ideally they should be complementary. The Export Salesman may go off on foreign trips full of product knowledge and market information yet be quite unbriefed on the financial considerations affecting his selling activity. The Credit Manager may be overly concerned with cash collection performance and therefore 'plays it safe' with restrictive credit terms and strident collection routines. The result, all too often, is to have confused customers, contractual errors, and inaccurate documents, all the very elements that lead to payment delay and profit erosion. Mutual communication is essential to bring together the commercial and financial effects, so that better profits result.

Above all, professional credit management means being commercially orientated, anxious to 'make a business', to support the sales ambitions but at the same time to add a degree of financial prudence to the inherent optimism of sales staff. This requires a very real understanding of risk assessment and of its essential link with the payment conditions on the client.

By its very nature, exporting means that the Credit/Finance Manager must have a sound working knowledge of currency operations and the foreign exchange market. The days of exporting only in Sterling almost as of imperial right have long gone. Today we see many more considerations as Sterling strengthens or weakens against other major currencies. Skill and knowledge are essential for minimizing the risk of exchange loss whilst using the marketing tactic of selling in the customer's own currency.

One of the major problems with export credit is that, for most of us, human frailty makes it quite impossible to retain all the information sources available and to remember all the routines essential to a proper financial management, so we require some compendium, easily referenced, to provide the answers. No matter how large or small our business, we still need checklists for in-house routines, addresses of useful organizations, to know what help we can get from government and the banks, the Incoterms definition of, e.g. FOB, the advantages and costs of financing export debts, and so on.

Happily, this most excellent of books provides the answers to all these questions and to many more. Throughout my long career in the practice of credit management, I have read a wide variety of books on the subject and related matters. Never have I been privileged to read one so totally complete, so very informative over the whole spectrum of its title or so stylishly and amusingly written. It was a pleasure to read a text-book that frequently brought a wry smile. Burt Edwards, its expert author, is to be most heartily congratulated.

Hopefully, this book will be read carefully by everyone concerned with exporting as its relevance extends far beyond that of the credit department alone. It is in fact all about 'shortening the odds'. Would that it had been published thirty years ago when I would have made far fewer mistakes when learning the hard way.

Gratefully,

W.V. (Bill) Adams, FICM, MIEx
former Council Member – Institute of Export
Vice-President – Institute of Credit Management

1 Some introductory thoughts

'Exporting is fun', we heard from our politicians in the sixties, as they exhorted more British firms to start exporting.

Far from being 'fun', exporting is deadly serious, both for companies and nations. In the austere fifties, Chancellor of the Exchequer Sir Stafford Cripps said 'Export or die', in the context of post-war recovery; and in the seventies, President Richard Nixon predicted the impending record US foreign debt when he said: 'we must master world trade before it masters us'. Sadly he was too late and subsequent administrations have mortgaged the future of young America by borrowing massively from abroad to balance the government's cash flow.

It is interesting that in 1660, Charles II formed the 'Councell of Trade', forerunner of the Board of Trade and DTI, with a list of twelve commandments, item 7 of which stated 'you are seriously to arrange that the importacion of forreigne commodities do not overballance ye exportacions of such as are native'. A wise approach three hundred years ago, and even more necessary today!

The awful international debt crisis has stayed unresolved since 1982 because some 150 of the world's 204 nations are in permanent net debtor positions, that is, they are permanent net importers with growing populations. They are thus unlikely ever to be able to repay past billions and have to ration severely their current imports and hard currency payments for them. One result is that competition has intensified to sell more to the remaining few markets which are able to buy more and remit foreign exchange, mainly in Western Europe and North America.

The profitability of exporting companies has been hit by the cost of borrowing at high interest rates to finance the credit periods and delays of exports. Experienced exporters have observed that export cash has become slower in recent years and the Days Sales Outstanding Ratio, or collection period, is usually longer for export sales than for home trade business.

Trade expansion within the UK has been so weak in recent times, particularly in the manufacturing sector, that increasing numbers of British companies each year have sought foreign orders for the first time. The BOTB commissioned the 1987 Bannock Report to examine the exporting potential of small and medium-sized companies and find out the apparent barriers. The report, called 'Into Active Exporting', makes extremely interesting reading, and concludes that the biggest disappointment and deterrent by far is 'Finance/Delays in Payment'.

Payment difficulties in foreign trade are very real. Large companies employ specialist Credit or Finance Managers, so that adequate time and brain-power can be applied to the task. Smaller companies cannot afford such luxury, yet are still exposed to the same risks.

An exporting company invests a large part of its capital to support credit allowed to customers. The dividend on the investment is simply the profit on each sale. The investment period begins when the first cost is incurred (pricing? quoting? advance marketing?); it lasts throughout the production, delivery and credit period phases, and only matures when the proceeds are actually received into the firm's bank account. The planned Return On Investment is eroded by unplanned payments delays and totally lost when the expense of borrowing exceeds the margin on the sale. Actual bad debts not only lose the margin on those sales but also on many other, innocent, transactions.

The UK national average net profit margin is around 5% of sales. The true figure for exports alone is not available, mainly because costs cannot always be allocated between home and export sales. However, it is fair to assume that exports are less profitable than home sales because of all the extra costs and delays, so an export margin lower than 5% is extremely fragile and vulnerable to unmanaged costs.

The focal point for exports must be profitability, not turnover alone. There is no point in going flat out for sales growth if the result is to suffer losses which drain the firm's home trade profits. Export pricing has the double-edged sword effect of having to be competitive yet take account of all true costs – not just the interest on borrowings for export credit, but also the costs of commissions and fees, documents, shipping and customs charges, and the many external services, such as business information, credit insurance and specific finance.

The approach of the single European market of 1992 means a radical reappraisal of credit terms and conditions. Already, in any country, exporters have to compete with credit allowed by foreign and local suppliers. Fiercer competition in a single market atmosphere in the EEC will, no doubt, encourage a standardization to longer credit arrangements and the resultant effects on profit and cash flow. Many firms have already established policies to cope, putting a greater duty onto local agents and associate companies to act promptly.

Managing export credit really means making sure of getting paid the intended price on the intended date. This rather basic statement, in practice, requires somebody to oversee or influence all the company activities which affect that achievement. It is for individual companies to decide exactly where, for them, the task of managing export credit should begin.

More and more companies employ professionally qualified credit managers and unless a firm is too small to afford any specialists, it rarely makes sense to load credit responsibility onto either sales or accounting staff. A good export credit manager will bridge that critical gap between commercial and financial priorities, and build the necessary fund of other skills, such as in legal, shipping, banking and documentation areas. The specialist qualifications for those making a career in international credit are membership of two bodies, the Institute of Credit Management and the Institute of Export .

Most of the booklets available from banks and export services agencies, whilst very clear and helpful, have allegiances to the sponsoring organizations. This book covers the range of export credit functions as seen from the desk of a corporate manager or businessman. Its first edition in 1979 was the first comprehensive guide to UK export credit management. Its aim is still to help speed up cash flow and minimize the risk of reduced or lost profit, yet recognizing the pressures of sales growth and company politics.

Each chapter has detailed sections on separate features of export credit and a large number of checklists have been provided. Thus, the book is a training guide for those learning export skills, a working guide for experienced managers, and a source of reference for all.

2 Export credit policy

The need for a planned approach

There are two good reasons for applying senior management effort to the investment of capital in credit for export sales

1. Uncontrolled export selling and/or credit granting produces unplanned costs which erode the hard-earned profit in the rest of the business

    and, more positively,

2. The specific identification of solvent, growing customers and markets helps sales staff to find more profitable business.

Surveys by business information companies have shown that companies with significant exports generally have slower debtor/sales ratios and higher borrowing ratios than non-exporting companies. Being relatively less competitive, their market share is at risk and they are more vulnerable to re-organization, acquisition, or insolvency.

Delayed cash is not available for further profitable use in the business and exporters carry a higher risk of bad debt losses, since the longer a debt is unpaid, the greater the chance of it never being paid! The interest cost of overdues is usually at least 10 times bad debt losses and may alone make the export activity unprofitable.

Sales development of customers and markets is expensive and takes time. Exporters usually prefer strong, growing customers in countries where sales increase is possible. Resources are wasted when applied blindly to product design and marketing for weak customers or for countries where imports are likely to be restricted.

Getting paid nearer to due dates requires several activities:

● Checking customers and markets before and during trading;

- The right payment terms and credit periods, to match varying degrees of knowledge and trust;
- Cost-effective external services, especially financing;
- Trained staff;

and not least,

- Collecting debts promptly through the banking system.

Having said that the key word for exporting is profitability, the key requirement for profitability is to *focus management attention on generating cash.* Increasing cash flow allows less time for risks to mature, it reduces interest expense and makes more cash available for other needs.

While export sales staff are putting skill and expense into getting orders, there is often a quite separate operation whereby the finance function arranges the large borrowings to fund the company between production and customers' payments. Better co-ordination and planning can improve the time of borrowing and reduce its expense.

Apart from poor balance sheet ratios that disturb lenders, the expense of financing waiting periods and the cost of actual bad debts significantly reduce available profits. Even with ECGD cover, the 10% self-retention can exceed the net profit these days. These disappointing effects frequently delay or postpone company expansion.

The lesson learned usually the hard way by exporters is not to compete with credit terms, nor lead a credit race or a terms auction. Sales competition should be all about price, delivery, quality and service, but not cash. Cash is life-blood, and the shortest possible cash base is needed at the outset because of all the delays occurring later.

A vital step is to have a *senior managerial link* between Sales and Finance. Large exporters nowadays have professional credit managers, or trade-orientated treasurers, with authority to influence sales decisions to benefit overall profit. Their task is to operate the techniques required, influence sales towards low risk customers and countries, and filter out for special treatment those with a poor return after interest expense. Despite their offers of comprehensive services, banks cannot do these things for exporters. They involve the daily hurly-burly in the office and sometimes the involvement at short notice of senior management.

Exporting involves credit risk; credit risk affects collectability of sales; and delays cost dearly. Between order-taking and cash receipt, there is a jungle of problem situations, where efficiency increases profit and slackness erodes it. A planned policy is needed.

The role of top management

The balance sheet and P & L items most directly affected by allowing customers time to pay are the Debtors, or Receivables asset, the related form of finance, profit on sales and interest expense.

Ideally, exporting companies would calculate their planned sales, apply the agreed credit terms per customer, then arrive at a Debtors figure for each month ahead, thus projecting the required borrowings and interest cost. In the real world, most companies sell first, then try to collect the proceeds. Whilst some companies have ample borrowing powers, others feel the strain if the Debtors asset, normally the largest on the balance sheet, is too large in relation to sales.

Despite the many different kinds of businesses and the wide range of profit margins, the common requirement for all exporters is to *make sure that sales turn into cash at the planned rate.*

That requires a plan of some kind and also the authority delegated by the Board to an executive to achieve the plan.

In particular, exporting companies should have the following set-up:

- A written *policy statement* on granting credit to customers.
- *Corporate Objectives,* varying from time to time, for the levels of Debtors to Sales, Bad Debt losses and related expenses.
- *Detailed targets* for individuals at the working level.
- *Monthly results,* reported in a brief usable style.
- *Action meetings,* monthly, to review results and take action to control major problems and trends.

The recognized sequence of events operated at Board level and by all affected departments, especially Sales, Credit and Production should be to *plan – measure – review – improve,* month after month, reliably and consistently.

Factors affecting export credit policy

Payment terms

These involve *time* and *security.* Policy should be to allow the terms that are normal for the market, but the customer may demand longer or less secure terms, or salesmen or agents may concede them to 'get the business'. Demands should always be quantified in terms of cost and, if necessary, converted into price or other concessions instead. Changing security of terms needs special decisions which may be affected by country risks.

Country risks

Political and economic risks, especially of soft and weak currencies; the inability of central banks to generate hard currency at due date; exchange losses if local currency is accepted; cancellation by governments of orders or import licences; foreign attitudes to trade with UK; the availability of ECGD cover; the ability to get letters of credit confirmed in London; etc, etc.

It is good practice to allocate simple risk codes such as A,B, or C and use in credit policy for marketing and payment terms.

Credit worthiness of customers

Can they pay *on time?* Will they become *insolvent* during the life of the contract or the expected business? Is *development* justified? Policy should be to: obtain reports for credit exposure; obtain ECGD cover where needed; apply secure terms to high-risk customers; shorten credit periods to reduce perceived risks.

Pricing of costs after ex-works

Selling terms such as FOB or FAS involve transport, packing and documentation costs. C + F, CIF and others also involve onward costs.

Policy should be not to rely on lump sums or percentages, but to calculate or estimate costs before quoting or confirming orders; be clear on pricing at quotation stage, since add-ons lead to disputes which delay payment and increase risks.

Pricing of credit period

Standard prices may assume, say, 30 days credit. The 'credit period' for pricing is the total DSO experienced between shipment and cash receipt, including all delays, especially those of foreign bank remittances. 60 day terms may result in 120 days or more waiting time. Policy should be to include the cost of credit in prices at the forecast interest rate, say 1% per month for the full actual DSO. (If uncosted, the 120 days experience on 60 days terms can mean 2% off the bottom-line.)

Sterling value

The exporter expects 100% payment. At sterling prices, the customer has a currency risk, i.e, how much of his own currency to find several months after placing the order. He may not have a forward FX market. This may lead to delays or deductions. (A disputed invoice can mean three months delay before payment, i.e. 3% off the bottom line.)

If pricing is made more attractive to customers by quoting and invoicing in their own currencies, the cost of hedging (e.g. by selling receipts forward) can usually be built in.

Marketing in non-creditworthy markets

Glamorous or traditional countries should not be marketed at great expense when there is little possibility of prompt payment. Policy should be to avoid commitment to non-creditworthy business by unauthorized staff; and to avoid loose verbal commitments regarded by customers as legally binding.

Authority to non-financial staff

So that the wrong staff do not give commitments on prices, terms or other conditions which may incur losses or penalties, be clear on who can authorize what and have a checklist approach to confirming orders. Use escape clauses during visits, if need be, e.g. 'subject to written confirmation within 14 days'.

Local representation

The agent or local representative's specific duties are risk items. If orders taken locally commit the company to a contract, ensure that credit checks are made, with recommendations as to risk and terms.

A complete agreement should be devised which gives the agent local prestige and freedom of action, but obliges him to meet required terms and conditions and also to make personal contact with customers at any time as needed, to achieve acceptance of drafts, to collect or enforce payment on due dates, or follow up bank activity. The equitable control is to pay commission only when the sale is complete, i.e. when the exporter is paid.

Customer contact

The secret of good export credit management is *immediacy*. The cost of a problem causing a delay is at least 1% per month. All customer contact should be with a known person, either direct from UK or by the local agent. It is cheaper to telephone than to wait for a postal reply that has not even been sent. It is cheaper to take a plane to visit than bear the interest expense on a very large overdue account, or worse, the cost of a bad debt incurred through inactivity after due date.

Contract conditions

Buyers' purchase conditions should be checked on receipt and challenged if unacceptable, particularly penalty clauses for late deliveries and defects. Exporters' conditions should supersede buyers' ones and be governed by English law, with arbitration allowed for. Retention of Title should be agreed wherever possible. Progress payments should be requested where high costs are incurred before shipment date. Charges for contract cancellation should be defined. Clauses should be inserted for interest on late payments and for exchange shortfalls to be the customers' responsibility.

Documentation

This must always meet order requirements, otherwise security may be lost, e.g. on a letter of credit. Bills of exchange need expert attention at all stages of processing. Somebody in the credit area should be responsible for assembling all documents needed for payment.

Expertise of staff

It is usually better to avoid mixing staff on home and export duties, as this may lead to preference for familiar home trade tasks and neglect of export dates or actions. Export expertise is best built up on concentrated daily experience. It is better to reallocate duties to separate home and export people, or if there are not enough people to do that, to allocate special times for export work.

Credit approval of orders

It is essential to identify undercapitalized buyers, slow payers and difficult customers who deliberately introduce minor problems to delay large payments.

Some countries have exchange controls or hard currency shortages. Credit assessment should be made at the earliest stage to avoid wasted effort. Orders should be confirmed only after credit has been approved as a justified investment. The assessment process must be quick but allow for compromises. Ways must be found of saying 'yes' rather than rejecting any order. (This may mean splitting shipments, changing terms, some fast telephoning or a visit, using finance bodies, etc.) The use of credit limits must allow for orders in the pipeline. Good advance analysis allows fast order decisions. Automatic approval can be given for small orders. ECGD conditions must be followed to preserve cover. Good credit drills allow the factory to go ahead with confidence.

Bank collection efficiency

To reduce problems of bank 'float-time' on international payments, use should be made of the ICC Uniform Rules for Collections which lay down responsibilities for exporter, customer and bank. Prompt advices of draft acceptances followed by prompt collection advice should be insisted upon with the bank. Track records on collections should be studied and different banks used, according to their specialization in certain countries. Banks have to be pressurized from time to time to improve their performance, based on unsatisfactory cases. Consideration should be given to sending collections direct to foreign banks, especially where there is a local agent. Use should be made of the fact that banks compete for collection work.

Open account collections

It makes sense to try to find out the bank to be used by a buyer and give to both buyer and bank the exact details of the exporter's bank name, address, sort code and account number to receive transfers.

Policy should be to insist on TTs or telex transfers, paying cable fees if needed (cheaper than delays). Copies of all open account invoices should always be sent to local agents who should be instructed to telex advice of payments sent or reasons why not. Close contact should be kept with the bank for news of receipts and payment details used to follow up delays. Excessive bank delays justify claims on the responsible bank for interest.

Selection of financing options

The method of finance should match the waiting period and the risk. The aim should be to get the fastest cash onto the balance sheet at the lowest cost. It is usually inefficient to tie up the overdraft for export credit. Foreign currency risks are best hedged by being financed by Eurocurrency loans. Interest rates are those of the currency country, usually cheaper than sterling. Alternatively, expected currency can be sold forward, i.e. the sterling value fixed at the date of contract or shipment.

Return on investment

Planning future export receivables requires disciplines to be imposed on other company activities, e.g. sales policies needs to decide:

- Can we afford to sell into that market with its weak currency?
- Can we compete effectively on our existing credit terms?
- Are we competently represented locally for all eventualities?
- Do we do all the right things when taking orders?

There are three basic 'attitude' questions to be considered:

- Does it matter if customers pay late?
- Do overdues affect profit performance?
- Do bad debts affect company health?

Does it matter if customers pay late, as long as they pay? (this question is heard from time to time, along with 'don't worry about XYZ Ltd, they'll pay in the end, they're all right!')

The answer is that exporters need cash on time, to avoid the cost of extra borrowings needed when excess receivables are created by slow payers. The Return on Investment ratio used by banks, lenders and analysts judges the efficiency of an exporter in managing his total assets. Faster collections doubly benefit the ROI by:

(a)   Increasing the 'Return' by reducing interest costs;
and
(b)   Reducing the 'Investment' by reducing receivables.

It is vital to maintain the shortest possible credit base in export receivables, both for ROI reasons and to avoid encouraging an international credit race, whereby firms compete with longer and longer credit terms and subsequently run out of cash.

The following example illustrates how a company progressed after producing a credit policy. The third column indicates what might have happened if they had continued in the old, unplanned way.

Example

£	Actual 1980	Actual 1986	1986 @ 1980 DSO Level
Export Sales	8 million	14 million	14 million
Net Profit (Return)	400 000 (5%)	840 000 (6%)	506 000 (3.6%)
Assets (Investments)	6 million	8 million	10.2 million
Export Receivables	2 740 000	2 570 000	4 795 000
Days Sales Outstanding	125	67	125
Return on Investment	6.7%	10.5%	5.0%

Sales growth over six years was good but if customers in 1986 still took the 125 days to pay as in 1980, export receivables would be £4 795 000. Borrowed finance at 15% per annum in 1986, on extra receivables of £2 225 000, would have cost an extra £334 000, leaving a profit of only £506 000 or 3.6% on sales, and a ROI of only 5.0%. Cost pressures in later years could even reduce net profit to a point where the receivables level of 1980 would produce a loss.

Do overdues affect profit performance?

A company borrowing at 15% per annum and producing 5% net profit makes a loss when debts are four months overdue (see Figure 2.1). With borrowings at 18% and profits at 3% losses are incurred at only two months overdue! The export credit manager can use the chart to show when the overdue period, according to borrowing rates and profit margins, produces a loss on sale. Figure 2.2 shows the interest cost of credit as a flat percentage of sales value.

The policy on payment arrangements should address this profit drain.

Do bad debts affect company health?

Although the major profit leak comes from slow-payments rather than bad debts, any bad debts at all place a heavy burden on the sales department to replace the profit level.

An exporter with a 5% net profit margin, who suffers a bad debt of £10 000, must sell a further £200 000 to regain the lost £10 000 just to stand still. Pity the poor salesmen!

Figure 2.1   How To Measure When Overdue Cancel Profit

Net Margin	1%	2%	3%	4%	5%	8%	10%	12%	15%
Cost of Borrowing pa									
10%	1.2	2.4	3.6	4.8	6.0	9.6	12.0	14.4	18.0
11%	1.1	2.2	3.3	4.4	5.5	8.7	10.9	13.1	16.4
12%	1.0	2.0	3.0	4.0	5.0	8.0	10.0	12.0	15.0
15%	0.8	1.6	2.4	3.2	4.0	6.4	8.0	9.6	12.0
18%	0.7	1.3	2.0	2.7	3.3	5.3	6.7	8.0	10.0
20%	0.6	1.2	1.8	2.4	3.0	4.8	6.0	7.2	9.0

Period in months after which profit is absorbed

Method:
Find column across for rate of profit on sales.
Align with current borrowing rate on left.
Meeting point shows where interest expense cancels profit.

Figure 2.2   The Cost of Financing Credit Taken as a Flat Percentage of Sales Value

	Rates for Borrowing Funds (per annum)					
Credit Taken (days)	10% per annum	12% per annum	14% per annum	16% per annum	18% per annum	20% per annum
30	0.8	1.0	1.2	1.3	1.5	1.6
60	1.7	2.0	2.3	2.7	3.0	3.4
90	2.5	3.0	3.5	4.0	4.5	5.0
120	3.3	4.0	4.7	5.3	6.0	6.6
150	4.2	5.0	5.8	6.7	7.5	8.4
180	5.0	6.0	7.0	8.0	9.0	10.0
210	5.8	7.0	8.2	9.3	10.5	11.6
240	6.7	8.0	9.4	10.7	12.0	13.4
270	7.5	9.0	10.5	12.0	13.5	15.0
300	8.3	10.0	11.7	13.3	15.0	16.6
330	9.2	11.0	12.8	14.7	16.5	18.4
360	10.0	12.0	14.0	16.0	18.0	20.0

To use chart: Select credit taken period on left.
Move across to column headed with current cost of borrowing funds. The resulting figure is the percentage of the sale value eroded by interest.

Note: 'Credit Taken' consists of entire period from recording sale to receipt of funds into bank.
It can be roughly calculated as Total Sales ÷ Receivables × 365.

Example: If customers take 120 days' credit on average, and the company borrows at 16% per annum, then credit costs are 5.3% of the sale value.

Figure 2.3 shows various loss effects.

The calculations in Figures 2.1, 2.2, and 2.3 show the need for an investment approach to export credit, and demonstrate the difference between the outdated way of just selling and the progressive way of managing export sales risks, collectability of cash and net profit.

Figure 2.3   Extra Sales Needed to Recover Bad Debt Losses

Bad Debt Loss	£100	£500	£1 000	£5 000	£20 000	£50 000
Net Margin						
1%	10 000	50 000	100 000	500 000	2 000 000	5 000 000
2%	5 000	25 000	50 000	250 000	1 000 000	2 500 000
3%	3 333	16 666	33 333	166 666	666 666	1 666 666
4%	2 500	12 500	25 000	125 000	500 000	1 250 000
5%	2 000	10 000	20 000	100 000	400 000	1 000 000
8%	1 250	6 250	12 500	62 500	250 000	625 000
10%	1 000	5 000	10 000	50 000	200 000	500 000
15%	667	3 333	6 666	33 333	133 333	333 333

Planning receivables

The level of investment can be planned a long time ahead, in most businesses, by combining the planned sales with the average export days sales outstanding (DSO). This can be for each month-end, for each market or organizational region, and by customer if necessary. In other words, sales value x average DSO at a given future date will reveal the total debtor value to be financed.

Similarly, probable interest costs can be computed, by taking the future debtor level x the expected cost of borrowing.

In planning or budgeting export receivables it makes sense to combine the marketing and credit knowledge. This is the time for each function to persuade each other of its priorities and needs. Figure 2.4 suggests some useful steps in budgeting receivables.

Figure 2.4   Key Stages for Budgeting Receivables

(i)	Discuss the credit and marketing assumptions at a very early stage.
(ii)	Obtain the sales plan for the period involved, with as much detail as possible of:

        customers within countries
        sales by month
        product margins if terms differ.

(iii)   Apply existing DSO period to each customer or country (estimate DSO from experience, for new customers or countries).

(iv)   Calculate period-end receivables balances for each customer, country, region or just total exports by counting back sales value for period of DSO.

(v)   Calculate any other details required for budget, e.g. overdues, disputed debt levels, interest costs, ECGD premium, etc.

(vi)   Make a top-level company decision on acceptance of the budget. (If levels are too high or unbalanced, this is the time to amend sales plans, rather than just prior to delivery.)

Budget assumptions

You have probably been exporting for some time. (If not, talk to a contact who has.) It is likely that people in marketing and in credit have views about customers and countries such as good, bad, efficient, slow, growing, declining and so on. Now do the following:

- Agree a date for an intensive discussion between marketing and credit.
- Write down the countries to which you sell.
- List the customers or planned customers in each country.
- Make a note of present sales, payment terms and experience.
- Pull out the files of economic views of each country, or get hold of regularly published bank bulletins.
- Get the marketing man to indicate sales trends for the next year.
- Notate expected changes in payment terms.

You now have a useful document which can be circulated to general management for comment and held for the next budget stage.

Sales plan

Insist that by, say, November, your company produces its export sales plan for the following year. It may only be approximate, or may only be detailed for 75% of sales, but it is essential for planning export finance. Try to pin down the sales manager to analyse the sales into months, into countries, into customers and, if credit terms differ by product, into product groups.

Compare the sales plan with the 'assumptions' made earlier and discuss any major variations.

If there is not even a sales plan for exports, the need for a receivables investment budget can encourage sales/marketing staff to develop their own planning.

Apply DSO periods

Now comes the tricky part. If the DSO technique is not already in use, start it now, as follows:

● Decide if you are going to budget receivables by each customer, each country or just total exports.
● Take existing data from the sales ledger for receivables and sales for previous 12 months.
● For each month, take receivables balance and by counting-back sales made, see how many days of sales value are represented by the receivables balance. Remember to use total sales, not just those unpaid.

Example

Export	Receivables: December 31st	£4 250 000	
	December sales	£1 375 000	(31 days)
		£2 875 000	
	November sales	£1 200 000	(30 days)
		£1 675 000	
	October sales	£1 400 000	(31 days)
		£275 000	
	September sales (£1 650 000)	£275 000	(5/30 days)
Total Days of Sales	Outstanding:	—	97 days

● You may think your terms average, say, 60 days, but this shows that customers did not pay for an average of 97 days. If this level is consistent and if you have done nothing significant to speed up payments, it is only sensible to use this level to plan future receivables.
● In case there are seasonal variations, it is better to calculate DSO periods for several different months.

Calculate total receivables value

By taking recent actual DSO periods, it is now possible to apply the ratio to the planned sales for each customer, country or total, to arrive at intended receivables balances for future months.

This produces the probable month-end balance that must be financed by bank overdraft or other loans. If the finance is interest bearing, the cost can now be budgeted.

Example

	1988 DSO Results (days)	1988 Planned Sales (£000's)	1989 Planned Receivables (£000's)
January	92	1400	3975*
February	85	1500	4053*
March	82	1500	3994
April	88	1700	4596
May	87	2000	4958
June	90	1800	5443
July	94	1600	5510
August	98	1400	5187
September	97	1500	4800
October	95	1600	4655
November	95	1600	4880
December	97	1700	5150

*These require sales of late 1988 incalculation.

The example given above assumes that the monthly levels of credit taken in 1987 will continue in 1988.

You may decide to reduce the balance sheet Receivables and borrowings by planning improvements in payment terms and collection methods. The reduced DSO can then be used.

Calculate other budget detail

The receivables budget should contain more than just balances and DSO levels. As it will be used later for monthly action to correct variances, now is the time to include all the intended detail, such as:

● Overdues, by percentage of total and also by value.
● Ageing of overdues, into 1 to 30 days, 31 to 60, 61 to 90, 90 plus.
● Suspense or Doubtful Debts, based on experience and the risks identified in the 'assumptions' exercise.
● Bad Debt Reserve, by whatever policy dictates.
● Currency Balances (although converted to Sterling to fit the budget) may be subject to forward currency contracts or other uses.
● Special Terms accounts, with longer or shorter credit than usual, distorting DSO levels.

- Discounted Debts, which may be eliminated from the Balance Sheet but still require collection. These need a separate budget section.
- Bills Receivable, which must be included in the total investment and DSO period, even though they are recorded off the ledger.

Planning the receivables realistically also helps to decide the resources required in people and systems.

Company performance can really begin to sparkle when expert people are encouraged to put their expertise into quantified plans. The process tends to dispose of wishful thinking and generates actions in good time to be effective.

Targeting collection of funds

Achievement of the budget, or receivables plan, should be the prime motivation for the collection function. As the year progresses, and the period lengthens since the budget was prepared, sales variances and collection performance will produce quite different balances from those budgeted. What matters is that the planned DSO *level* of receivables is achieved.

The DSO ratio can be used each month *in advance* as the most useful way of calculating the cash required to achieve the budget level of receivables.

Taking the budget example shown previously, the following situation can be imagined:

	Sales		*DSO*		*Receivables*	
Month	*Planned*	*Actual*	*Planned*	*Actual*	*Planned*	*Actual*
May	2000	1950	87	86	4958	5020
June	1800	1900	90	88	5443	5300
July	1600	1750	94	90	5510	5474
August	1400	?	98	?	5187	?

How much cash must be collected in August to achieve 98 DSO?

The actual August balance is unlikely to be 5187, because July was already running at 90 DSO, four days better than budget, and recent sales have been quite different from budget. So there is no point in calculating the cash needed to arrive at the planned *balance* of £5187 (i.e. £5474 + 1400 − 5187 = £1687 cash). The task is to calculate the cash needed to achieve

98 DSO. The receivables balance should represent the equivalent sales of the previous 98 days, i.e.:

> 31 days August
> 31 days July
> 30 days June
> <u>6 days May</u>
> = <u>98 days sales</u> outstanding

The cash required to achieve this level is:

Actual receivables at July:		£5474
Less equivalent July Sales	£1750	
Less equivalent June Sales	£1900	
Less equivalent 6/31 May Sales	£377	£4027
Cash required:		£1447

If £1447 is collected in August, whether current or overdue, then regardless of actual sales in August, the resulting receivables balance will represent 98 DSO — the planned level. If collections are greater than £1447, the DSO ratio will be fewer days, and conversely if less is collected, the DSO will go up.

Are there other ways of targeting cash?

There are several. The method shown above is a straightforward calculation of the cash intake needed to achieve a previously planned *ratio* of receivables to sales. It is the culmination of planning all the elements of credit terms, sales and collection techniques.

However, although the DSO is a great motivator to collect the cash needed to achieve the planned level, its principal defect is that it does not strictly relate to *collectable* cash.

The 'DSO Targeting Technique' can be regarded as a 'top-downwards' approach. Any non-involved person, can take the sales and receivables balances and, given the DSO plan, calculate the cash needed. The 'bottom-upwards' technique, requiring job-knowledge and detailed information on each export account is 'Assessing Collectable Cash'. Two possible methods follow:

Getting Paid for Exports

1 ASSESSING COLLECTABLE CASH ACCOUNT BY ACCOUNT
(a) As soon as a month has ended, take the ledger, and Bills Receivable file if necessary, and list the debts becoming due in the following month. Result = Total Cash Due.
(b) Against each account, notate the known disputed debts which may not be resolved in time for payment next month.
(c) Against each non-disputed account due in the next month, assess the amounts unlikely to be paid, from previous experience of time taken between due date and date of receipt.
(d) For each overdue debt, review follow-up file and assess the probability of non-receipt in the next month.
(e) Add together items in (b), (c) and (d) and deduct them, as non-collectable, from the Total Cash Due in (a). The result will be the 'grass-roots' opinion of the Collectable Cash. Ideally, it will achieve the DSO. The defect in this method is that it will be conservative, to protect the collector.

The sensible management action is to use the DSO Technique *and* the Account by Account Assessment, to see if any shortfall looks likely. Action can then be taken to deal with the problems in good time.

2 ASSESSING COLLECTABLE CASH–PROBABILITY METHOD
Either for individual accounts, or for the total ledger if terms are fairly standard, calculate the *rate of payments* on recent months' sales.

By using the average percentages in the example, the month of May could be forecast to produce cash of £1546 on the basis of:

7% of May	£2000	=	£140
8% of April	£1700	=	£136
27% of March	£1500	=	£405
53% of February	£1500	=	£795
5% of January	£1400	=	£70
			£1546

On a statistical average basis, the same percentages can be applied to sales value to produce the forecast of probable cash receipts in subsequent months.

There are other statistical methods of improving the quality of the forecast, such as taking the percentage of *the number of invoices* paid on time, one month late, two months late and so on.

The defect in statistical methods is that they repeat history and take no account of current trends and resources.

Example

		Actual Amounts Paid				
Month of Sales	*Sales*	*Same Mth*	*2nd Mth*	*3rd Mth*	*4th Mth*	*5th Mth*
January	1400	100	100	300	800	100
February	1500	120	90	500	750	40
March	1500	115	110	400	800	75
April	1700	90	130	400	850	230
May	2000	150	200	600	1000	50
June	1800	140	180	500	950	30
July	1600	130	150	400	900	20
August	1400	100	120	300	800	80
September	1500	110	130	400	800	60
October	1600	110	140	500	850	—
November	1600	120	130	400	850	100
December	1700	140	150	450	900	60
Average	1600	120	135	430	845	70
Average %	100%	7%	8%	27%	53%	5%

Measuring performance and reporting results

Every company investing in export credit should develop an inexpensive but effective system for providing management information at regular intervals.

The objectives should be, for example:

- Measure Receivables performance, using data readily available.
- Report results to management and staff.
- Compare results with budget and recent periods.
- Obtain 'exceptional need' data on serious problems.
- Take prompt action to correct variances and defects.

It is difficult to specify the reporting format required by different businesses. Even the intention to examine results and to report on defects will be derided or played down in some companies. But let us assume that top-management believes in communication and visibility!

CREATE AN INFORMATION TREE

An Information Tree takes data from the roots and passes it right to the top. If the Tree is properly treated it will achieve the correct shape and thrive for years. If it is abused, it will be lop-sided, and will need frequent pruning and re-shaping. The general principle for management information is to distribute freely to all related parties the briefest data necessary for their roles and to be able to provide more detailed backup if required. As a rule, the more senior the management level, the less frequent but more urgent will be the need for information. Figure 2.5 shows a sample Information Tree.

Figure 2.5 Sample of a Healthy Information Tree

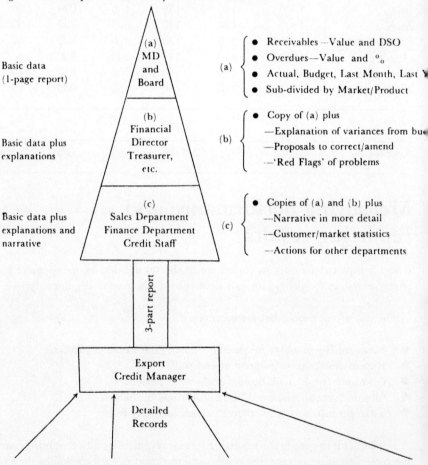

Note: This system keeps others regularly updated but transfers to them the responsibility to request any extra data. The habit of sending everything to everybody 'just in case', should be strictly discouraged.

The main items to measure and report monthly are:

- Days Sales Outstanding in receivables.
- Overdues, Total and as percentage of receivables.
- Aged Analysis within total overdues.
- Disputed Debts as percentage of receivables and as DSO.

Subsidiary data for a report might be:

- DSO for products, divisions, countries or regions.
- Aged Analysis by customer credit risk category.
- Aged Analysis by country and/or risk code.
- Overlimit accounts.
- Debts paid in local currency, not yet transferred to UK.
- Bad Debts written off.

DAYS SALES OUTSTANDING (DSO)

Already described in targeting section (c), this is the simplest ratio of credit efficiency. It relates the receivables asset to latest sales and expresses the combination of credit periods granted, the time taken to pay and transmission delays. The DSO is the average time taken to turn sales into cash and means that today's sale will be paid on average at a future date equal to the DSO period. Variances from budgeted DSO or that for previous periods can be analysed to see whether they are caused by credit terms, collection methods or banking delays.

OVERDUES IN TOTAL AND AS PERCENTAGE OF RECEIVABLES

Percentage overdues are commonly quoted in a company but any percentage is deceptive on its own, as it fluctuates with latest sales, e.g.

Total Receivables	£5 000 000
Overdues	£500 000
% Overdue	10%

But, if latest months' sales were £1 000 000 greater, this becomes:

Total Receivables	£6 000 000
Overdues (still)	£500 000
% Overdue	8.3%

Yet the overdues have not improved at all!

The overdues figure and percentage should be reported, but read together with the DSO and the Aged Analysis.

Figure 2.6 shows a typical monthly report format and Fig. 2.7 shows a method of recording useful credit performance data for planning future performance.

AGED ANALYSIS WITHIN TOTAL OVERDUES
This shows the relative quality of overdue debts and is some measure of collectability, since an older overdue carries more risk of going bad than a recent one. Ideally, if any debts are dishonoured at due date they should be paid soon afterwards, i.e. never more than about one month late. But this is not realistic and it is necessary to know whether debts are sliding back or getting more up-to-date. The trends can be a sign of customer behaviour, or collectors' efficiency, or both!

Example

Total Overdue	1–30 Days	31–60 Days	61–90 Days	91 + Days
April £500 000	£360 000	£90 000	£30 000	£20 000
100%	72%	18%	6%	4%
May £510 000	£357 000	£102 000	£20 000	£31 000
100%	70%	20%	4%	6%

Variances in the percentage should be monitored to control any slide towards the right and to plan a monthly improvement to the left.

DISPUTED DEBTS AS PERCENTAGE AND DSO
Disputed claims for non-delivery, or defects, or price errors or a multitude of other dissatisfactions tend to block cash flow and distort normal ratios. A dispute is usually worth two to three months' extra credit to the customer, pending resolution, and it is well worth setting up a rapid clearance system with the sales or shipping departments, in view of the effect on both profits and customer service levels.

Meanwhile, the disputes can be measured and reported in the main monthly report as a percentage of total receivables and as the equivalent sales days. Thus cost can be measured and the guilty departments shamed into action to help release valuable funds.

Example

Total Receivables	£5 000 000 = 92 DSO	
Disputed Receivables	£150 000	
	= 3% or 2.8 DSO	

An accurate listing of disputed debts should always be to hand. It should not be necessary to analyse disputes *by age* as there should be none remaining after the next reporting month. In exceptional cases, long-lasting disputes should be reported separately.

Figure 2.6   A Typical Front Page of a Monthly Report

BRITISH EXPORTERS LIMITED				
Export Receivables		as at	30th June 19	
£000's	This Month	Budget	Last Month	Last Year
DAYS SALES OUTSTANDING	92	94	91	95
OVERDUES %	10%	10.5%	9.5%	11%
AGED ANALYSIS OF OVERDUES				
1–30 days	£360: 72%	75%	70%	68%
31–60 days	£ 90: 18%	20%	19%	17%
61–90 days	£ 30: 6%	3%	6%	7%
91 + days	£ 20: 4%	2%	5%	8%
Total	£500: 100%	100%	100%	100%
DISPUTED DEBTS				
VALUE	£150	£54	£120	£71
%	3%	1%	2.4%	1.6%
Total Receivables	£5 000	£5 400	£4 950	£4 500
Overdue Receivables	£ 500	£ 567	£ 470	£ 495
Sales	£1 550	£1 600	£1 750	£1 350
Cash collected	£1 700	£1 610	£1 680	£1 430

Subsequent pages might explain variances, give detailed account situations and propose actions

Exception reports for action

There is no time to look at all accounts all the time. It is necessary to decide priorities according to resources available for action. For daily information,

Figure 2.7   Export Receivables Data Sheet

EXPORT RECEIVABLES DATA SHEET

		Jan	Feb.	Mar.	Apr.	May	June	July	Aug.	Sept.	Oct.	Nov.	Dec.
SALES:	Budget												
	Actual												
	Last Year												
RECEIVABLES:	Budget												
	Actual												
	Last Year												
OVERDUES:	Budget												
	Actual												
	Last Year												
DSO:	Budget												
	Actual												
	Last Year												
DISPUTES:	Budget												
	Actual												
	Last Year												

This can be usefully maintained by the Export Credit Manager for:
● monitoring trends in the year,
● comparing variances with budget and previous year,
● compiling future plans or budgets.

reports should be produced on an exceptional need basis. It is a good policy to determine 'Red Flag' definitions for the computer and for staff, i.e. those situations which require attention fairly quickly. Examples:

- Credit limits exceeded by a certain value.
- High risk accounts overdue 60 days.
- Bills dishonoured in certain countries.
- Sales made to high-risk customers.
- Incorrect credit terms printed on documents.
- Orders received from overdue customers.
- Orders held for credit reasons.

Cash collection monitors

For monitoring Cash Intake against targets or budgets, two documents suffice:

(a)   a Collection Progress Sheet,
and
(b)   a Cash Graph.

They should both be used for the current month only and be produced and maintained by the collection person as prominent visual aids.

The Collection Progress Sheet (CPS) should list collectable accounts individually above a certain value, accounting for, say, 80% of the cash requirement, then a subtotal figure for accounts providing the balance of 20%. The CPS should show the Balance, the Current Debt and the Overdue Debt. The collector should use the sheet during the month to notate cash paid, payments promised or arranged and follow up action taken. It is then relatively simple, at any time, for the collector or the manager to look at the blank spaces, or the unpaid accounts, to decide what step should be taken next.

A separate CPS focuses the mind on the important debts and is far more effective then having to study the entire ledger. (see Figure 2.8 for a suggested format.) The Cash Graph (Figure 2.9) should show the days across the sheet and the cash required in the vertical graduations. Collection actions can be noted, e.g. 15th = telexes sent, 20th = agents telephoned, 22nd = review with manager, etc. The cash intake is plotted as the most distinctive line on the graph. The majority of cash arrives, but it is the reliable achievement of the percentage which is the potential shortfall that motivates the collector and puts the company in a much better competitive position.

Any visual aids should be simple working tools and not elaborate works of art or ritual clerical chores. Their purpose is to motivate staff, provide instant pictures of progress for management, and stimulate improvement actions.

Figure 2.8   Export Collections Progress Sheet

Month: MARCH		Collector: MARY		TARGET: £972 000		
Account No.	Name	Total	Current	Overdue	Agreed	Received
0001	ABC	25 000	20 000	5 000		
0023	XYZ	7 000	7 000	—		
0038	QPR	38 000	18 000	20 000		
0052	WBA	34 000	10 000	24 000		
0061	CIF	54 000	54 000	—		
0084	NBG	9 000	5 000	4 000		
0102	DOA	38 000	37 600	400		
0369	VIP	4 000	3 000	1 000		
etc.	etc.	etc.	etc.	etc.		
185 a/cs Sub-Total		900 000	808 000	92 000		
815	Others	£225 000	£204 500	£20 500		
Ledger (1000 a/cs)	Total	£1 125 000	£1 012 500	£112 500		
TARGET: RECEIPTS		£972 000	£872 000	£100 000		

Note: This CPS identifies all balances above £1,000. If the top 185 accounts are collected, 80% of cash is in.
(a) *Produce* sheet at beginning of month.
(b) *Log* agreed amounts daily.
(c) *Delete* agreed amounts when received.
(d) *Shows always* – situation of cash in + agreed payments v. target.

The different policies of small and large exporters

The distinction between small and large, for this purpose, could be that a small firm has so few staff that they interchange to do all the tasks and it is not economical to employ specialists.

We have seen how a sales plan is converted into a cash borrowing requirement. The ability to borrow the required capital and to repay the interest expense out of export profits is a prime management task for a company of any size.

Figure 2.9   Example of a Cash Graph

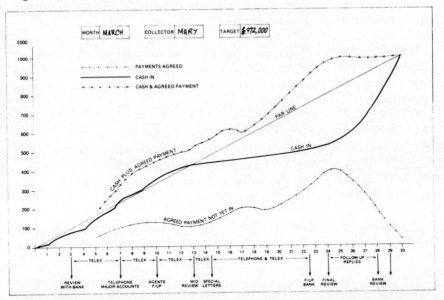

Extra working capital is needed *at the same time* as sales growth. Profit to retain and use is only a small part of the extra sales. It takes a long time to acquire enough extra profit to be able to reduce external borrowings—perhaps never. The dangers of over-trading (increasing sales faster than they can be financed) are illustrated in the following graph, some times referred to as the 'financial time-bomb'.

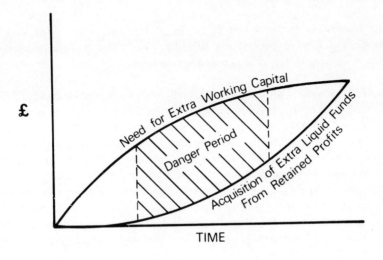

Correct management policies and clear operating drills for staff are needed if the expansion is to be worth the pain. Our approach is to develop step-by-step decision paths and operating checklists.

Whatever the size of an exporter, there are common factors which will influence the policy-making and guidelines or directives. Companies should segregate the different classes of export risk and payment performance inherent in sales made:

- directly to end-customers and distributors in foreign countries
- to end-customers looked after by local commission agent (who may be on a 'del-credere' basis, i.e. taking the credit risk himself)
- to foreign associates or subsidiaries for local resale.
- to UK-based specialists for onward delivery.

A review of the customers in these categories will present a picture of the risk of insolvency and the delays in payment and, therefore, the strength of control required to reduce the worry to a manageable size.

Sales made directly to foreign end-customers, without the active involvement of local agents, will require the classic risk assessment, appropriate payment terms and collection methods covered in this book. There will probably be a high 'worry' factor and a high cost of interest in payment delays. Against this, there is the saving of 5%–15% in commission not paid to an agent. At the other extreme, exports made through UK merchants or confirming houses will have low risk and, provided the merchant's fee have been fully costed, there will be few unplanned interest expenses. But the middle-man's fees will have been incurred.

The interesting business will be in the middle two cases, of exports for resale through foreign associates or subsidiaries and to appointed distributors or end-customers where local agents are responsible.

Sales to associates/subsidiaries are usually on a territorial basis, e.g. Bloggs (UK) Ltd, will export to Italy through Bloggs (Italia) s.p.a., who may also cover Yugoslavia and Malta with their sales force. Italy will pay UK a price which guarantees the Italians their required operating margin, e.g. 10%, but will pay strictly to policy on intercompany terms, e.g. 90 days from invoice. They will also carry bad debt reserves within their margin, so there is no risk for the UK company (who may operate in exactly the same way for imported products or associates. Sometimes international groups have 'limited bad debts' policies, where for example the Italian company absorbs bad debts up to, say, 1% of sales, or a stated order value and charges any extra losses back to the UK associate.

In cases where the foreign associate has the right to charge back all or part of local bad debt losses, the UK company will be entitled to assess the end-customer credit risk before local sales take place. And should do so!

In the case of distributors and agents, a lot of confusion exists with a resulting bad export management. Both are sometimes loosely referred to as 'our agents'. Exports are made *through* agents, or are made *to* distributors. The simple test is to ask: who is contractually responsible for payment?

With a distributor, there is just one account, one payment and one risk, albeit usually a large risk. As the firm has been appointed and trusted with selling rights for an area, there is usually a signed agreement with privileges, concessions, perhaps some rights to unsold stocks and possibly a legal charge over the distributor's assets.

An agent, strictly speaking, is part of the exporter and acts on his behalf. There are several customer accounts, several payments and different credit risks. Perhaps even the risk assessments were based on the agent's own report, and he may have no responsibility for payment at all, unless he is a 'del-credere' agent (must pay if customer fails). Agents are usually 100% engaged in selling and may not chase very effectively for overdue debts on behalf of the UK exporter, if this risks offending good sales prospects. Agents' commission should be credited at time of invoicing customers, but not actually paid until the exporter has received payment.

The apparently attractive prospect of selling through a single prompt-paying distributor may become less attractive when the sales grow. That very success will be constrained by the liquid funds the distributor has available. As somebody once said: 'the better job a distributor does, the sooner he is unable to do it!'

The exporter then faces a choice of: restricting or reducing the distributor's territory and appointing another; giving longer credit terms (i.e. supplying the extra finance); selling on a consignment stock basis; or agreeing to nil growth in the area; or selling directly to customers as well as to the distributors – an unsatisfactory marketing approach.

So, the exporter's choice of selling methods will certainly affect his investment in controls and information systems.

Small or new exporters may not yet realize that the traditional skills of sales and accounting staff are not necessarily adequate to cope with export credit problems. The ever-changing legal differences, documentation and financial habits in the international market-place, require exporters to apply special effort and expense to matters which simply do not exist in the home trade. There is no myth or magic involved, simply a need to understand and specialize.

Many exporters in recent years have appointed specialist managers to handle credit risk and payments, having realized that the time needed by sales staff to keep abreast of financial matters is better spent on customers and product matters.

Since uncontrolled export credit can hurt a firm's progress it is important that top management sets up and supports the role of export credit management. Whereas this is easy in a large firm, full of other specialists, it is usually not possible in a small firm, where the answer is for the Financial Controller, or Commercial Manager (whatever the title may be) *to allocate a specific part of his time* to manage credit.

The basic tasks of export credit management are:

- To assess the financial worth of customers.
- To set the most appropriate payment terms.
- To run an accurate ledger information system.
- To collect debts on time.

These four tasks must not be under-estimated.
Closely related to these is the need to be accurate in all documentation; to purchase cost-effective external services and to work well with the banking system.

The person made responsible must be given the authority to be effective. As it would be pointless to the firm's aim to allow a sales person to override the proper credit decision, the credit person should be at the same decision level as the top sales person, below Board level. Any disagreements can then be negotiated sensibly and referred to the Board by either person if a point of principle is at stake.

The export credit person will be vastly more effective if he (or she) is seen to be the credit-granter and the commercial person in the financial area. The worst image is that of a debt collector who sweeps up 'after the marketing coach has rolled past'. As a simple rule, cash intake is far easier if the correct actions have been taken at the front end of a sale. Conversely, it is unfair to expect a credit person to collect efficiently if he is demotivated by having accounts subject to vague terms and private agreements.

A mature, experienced financial executive with a commercial leaning will be expensive. Export credit management is a relatively new specialist profession and good executives will be in great demand until their numbers increase substantially.

Let us look at four typical policy matters:

(i)   What terms are normal for our customers in *their* markets?
(ii)   What level of exposure can we risk in a country and overall?
(iii)   Which of the firm's products need special support, via special payment terms and/or liberal credit?
(iv)   What is the competition doing?

These require market and product knowledge, not available by sitting at a desk in the accounts department. The export credit person must have a commercial curiosity and acquire enough knowledge to be able to argue his case convincingly with the sales or production person and sometimes the customer.

Regular meetings between other departments and the credit function are excellent for promoting a strong export credit policy. At a monthly export Receivables meeting, for example, there should be representatives of:

Sales
Customer Service
Production
Finance

with the export credit person in the chair. The agenda will obviously vary with current needs and a typical one is given in Figure 2.10.

This is far better than the non-communication situation where sales staff operate independently and credit staff block deliveries after a commitment has been given to factory and customer. The abuse of controls is a serious defect.

Commercial export strength develops from training credit and sales staff in each other's skills; by special presentations, and in-house training sessions. Also effective is the simple technique of copying sales bulletins to credit staff, and vice versa, so worded as to 'sell' their requirements to the other function.

Small firms

Many small firms are profitably exporting every day. They have found their niche in the world market-place, learned how to price and promote their products and which customers to trust with credit so as to get paid on time. Why cannot all small firms do that?

Figure 2.10   A Sample Agenda of Monthly Export Credit Meeting

---

(a) State of export Receivables—report by credit manager.
- number of active customers.
- total debts, DSO, overdue value, ageing and percentage.
- bad debts.
- comparison with budget or previous meeting targets.

(b) Orders held for credit reasons—report by sales or production person.
- show customer, country, value.

Discussion on reasons.
Explore ways to achieve release.

(c) Proposed orders/new customers— report by sales person
- explain plans.
- 'sell' marginal cases to others.
(valuable early warning to avoid delays later)

(d) Customer claims/disputes—report by customer service person

(a dispute of debt means an unhappy customer so this is of interest to all present to solve)

Note: The meeting should be minuted. It should issue work assignments and require action by deadline dates.

Small firms who struggle with export often complain that they find the techniques complicated, or they cannot finance the extra costs.

A BOTB survey in 1987 produced an excellent Occasional Paper 'Into Active Exporting', a very readable yet thorough review of the attitudes and difficulties of small firms in the export trade. Every firm, regardless of size, would benefit from studying the Paper and comparing their own experience. The report looks at barriers, real and imaginary, profitability, how firms started to sell abroad, etc., and a potential for massive extra sales by 3800 'passive' exporters (i.e. those with less than 15% of total sales) in 14 different product sectors. An extremely interesting observation is that the events feared by less successful exporters are not actually experienced by successful ones, eg. Credit Risk is a deterrent to some, but is successfully handled by others.

Another BOTB Occasional Paper which is brimful of helpful advice for small exporters is 'Exporting for the Smaller Firm' (1986).

The official government booklet for small exporters is 'How to Start Exporting' issued by the Small Firms Service of the Department of Employment. It is deliberately brief but effectively refers to other documents and sources of information.

So, the main export guideline to small firms is:

> Do not struggle alone to export or to finance your exports. There is no need to agonize in isolation nor should you try to re-invent the wheel. It has all been done before. There is plenty of advice available. You may not like what you hear, but DO LISTEN.

The Small Firms booklet asks: 'Do you really want to export?' and goes on to say: 'Exporting can be highly profitable and can strengthen the basis of your business. *These are the only valid reasons* for a small firm to export. It will stretch your financial commitments and strain your financial and marketing expertise. Few exporters do not regard their overseas operations as more demanding than trading in the home market. The decision to export is a cold, hard calculation of a major *long-term* decision of critical importance to the survival of your firm. It should not be taken unless you give it top priority. It will often seem irritating, frustrating and unrewarding.'

Hard words, perhaps. But the insolvency courts are littered with companies that treated exporting as glamorous globe-trotting or as a useful outlet for spare production. Some of them marketed seriously but neglected financial preparation.

The management of a small firm looking at export growth should ask three important questions:

- Do we have the staff skills, or can we get them quickly?
- Do we have market knowledge?
- Do we have adequate bank support for finance?

If the answers cause a shudder of apprehension but still a determination to export, the next step *could be* to go to a Confirming House.

The British Exporters Association will provide a list of member companies in the UK who buy goods and export them, relieving the small manufacturer of all three of the above worries, because sales become UK orientated. The member companies place orders in the UK for foreign customers and pay on cash or fairly short credit terms in return for a small fee. They are also willing to look for foreign customers on behalf of manufacturers.

Exports are still mainly financed out of overdrafts and small firms are often surprised at the total length of credit involved in a transaction and the extent to which overdrafts are tied up. The time between receipt of order and delivery date can be up to three months in manufacturing industry, the shipment period may be up to six weeks and the credit period anything from a few days to six months. The funds can then take two or three weeks to arrive in the exporter's bank account. So from order to receipt of funds, it is possible for several months to elapse. If money is borrowed at 15% per annum, the interest burden can be from 5% upwards of the price. In addition, the working capital tied up may prevent other orders being taken.

Here is the dilemma. Small firms can least afford to be out of their money yet have the least 'muscle' to speed up its flow. The solution is a combination of:

- Knowing the best banking techniques.
- Cultivating first class customer relationships.
- Being dedicated to a short credit policy (not competing on longer and longer terms which only hurt in the end).

A remarkably useful leaflet is 'How to Control Floating Money', produced by SITPRO and a committee of experts, including major banks, which shows several good drills for speeding up the flow of payments.

When quoting, or negotiating credit terms, the small exporter must (a) achieve the shortest possible cash turnaround and (b) cover his credit cost in the price.

The approach on payment terms should be:

- Request a letter of credit payable in London on shipment.
- Failing this, request payment by Sight Draft on arrival of goods.
- Failing this, if credit must be granted, request acceptance of a bill of exchange dated from shipment. (This can be discounted for fast cash.)
- If all the above fail, allow open account with a specified date from shipment, but only to first class buyers in rich countries.

Apart from the letter of credit method, all others should require the funds to be remitted to the exporter's bank by Telegraphic Transfer (TT). This is far quicker than normal transfer and the cable cost is cheaper than waiting for slow funds to arrive.

The chapters that follow on export finance, credit risk assessment, payment terms and collection techniques are as valid for small firms as for any other size.

Checklist: Export Credit Policy Points

- Has the working capital required to support Receivables been calculated by production of a debtor's budget (by multiplying planned sales by the credit terms)? How about pre-shipment finance?
- Have you specified one individual or department on whom you will build the company's export expertise?
- Is there a written company guide showing authority, responsibility and procedures for order approval, credit terms, collection methods and financing?
- Do all relevant staff and departments have a copy of it?
- Who can visit customers, telephone them and write to them?
- Have you decided how to involve agents or associated companies?
- Have you specified the possible range of payment terms for each market? (If you have an ECGD Policy, is your range of terms permitted?)
- Have *all* cost elements been included in prices quoted?
- Is pricing to be in Sterling or local currency? For which markets?
- Do you show payment terms and the price basis on all quotations and acknowledgements?
- How are new customers checked for creditworthiness? Has a suitable list of credit questions been developed for information-gathering by the salesman?
- Do you have reliable local representation in each market to obtain credit data and help to collect if asked?
- Are you satisfied with the customer credit reports you get from credit agencies and banks?
- Do your rules for credit approval of orders avoid overstrictness (which loses orders) and overliberality (which loses profit)?
- Are all customers given credit limits, to avoid overtrading? If so, are limits reviewed regularly?
- For marginal risk customers, when do you ask for guarantees, or reduce or refuse credit?
- Who can authorize credit extensions or agree longer terms on orders?
- Is a reliable customer record system being developed to show basic data plus sales and payments history?
- Do you produce effective invoices showing payment terms and international data clearly?
- Have you arranged for bank documentation (invoices, packing notes, Bills of Lading, Certificates of Origin, etc.) to be obtained rapidly and coordinated accurately for the bank?
- Is there a fast, accurate sales ledger for exports, with invoices and receipts recorded daily?
- Does the sales ledger provide management data on export customer performance promptly each month?
- Is the export Receivables report reviewed critically by management each month?
- Are overdue accounts followed up immediately and at frequent intervals?
- Is your policy clear on charging interest on overdues, using agents and associates to collect, protesting bills of exchange, and responding to bank advices of dishonour?
- Is the total cost of staff, ledger, documentation and export finance assessed and related to profits?
- Is your bank manager frequently shown the export Receivables situation as a basis for discussing financing methods?
- Has export factoring been considered as a cheaper credit management and cash flow system?
- Who will review alternative financing methods and how often?

These 29 questions are worded so as to imply what should be done. Discussion will lead to the policy decisions appropriate to a particular firm. From these, the necessary working drills can be formulated.

Large firms with few exports

Large firms are defined here as companies established for some years, with a substantial turnover in the UK and an organizational structure with the usual specialist departments or managers.

In recent years, problems of growth and market share in the UK have led many firms to look abroad for new markets.

Some of the operating problems for large firms with few exports are:

● Management and staff sometimes have a home trade orientation, so that exporting is regarded as a temporary nuisance.
● Production is not specially allocated for export, so that delivery dates are often not met.
● Staff are hard-pressed for time, so the less familiar export paperwork is neglected, or delayed.

The senior management of a large company exporting less than, say, 10% of its production, should organize an objective study of its methods, then develop a policy and enforce it with clear operating procedures for staff.

Large firms usually have the resources, and the negotiating 'muscle', to achieve efficient export credit management and to turn their exports into cash faster; provided it recognizes the need to do so and does not simply worship the god 'More Sales'.

Theoretically, if exports are properly priced, orders looked at objectively before acceptance and resources organized to collect on time, the decision to export will be justified by the healthy flow of foreign cash into the business. If any god is to be worshipped, it should be 'More Export Profits'.

In practice, what often happens to large firms exporting only a small proportion of their total sales is:

● Exports get a low priority from management.
● Costs get mixed in, so that export profitability is hidden.
● A disproportionate amount of working capital is tied up in exports, compared to home sales.
● True export profitability is low or even negative.

So, the requirements of firms that fit the above profile can be summarized as:

- An objective management decision on whether to export or to put resources into domestic profitability.
- If committed to exporting, a separation of the expertise from the domestic operations.
- An Action Programme, resulting from the Objective Policy Study (Figure 2.11), with a strong commitment to increase export profitability.

Any perceptive shareholder will demand nothing less!

Figure 2.11   Procedure for an Objective Policy Study

---

1   Call together the Sales, Production and Accounting managers to discuss the company's exports, i.e. methods, priorities, progress, etc.
2   Produce statistics to show: market penetration
                                   profitability
                                       (Return on Sales)
                                   working capital required
                                   future growth forecasts.

Now for credit and finance!

3   Compared with the home trade, each £ of export sales value requires more cash to be tied up for longer; so make a realistic budget for export receivables, using the sales plan and the payment experience for each customer or market.
4   Look at the resulting level of borrowing needed to support export sales and its effect in interest costs on the P & L.
5   Decide policy on: markets, agents, product pricing, and production allocation. Decide also on staff resources and concentration to handle export orders, billings documentation and shipping.
6   Items 1 to 5 will enable budgets to be made for Sales, Capital, Marketing Expense, Staff Expense and Distribution Methods.
7   If exporting is still considered worthwhile, decide a forward growth policy to include:

- Which customers to cultivate for growth (or perhaps product lines).
- Which markets to develop or withdraw from.
- A range of permitted payment terms for each market.
- The cost of finance to be built into prices.
- Authority levels of staff to take credit decisions.
- Use of agents, salesforce and others to enforce terms.

8   Put responsibility for export credit management clearly on to one person.
9   Decide how many staff and what systems are needed to:

- Approve export orders for credit.
- Investigate new and existing customers' creditworth.
- Operate an ECGD policy, if there is one.
- Control export documentation.
- Plan, target and achieve export collections.
- Maintain up-to-date contact with banks and information agencies.
- Obtain export finance at best rates.
- Report monthly on results to required levels.

(In considering item 9 of the Objective Policy Study it would be useful to go through the policy checklist given previously for small firms.)

Large exporters

Large exporters will have achieved mostly correct marketing decisions, organized a professional export credit management function and arranged adequate financing. So, apart from the occasional reviews and re-thinks beneficial to any operation, the main requirement for such firms is:

to operate the most up-to-date efficient credit, collection and financing techniques available for their needs.

Their detailed requirements can be summarized as:

(i)   The Board should delegate to an experienced executive, best called the Export Credit Manager, responsibility for managing the company's investment of funds in export credit sales. His responsibility should include coordinating those parts of any activity in the firm (e.g. sales, accounting, shipping, etc.) which influence the investment.

(ii)   An expenditure budget should be agreed annually to allow the export credit manager to maintain relations at the correct level with banks, institutions and export agencies, as well as the travelling necessary to deal with important problems, and the information systems required to keep the company aware.

(iii)   An export receivables budget is an annual requirement, with the essential participation of the export credit manager, who will then be responsible for its achievement.

(iv)   A reporting system is required, based on results compared to the budget, which converts variances in figures to actual operational situations, for review by the Board or functional managers.

(v)   A company-wide understanding must be achieved, that export credit is a combined Marketing/Finance function. Both departments have vital responsibilities to each other and friction over specific differences must be resolved rapidly so that customers see only a single stance on matters of credit and payment.

(vi)   Within the expense allocation, the export credit manager must organize the correct number and calibre of staff needed for the firm's exports. The duties can be broadly classified as:

- Giving advice to salesmen on customers and countries.
- Investigating proposed customers, and contact with information sources.
- Approving orders and particular contract clauses.
- Monitoring export documentation.
- Collecting accounts, and contact with banks, agents, customers.
- Input to computer and accounting systems.
- Reports and analysis.
- Meetings–planning, information, problem-solving.

By kind permission of the Institute of Credit Management, Figure 2.12 reproduces their own recommendation of a Job Description for export credit managers.

Figure 2.12　Export Credit Manager's Job Description

Objective

To protect the overall quality of export debtors. To act as adviser in the arrangement of export finance and currency invoicing.

Responsibilities

He/She will:
(a) In liaison with Sales and Marketing, recommend the most suitable payment terms for new and existing customers, having regard to market risks and conditions, the financial standing of the buyer and the cost of credit to the company.
(b) Maintain updated status files on all active buyers.
(c) Maintain up-to-date information files on all markets/countries in which the company has an interest.
(d) Set limits for all buyers appropriate to their financial condition, having regard to the terms of payment and the level of business. Review credit limits not less frequently than once a year.
(e) Monitor the payment performance of all buyers, arranging follow-up wherever necessary.
(f) Make the best use of bank facilities to ensure that cash-flow into the company's UK bank account is as fast as possible.
(g) Be thoroughly conversant with ECGD and other credit insurance facilities, in order to make recommendations for or against a policy and subsequently any special endorsements.
(h) Have sufficient knowledge of the sources and workings of export finance to be able to give advice to Sales and Marketing and if need be to participate in contract negotiations.
(i) Have sufficient knowledge of the foreign exchange market to be able to give advice to Sales and Marketing on the use of non-Sterling currencies and to control and maximize cash-flow from non-Sterling business.
(j) Maintain constant liaison with the company's overseas agents, to ensure that they act as a source of commercial information and assist in any follow-up activity on outstanding accounts.

(k) Prepare such reports as are required by the Credit Manager relating to the level and quality of export debtors.

(l) Maintain the Bills Receivable File in good order.

(m) Liaise closely with Sales and Marketing on all customer problems with particular reference to political or transfer risks. On this latter point, Financial Management should also be informed.

(n) Produce at regular intervals a schedule of any items that should be considered as Bad and Doubtful debts.

(o) Ensure that his/her staff receive adequate training in all aspects of export credit control relevant to their functions.

(p) Professional qualifications: Membership of the Institute of Credit Management (MICM) and the Institute of Export (MIEx) is highly recommended.

The ICM is the national UK professional body for credit management, and its Export Committee has published an excellent guideline document for issue to staff and others giving broad guidance but requiring referral to the company credit experts on detailed matters.

By the kind courtesy of the ICM, the document is reproduced in the Appendix (p.348).

Checklist: General Points for Export Credit Policy

- If there are not enough staff to have specialists, reorganize tasks so that export matters are concentrated on very few people.
- Develop a picture of risk, terms and methods for the different classes of export: via agents, associates, UK export houses or direct to end-buyers.
- Consider how to: assess customers' worth; set appropriate terms; operate accurate ledger; collect debts on time.
- Give the export credit person top backing to prevent out-ranking by sales or production staff.
- Expect to pay well to hire or keep an experienced export credit person.
- Build into policy: normal terms for buyers' markets; level of investment allowable by risk and overall; support for certain products; knowledge of the competition.
- Fix a monthly get-together of sales, production, service and credit to build a strong export function.
- Train sales and credit staff in each other's needs.

Conditions of sale

The seller and the buyer are both legally committed to the conditions of a contract as soon as it is made, whether verbally or in writing.

Basic requirements

Export orders should be subject to export Conditions of Sale. This rather obvious assertion is made because many companies place themselves at risk by taking orders and delivering without any conditions at all and others trade on standard home trade conditions.

International trade, despite its hotchpotch of languages, religions and legal traditions around the world, has, over the years, developed a fairly sophisticated set of standards. There is always a small risk that some governments or regimes will defy international goodwill and ride roughshod over legal contracts, but UK exporters can generally operate with confidence if:

● Quotations, and sales literature show Conditions of Sale.
● Customers' orders are scrutinized for unacceptable purchase conditions, and differences negotiated out.
● Orders are acknowledged, in every case, with Conditions of Sale, either standard, or tailored to suit the contracts.
● Conditions of Sale show that *Incoterms* (see later) apply.
● Conditions of Sale are subject to English Law, with provision for arbitration by the International Chamber of Commerce.

There are possible legal complexities in drafting some Conditions of Sale and Professor Schmithoff, in 'The Export Trade' (Stevens & Sons Ltd) is the recommended authority on international law and its interpretation. But exporters should not be deterred from issuing standard contract conditions.

This section concentrates on the Conditions of Sale affecting credit and payments risks. In addition to the Incoterms definitions, clauses on Interest, Currency, Price Escalation, Case of Need, Retention of Title and arbitration are considered. As a very important condition, Payment Terms have a separate chapter, including a section on Bills of Exchange, which carry their own legal conditions under the Bills of Exchange Act of 1882.

Acknowledgement of order

Since orders arrive in a variety of ways, by letter, telex, telephone or verbally, it is useful to standardize their legal acceptance at the first opportunity. The ideal document for this is the order acknowledgement.

All export orders should be acknowledged in writing by the exporter confirming the customer's requirements in terms of the exporter's selling conditions. The document should include the correct description of the goods, with any specialist part numbers and codes, and then show clearly the Conditions of Sale.

Credit risks may be reduced and collections improved by conditions as to:

- Payment terms.
- Price basis, e.g. FOB or CIF, etc.
- Packing and carriage charges.
- Contractual retentions, percentage and dates.
- Time allowed for notification of shortages or damage.
- Interest charge basis.
- Reservation of Title until payment.
- Currency shortfall responsibility.
- Price-escalation basis.
- Arbitration on disputes.
- A reference that Incoterms apply.

The exporter should always check his buyer's conditions on incoming orders and negotiate out of unacceptable requirements, to avoid later conflict when financial claims become related to printed conditions.

The real test of an effective Order Acknowledgement is that it is acceptable to both parties as a reference source to resolve any dispute.

Incoterms clause

The Order Acknowledgement should state that Incoterms apply.

Incoterms are a set of international standard rules which define the obligations of exporters and importers under fourteen kinds of selling terms. Export pricing must take full account of the contractual costs implied in the terms, which identify the point in the transaction where the buyer becomes responsible.

Incoterms were first developed by the International Chamber of Commerce in 1936 and updated at intervals, the latest being 1980. ICC Publication No. 350 gives full details, with illustrations, of each trade term.

Sea Transport

Free alongside ship	FAS
Free on board	FOB
Cost and Freight	(C&F) CFR
Cost, Insurance and Freight	CIF
Ex. Ship	EXS
Ex. Quay	EXQ

Air Transport

FOB Airport	(FAD) FOA

Rail Transport

Free on Rail/Truck	(FOT) FOR

All forms of transport (incl. Road)

Ex Works	EXW
Free Carrier (Named point)	FRC
Freight paid to (Named point)	DCP
Freight v Insurance paid to (Named point)	CIP
Delivered at Frontier	DAF
Delivered Duty Paid	DDP

The exact wordings are available in the ICC booklet, but for the guidance of credit managers, the following notes may be useful.

FAS – FREE ALONGSIDE SHIP

The exporter's obligation is to transport the goods to 'alongside' the nominated ship. Risk and costs pass to the buyer from that point. The document provided to the buyer, evidencing a clean delivery, is a warehouse receipt or a dock warrant.

The credit manager's situation is the same as in FOR or FOT, except that disputes are more likely than on rail transport as the buyer may delay in nominating a carrier or vessel.

FOB – FREE ON BOARD

The exporter's duties and costs include placing the goods on board ship to the buyer *at a port named in the contract.* The exporter must also provide any export licence required, provide a clean on board receipt and pay loading costs not included in the freight. The buyer assumes all risks and costs once the goods are loaded.

From a credit viewpoint, problems can be encountered if the buyer does not nominate a ship at a port in time to meet the agreed delivery date. The buyer may dispute a credit period dated from shipment date if loading was at a much later date. It is better to date credit terms on FOB contracts from the invoice date.

Quotations and acknowledgements should avoid stating just 'FOB' or 'FOB UK Port'. They should show the intended port of shipment, e.g. 'FOB Felixstowe', so that correct costing and pricing is possible. Then, if the buyer changes to a vessel from, say, Liverpool, the exporter can properly charge for extra inland costs and port charges.

C AND F – COST AND FREIGHT
CFR – COST AND FREIGHT

The exporter must pay the costs and freight necessary to get the goods to the contracted destination, and any unloading costs included in the freight charge. The buyer must accept delivery on receipt of the Bill of Lading and assume ownership and risk when the goods are loaded.

From a credit management viewpoint, the goods in a C and F sale are represented by the documents. The credit terms should be arranged to take account of this, e.g. where Open Account terms are agreed for a 'good' buyer, the document can be sent to the buyer, but where Bill terms apply to a 'risky' buyer, documents will only pass when the Bill has been accepted or paid via a bank.

CIF – COST, INSURANCE AND FREIGHT

The exporter behaves as in C and F above, but also provides insurance to destination. As risk passes to the buyer at port of loading, any insurance claim must be made on the exporter's insurer.

Credit risk is the same as in C and F above but there may be disputes or payment delays whilst claims from the buyer for damage or loss are passed to the insurer. The insurance aspects of CIF contracts are well worth the attention of the credit manager, to ensure that correct arrangements are made.

For example, all staff should be aware that contractual payment responsibility is not affected by marine insurance claims.

EXS – EX-SHIP

This provides an 'arrival' contract, whereby the exporter contracts to make the goods available *on board ship* at the port of destination. The exporter bears the costs and risks of transport to that point and the buyer from then.

This term is less common and is used where there are specific local unloading facilities, e.g. for grain or cement.

An extra risk for the seller is 'demurrage', or ship's waiting time. If the vessel cannot get to the agreed unloading point for any reason, the EXS term enables the charge to be passed to the buyer. The EXS basis is sometimes the cause of disputes as to precise dates of arrival and responsibility for costs.

EXQ – EX-QUAY

This term takes the exporter's costs and risk one stage further than Ex-Ship, i.e. to the quay of unloading. The extra costs are in unloading and insurance of this activity. Customs duty has to be agreed in the contract, either as 'Ex-Quay Duty Paid', or 'Ex-Quay (duty for buyer's account)'. This price basis is useful for exporters who want total freedom of choice in how they get goods to the destination.

FAD – FOB AIRPORT

The same risks and obligations using air transport as for FOB. Instead of 'ship's rail', the delivery point becomes the air carrier at the airport of departure.

From a credit viewpoint, there are extra risks because of difficulty in retaining possession of goods delivered by air. The carriage document is an Air Waybill which does not evidence title, as a Bill of Lading does. A typical solution is to consign the goods to a bank or agent, for release to the customer only when agreed.

FOR – FREE ON RAIL
FOT – FREE ON TRUCK

Used where goods are exported by railway truck. The exporter must pack the goods and deliver them to the railway company, pay for any checking and provide rail documentation to the buyer. The buyer must state the required destination, pay the freight, accept the goods when delivered to the railway on receipt of the transport documents, pay the exporter for Certificates of Origin and consular invoices and obtain any export licence.

EX-WORKS

A price basis for a sale in the exporter's country. For this price, the exporter must make the contracted goods available at his own premises, paying for packing and any checking operations. The buyer must bear the costs and risk of transferring the goods to destinations and pay the exporter for any documentation provided (export licences, certificates of origin, etc.).

DCP – FREIGHT OR CARRIAGE PAID TO ...

The same as C and F (for sea carriage) when applied to overland road, rail or inland waterways. Where there is more than one carrier on the total route, the exporter's delivery is fulfilled on delivery to the first carrier.

DAF – DELIVERED AT FRONTIER

This term is normally used where the goods travel by road or rail and means that the exporter's obligations and risks end when the goods arrive at the 'frontier' but before the customs barrier. It is a more accurate description of the loosely used 'Free border' or, worse still, 'Franco border'. These terms should *not* be used. The exporter must pay for everything necessary for delivery of the goods to a *named* place at the frontier, and can nominate the delivery point, providing it has customs facilities.

DDP – DELIVERED DUTY PAID

The most convenient term for a buyer, as a total 'delivered' price. It is the extreme opposite of Ex-Works. It requires the maximum obligation for the exporter when followed by the buyer's named premises. Any method of transport can apply. The exporter assumes all expenses, obligations and risks, including customs clearance and duties up to local delivery into the buyer's premises; thus having similar role to a domestic supplier in the buyer's market.

The credit situation here is difficult. Not only are the goods handed to the buyer, who must, therefore, be absolutely creditworthy, but the transit period cannot be precisely calculated in advance. A sensible credit cost must be included in prices to cover an uncertain shipment period, if credit begins from arrival. It is always preferable to agree credit terms to begin at shipment, not arrival.

Arbitration clause

The importance of making an export contract subject to English law is that a defaulting buyer is, even internationally, in breach of the English contract and this will weigh in favour of the exporter in a court action. But increasingly, the laws of foreign countries produce complexities which block the local enforcement of English law, thus deterring exporters from going to court. This is where arbitration will usually produce a speedier and cheaper result to a dispute between the parties. It also has the advantage of privacy, in case publicity is not in the interests of either party.

Exporters are recommended to include in their Conditions of Sale a wording such as:

> 'All disputes arising in connection with the present contract shall be finally settled under the Rules of Conciliation and Arbitration of the International Chamber of Commerce by one or more arbitrators appointed in accordance with the said rules.'

The clause may be supplemented by details of the place of arbitration and the number and type of arbitrators.

Apart from the legal force of the arbitration clause itself, its presence in a contract may well deter a buyer from commencing a dispute.

Cost escalation clause

Where there is a long period of time between quotation date and final delivery, an exporter requires protection from the ravages of cost inflation, in material and wages, currency effects on imported raw materials and components, and world prices for valuable metals, such as gold and copper.

The two basic methods of protection are to inflate quoted prices by a sufficient margin to cover all possible increases; or to put a price increase facility in the contract. The inflated price approach is usually uncompetitive against companies in countries with lower inflation rates and stronger currencies. The more attractive approach to a buyer is a Cost Escalation Clause, which defines an allowable price increase, with either monetary or percentage limits for each cause based on reliable indexes. Subsequent invoices should refer to the Condition of Sale and provide the index justification. Where the cost increase requires certification in the UK, the contract should state which party is responsible for the fees involved.

Case of need clause

This quaint expression applies to a person or firm that is the exporter's agreed representative in the buyer's country. It originates from having to contact somebody 'in case of need'. With documentary collections through banks, it is useful for the exporter's bank to be able to contact the Case of Need, whose delegated powers may range from unconditional authority to act for the exporter in that market, down to precise, particular duties such as taking delivery of unwanted goods. It is advisable for exporters to include, in Conditions of Sale, a reference to the existence of the Case of Need. The Condition may be specific to the particular needs of a contract or it may say, more generally:

> 'The Case of Need has authority to deal, on our behalf, with any matters concerning our products or related documentation following arrival in the buyer's country, provided such action does not supersede in any way these Conditions of Sale.'

Such a condition will strengthen the local representation of the exporter in the eyes of the customer but it must be supplemented with a strict instruction from the exporter to the agent as to his real limits of authority.

Interest clause

The Conditions of Sale should be clear on when interest, in addition to the price, is payable by the buyer. Extra charges may apply for the period of credit and/or late payment.

Some countries have strict rules on acceptable rates of interest payable locally to foreign interests and there may be a local withholding tax on interest paid.

A typical interest condition might read:

> 'Interest will be charged at the rate of...% per annum on the credit period agreed in the contract.'

There is obviously a marketing/customer relations point of view in imposing this condition and it is usually far better to include the basic cost of credit in the price.

For penalty interest on payments made after due date, the rate should be higher, e.g. 2% per month but not so high as to be considered usurious by a court. Again, the deterrent effect is important.

A Penalty Interest clause might read:

> 'In the event of payment not being made at the contracted due date, interest will be charged at the rate of 2% per month on the overdue debt from the due date until payment is received by our bank.'

Currency clause

There are several different situations on exchange fluctuation which should be covered by clauses to protect the exporter. Most of these clauses are placed on bills of exchange and are dealt with in another chapter. The protection required by an exporter is that:

(a)   The invoice is paid in the currency of the invoice and no other.
(b)   The invoiced amount is paid in full, regardless of the extra local currency needed at due date.

A suitable Condition of Sale might read:

> 'Payments under this contract must be made in full, in the currency stated in the contract. Any difference in exchange at the date of payment will be for the account of the buyer.'

This condition combines the two requirements and says, equitably, that the buyer keeps any gain or pays any loss incurred if there has been a movement in exchange rates between contract and payment.

Retention of title clause

This is a clause to retain ownership of goods supplied until payment is received.

The case of Aluminium Industrie Vaasen BV and Romalpa Aluminium Ltd, in 1976, alerted UK companies to the use of the protective Retention of Title clause, which Germans, Dutch and others have used for years (referred to in Germany as 'Eigentumsvorbelhalt'). In the Romalpa case, the Dutch supplier's conditions of sale retained property in the aluminium foil supplied until it was paid for. The customer became effectively an agent and was obliged to keep funds separately until paid to the supplier; who duly had priority in the insolvency over normal secured lenders. The Dutch clause was held to be valid by a UK court. In another famous case, the Court of Appeal overturned a similar judgement where resin had been supplied to a chipboard manufacturer. The court held that the resin ceased to exist upon manufacture and thus the seller could not trace into the chipboard. Exporters should take legal advice on the correct wording of their Retention of Title clause. The clause must be acknowledged by the customer; must be clear; the goods must be identifiable; the goods recovered must be the actual ones unpaid; and must, of course, be available.

Summary

We have looked at some factors in export orders which affect credit risk and collectability. The commercial relationship also affects these, as does any badly worded Condition which results in a dispute. The person managing export credit should participate in *any* management area which affects credit and profitability.

Agents, distributors and subsidiaries

It is important not to deal at long distance. Local representation is useful for obtaining information on customers and Central Bank regulations; following up overdues and disputes on the spot; acting with a collecting bank; and responding instantly to any need of the far away exporter.

Because the terms 'agent' and 'distributor' are bandied about rather loosely, it may be useful to pinpoint the essential differences between them, as well as the role of a foreign subsidiary or associated company.

Agents are different from distributors or customers. An agent is appointed to act on behalf of the exporter. The terms of reference may be narrow or wide, but in all cases, the agent *is* the exporter. Most agents promote products and obtain orders from customers. They are not a party to the contract. They get commission on sales. That is a separate contract. An agent should not owe the exporter money. If he buys on his own account, he is a customer for that deal, not an agent. A del credere agent is responsible for the debts of customers he has obtained. Sales commission can be credited at invoicing, but should not be paid until the exporter has been paid. Agent agreements should list all required financial duties and local responsibilities.

Distributors are independent customers who receive special support from exporters in order to promote products, usually in a defined territory. They buy on their own account and may receive extra credit as a form of support. They do not necessarily have any obligations to the exporter for supplying information and acting locally as agents do.

Subsidiaries, wholly or majority owned, may be required to act locally for an exporting parent company or for sister subsidiaries, in obtaining information and collecting overdues. Some groups operate at arms' length, where subsidaries have to be persuaded, or paid, to act locally on independent sales. Others decree it, depending on organization, policy or marketing preference.

Associated Companies are minority shareholdings, where daily contact by minority shareholders is not usual. Associates are far less likely to be willing to act for foreign parents, but arrangements should always be negotiated on a fee basis, to ensure a local presence.

3   Export documents

Introduction

Sending goods across national borders and over large distances requires a variety of documents: to move the goods, to prove their origin, to insure them, to show who has legal title to them en route, and, most important of all, to get paid.

In most cases, the documents must be precisely correct. Incorrect documents can cause payment delays, through no fault of the customer, and even cause the goods to remain in foreign customs, out of reach of the intended customer.

Earlier, we recommended that the export credit manager should influence other functions which can affect payment. Documentation is a case in point. Although invoices, air waybills, insurance certificates, etc., may be produced elsewhere, the export credit department should collect them into sets and check them for accuracy before despatch to the bank or customer. Others will be relaxing, having done their job. The credit department has the motivation to get the documents exactly right in order to get paid on time. Errors or missing items should be corrected right at the outset.

Although there are no international standards for documents, there are many established good practices. Exporters should review thoroughly their documents for accuracy and to weed out errors that have crept in over the years.

The Simplification of International Trade Procedures Board, SITPRO, has been working hard for years to encourage simplified, standard documentation. Their aligned documentation system is based on a single master document from which most of the others can be produced. This reduces checking and the risks of transposition errors. Their publication 'Systematic Export Documentation' is available from chambers of commerce or from SITPRO: Almack House, 26–28 King Street, London SW1Y 6QW (telephone: 01 930 0532).

The most popular manual on documentation in daily use is Croners Reference Book for Exporters, which is updated monthly with documentary and other requirements for 153 countries. It is available from Croner Publications Ltd, at Croner House, 173 Kingston Road, New Malden, Surrey KT3 3SS (telephone 01 942 8966).

Documents can be roughly segregated between:

INVOICES   – Proforma; Commercial; Consular; Legalized; Certified

TRANSPORT   – Ocean Bill of Lading; Combined Transport B/L; Through B/L; Air Waybill; Road Transport Notes; Rail Transport Note; Parcel Post Receipt; House B/L

INSURANCE   – Policy; Certificate; Broker's Certificate; Cover Note

CERTIFICATE   – Origin; Blacklist; Weight; Inspection; Analysis; Packing List; Health; Industry Standard; Special

BILLS OF EXCHANGE   – Sight Draft; Term Draft

LETTERS OF CREDIT   – Confirmed, Irrevocable (CILC); Irrevocable (ILC); *Revocable (RLC)*

Invoices

There are five basic kinds of export invoices: Pro Forma, Commercial, Consular, Legalized and Certified.

Pro forma invoice

This is used to give advance information to a customer:

- To support a quotation.
- To help the customer prepare a Letter of Credit.
- For the customer to obtain a foreign currency allocation.
- For the customer to obtain an import licence.
- To ask for payment in advance.
- To invite a tender opportunity.
- (Unpriced), to invite an offer for special goods or services.

It should clearly state 'Pro Forma' and its details copied precisely if it later becomes a commercial invoice. Foreign authorities may delay imports or payments if their original approval of a Pro Forma is abused by subsequent changes.

Commercial invoice (see Figure 3.1)

One of the vital documents of export. Several copies may be required for the buyer and other agencies. The exporter may be free to use his own form, or he may have to use a style stipulated by the buyer's country, and the invoice may have to show clauses or customs declarations in specified languages.

The commercial invoice's purpose is to describe the despatch in conformity with the contract and should show:

- Customer's name, address and order reference.
- Date and Invoice Number.
- Complete description of the goods.
- Price and price base (e.g. CIF Hong Kong).
- Total value, including all charges.
- Currency of payment.
- Weights and quantities, certified if required.
- Name of vessel or airline, if required.
- Shipping marks and numbers.
  and particularly
- PAYMENT TERMS

Some commercial invoices may be required to show:

- Origin of goods (sometimes as a CVO – Combined Certificate of Value and Origin).
- Agent's commission (some can only be paid locally in soft currency).
- Separate freight and insurance.

Consular invoice

Some countries, notably in South America, require consular invoices to enable goods to be cleared from customs on arrival. The purpose is for official checks on prices (e.g. for anti-dumping measures), origins of goods and to calculate import duties.

Exporters must obtain specially printed consular invoices at a charge from UK consulates or embassies of those countries. There are commercial agencies who will obtain these rapidly for exporters.

Figure 3.1 Commercial Invoice

SPECIMEN

INVOICE	FACTURE FACTURA	RECHNUNG FACTUUR

Seller (Name, Address, /AT Reg No) Speirs and Wadley Limited Adderley Road Hackney London E8		C C C N No 85.05
	Invoice No. and Date (Tax Point) 124 11 Aug 19	Seller's Reference Job No. 5678
	Buyer's Reference	S/291

Consignee Woldal Limited PO Box 666 Broadway Hong Kong	Buyer (if not Consignee) Woldal Limited PO Box 666 Broadway Hong Kong

Notify Woldal Limited PO Box 666 Broadway Hong Kong	Country of Origin of Goods United Kingdom	Country of Destination Hong Kong
	Terms of Delivery and Payment C.I.F. Hong Kong Irrevocable documentary credit FDC/2/6789	

Vessel Aircraft etc Cardigan Bay	Port of Loading London
Port of Discharge Hong Kong	

Marks and Numbers Numbers and Kind of Packages. Description of Goods	Quantity	@	Amount (State Currency)
WI 124 HONG KONG 1/5	5 Wooden Cases Said to contain ELECTRIC POWER DRILLS Model LM425 2 speed (900 RPM and 2400 RPM) 425 watt high-torque motor 2 chucks – 12.5mm and 8mm supplied with each drill	400	£ 10.00 each	£4000.00
	Freight charge and export packing			£ 96.00
	Insurance			£ 12.00

TOTAL £4108 Sterling

Gross Weight (kg) 950	Cube (m³) 2.376

Name of Signatory J McDonald, Chief Clerk
Place and Date of Issue London   11 Aug 19
Signature J McDonald

It is hereby certified that this invoice shows the actual price of the goods described that no other invoice has been or will be issued and that all particulars are true and correct

380 1

SITPRO OVERLAYS 1981 V1

COMMERCIAL INVOICE

Legalized invoices

Some countries, notably in the Middle East, require a copy of the exporter's commercial invoice to be 'legalized' by stamping at the UK consulate. The purpose is for official records of the buying country. If deadlines are involved, such as in a LC transaction, exporters should be aware of consulate office hours and public holidays.

Certified invoices

Contracts may require invoices to be certified as to almost anything at the whim of the buyer as his government, e.g. origin of goods, blacklist countries, quality of goods, etc.

Certified invoices also exist for specific destinations, e.g. CVOs used for Commonwealth trade, others for the EEC and LAFTA areas for the purpose of lower duties than apply for nonaligned exporting countries.

Chambers of commerce in most cities can help exporters obtain stampings and certificates for export invoices.

Transport documents

The several methods of transporting goods each have their own document. Most methods are subject to international conventions which define the responsibilities of consignors and carriers, and the rights of consignees. They are:

By Sea:	Bill of Lading (various):	Hague–Visby Rules
By Air:	Air Waybill:	Warsaw Convention
By Road:	Road Consignment Note:	CMR Convention
By Rail:	Rail Consignment Note:	CIM Convention
By Post:	Parcel Post Receipt	

By more than one method: Combined/Through Bill of Lading

Note: It is unwise and often illegal to take goods (except samples) personally, e.g. in a briefcase, into another country. Payment may not be possible.

Bill of lading (see Figure 3.2)

A Bill of Lading is a combined receipt for the goods, evidence of carriage and the document of title to the goods. It is used for sea transport and is issued by the shipping company or its agent in a set of two or three originals, any of which give title, and are negotiable. As the consignee must produce the Bill of Lading to obtain the goods on arrival, the payment terms can give the exporter security, in that the importer can be required to pay the value or accept a bill maturing later, before being given the Bill of Lading. Note: There is no similar security for air freight or parcel post, although alternative security can be arranged (see 'Payment Terms').

The Bill of Lading shows the shipper, the date and place of shipment, the name of the vessel, the port of destination, description of the goods and the shipping marks. It states whether freight has been paid or is collectable forward and may show the name of the consignee but usually is 'to order', i.e. the shipper can endorse it in blank, thus making it transferable.

Where payment terms are non-secure, e.g. 'Open Account – 90 days from invoice date', the Bill of Lading to the order of the buyer is sent directly to him so that he can claim the goods on arrival.

Any number of non-negotiable copy Bills of Lading can be produced for information purposes or for other parties.

Where documentary terms are involved, requiring payment or acceptance of a Bill of Exchange controlled by a bank, the Bill of Lading made 'to order' (and endorsed by the exporter) is sent to the bank with the documents accompanying the Bill.

A 'clean' Bill of Lading is one which is not claused by the receiving shipping company to indicate damage or defects. Most Letters of Credit require clean Bills of Lading, as a means of protecting the buyer.

A 'shipped on-board' Bill of Lading confirms that the goods have been actually despatched on a named vessel.

A 'received for shipment' Bill of Lading confirms only that the goods are held by the shipping company pending a future shipment. Such a Bill of Lading may not be acceptable to a buyer and is usually not permitted under a Letter of Credit. For payment reasons, exporters should expedite shipment so that the Bill of Lading can be converted to a 'shipped' version before the deadline date.

A 'short-form Bill of Lading' is one which does not display the detailed conditions of carriage of the shipping company but is usually acceptable under Letters of Credit.

Figure 3.2   Bill of Lading

BILL OF LADING FOR COMBINED TRANSPORT SHIPMENT OR PORT TO PORT SHIPMENT

Shipper		
Speirs and Wadley Ltd., Adderley Road, Hackney, London E8	**OVERSEAS CONTAINERS LIMITED**	B/L No. **45969648** Booking Ref: **1234567** Shipper's Ref: **Job 5678**

OCL

Consignee		
To Order	**SPECIMEN**	

Notify Party/Address	Place of Receipt (Applicable only when this document is used as a Combined Transport Bill of Lading)
Woldal Ltd., PO Box 666 Broadway, Hong Kong	Container Base Barking Ltd., Box Lane, Renwick Road, Barking, Essex IG 11

Intended Vessel and Voy. No.		Place of Delivery (Applicable only when this document is used as a Combined Transport Bill of Lading)
Cardigan Bay	0415	Modern Terminals Ltd., Number 1 Berth, Kwai Chung, New Territories, Hong Kong
	Intended Port of Loading London	
Intended Port of Discharge Hong Kong		

Marks and Nos. Container Nos.	Number and kind of Packages, description of Goods	Gross Weight (kg)	Measurement (cbm)
OCLU0707070 WI 124 HONG KONG 1/5	5 Wooden Cases Said to contain ELECTRIC POWER DRILLS	950	2.376

2 AUGUST 19..
SINCE SHIPPED
O.C.L.

ABOVE PARTICULARS AS DECLARED BY SHIPPER

*Total No. of Containers/Packages	
Packages or pieces	5

Movement
LCL. Depot/LCL. Depot

Freight and Charges (indicate whether prepaid or collect)

Origin zone transport charge ...

Origin Terminal Handling/LCL Service Charge   Prepaid

Ocean Freight   Prepaid

Destination Terminal Handling/LCL Service Charge   Prepaid

Destination zone transport charge

ICS
CT B/L
April 78

Received by the Carrier from the Shipper in apparent good order and condition (unless otherwise noted herein) the total numbers or quantity of Containers or packages or units indicated opposite ‡ stated by the Shipper to comprise the Goods specified above, for Carriage subject to all the terms hereof (INCLUDING THE TERMS ON THE REVERSE HEREOF AND THE TERMS OF THE CARRIER'S APPLICABLE TARIFF) from the Place of Receipt or the Port of Loading, whichever applicable, to the Port of Discharge or the Place of Delivery, whichever applicable. On presentation of this document (duly endorsed) to the Carrier, by or on behalf of the Holder, the rights and liabilities arising in accordance with the terms hereof shall (without prejudice to any rule of common law or statute rendering them binding upon the Shipper, Holder and Carrier) become binding in all respects between the Carrier and Holder as though the contract contained herein or evidenced hereby had been made between them

Number of Original Bills of Lading
Two   (02)

Place and Date of Issue		
London	01 08 19..	

IN WITNESS of the contract herein contained the number of originals stated opposite has been used, one of which being accomplished the other(s) to be void

For the Carrier   A.J.S.Gilbuey

SPECIMEN ONLY

As Agent(s) only

A 'stale' Bill of Lading is one presented late to a consignee, e.g. after goods have been unloaded from a vessel, causing storage charges or fines. The Uniform Customs and Practice for Documentary Credits (L/Cs) allows documents to be rejected if presented to banks more than 21 days after the Bill of Lading date.

A 'Through Bill of Lading' covers shipment all the way from the exporter's to the consignee's premises, e.g. including road, rail, sea or other carriage. The sea carrier arranges the other transport stages on behalf of the shipper, but is not responsible for their performance.

A 'Combined Transport Bill of Lading' covers container shipments from exporter to consignee. Even though other modes of transport may be used, the sea carrier is responsible throughout to the shipper.

A 'Groupage' or 'House Bill of Lading' is issued by a freight forwarder when he combines several loads into a container to make full use of it. He receives a Groupage Bill of Lading from the carrier and 'deconsolidates' the shipments into individual 'House Bills' for each supporter.

Note: House Bills of Lading are not documents of title and are usually not acceptable by banks under L/Cs. The FIATA Bill of Lading, or FBL, has been developed to overcome this problem and should be stipulated in L/Cs where groupage is certain to take place.

Problems for the credit manager arising out of Bills of Lading:

- Banks do not usually accept, for Letters of Credit, Bills of Lading issued by forwarding agents, or Charter Party Bills of Lading.
- Under CIF and C and F contracts, 'freight prepaid' must be shown on Bills of Lading, otherwise, in the interests of the buyer, the bank will refuse payment on a Letter of Credit.
- Letters of Credit specify a deadline date after shipment for presentation of documents and delays in receipt by the exporter of the Bill of Lading from the shipping or forwarding agent can frustrate payment.
- Where the exporter's goods are expected to be stowed on deck, it is essential for the buyer to allow this in the terms of the Letter of Credit. Otherwise, the 'claused' Bill of Lading will mean refusal by the bank.

These problems can be avoided by care and prior checking by the credit manager, but where unavoidable, it is usually possible to issue a Letter of Indemnity to the bank to obtain payment pending agreement by the buyer.

Air waybill (see Figure 3.3)

Airfreight is now widely used for all but heavy, bulky goods and some traditional commodities. Unfortunately, the classic security of the Bill of Lading for sea transport does not apply to aircraft.

The Air Waybill is not a document of title. It is only a receipt for the goods and evidence of the carriage. It is issued in triplicate or greater (for the exporter, the airline and the consignee) and goods are released to the named consignee at destination.

To control release of the goods only after payment or acceptance of a bill of exchange, it is necessary to consign the goods to a bank or agent, for release upon instruction. The advantage of speed in airfreight makes this technique seem cumbersome on occasions, but it may be justified for a risky credit customer.

Rail consignment note (CIM note) and road consignment note (CMR note)

The situation is the same as with the Air Waybill. The rail or road carrier taking exports through a continuous journey to the foreign destination will release the goods to the named consignee at the arrival point.

For the credit manager requiring security, it is necessary to name a bank or agent as consignee.

Parcel post receipt

For many small products, the international Parcel Post is the fastest and cheapest method of getting to the buyer.

The Post Office receipt will show date of despatch; signature of receipt; the name and address of the consignee; identification numbers and the postage paid. Goods will be delivered to the consignee at destination or held, on advice, for his collection.

Two problems arise for the credit manager:

(a)   Most foreign post offices do not deliver, but await collection by buyers, goods can deteriorate and there is no certainty that buyers will collect.

Figure 3.3 Air Waybill

125- 3656 6773 | LHR

| | | | | | For Carrier use only | | 125- 3656 6773 |

Flight/Day | Flight/Day

Airport of Departure (Address of First Carrier) and Requested Routing	Airport of Destination	Flight/Day	Flight/Day
HEATHROW	KENNEDY	BA 23	1/8
			Booked

Routing and Destination

| To | | By First Carrier | BA | To | By | To | By |

Consignee's Account Number | Consignee's Name and Address

WOLDAL INCORPORATED,
BROADWAY,
NEW YORK,
U.S.A.

Shipper's Account Number | Shipper's Name and Address

SPEIRS AND WADLEY LTD.,
ADDERLEY ROAD,
HACKNEY,
LONDON E.8.

Issuing Carrier's Agent Account No | Issuing Carrier's Agent Name and City

BRUNSWICK AIR, ASHFORD ROAD,
HOUNSLOW, MIDDX.

Agent's IATA Code
93-6-3331

| Currency | Declared Value for Carriage | Declared Value for Customs |
| UKE | N.V.D. | N.V.D. |

British airways

Air Waybill
(Air Consignment note)

Issued by British Airways, London
Member of International Air Transport Association   Not negotiable

If the carriage involves an ultimate destination or stop in a country other than the country of departure, the Warsaw Convention may be applicable and the Convention governs, and in most cases limits the liability of carriers in respect of loss of or damage to cargo.
Agreed stopping places are those places (other than the places of departure and destination) shown under requested routing and/or those places shown in carrier's timetables as scheduled stopping places for the route. Address of first carrier is the airport of departure.
SEE CONDITIONS ON REVERSE HEREOF.

The shipper certifies that the particulars on the face hereof are correct, agrees to the CONDITIONS ON REVERSE HEREOF, accepts that the carrier's liability is limited as stated in 4(c) on the reverse hereof and accepts such value unless a higher value for carriage is declared on the face hereof subject to an additional charge

a. Hinton   pp BRUNSWICK AIR
Signature of Shipper or his Agent

Carrier certifies goods described below were received for carriage subject to the CONDITIONS ON REVERSE HEREOF. the goods then being in apparent good order and condition except as noted hereon

Executed on   1-8-19..   LHR
(Date)   (Place)

M.Ellis
Signature of Issuing Carrier or its Agent

Copies 1, 2 and 3 of this Air Waybill are originals and have the same validity

Weight Charge and Valuation Charge		All Other Charges at Origin		Accounting Information	
Prepaid	Collect	Prepaid	Collect		
XX		XX		REF. 1307660	NY 32256

| No of Packages RCP | Actual Gross Weight | kg lb | Rate Class Commodity Item No | Chargeable Weight | Rate/Charge | Total | Nature and Quantity of Goods (incl Dimensions or Volume) |
| 5 | 254 | K | | 254 | 1.765 | 448.310 | 5 CASES ELECTRIC DRILLS 1m x 1m x 1.5m |

| | Prepaid Weight Charge | Prepaid Valuation Charge | Due Carrier | Total other Prepaid Charges | Due Agent | Total Prepaid | For Carrier's Use Only at Destination |
| PREPAID | 448.310 | 2.000 | | 0.750 | | 451.060 | |

	AWB Fee and Code	Clearance and Handling	Cartage	Other Charges (except Weight Charge and Valuation Charge)			Collect Charges in Destination Currency
	0.750	2.000(c)					
							COD Amount
	Disbursements	COD and/or Disb Fee					Total Charges

	Collect Weight Charge	Collect Valuation Charge	Due Carrier	Total Other Collect Charges	Due Agent	COD Amount	Total Collect
COLLECT							
	CA Number 32256	Attached EEC Transit Documents	Type	Customs Reference Number	In Envelope	Yes	No

5 CASES   SW/WOL. INC./NEW YORK   1-5

Handling Information

T 327 (12th)   Original 3 - (For Shipper)   125- 3656 6773

(b)   The technique of sending documentary collections c/o a bank is not effective because foreign post offices do not agree to hold goods 'to the order' of the banks.

Insurance policies and certificates
(see Figure 3.4)

Under CIF contract terms, the exporter must hold an insurance company certificate or the actual policy, to cover damage or loss during the carriage. A broker's certificate or cover note is not acceptable to banks on documentary collections or to the courts in the event of litigation.

Note: For marine insurance to be valid, the cover must be dated prior to the sailing of the vessel.

The exporter should insure the goods for as long as they remain in his possession and at his risk. The Incoterms price basis will define this period. However, prudent exporters purchase 'contingency' or 'seller's interest' cover outside of their own liability, e.g. if the buyer does not take up the goods and they have to be re-sold locally or returned to the UK.

Some Incoterms effects are:

Ex-Works: Risk passes to the buyer when the goods are made available to him.
FOB: Exporter insures up to the ship's rail and the buyer bears the risk from there.
C&F: As for FOB.
CIF: Exporter insures for the entire transit.
DDP: Exporter insures all the way to a named destination, often the customer's premises.
FRC: (Free carrier) For road transport to the Continent, the FOB term is inappropriate. Risk passes from the exporter at a named point where goods are handed to the carrier.

The old expressions of 'With Average', 'Free from Particular Average', 'All Risks', etc. were abolished in 1982 in favour of the Institute Cargo Clauses A, B or C. 'A' Clauses provide the most comprehensive cover and 'B' and 'C' clauses are used for specific risks and normally refer to total loss only.

Figure 3.4 Certificate of Insurance

ORIGINAL

Lloyd's Agent at **Hong Kong** is authorised to adjust and settle on behalf of the Underwriters, and to purchase on behalf of the Corporation of Lloyd's, in accordance with Lloyd's Standing Regulations for the Settlement of Claims Abroad, any claim which may arise on this Certificate

LLOYD'S

Exporters
Reference

THIS CERTIFICATE
REQUIRES ENDORSEMENT

Certificate of Insurance No. C 8700/

This is to Certify that there has been deposited with the Committee of Lloyd's an Open Cover effected by *Barclays Insurance Brokers International Limited* of Lloyd's, acting on behalf of Speirs and Wadley Limited with Underwriters at Lloyd's, dated the 1st day of January, 19 , and that the said Underwriters have undertaken to issue to *Barclays Insurance Brokers International Limited* Policy/Policies of Marine Insurance at Lloyd's to cover, up to £100,000 in all by any one steamer or sending by air and/or post and/or road and/or rail and/or conveyance and/or location, machine tools, other interests held covered

to be shipped on or before the 31st day of December, 19 , from any port or ports, place or places in *the United Kingdom* to any port or ports, place or places in *the World or vice versa, other voyages held covered* and that are entitled to declare against the said Open Cover the shipments attaching thereto.

Dated at Lloyds, London, 2nd October 1979

for the Committee of Lloyd's

Conveyance	From
Cardigan Bay	**London**

Via/To	To	INSURED VALUE/Currency
Hong Kong	**Warehouse, Hong Kong**	**£4520 Sterling**

Marks and Numbers	Interest
WI 124 HONG KONG 1/5	5 Wooden Cases Said to contain 400 ELECTRIC POWER DRILLS Model LM 425 2 Speed (900 rpm and 2400 rpm) 425 watt high-torque motor 2 chucks – 12·5mm and 8mm supplied with each drill

We hereby declare for Insurance under the said Cover interest as specified above so valued subject to the terms of the Standard Form of Lloyd's Marine Policy providing for the settlement of claims abroad and to the special conditions stated below and on the back hereof

Institute Cargo Clauses (A) (1 1 82) or Institute Cargo Clauses (Air) (excluding sendings by Post) (1 1 82) as applicable
Institute War Clauses (Cargo) (1 1 82) or Institute War Clauses (Air Cargo) (excluding sendings by Post) (1 1 82) or Institute War Clauses (sendings by Post) (1 1 82) as applicable
Institute Strikes Clauses (Cargo) (1 1 82) or Institute Strikes Clauses (Air Cargo) (1 1 82) as applicable
General Average and Salvage Contribution payable in full irrespective of insured or contributing values

Underwriters agree losses, if any, shall be payable to the order of Speirs and Wadley Limited on surrender of this Certificate.

In the event of loss or damage which may result in a claim under this Insurance, immediate notice should be given to the Lloyd's Agent at the port or place where the loss or damage is discovered in order that he may examine the goods and issue a survey report.

(Survey fee is customarily paid by claimant and included in valid claim against Underwriters.)

This Certificate not valid unless the Declaration be signed by

Speirs and Wadley Limited

Dated at

London, 30th July 19 ..

Signed **W. H. Nevin**

pp Speirs and Wadley Limited

Brokers Barclays Insurance Brokers International Limited
India House, 81/84 Leadenhall Street, London EC3A 3DJ

14478/9

CERTIFICATE OF INSURANCE – SEE PAGE 18

Figure 3.5 Arab–British Chamber of Commerce Certificate of Origin

Consignor: ‏المرسل :‏ [1]	**B/ 380953** Consignor's ref. [4]
	شهـــادة منشــأ **CERTIFICATE OF ORIGIN**
Consignee: ‏المرسل اليـه :‏ [2]	تشهد السلطة الموقعة بأن البضائع الوارد بيانها أدناه The undersigned authority certifies that the goods shown below originated in: ‏منشـأها :‏ [5]
Consigned by: ‏مرسلة بواسطة:‏ [3]	غرفة التجارة العربية البريطانية **ARAB-BRITISH CHAMBER OF COMMERCE**

Marks and Numbers: ‏الأرقام و العلامات‏	Quantity and Kind of Packages: ‏كمية ونـوع الطرود‏	Description of Goods: ‏مواصفات البضاعة‏	Weight (gross & net): [6] ‏الوزن (الصافي والاجمالي)‏

غرفة التجارة العربية البريطانية
ARAB-BRITISH CHAMBER OF COMMERCE

‏مكان وتاريخ الاصدار‏
Place and Date of Issue

Issuing Authority   ‏سلطة الاصدار‏

Figure 3.6 European Communities Certificate of Origin

Consignor: (Expéditeur:)			SPECIMEN	**B** 629546

Speirs and Wadley Limited,
Adderley Road,
Hackney London.

EUROPEAN COMMUNITIES
(Communautes Europeennes)

Consignee: (Destinataire:)

Compania de Dowal
Av. Grande 1124
Madrid, Spain

CERTIFICATE OF ORIGIN
(Certificat d'origine)

Consignment by: (Expédition prévue par:)

Ship – IONIAN

THE LONDON CHAMBER OF COMMERCE AND INDUSTRY

THE UNDERSIGNED AUTHORITY certifies that the goods shown below
(L'AUTORITE SOUSSIGNEE certifie que les marchandises désignées ci-dessous)

Serial No.	Packages		Description of goods	Weight (1)	
	Number and kind	Marks and numbers		gross	net
	5 cases	SW CIA DOW MADRID 1 TO 5	Electric Drills	254 Ks.	240 Ks.

originated in:

(sont originaires de:)   European Communities – United Kingdom

L. Griffiths.

London, 3rd August, 19 ..	The London Chamber of Commerce and Industry
(Place and date of issue)	(Name, signature and stamp of competent authority)

(1) This entry may, where appropriate, be replaced by others allowing identification of the goods.

CERTIFICATE OF ORIGIN

Certificates

Certificate of origin

These are required by many importing countries as evidence of the origin of goods. Customs clearance cannot take place without them in these places and payment depends on their submission, e.g. in Letters of Credit.

The two types in use currently are:

- The Arab–British Chamber of Commerce C/O for the 19 countries of the Arab League (see Figure 3.5).
- The European Communities C/O for all other countries requiring them (see Figure 3.6).

Blacklist certificate

Required by some foreign governments in conflict with others, to show that goods did not originate from the offending country, or that the parties involved in the contract are not individually 'blacklisted', or that vessels will not call at prohibited ports en route.

Packing list/specification

Show how the goods are packed and assist foreign Customs authorities to check complex consignments. They do not usually show values.

Inspection certificate (see Figure 3.7)

A number of importing countries require a report from an Inspection Agency chosen by them to operate in the exporter's country. Goods are inspected prior to shipment to check quality, quantity, condition, price, etc. Typical agencies are Cotechna and SGS. They issue a 'Certificate of Clean Findings' which is often specified in documentary payment arrangements.

Single administrative document (SAD)

In January 1988, this new document entered the scene to replace the multitude of previous customs documents in use in the EEC. It is an 8 page document

Figure 3.7 Inspection Certificate

CERTIFICAT D'INSPECTION

N° 4.370.843

GENERAL SUPERINTENDENCE COMPANY LTD.

TÉLÉGRAMMES
SUPERVISE

SOCIÉTÉ GÉNÉRALE DE SURVEILLANCE

Société Anonyme au Capital de 12 000 000 de Frs

SIÈGE SOCIAL À PARIS 16, RUE DU LOUVRE (1er) 75054 PARIS CEDEX 01   B.P. 278   R.C. PARIS B 552051050

CERTIFICATE OF QUALITY/CONDITION AND ANALYSIS OF SHIPMENT SAMPLE BASED ON
MINIMUM TWO PERCENT OF THE CARGO
••

We undersigned SOCIETE GENERALE DE SURVEILLANCE SA certify that the quality
inspection had been carried out at the mills and just before loading of :

169.000 bags of flour weighing gross 11.316 LT. 2.160 lbs
                                 tare   169 LT. 1.690 lbs
                                        ----
                                 nett 11.147 LT.   470 lbs

New single strong jute bags marked DRB/JTW.

According to the various analyses made on 2% minimum of the cargo, the flour
conforms in every respect to the specification laid down in the contract of sale
n° F.105 dated 29.01... addendum n° 3 dated 16.04

FRENCH WHEAT FLOUR milled from wheat of fair average quality of the current
season in sound and merchantable condition and fit for human consumption at the
time of shipment.

Extraction   72 % maximum
Ashes   0,520 % maximum on the dry substance
Protein   11 % minimum
Moisture   14 % maximum

The above quantity has been loaded at ROUEN under the supervision of our correspondents on the S/S ETERNITY to Colombo as per bill of lading N° 1 dated
ROUEN 24.05....

SPECIMEN

PARIS 25th May 19..
SOCIETE GENERALE DE SURVEILLANCE

P.pen

INSPECTION EFFECTUÉE EN AME ET CONSCIENCE MAIS SANS RESPONSABILITÉ DE NOTRE PART. LE PRÉSENT CERTIFICAT NE LIBÈRE PAS LE
VENDEUR DE SES RESPONSABILITÉS CONTRACTUELLES. PARTICULIÈREMENT EN CAS DE VICE CACHÉ DE LA MARCHANDISE. NON DÉCELÉ
AU MOMENT DE L'INSPECTION.

used for all Intra-Community trade and also for exports from EEC countries to non-EEC countries and for imports from non-EEC countries into the EEC. It is not used for transactions between countries outside the EEC.

As business grows in both directions between the UK and the rest of the Community, especially with the 'single market' concept of 1992 approaching, it is useful that a single document can simplify the form filling for journeys across Europe, to minimize customs delays and thus speed up the receipt of goods by customers and the resultant cash flow.

The bill of exchange (see Figures 3.8, 3.9, 3.10 and 3.11)

This is the exporter's friend – the document which most successfully achieves payment for goods exported on credit.

According to the Bill of Exchange Act 1882, it is 'An unconditional order in writing, addressed by one person (the drawer) to another (the drawee), signed by the person giving it, requiring the person to whom it is addressed to pay on demand or at a fixed or determinable future time a sum certain in money to, or to the order of, a specified person (the payee), or to a bearer.'

That definition has stood the test of time and has been copied, with little amendment, by many other countries. The standard format of bills has become internationally recognized.

In a normal transaction, the exporter draws the bill and sends it either directly or via a bank to his customer who, according to its payment term, either pays its value or accepts it, by signing across its face, as payable on a future date (either a specific date or determinable, e.g. 90 days from shipment). The buyer may dishonour the bill by neither paying nor accepting it.

Through the banking system, the exporter can use bills with the documents of title to control the release of goods. Accepted bills can be discounted to provide cash and bills can be claused to charge interest up to payment date and to cover currency shortfalls.

When a bill is sent through the banking system for collection the accompanying instructions to the collecting band state the required method of remittance, i.e. mail or cable, and the name of a local contact in the event of difficulties, and who should bear the charges at each end (see Figure 3.8).

Figure 3.8 Bill Instruction Form

From: **National Westminster Bank PLC**

Branch

Date

To: Overseas Branch, Bills Department

Branch Reference Number

Please **Collect** the following Foreign Bill (with or without Documents) or Cheque(s)/Drafts payable abroad, subject to instructions marked [X] to special instructions below, and to General Instructions overleaf

Drawee		Town	Tenor	Amount
Drawer		Name and address of Bank to be used (If unspecified your usual correspondent should be used)		

State-ment	Freight note	Invoice	Cons. Inv	Cert. of Origin	Insce. Cert./ Policy	Bills of Lading	Other Documents

Unless otherwise instructed original documents should be despatched by registered airmail - duplicates by unregistered seamail.

Covering

X	**Care of Goods** Any consequent expenses to be claimed from the drawee but if not paid by them to be charged to me/us.	Postal charges are for the account of the **Drawer/Drawee**		Collection charges are for the account of the **Drawer/Drawee**
	Deliver documents against	Acceptance Payment may be deferred until arrival of goods	**Overseas Branch Use Only**	
	Remit Proceeds by Sterling	Remit proceeds by **Telegraphic Transfer** at		
	Mail Transfer	the expense of the **Drawer/Drawee**		
	Charges may	Collect interest at	No Protest for	Non-acceptance	Non-payment	Protest for	Non-acceptance	Non-payment
	be waived	from date of draft to approximate date of receipt of proceeds in London		
	Forward original documents by air mail	Insurance covered by drawee. Please see that goods are still insured if not taken up immediately on arrival	Insurance covered by drawer	**X**	See General Instructions Overleaf

Special Instructions: In case of need refer to

whose instructions may be followed unconditionally.

who will co-operate in obtaining payment.

I/We agree that this business, if undertaken by the Bank, will be subject to the conditions printed on the back hereof

NWB1706 Rev Apr 82-1

Customer's Signature

Authorised Signature

The following **General Instructions** are given by the Bank to its correspondents in connection with all Collections, and are applicable except in so far as they may be modified or contradicted by any Special Instructions given by customers or appearing on the Bill itself:

Presentation for Acceptance. – Term bills, not already accepted, should be presented for acceptance immediately on receipt, unless contrary instructions are given.

Advice of Acceptance. – Please give us prompt advice of acceptance, stating date of maturity.

Non-Acceptance and/or Non-Payment. – Advise non-acceptance or non-payment promptly by mail, unless otherwise instructed, giving definite reason for refusal, and stating whether the case of need (when given) has been advised.

Protest. – Unless contrary instructions are given overleaf, or on the bill itself, please proceed as follows:

Protest accepted bills if unpaid at maturity.
Do not protest bills for non-acceptance.
Do not protest cheques or drafts at sight or on demand.

Care of Goods. – If documents of title are attached and these are not taken up on arrival of the consignment, or any difficulty arises, please advise us immediately, stating the reason. Meanwhile please see that the goods are properly protected but do not insure them unless specific instructions to do so are given. All consequent expenses to be claimed from drawee.

Charges. – Where charges, including collection commission and Bill Stamps, are not paid by the drawees such charges will be debited by the Bank to its Principals.

When goods are insured by Drawee, the following instruction is given:

Insurance covered by drawee. Please see that goods are still insured if not taken up immediately on arrival.

Collections are handled subject to Uniform Rules for the Collections (1978 Revision) International Chamber of Commerce Publication No 322.

A great advantage of the bill of exchange is that it stands alone as evidence of a debt, for example, if legal action becomes necessary. There is no need to prove a contract existed or that delivery was made; the court simply needs to prove that the debtor accepted the bill.

In many markets, dishonoured bills have to be 'protested', i.e. recorded by a notary public in the official record, before they can be taken to court action. There is usually only a brief time from due date allowed for protest action, so the decision to protest or not has to be given in the Bill Instruction Form to the collecting bank.

For documentary Letters of Credit, bills may be specified and may be required to be drawn on the opening, advising or confirming banks, or on the customer. The LC instruction has to be followed.

A Promissory Note is often confused with a Bill of Exchange, but is not the same thing. It is drawn by the customer, promising to pay the exporter or other beneficiary and, as such, does not meet the above definition of the Bill of Exchange Act.

Figure 3.8 shows a Bill Instruction Form, which accompanies bills sent through the banking system;
Figure 3.9 is an example of a Sight Draft;
Figure 3.10 is an example of a Term Draft; and
Figure 3.11 shows the same draft, but accepted by the drawee.

Letters of credit

A documentary credit is a conditional bank undertaking of payment.

More fully, it is a written undertaking by a bank (issuing bank) given to the seller (beneficiary) at the request, and in accordance with the instructions, of the buyer (applicant) to effect payment up to a stated sum of money, within a prescribed time limit and against stipulated documents.

These stipulated documents are likely to include those required for commercial, official, insurance or transport purposes, such as commercial, invoice, certificate of origin, insurance policy or certificate and bill of lading or combined transport document.

Because the documentary credit is a bank undertaking, the seller can look to the bank for payment, instead of relying upon the ability or willingness of the buyer to pay.

Figure 3.9 Sight Draft

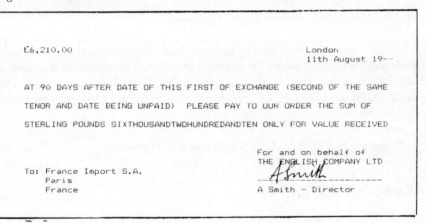

Figure 3.10 Term Draft

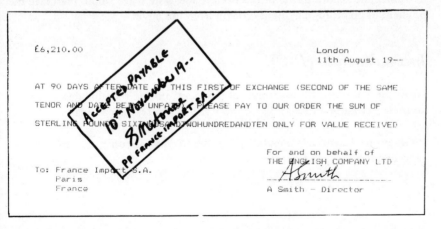

Figure 3.11 Accepted Term Draft

However, because the undertaking is conditional, the seller only has the right to demand payment if he meets all the requirements of the credit. It is, therefore, unwise for the seller to proceed with shipment until he is aware of the requirements – and is satisfied that he can meet them.

The L/C document is normally issued on the letterheading or special form of the advising or confirming bank. It is perfectly valid when notified to the seller by telex.

The documentary credit achieves a commercially acceptable compromise between the conflicting interests of buyer and seller by matching time of payment for the goods with the time of their 'delivery'. It does this by making payment against documents representing the goods rather than against the goods themselves.

An irrevocable documentary credit (especially a confirmed one) is, therefore, an excellent instrument of payment.

Above all, the beneficiary (seller) must remember that the credit undertaking to pay, accept or negotiate is conditional upon his compliance with all the terms and conditions of the credit. Since it is issued 'subject to UCP' (Uniform Customs and Practice for Documentary Credits), this means compliance with the requirements of 'UCP' also.

There are two kinds of L/C, Revocable and Irrevocable.

Revocable credit (RLC)

Involves risk, as the credit may be amended or cancelled while the goods are in transit and before payment has been made. The seller would then face the problem of obtaining payment directly from the buyer.

Irrevocable credit (ILC)

Gives the seller greater assurance of payment: but he remains dependent on an undertaking of a foreign bank and its ability to transfer funds.

Gives the buyer less flexibility, as the credit can only be amended or cancelled if the exporter agrees.

Confirmed irrevocable credit (CILC)

Gives the seller a double assurance of payment, since a bank in the seller's country adds its own undertaking to that of the issuing bank. This additional requirement on the part of the seller is more costly.

There are some special kinds of Irrevocable L/C, viz.

● *Revolving credit*
Where the amount is renewed or reinstated automatically without specific amendment to the credit being needed.

● *Red clause credit*
A credit with a special clause that authorizes advances to the beneficiary before presentation of documents. The clause is incorporated at the specific request of the applicant, and the wording can be negotiated between the parties.

● *Transferable credit*
Can be transferred by the original beneficiary to one or more second beneficiaries. It is normally used when the first beneficiary does not supply the merchandise himself, and wishes to transfer part, or all, of his rights to the actual supplier(s) as second beneficiary(ies).

This type of credit can only be transferred once, i.e. the second beneficiary(ies) cannot transfer to a third beneficiary. The terms of the original credit must apply, except that:

● the name of the first beneficiary may be substituted for that of the applicant for the credit.
● the amount of the credit and any unit price may be reduced to enable the first beneficiary to obtain his profit.
● the validity and the period for shipment may be shortened.

● *Back-to-back credit*
If a LC is not transferable, and the seller needs to purchase the goods from another supplier, it may be possible to use a 'back-to-back credit'. This involves the issue of a second credit by the seller in favour of his supplier. The seller, as beneficiary of the first credit, offers it as 'security' to the advising bank for the issuance of the second credit. The seller is responsible for reimbursing the bank for payments made, regardless of whether he himself is paid under the first credit. There is no compulsion for the bank to issue the second credit.

Checklist: Export Documents

Croner's Reference Book for Exporters defines the penalties of poor export documentation as: Delays in transit; Fines; Increased costs; Time spent sorting out problems; Loss of goodwill; Missed deadlines; Non-payment by customers.

Every export management, at least annually, should ask itself:

- Which documents do we produce ourselves?
- Which documents are provided to us by others?
- Are our documents clear?
- How can we make them more effective?
- Do we receive external documents quickly?
- Do we produce, assemble and despatch documents efficiently?
- What complaints, errors or losses have we had in the past 12 months, caused by documentation problems?
- Are we absolutely clear on documentary requirements for each of our export markets?
- Do we accurately perform to documentary requirements specified in customers' orders?
- *Action assignments:* Senior staff should be detailed to put right any defects arising, without delay.

Note: Many exporting firms keep special records of documentation errors and lateness on Letter of Credit presentations. Since L/Cs define contractual and customer requirements, they are a microcosm of all export transactions. If each failed presentation is used to correct the next shipment, the failure rate on L/Cs should reduce progressively, and performance should improve on documentary bills and open account transactions.

4 Export credit risks

An overview of credit risks and their management

'Will we get paid?' The most important question in business. The decision to transfer shareholders' funds to customers in the form of trade credit is indeed a serious one, concerned with trust (the Latin root of credit means 'to trust'). The belief that the funds will come back with profit attached should be positive, based on knowledge, not wishful thinking or total ignorance.

The credit manager's task is to find out *early* if payment problems are likely *and do something about them*. In other words, *managed credit*, not reactive firefighting. If a potential customer is already in financial straits and pays other suppliers only when threatened with legal action, it makes sense to know that and take steps in good time – a special discussion for preferential payments, or pre-payment, or Letter of Credit, or a reliable third party guarantee, and so on. Just to proceed as if there were no risk, or worse not to bother to find out the customer's situation, is *irresponsible management* of shareholders' funds.

The same logic applies where customers may be first-class but their country is declining in ability to transfer Sterling for imports. The financial press reports all such cases, the banks certainly advise on transfer risk situations, so do various commercial agencies and the credit insurance companies. There is no shortage of intelligence on risk situations, so it is rather surprising that so many exporters claim to be taken by surprise.

The attitude of a leading supplier of business information is that

INFORMATION = MANAGEMENT OPPORTUNITY, and
MANAGEMENT OPPORTUNITY = PROFIT MAXIMIZATION

So, credit management needs information, and in a progressive company culture that recognizes that sales revenue is always at risk to some degree, needs to use the information to help maximize profit performance.

Credit risk obviously influences sales planning and expense. Company funds and management brain-power are spent on product design for export markets, on market research, on cultivation of customers and on production planning. When customers go into decline, or actually fail, there is an expensive set-back to company plans and an indirect write-off of expense to date. The same situation applies to markets and their ability to import and find hard currency at the right times.

Since the plague of foreign debt crises afflicting so many countries in the 1980s, market risk comes before customer risk in order of importance. In his book 'Credit Management', Dick Bass wrote that 'the market risk should be considered first because if it proves unacceptable and unavoidable, there is no point in looking at the buyer risk'.

There is an increasingly valuable case for credit and sales managements to work together to identify good, growing prospects and avoid the time-wasting, albeit sometimes glamorous, customers and markets which simply cannot provide the necessary business growth.

The approach should be to look at existing and prospective customers and ask:

1. Is the customer about to go bust? If not:
2. How much capacity does the customer have to buy from us and pay promptly on our terms?

    If the answers are looking good so far, then:

3. Is the customer growing or declining, and how fast?

All these questions of course are preceded by a view of the market, i.e. for our projected sales and terms can that country generate adequate Sterling (or other hard currency)?

If, by magic, an exporter had the answers instantly on all customers, the profile would probably be disturbing. Few sellers are insulated from the company insolvency and market restrictions which are now a part of business life. In Germany, a company fails every 5 minutes or so of the working day. In the USA it is every 3 minutes. For every company that goes bust there are at least ten which are struggling, i.e. are delaying payments and may be the next failures. Similarly, about 150 of the world's 208 countries were restricting their release of foreign exchange in various degrees in 1988, resulting in slow revenue for exporters.

It would be quite typical for an exporter selling to, say, 100 countries in all parts of the world, with, say, 1000 customer accounts, to find a profile of:

	Markets	Customers
No Risk	15%	10%
Average Risk	35%	60%
High Risk	50%	30%

Good credit management identifies the risky customers and markets, but (a) emphasizes the scope in all the other, solvent and liquid ones and (b) tries to make satisfactory payment arrangements for all the problem cases, so that few sales are lost.

But the message for sales staff is to recognize the real limitations of some customers and markets and to apply their skills to compete better in the more profitable cases.

Very few risk events are total surprises – the warning signs are there but somebody must take the trouble to find them. Most risks that delay payment can be identified at the order entry stage by proper investigation. Credit managers need good, selective information and a system for using it positively.

An exporter's credit policy should define, inter alia:

(a)   How often information should be obtained: e.g. Once a year; all the time, progressively; only when something of interest occurs; when new accounts are opened, etc.

(b)   On which Customers and Markets: e.g. all; those providing 80% of revenue; only high values, etc.

(c)   Which types of data and delivery system to use: e.g. internal, external, free sources only, agencies, referees, banks, ECGD, financial analysis, etc; by post, telephone, telex, fax, computer screen, visit, etc.

(d)   How to systemize and use information: e.g. computer or manual codes; whom to copy; use of credit limits; use of risk categories; credit insurance requirements; order entry and/or pre shipment; analyses and reports, etc.

Any system for risk assessment should bear in mind the Golden Rule:

KEEP THE ORDERS FLOWING

There are two features to this:

1.   Use the 'Exception' approach, where only problem cases get held for action – all others go through automatically.

2. On problem cases, look for a fast turn-round and ways to achieve the
    sale.

Credit management is the art of finding acceptable ways of saying '*yes*' to
risky business.

Credit risks – a full list

We have said that the risks are the *insolvency, illiquidity* and *lack of growth* of
customers and the *lack of foreign exchange* of countries.

The credit insurance companies have to be more precise, since they offer
protection to exporters against a wide range of credit losses. The main risks
covered by credit insurers can be grouped thus.

Buyer

- Insolvency
- Default at due date
- Repudiation of contract

Buyer's government

- Cancellation of import licence
- Imposition of import licence
- Non-transfer of sterling
- Moratorium on external debts
- Law preventing contract performance
- War/Civil disorder
- Contract non-ratification
- Expropriation/damage to Plant/Property
- Unfair calling of bonds

Exporter's government

- Cancellation/imposition of export licence
- Prevention of contract performance

Any government

- Actions preventing contract performance

Collecting credit information

In accepting an order for future payment, some exporters completely by-pass the stage of a conscious credit decision, while others go to the extreme of collecting masses of data they will never use.

A good system is one that provides up-to-date information at a cost which relates economically to the business involved.

The many sources should be used to channel selected information into:

(a) Country Files: indicating economic conditions, political risks, currency transfer situations, local payment terms, and any special ECGD requirements.

(b) Customer Files: showing correct name, address, telex, telephone and fax numbers, names of contacts, payment terms, and any special clauses or conditions. Also the stock of financial data from agencies, banks, visit reports, etc. and for large exposures, balance sheet details. Where credit insurance cover is held, the terms and renewal dates, etc. should be clearly shown, so that cover is not lost.

The system should be kept simple and highly visible. Outdated reports should be consigned to a 'History' file and dumped after three years.

Exporters should guard against allowing bureaucratic systems to develop whereby every possible report is purchased and full sets of data gathered on every customer regardless of value. The resulting mass only delays and obscures the essential work.

We therefore examine sources of information with particular regard to cost and availability.

Checklist: Sources of Information	
Customers	*Countries*
• Credit Reporting Agencies	• 'International Risk and Payment Review' • Specialist political risk agencies
• Credit Insurance companies • Bank references • Trade references • Balance sheet analyses • Sales Ledger Information • Visit Reports • Trade Credit Groups • Local agents/subsidiaries	• Credit Insurance companies • Bank Country Reports • Bank Reviews/Bulletins • IMF Monthly Bulletins • ICM Export Workshops • FCIB Round Tables • Trade Credit Groups • Local agents/subsidiaries 'Financial Times' 'Economist'

Customer information

Credit reporting agencies

There are several well established companies providing business information on foreign entities. Recent years have seen a variety of mergers and associations of agencies across Europe, partly to combine their databases, and achieve economies in collecting and analysing future data, and partly to present more substantial and comprehensive facilities to clients.

The great advantage offered by the larger credit agencies is the combination of several types of information in a report, e.g.:

• Confirmation of the subject's exact name, address, activity, directors, etc.
• Latest Companies Registry data.
• Estimates of interim results from authorized officers of the subject company.
• Payment experience of other suppliers.
• Legal charges, judgements etc.
• Financial ratios and trends over 3 years.
• Comparison of performance with subject's industry average.
• Credit rating.

Obviously it is costly for agencies to collect data continuously on all possible companies without even knowing if it will ever be purchased by anybody, or how many times. It is thus understandable that credit reports appear expensive and that some agencies sell selected sections at lower prices. The cost has to be compared to the alternative of collecting separate data from several other sources.

However, most credit managers agree that money is only spent on agency reports for substantial exposures.

The method of delivering credit information has become a competitive factor in recent years. The traditional procedure has been to phone an agency, or send them a printed form, then receive a multi-page report through the post a few days later. That method is still used by some as the most economical for non-urgent cases. However, delivery can now be by courier, telex or fax the same day as the request.

Some agencies offer data on-line to a computer terminal in the exporter's office, charging either on a time-usage basis or on a standard charge per report. Dun and Bradstreet International, the world's largest agency, also offers the DUNSVOICE service, where the exporter telephones the database and receives recorded spoken answers to pre-set questions, using the telephone buttons as codes for various kinds of data.

There is a mixed opinion of the value of credit agencies, when their charges for reports is compared to the sometimes out-of-date nature of the information, and the limited data for some markets. In fact, the best agencies can only collect what is available and try to fill any gaps with comments from authorized officers of the companies under enquiry. Agency reports are as good as the information available. Compare the Middle East with the USA. In the Gulf states which lack legislation on financial disclosures, tax and competitive reasons cause companies to reveal very little about themselves. The concept of showing the world how credit-worthy they are has not yet become necessary. Estimates are made by agencies of items such as Sales and Net Worth. Two agencies may come up with different estimates. It is little wonder that even rich companies in Kuwait, for example, are asked for Letters of Credit, because their true solvency cannot be established by creditors.

Reports on companies in the US present a very pleasant contrast, with several pages of the fullest disclosure of financials, products, directors' families and education, statements on current progress and corporate plans, and so on. This is simply the evolution of credit-dependence in the USA, where companies have got used to the need to explain themselves to justify bank and trade credit.

Some exporters routinely request an agency report on all new customers. This is not always wise if there are small value accounts as the cost may not be covered by the profit on the transaction. For example, the average net margin ('bottom-line') of UK companies is about 5%. The £40 average cost of a standard agency report would use up the profit of any orders less than £800 – and there are many other demands on the margin besides agency reports.

Similarly, most exporters routinely use the same agency for all reports, when there may be better, faster or cheaper reports available from other agencies, particularly those situated in buyers' own countries and especially in Western Europe and North America.

Credit managers should run trials with different agencies and decide which to use for each market.

Purely for illustration we can examine the services of some major European credit agencies, *Dun & Bradstreet; Internet; Graydon; Infocheck; Infolink.*

1.   DUN AND BRADSTREET INTERNATIONAL, 26 CLIFTON STREET, LONDON EC2P 2LY (DESTINED TO CENTRALIZE FACILITIES AT HIGH WYCOMBE IN 1990)

Estimated by 'Credit Management' magazine in August 1988 to have 38% of the European business market, with information stored on 7 million companies plus a further 9 million in the USA. They have the most comprehensive mix of data in reports, especially on current payment experience of other suppliers, important when filed accounts are old or indicate risks. In the UK, D & B ask all subscribers to volunteer their sales ledger records monthly, in full confidence, to help build a remarkable database of payment practices of millions of companies. D&B believe in the 'pre-payment by unit' method of charging whereby subscribers estimate their usage and pay a price according to volume. The various products are then charged as 3 units, 7 units, etc., which makes price comparisons difficult.

D & B's range of delivery systems is unique, with DUNSVOICE - the telephone response; DUNSTEL - subscribers discuss needs with D & B analysts by phone; and DUNSPRINT - where printed reports are sent by courier, post, fax, telex or computer terminal.

2.   INTERNET (PART OF CCN SYSTEMS, TALBOT HOUSE, TALBOT STREET, NOTTINGHAM NG1 5HF)

A consortium of ten leading business information companies in Europe, to provide expert national credit reports to UK exporters in English and in standard format. Delivery is by post, fax or telex and costs from £28 to £115 depending on market and speed of service. An obvious advantage of the Internet scheme is the interpretation of balance sheet oddities by national experts – allowing credit managers to make their own credit decision with more confidence.

The European partners of CCN in Internet are:

- Norway   – Creditreformfereningen A/S
- Finland   – Luottotieto r.y. – Creditinformaation
- Sweden   – Upplysningscentralen UC AB
- Denmark   – Kobmandstandens OB A/S
- Germany   – Creditreform
- Netherlands   – IS Nederland
- France   – SNRC
- Spain   – INCRESA GROUP
- Portugal   – INFOCOMER

3. GRAYDON - ATP INTERNATIONAL LTD, HYDE HOUSE, EDGEWARE ROAD, LONDON NW9 6LW

Formed in 1986 by the merging of the two Dutch credit agencies, followed by acquisition in 1987 of ATP in the UK. An interesting strategy was that one of the Dutch agencies was owned by NCM, the famous Dutch credit insurance company, who believe that the need for credit insurance in Holland will reduce as companies improve their credit management based on good business information. Graydon has subsidiaries or joint ventures in USA, Italy, France, Spain, Japan and Scandinavia. Reports are delivered in hard copy or on-line, and the emphasis is on high-quality information with a lot of flexibility and selectivity to exporters.

4. INFOCHECK

Smaller than the others, with representative offices in all European capitals, Infocheck specialize in slimmer reports containing what their experience says that credit managers require, at 1/3 to 1/2 cheaper than the larger agencies. They also claim a very high 'availability' rate and a fast response to all enquiries.

5. INFOLINK LTD, COOMBE CROSS, 2, SOUTH END, CROYDON, CR0 1DL

Very large in the UK with a combination of database facilities on consumers and businesses of all kinds (sole traders, partnerships and limited companies). They are organized in an international reporting service with agents in most major countries and their speciality is providing a credit picture on non-limited companies, which do not have to register their accounts officially. Secondly, Infolink have a sophisticated delivery system to dedicated computer terminals in exporters' offices, as well as viewdata by subscription, and telex or post.

Checklist: Using Credit Reporting Agencies

- Find out services provided by several agencies.
- Select and use more than one agency.
- Consider going direct to agencies in other countries.
- Insist on good 'hit rate', otherwise change agency.
- Decide on frequency of updates and economical values.
- Decide on best delivery system to suit your decision process.
- Do not expect accurate data from developing countries.
- Communicate report contents to all interested parties.

Credit insurance companies (ECGD, Trade Indemnity Co, etc.)

If the exporter holds a credit insurance policy he will apply for a Credit Limit if the proposed business gives an exposure above the discretionary limit. Although insurers do not supply actual customer information, their response to a request for, say, '£50,000 on 90 days D/A terms' will indicate the customer's strength. In urgent cases a reply can be obtained by telephoning or telexing the local office. If the answer is not so readily available, it may take two to three weeks to obtain, or even longer, since insurers have to apply to similar sources abroad as the exporter would use.

Bank reports

Foreign bank reports are usually more informative than UK ones ranging from lengthy and detailed reports on USA companies, to short European reports and almost UK style brief language from Commonwealth countries. They are free and fairly rapid. Exporters have a choice of applying through their own bank, naming the customer's bank, or applying directly to the customer's bank, who will only reply to the exporter's bank, which should be named in the enquiry.

It is both courteous and efficient to tell the customer that his bank will be approached for a reference since the bank may ask the customer's permission to release financial data. There is the usual banker's code of confidentiality in most countries, which is why exporters may receive two kinds of report from the same foreign bank. A general report on a customer's reputation and business activity will be given when the customer refuses a request for specific financial data, but if the customer agrees, fuller reports may quote trading profits, bank balance, payment habits and size of payments.

American banks freely quote account details which would embarrass their European counterparts and this is accepted by US firms as a normal credit assessment routine. To be fair to European banks, particularly in Italy and Spain, their views are limited by the knowledge that companies maintain accounts at several banks. And in some countries, e.g. Sweden, banks are forbidden by law to issue references.

It helps foreign banks to give better answers if the exporter asks precise questions.

WRONG *Question:*	'Can you please give me your opinion on El Bloggo Ltda (and address)?'
CORRECT *Question:*	'Do you consider El Bloggo Ltda (and address) a good credit risk for Ptas 1 million on 90 days D/A terms?'

Even if selling in Sterling, always express the amount in local currency, which is more relevant to the customer's bank.

Where exporters can organize it, via local subsidiaries or agents it is often possible and more informative to obtain a verbal opinion from the customer's bank.

Some credit managers believe it is beneficial to tell a customer that his bank is being asked for a reference as it increases respect for the supplier's thoroughness.

Trade and professional contacts

These sources of information can be classified into trade references, industry groups and professional credit bodies.

Trade references on export customers can be obtained from other UK suppliers or from suppliers in the customer's country, although foreign trade references are not usual in some areas, e.g. Middle East states and Latin America, where competitive secrecy is maintained. In applying for references it is always preferable to be polite and brief, and ask the other company these basic questions:

- How long have you known the customer?
- What is your monthly/annual sales value?
- What payment terms apply to your business?
- Does the customer pay promptly?
- Do you consider the customer able to pay £—— (or currency) on terms of (quote proposed payments terms)?

The names of referees may be supplied by the customer, in which case they are possibly, but not necessarily, accounts specially cultivated for references. It is preferable to apply for references to firms that you already know as suppliers to your customer, e.g. names obtained by the salesman or noticed on a visit from documentation or packages on the premises.

The flimsy nature of trade references means they should not be the sole source of information. Their value is in supporting or amplifying other reports.

Industry Credit Groups exist in the UK where members of firms competing in the same industry meet to exchange experiences of customers, names of contacts and useful techniques. There is no illegal restrictive practice involved, provided the purpose is to exchange information with no intention to collaborate against a customer. It follows that credit information obtained from such a close-knit group is more reliable than external references. For some industries, similar groups exist in countries such as France, Belgium and Germany, and a really solid basis for credit exchange can be developed.

Balance sheets

Internationally, these are usually called 'Financial Statements' or 'Company Accounts'.

Where a proposed credit exposure is significant or where a special trading relationship is envisaged, it is essential to understand the financial worth of the customer. The UK habit of £2 issued capital and masses of trade credit is not possible in other countries, but trends towards insolvency and illiquidity are still the risks for the exporter to detect, particularly on a comparative year-on-year basis.

The reason that exporters traditionally just 'get a Bank Report and a Bradstreets' is that they want to buy ready-made decisions, however limited or in summary form. Not many exporters have the skill or the time to analyse Balance Sheets and, therefore, have not demanded them from customers. Therefore, customers have not been used to releasing such data and sometimes react hostilely against such requests.

Exporters should tactfully ask customers for copies of their latest Balance Sheets; but if they find this difficult, they can readily obtain copy documents or salient details from official or commercial bodies in most of the developed countries. The classic problems of lateness and out-of-dateness apply in all countries.

There is a direct contrast between North American standards, where firms readily disclose data to justify credit ratings, and Europe (excluding the UK) where perfectly sound companies see no reason to disclose their status. To reduce tax liability, assets are often understated and reserves maximized. In some countries, such as Germany, reserves on some assets are allowed by law to a certain percentage. In most countries of Europe the companies in a group are not consolidated for report purposes.

Because Balance Sheets are invariably published in the native language, Chapter 12 shows the English equivalents of some Balance Sheet expressions. For exporters puzzled by a foreign Balance Sheet, the multi-national firms of auditors will usually assist in interpreting key features.

The company structure in a number of the more industrialized countries and the availability of accounts is given in Chapter 12.

Visits and account records

Personal visits to foreign customers by credit staff can only be justified on large contracts, or to cover an entire territory of several customers in a visit. If credit staff cannot visit, they should frame questionnaires very carefully for salesmen or others to obtain precisely the data required on customers. The value in a personal visit is to fill in all the gaps in a credit 'picture' and to establish goodwill and confidence in a business relationship. Basic financial data not available from banks or agencies will often be released person-to-person and there is the opportunity to study the offices, factory and equipment of the customer. Are the premises in a prime site or in a poor area? How well are they maintained? What is the morale of staff like? Is the production area buzzing with activity or sluggish? Are there excessive stocks of components or finished goods visible?

It should not be assumed that unfavourable observations mean a poor credit risk, but they form a natural basis for discussion and may reveal trends not yet visible in financial reports. In all visits, a credit man should be accompanied by a sales person or the local agent if possible. Not only does this smooth the introductory stages and possibly provide technical explanations, but also the sales person can experience the credit man's approach at first-hand. Most important of all, the customer will see a united sales/credit combination and will not be able to play one off against the other.

Visits can happen in reverse. When a foreign customer is due to visit the UK operation, arrangements should be made (beforehand) for him to see the credit manager. If he can bring his latest financial statements with him, it is very useful to be able to discuss them responsibly in the exporter's own financial atmosphere. The best theme for such a discussion is a review of payment terms and credit rating, with the implication of an up-grading subject to the data being satisfactory.

Whether the visit happens in the UK or the buyer's country, the account history should be used in the discussions. A neat, clear summary of the recent sales, due dates and payment performance is far more effective than hours of talking, in focusing attention on the problem at hand.

Agents and subsidiaries

Territorial representatives, whether agents or operating subsidiaries, acquire considerable knowledge of customers, actual and potential, and are better placed than the exporter to interpret 'reputation' and reported results. Local representatives are relatively obedient and should be used far more than at present, to gather data for the exporter, in a *specified style*. It is good practice to include a local report in the dossier on all new customers, and to require an annual report on all major customers in a territory, as part of an agent's standard performance. Wherever possible, the credit manager should develop a form of simple training in the information to be acquired by the agent and how it is used to help formulate risk decisions and assist sales.

Foreign subsidiaries or associated companies are very well placed to obtain credit information on customers, whether from their own records, from local agencies or from the customer directly. Usually the communication links between UK credit staff and their foreign colleagues are not as well developed as those between commercial and technical staff. Once a professional working relationship has been established, telephone and telex can be used to get rapid opinions on customers, enough to pass or reject orders or shipments, with full reports to follow later.

Country information

All countries of the world pay for their imports with external funds obtained from:

- Exports or 'invisibles', e.g. services or tourism.
- Foreign aid, whether from other countries, international banks or controlled systems, e.g. Comecon (The Council of Mutual Economic Assistance – the Communist 'bloc').
- Usually, a combination of both.

Strong countries export more than they import, earn a surplus of foreign funds and require no international loans. Thus their currency remains at a premium to others and their domestic economy normally strengthens. It is usually the case that their governments remain stable and policies can be reliably forecast a long way ahead. Examples are Germany and Japan.

Countries with little to export have to fund their domestic needs with foreign aid or loans and indulge in a political race against time to find a way of paying back those loans when due. Their currencies remain weak, not required by others and usually not convertible, i.e. not freely traded in London. Their governmental system is always at risk and no long-term investments can be planned by foreign businesses. In recent years, Brazil and Mexico have had to negotiate massive re-scheduling of international debts.

Most nations are situated between the two extremes, laboriously trying to plan growth, stimulate exports and control their economies. However strong the status of a particular customer is, the export credit manager must keep well abreast of the international economic and political scene, to be sure that a customer's national Central Bank is able to remit Sterling or other preferred currency on the due date, and that a reliable forward view can be taken.

'International risk and payment review'

Several commercial organizations sell services relating to financial and political risk data on foreign markets. Dun and Bradstreet's 'International Risk and Payment Review' is a monthly digest sold on an annual subscription, which collates the opinions of several sources, including a panel of exporters, commercial banks, embassies, D & B offices abroad, and others. About 105 countries are included each month, with comments on 'Usual Payment Terms', including useful data on import licences and value restrictions; 'Transfer Situation', which quotes existing delays and gives advice on documents and procedures; and 'Risk Factor', which comments on political and civil disorders; forthcoming elections; coups d'état; and some economic performance details. If an exporter's time is limited for regular study of country risk information, the D & B I.R.P.R. is invaluable for a quick indicator of key points. Really significant matters can then be pursued elsewhere, if required.

Specialist political risk reporting agencies

Frost and Sullivan Inc., of New York and London, produce substantial Political Risk Reviews, available for selected markets by subscription.

Similarly, S. J. Rundt and Co. of New York produce political risk treatises, but on a more individual basis to cover subscriber's requirements.

Many multinational corporations and large exporters use agencies such as these to help with market planning, where it is vital to predict the degree of stability of economic programmes; the attitude of governments to exporters' countries; local investment opportunities; profit remittance from local subsidiaries, and so on. Underlying all these is the fundamental balance of trade situation and its effect on foreign exchange reserves, which influence government policies on interest rates, inflation, foreign investment, import priorities, etc.

Credit insurers (ECGD, Trade Indemnity Co, etc).

Policy-holders do not receive actual market reports or news of important developments, but ECGD's structure of cover gives a strong indication of the Department's view of each country. If ECGD says 'CILC terms only for Afghanistan', that is a clear warning that the economic 'mix' in Afghanistan makes it unwise to expect payment on a credit terms basis. Policy-holders receive a list from ECGD showing markets where credit restrictions apply. Sometimes measures are imposed by foreign governments to control imports, e.g. Argentina. In other cases, although the foreign country is only too glad to be funded by UK export credit, the history of prompt repayment is so poor that ECGD has to impose its own restrictions.

ECGD keeps a systematic watch on foreign economic and political developments, claiming some 180 countries in its portfolio. Data are collected from published sources, international authorities and British Embassies and consulates, supplemented by travelling teams checking markets at first-hand. All of this enables ECGD to anticipate good or bad trends with a fair degree of confidence, so exporters must be very sure of themselves before going against an ECGD market view.

ECGD's membership of the Berne Union, an international club of credit insurance organizations, encourages the exchange of information between member countries and helps to promote cooperation and prevent unfair competition – all in the interests of UK exporters.

The 'Consensus' Guidelines for medium term credit, reviewed annually by the OECD credit insurers, allocates all countries into Categories I, II, III according to per capita income – a good guide to their ability to pay for imports. The ECGD list of countries by category is a very useful guide to country risk and the need for prudence in setting payment terms.

Bank publications

All the major banks, many foreign banks both in UK and in their own countries and several merchant banks produce excellent regular bulletins on foreign market risks, to help their client exporters formulate decisions and act prudently. They are very well researched and clearly written and, best of all, they are free!

We select at random, the Natwest 'Exporters Bulletin' and Barclays market reports, for comment here. Others are equally good. All vary slightly in emphasis, so exporters should find two or three sources which appeal to their particular approach to market risk management.

The 'Exporters Bulletin' from National Westminster Bank covers export opportunities (products needed abroad) and recent publications, but principally its 'Foreign collections information' is the most useful part for credit managers. It lists all the countries where something has happened to influence collections. Two examples in the July 1988 issue:

'Nigeria – extreme caution is advised in first transactions with new importers, due to fraudulent documents at present emanating from Nigeria.'

'The Gambia – Commercial banks will accept payment in local currency, but not any responsibility for any shortfall due to fluctuation in exchange rates for provision of foreign exchange, which must be for the importer to provide. Exporters must give specific instructions to the collecting bank as to whether documents are to be released against payment in local currency or the currency shown on the Bill of Exchange.'

Both excellent pieces of advice which might not come the exporter's way by any other means.

The Natwest Bulletin also lists 25 countries where extreme delays are being experienced in the receipt of export proceeds due to FX control delays.

Under its 'Overseas Trade News', examples of items which affect market risk are changes in import controls, documentary requirements and exchange controls. It also announces lines of credit, e.g. £5 million for Czechoslovakia to buy UK capital goods, but as it is unlikely to promote such news of other banks' credits, exporters are advised to check credit lines with either ECGD or the 'British Business' magazine.

The Barclays Bank Country Reports consist of loose-leaf sheets for each market, summarizing significant changes in currency, import and exchange controls but mainly giving descriptions of economic developments and local production and agricultural crop news. This presents a picture which helps exporters into the industries covered and also aids assessment of the markets' total economic strength. The style of the reports makes them particularly easy to file and retrieve when needed.

Other bank publications concentrate on political developments and make various forecasts of trade and currency prospects. There is a wide array of documents on the market, all of them offering their range of services to exporters. It takes little time and costs nothing to investigate and order two or three suitable booklets.

Official publications

A tremendous effort has been made in recent years to provide exporters with adequate data on export markets, concentrated through the British Overseas Trade Board (BOTB), the export organization within the Department of Trade and Industry.

'British Business' (formerly 'Trade and Industry') is the weekly magazine published by the Government for exporters. It covers so many topics that export credit and market risk matters may arise almost anywhere within it; furthermore, it actually explains interesting developments and gives telephone numbers for further details.

The EEC in Brussels publicizes several booklets each year giving information on trade and finance in the Community; it also details the various loans and aid schemes to the LDCs, some of which can be accessed by exporters for payment soon after shipment of approved orders.

The IMF Bulletin is published in Paris and London each month. It is a mass of statistics but it is possible to plot the improvements or deteriorations in FX Reserves and Debt Service Ratios for any markets that exporters are involved in.

Credit management organizations

Two membership bodies of credit managers exist to help UK exporters. The Institute of Credit Management, has a growing membership of over 6000 qualified credit staff, many of whom are in export. Its direct aids to export information are through its permanent advisory service to members and its Export Workshops in London on an informal, round-table basis. Non-members may attend and questions are submitted either beforehand or at the session, with answers provided by those present, aided by a panel of experts from industry, Export Credit Guarantee Department and the banks. Its monthly magazine 'Credit Management' features topical export credit information regularly.

A European version of the same kind of forum is organized by FCIB, the European branch of NACM, The National Association of Credit Management of the USA. Forums take place three times a year in different capital cities and attract about 100 managers from European and US member companies. Apart from actual questions dealt with, personal contacts are developed which facilitate exchange of data at short notice later.

Financial press

From day to day, the world-respected 'Financial Times' is the best guide to country developments affecting credit risk. News items on overnight 'coups', foreign aid agreements, crop predictions, famines and floods are all indicators to the alert credit manager responsible for decisions to invest his company's funds in credit to those areas.

The weekly magazine 'The Economist' is also famous worldwide for its very well researched articles on situations 'behind the news'.

Checklist: Obtaining Credit Information

- Do not relax behind an ECGD policy – know all about your customer and his country.
- Build the cheapest (but adequate) information system with a dossier on each customer and each country.
- On customers, have *at least* a Visit Report and a Credit Agency Report. For substantial business, include a Balance Sheet Analysis.
- Get local experts (agent, subsidiary, auditors) to obtain and interpret Balance Sheets.
- On countries, the best quick guide is ECGD but for background, use the Bank Reviews plus daily reading of the 'Financial Times'.
- Be in a position to know: Can he pay on time? Will he go bust? Is he viable for several years? Can his country pay?

Using the information to assess credit risks

In approving orders, or making general reviews of risk, the credit manager should consider two stages:

(a)   The period between now and payment date of this order;
(b)   The future period of a sales plan, e.g. one year or five years depending on the period ahead the firm uses for planning.

It is always easier to recognize and deal with an immediate customer or market problem situation. A longer period risk ahead is harder to forecast and needs more courage to act upon. But just as the credit manager expects early warning of new business from the sales staff, he should give early warning of credit difficulties to them, to avoid wasted effort and expense.

So, first we look at country risks and try to find ways of avoiding them.

Country risks

Countries of the world can be roughly divided between the developed industrialized nations (e.g. W. Europe, North America and Japan), the less developed nations (in Africa, S. America and the Middle East) and the Communist countries.

They all have their risks for a UK exporter but, generally speaking, the governments of the developed countries do not cause the credit losses listed earlier. Surprisingly to some exporters, nor do the communist countries, where the state-controlled buying organizations may well negotiate fiercely on contract conditions but then honour them. In recent years, however, there has been increasing experience of payment delays from Eastern Europe, due to rationing of hard currency.

The main area of risk is the large number of emerging nations, newly independent governments and politically unstable regimes around the world. These are the countries that badly need foreign investment, machinery and services, yet are also the least able to pay for them out of their own foreign earnings.

Some very large contracts are offered by such countries with attractive profit margins for UK firms. The credit manager's role is to assess the probability of the contract being completed and he should use his carefully compiled country file.

For all countries, the market risks listed earlier and the two stages of risk, i.e. the order-to-payment period and the future marketing period, combine to ask two main questions:

(a)   Will the buyer's country experience war or serious internal strife?
(b)   Will the buyer's country experience problems in foreign exchange?

Examples of (a) have occurred in recent years in Argentina, Iraq and Iran, which were previously lucrative markets for UK exporters. Some who observed the worsening internal political situations had the courage to restrict credit sales and/or obtained Letters of Credit or third party finance. Some who did not and loyally continued supplying the same customers on the same credit terms were left with profit-draining slow or bad debts. An additional problem in country risk occurring is the sudden loss of a complete market outlet for products.

There are plenty of examples of (b) led by Brazil and Mexico, followed by most of South America and Africa, with about 150 countries in all. To different degrees, their international borrowings peaked in 1982 onwards with the realization that loan installments, and sometimes the interest alone, could not be repaid. The loans had mostly been to finance capital projects which in turn were meant to reduce imports and increase exports. But most projects were unfinished or unsuccessful and existing trade deficits meant severe inability to service loans.

Checklist: Managing Country Risks

- LIST the countries to which your company sells.
- COLLECT economic data on each in a Country File.
- ALLOCATE an I, II or III risk grade to each country.
  - I   = negligible risk.
  - II   = average risk.
  - III = high risk.
  - (Use ECGD country categories).

If not a policy-holder with ECGD, allocate grades as follows:
  - I Hard currency countries, i.e. freely convertible in London.
  - III Countries with existing or potential difficulty to fund imports; oil-dependent with small export earnings; single-crop exporters; dependent on aid from West or Comecon; military governments; rapid changes of administrations, and so on.
  - II All the others.

- USE categories as follows:
  - I   = any terms, any hard currency
         = good for marketing development
  - II   = care with terms, trade in Sterling or major currencies only.
         = good for short-term marketing
  - III = CILC or payment guarantee only.
         = marketing expense to be controlled but watch for good opportunity contracts.
- AMEND categories when source information justifies it.
- REVIEW categories at regular intervals.

It is easy to cite the well-known problem countries but much harder to spot future examples in time to re-negotiate credit terms. Companies with ECGD cover have a ready-made guide to market risks but should still make their own assessment. In the interests of facilitating UK exports, ECGD has been known to continue cover long after uninsured exporters have stopped dealing in a market, but even the insured exporter who continues to deal risks losing the self-retention of 5%.

Customer risks

Having established that a customer's country can pay for its imports, and is worthy of export development, it is necessary to assess customers, to enable objective sales decisions to be made.

Export sales are only accumulated costs until the cash is banked, when the notional profit can be safely counted. Expensive marketing programmes, perhaps involving appointment of agents, sample approvals and exhibitions, will be wasted investments if the customers do not survive to take the planned sales.

So, customer assessments should ask the questions:

(a)   Will they go bust before we are paid?   (Solvency)
(b)   Can they pay our bills on time?   (Liquidity)
(c)   Are they viable for a few years yet?   (Growth and stability)

The chief risks are insolvency, approaching fast or slowly, and default, whether temporary or serious. The instances of repudiation of goods on arrival can be classed as default in most cases.

ECGD cover is a superb long-stop technique, but it offers only a percentage of the loss and leaves the exporter with a self-retention percentage often greater than the net margin on the sale. It is no substitute for a strong relationship between exporter and customer, based on financial respect.

Even if ECGD cover is purchased, exporters should know their customers' financial prospects and judge their character, reliability and ability to pay their way. Compared with the assessment of UK firms, export credit analysis is usually difficult because of the unreliability of reported financial data.

An Information File on each customer should reveal a certain commonality between the opinions in the Visit Report, Bank Report and Credit Agency Report. The luxury of a recent Balance Sheet should lock all other pieces together. Any piece of the jigsaw that is wildly different should be further investigated. Whether flimsy or comprehensive, the dossier will create some 'picture' of the customer's size and reputation.

Credit assessment has been used by banks for many years to support loan decisions. Yet although industry makes lending (credit) decisions every day, there has been little acceptance until recently of the right of sellers to investigate customers and make value judgements. Banks demand Balance Sheets, charge interest and take security for loans, whereas industrial credit granters usually do none of these.

There is a geographical trend in credit risk analysis. The practice is well developed and widely accepted in the USA and Canada, becoming rapidly developed in the UK and gradually creeping across Europe. There Scandinavia, Holland and Belgium lead the way, with Germany, Switzerland and Austria following, France lagging somewhat and the Latin countries of Italy, Spain and Portugal coming last of all. In the rest of the world, the Commonwealth countries and those brought up on US-aid programmes are well used to credit analysis. In all the lagging countries, it is usually US-owned companies which are to be found pioneering its acceptability.

Thus, UK exporters can assume that where their customers have a domestic environment of risk assessment, they will also understand the exporter's 'need to know'. Gilbert G. Grandjean published, via the Credit Research Foundation of New York in 1977, an excellent study of the situation called 'A Proposal to Develop Better Credit Information in Europe'.

If reliable financial data is available on a customer, the exporter should make a comparative analysis, i.e. for at least three consecutive years, of the following ratios:

SOLVENCY

CURRENT RATIO
The number of times that Current Assets cover Current Liabilities. For significant short-term strength, take the CA cover of Total Liabilities. Anything less than 1.5 : 1 may cause concern.

STOCK TO SALES RATIO
The number of times that stocks are turned into sales in a year. Stocks are in Current Assets and a worsening of this ratio would affect the view of the Current Ratio above. In calculating the ratio, be careful to average the stock figure by adding opening and closing stocks and dividing by two.

OWNER'S LIABILITY RATIO
The ratio of Net Worth to External Creditors (trade and banks) indicates the cover for outside lenders of the company's assets. Anything less than 1 : 1 may cause concern.

OVER-TRADING RATIO
The ratio of Sales to Working Capital (Net Current Assets) indicates dangerous over-trading if Sales increase out of proportion to the increase in WC, i.e. a lesser chance of creditors being paid.

LIQUIDITY

LIQUIDITY RATIO (OR ACID TEST)
The number of times that Current Assets *without stocks* cover Current Liabilities or even Total External Liabilities. In other words, the coverage of cash or current receivables. At least 1 : 1 is desirable.

COLLECTION PERIOD (DSO)
By dividing Receivables by Sales per Day (Turnover ÷ 365), the average

period of cash intake for sales is indicated. This is a good indicator of ability to pay to particular terms.

GROWTH AND STABILITY

GEARING RATIO
The ratio of Interest-bearing Borrowings to Net Worth indicates how much of a burden it is to earn profits just to service borrowings.

SALES GROWTH
The simple year-on-year percentage of sales increase should produce the same or better percentage profit growth.

PROFIT GROWTH
The year-on-year percentage of increase in profit before tax.

It is worth repeating that credit managers, unless very experienced in foreign accounting, should enlist the help of local experts (subsidiaries, local agents or auditors) to interpret Balance Sheets, where significant exposures are planned. The actions to minimize tax in countries such as Italy, Sweden and Mexico mean that profits are marked down by asset reductions or extra reserves which are sometimes quite legal but invisible.

For ordinary exports where financial data is not available, or not reliable or out of date, the exporter must rely on his 'picture' in the dossier of other reports. The warning signal is the reported item which conflicts with other reports, e.g. a foreign Bank Report which speaks highly of a customer when Trade and Agency reports sound only average. It is not unknown for a foreign bank to overstate a client's worth, to encourage trade credit and thus reduce the bank's investment!

For existing accounts, a wonderful guide to risk is right on hand in the sales ledger or bill book, i.e. the customer's payment record. The best credit reference is a prompt payment record, particularly with increasing sales. Conversely, with a slow-paying or erratic account, the collection file may reveal genuine reasons for delays or perhaps a trail of broken promises.

The best warning of customer risk is a deteriorating payment performance and inability to keep to agreed terms.

Risk codes and credit ratings

It is naïve to believe that all customers are first class risks. For reasons of sales volume and market share it is necessary to sell to average and even marginal risk accounts.

To assist in rapid decisions, for order approvals and shipment release, many exporters apply Credit Ratings or limits to accounts and it is well worth extending this system to include Risk Codes, as follows:

- Risk Code 'A' = Nil or negligible risk of insolvency.
- Risk Code 'B' = Average risk.
- Risk Code 'C' = High risk of insolvency.

The Risk Codes can be decided by reference to the Customer Files and exporters may choose to incorporate the Country Risk in the coding system. Whatever the system, it should be reviewed at regular intervals and accounts regraded where justified.

A quick analysis of the Risk Codes at any time is helpful to the marketing function as well as to the credit man. A ratio of 20% 'A' codes, 60% 'B' codes and 20% 'C' codes would be a reasonable spread of prospects, but an unhealthy increase in 'C' codes or a frequent downgrading of 'B' to 'C' would tell the Sales Manager something of his outlets, or of his agents' work.

The Risk Codes may also be used for:

- Selection of appropriate payment terms.
- Different approaches in collection of overdues.
- Priorities in production or delivery dates.

Credit Ratings may be agreed with ECGD or self-imposed. It is always good practice to notify customers of their Ratings, as well as the Sales Department. If a customer or salesman is unhappy with a Rating, a discussion can be created to obtain extra data or to explain the reason.

There is no exact way of calculating a Credit Limit. The test is 'how much money can this customer generate to pay our sales on our credit terms, in view of his other commitments?' Since the exporter has only out-of-date information on the customer's financial position, the task is difficult! Some approaches are:

1. The amount likely to be unpaid (i.e. Sales x terms).
2. 25% of the total creditor's figure.

3. 20% of working capital.
4. 10% of net worth.
5. The credit rating set by a commercial agency.

Method 1 is lazy because it may be more than the customer can pay, or well below his capacity and require increasing every time sales go up. Methods 2, 3 and 4 are based on 'let us be owed only a proportion of the customer's balance sheet value'. Method 5 takes whatever unknown method has been used by the agency.

It follows, however, that longer payment terms permit fewer sales within a particular limit. For both sales and cash flow, payment terms should be negotiated as short as possible and overdues should be collected quickly, to avoid blocking further sales.

Because the cash flow pipeline for exports is usually longer than in the home trade, it is common to find a two-tier Credit Rating system, e.g. 'the Order Limit will be four times the Credit Limit'.

This permits more orders to be taken and production to begin, whilst waiting for current sales to mature into cash and is particularly useful when credit terms are in the 90 to 180 days area.

So, combining the above suggestions, accounts might be rated as 'A', £100 000 or 'C', £5000, or by introducing the Country Risk Code, perhaps as 'IIA', £100 000 or 'IC', £5000.

These simple codings can be applied to computer or manual systems (for example, by tagging or colour-coding) and exception reports can be produced to select out of the mass only the accounts requiring management attention.

Figure 4.1　　Credit Checking: Export Orders and Shipments

Event	Action
Enquiry Quotation Sales Visit Prospect }	Early warning to credit dept to allow time for brief check according to exposure
ORDER: New Customer	Assess Credit Limit Assess Risk Category Decide Payment Terms
ORDER: Existing Customer	Check Payment Record Check Stop/Referral List Compare value to: 3 x Credit Limit less Debt
SHIPMENT	Check ledger situation Check Stop/Referral List Compare value to: Credit Limit less Debt

Notes:　　　　　　This approach is very easily automated, so that business flows through without delay, except any orders or shipment which fail the checks.

Reducing insolvency losses and reserves

Correct risk assessment

By obtaining enough data to judge the viability and liquidity of customers, and having the commercial courage to restrict sales where the exposure is too risky, the exporter can minimize insolvency losses.

Early warning signs

As trading goes along, there are plenty of warning signs such as slow-paying accounts; bad or nil responses to reminders; adverse press reports; imbalance in financial ratios, and so on. It is important to watch for the signs, check them out when they occur, and then have the courage to act when verified. 'Act' means deciding how to treat orders on hand and current negotiations for business, and also how best to collect existing debts before failure occurs.

Sudden disasters

Despite correct assessments and watching for warning signs, exporters can be caught by the unexpected collapse: a withdrawal of substantial backing; the insolvency of the customer's main customer; excessive over-trading since the last report, and so on. This is where ECGD cover is a boon and where a sound reserve policy pays off. Setting aside the possible recoveries (from a dividend to creditors, from ECGD, from Retention of Title, etc.) it is only prudent to put away part of the export sales value into a Bad Debt Reserve.

Such reserves, correctly entitled Provisions, are subject to very different opinions in exporting companies. The principle is to take some already earned profit and place it in reserve against the possibility of some loss on *existing* debts. General opinion of auditors is that reserves should not cover *future* sales. Many companies have a *rolling* reserve system whereby reserves are topped up or depleted according to sales or balances at month-ends. It is recommended that the Export Credit Manager rotates export debt listings with opinions on country and customer risks prior to the reserves being allocated. At least annually it is prudent to assess the true *net* value of export debts by offsetting a reserve against likely losses, after deducting the proportion of ECGD or other insurance cover. It is unwise to over-reserve on debts, as the funds can be more profitably used elsewhere in the business.

Typical reserve policies are:

1   Maintain a constant reserve of, say, 1% of export balances not covered by ECGD, including the 10% self-retentions.

OR
2   Put funds to reserve according to the aged analysis of export overdues, e.g:

1–60	days overdue – reserve 10% of overdues.
61–120	days overdue – reserve 25% of overdues.
Over 120	days overdue – reserve 60% of overdues.

OR
3   Reserve specific problem accounts. Identify each month, any export balances considered doubtful collections and transfer them to a Doubtful Debt account. Reserve at 100%. Keep up collection efforts. Apply cash receipts to DDA and reduce reserve accordingly.

It can be seen that the investment in credit insurance or in credit assessment to the A, B, C level of identification, can effectively reduce the expense of Bad

Debt Provisions. Nearly all bad debts will arise in 'C' Category accounts and blocked transfers will be in Category III markets. Provisions need only be made for accounts in these categories.

Indirect or contingency risks

There are several events which are not normally classified as credit risks which can cause unexpected financial loss. They can be managed contractually and even insured with commercial insurance companies. Many exporters put this area of risk management under the control of the credit manager, as it is political risks that often lead to these losses.

Some typical contingency risks are:

● Contract Cancellation: Where the buyer unilaterally decides to repudiate a contract. The risk can be covered with a Contract Repudiation Indemnity.

● Penalty for Delays: A Delay Penalty Indemnity can be obtained to recover the penalty charged to an exporter for delays outside his control and not covered by a force majeure clause.

● Non-performance Penalty: A Performance Penalty Indemnity is available to cover an exporter whose contract imposes a penalty on him if the equipment supplied or built does not achieve the stipulated performance criteria, excluding experimental work. Similarly, where failures or non-standard performances by an exporter give the buyer the right to reject further supplies or construction, cover is available for the possible loss.

● Plant Confiscation: In some countries, UK contractors have reason to fear that the government or public body will confiscate their plant for local political reasons, or not allow its return to UK after a project is completed. For the latter risk, it is usual to amortise the plant value in the contract price, but in case of premature confiscation, private insurance cover is recommended in London.

● Force Majeure cancellation: Although good contracts have a carefully worded force majeure clause allowing, e.g. delays due to strikes, such clauses usually bring termination of the contract after a certain period of force majeure. Apart from wording clauses carefully, the credit manager can also insure in London against losses caused by such termination.

● Contract Ratification: A Contract Ratification Indemnity can be obtained to cover an exporter against losses sustained when orders placed by him on sub-contractors or suppliers have to be cancelled when his own main contract is not ratified. This usually occurs after a contract has been signed, with certain conditions to be fulfilled before it is legally effective. The conditions may include down-payments, inspections, specimen signatures, and so on. It is relatively easy for a foreign government to have a change of heart and avoid liability by causing one or more of the Conditions Precedent to be incapable of achievement.

5   Payment terms

Influences on payment terms

Exporters are trading in a multi-market place, where there are many more
competitive pressures and alien practices than in the home trade. Despite
well-planned credit policies it is unwise to think that payment terms can simply
be imposed on customers by 'Head Office' standard rules. The luxury of the
ivory-tower is only possible in a monopoly situation.

Conversely, it would be abdicating responsibility to agree always to the
terms demanded by customers. This applies whether the customer stipulates
terms personally or they are printed on an incoming order.

The right approach, as ever, is a commercial compromise; sensible terms
for the exporter, but taking account of the customer's needs, and the cost of
the credit period. Some factors influencing the choice of payment terms are:

- The usual terms in the customer's country.
  (e.g. in France, customers and competitors may all deal at 90 days)
- What competitors are offering.
  (Care! allegations of generous terms should always be checked.)
- The exporter's need for funds.
- Seasonal support.
  (e.g. agricultural products may need support with longer terms in the
  growing season than in the selling season.)
- Life of the product.
  (No credit period should last longer than the product.)
- Profit margin available.
  (The margin left after credit costs must still be acceptable.)
- Regulations in the foreign market.
  (Many poor countries stipulate specific terms for imports.)
- Foreign currency availability.
  (The greater the FX risk, the greater the need for shorter terms.)
- A means of minimizing credit risk.
  (Some terms can retain possession of goods until paid.)

As the object of exporting is profit, and time costs money, the credit base established by payment terms should be as short as possible, compatible with obtaining the order.

When the credit terms issue causes conflict, it is essential to negotiate with the customer and not just give in. Whether the exporter wins or not, he will have earned respect and set a standard for the future. As to who should negotiate terms, he may (wrongly) feel a conflict of loyalties; so unless he really can wear the finance hat, he should refer the problem to the credit manager.

ECGD have vast experience of credit terms in many countries and their 'ECGD Services' booklet deals clearly with the broader credit scene and the international rules for medium and long credit.

In the booklet, ECGD says, in effect: Buyers naturally seek the best terms they can get, so there is a constant danger of a credit race developing between sellers in different countries, to obtain business. Such a race would be damaging to the balance of payments of all countries involved. ECGD discuss the prevention of a credit race with the Berne Union, the OECD and the EEC.

The broad application of the policy is a maximum of six months' credit for consumer goods, raw material and semi-manufactured goods. There is no precise pattern for other goods, but ECGD cover between two and ten years depending on the value of the order and the established trade practice. Only for very large projects will ECGD agree terms over ten years or if such terms are being offered by competitors, not as part of an aid programme.

The major nations have adopted guidelines setting maximum payments by the time of delivery, interest rates and maximum terms for credit above two years. For these purposes, buyers' countries are divided into three groups, on a basis of per capita income. The view of the OECD group, known popularly as the "Consensus", is that for capital goods the longest credit allowed to customers in the 'Relatively Rich' countries is five years on 85% of the contract value; with eight and a half years for the 'Intermediate' countries; and ten years for the 'Relatively Poor'.

The Consensus Guidelines are reviewed every year and the more aware exporters obtain from ECGD the list of countries in Groups I, II and III, as an indication of risk, and thus the security need for credit terms, even for short-term credit.

Short-term credit: methods of settlement and credit periods

The credit manager should weigh up the risk factors involved and try the shortest possible period of credit in getting agreement to one of the following terms, listed in order of security.

High Risk	*Open Account*
	No terms of payment stated (!)
	Net x days
	x days from date of arrival
	x days from date of invoice
	x days from date of shipment
	Cash against documents (direct to customer)
	Documentary collection
	Draft at x days after sight
	Draft at x days after arrival of goods
	Draft at x days after invoice date
	Draft at x days after shipment
	Sight draft
	Cash against documents (through a bank)
	Documentary letter of credit
	Irrevocable by issuing bank in country of risk
	Confirmed by an approved bank outside country of risk
	Confirmed by a UK bank
	Cash on Delivery
	Cash before Shipment
Low Risk	*Cash with Order*

Broadly speaking, the alternatives divide between:

● open account - where the customer is trusted *and* his country has a good record on hard currency transfers.
● bills of exchange - where some risk is perceived.
● prepayment/letter of credit - where risk is high.

The degree of risk is influenced by the combination of the customer's liquidity and his country's foreign exchange situation. A blue-chip customer in Germany could be sold on open account, whereas one in Zambia, where the transfer delay is up to 6 years, would require L/C terms.

The period of credit may be from a few days up to six months for non-capital goods on any of the payment methods. The cost of the credit period, normally at least 1% per 30 days, is a major factor.

Payment terms considerations for the credit manager

Cash with order (CWO)

Ideal for avoiding credit risk on small orders from new buyers or when credit has been withdrawn for any reason, or when there is doubt about foreign exchange availability. Some countries expressly forbid imports on cash in advance terms, however.

If significant production expense is involved, all or part payment should be received before manufacture begins. If the product is standard, it is helpful to the customer, and no more risky for the exporter, to ask for 'Cash before Shipment' instead of 'with Order'.

Because the availability of credit is almost taken for granted these days, it may not occur to some exporters to ask for cash 'up front', or they may believe the customer will be upset by such a requests. However, in any situation justifying advance payment, the customer will almost certainly have had such requests from other suppliers.

Cash on delivery (COD)

Semi-secure terms, whereby small-value goods are exported via the Post Office parcel post through the postal service of the foreign country and the goods are only released to the buyer against payment of the involved amount plus COD charges.

Commercial carriers do not usually operate COD facilities and many foreign countries do not provide the service required; exporters should check the current Post Office list for availability. The usual practice abroad is for the local Post Office to advise the customer of the arrival of a parcel and to expect it to be collected, rather than deliver it, as in the UK. There is little urgency and no automatic report back to the UK if the parcel is not delivered. Before using postal COD terms, exporters should check that re-export of uncollected parcels is possible.

Documentary letters of credit

This form of payment almost went out of fashion in the boom years of the sixties and seventies, having been a standard method of security for export payment for well over two hundred years before that. Then the world debt crisis after 1982 created a sudden rush back to safer terms for sales to many countries with inadequate foreign exchange.

Letters of Credit provide the most security, except for the rare cash with order term, and the fastest payment, since funds are usually made available at major London banks soon after shipment.

A Letter of Credit is an undertaking by the buyer's bank to pay a specific amount to the exporter, provided that the conditions listed in the Credit are met. The Credit is advised to the exporter by a bank in the UK which has a correspondent relationship with the opening bank. Better still, if the UK bank actually confirms the Credit, it takes responsibility for payment if the opening bank does not pay.

Letters of Credit are legal contracts subject to well-established international law and universally understood. The banks involved deal in the specified documents and not in checking, shipping or storing the actual goods.

When the customer agrees to open a L/C in favour of the exporter, he is incurring a borrowing cost, usually for three months, and tying up a portion of his borrowing capacity at his bank. This is the main disadvantage for the customer. The big advantage is that the customer is dictating efficiency in that the exporter must ship within the specified date, using the specified methods of carriage and insurance, providing specified documents and keeping to any protective conditions the buyer cares to stipulate.

The advantage to the exporter is that he can safely manufacture and ship, knowing he can collect his cash from the advising bank in the UK, simply by presenting the proper set of documents on time.

Letters of Credit are usually payable at Sight but even if payable at future dates up to, say, 180 days, the bank will usually discount the payment for immediate cash.

REVOCABLE LETTER OF CREDIT (RLC)

Really just an instrument of payment and provides no security, as it can be cancelled or amended by the buyer at any time. They are still used by importers in the Singapore/Malaysia area, for example, and can be accepted where the customer is trusted and the contract is not particularly onerous.

IRREVOCABLE LETTER OF CREDIT (ILC)

The most common type of credit. It cannot be revoked or amended after issue without the agreement of the exporter. The foreign opening bank is responsible for paying the exporter, once the credit conditions have been met, but arranges for a UK bank to 'advise' the credit to the exporter. The advising bank will make payment upon presentation of documents or it will send them for foreign collection if it is not in funds from the opening bank.

Banks simply advising credits are usually careful to show the clause 'this does not bear our confirmation'.

So the ILC is as sound as the bank that issues it.

Some exporters accept ILCs as long as the foreign bank is listed in the Banker's Almanac. Although this gives some indication of strength, there have been classic cases in recent years of foreign banks collapsing, or of foreign governments preventing credits being honoured.

Unless the opening bank is one of the world famous banks in one of the hard currency countries, the exporter should seek confirmation of the credit by a UK bank.

CONFIRMED, IRREVOCABLE LETTER OF CREDIT (CILC)

The CILC is irrevocable, as above, but instead of only being advised by a UK bank, it bears its confirmation, i.e. its full liability for payment, if the conditions are met, regardless of the solvency of the opening bank or its country. The exporter has no need to check the strength of the opening bank and there is no currency or transfer risk, since the value is paid in London by a major bank.

There may well be difficulty in getting a credit confirmed. The exporter may arrange CILC terms and then receive an ILC, because:

(a)   the customer was unwilling to incur the expense of a confirmation, or

(b)   the opening bank did not have Sterling in London.

The customer should always be pressed to arrange for the credit to be confirmed, but because of the great advantages, the exporter may offer to pay the London charges. Also, it is possible for an exporter to ask a UK bank to confirm a foreign ILC, in which case the bank may agree to contact the opening bank; but it makes more sense to involve the buyer in achieving a CILC situation.

Bills of exchange

The various listed terms of Documentary Sight Draft and Term Drafts all involve the use of a bill of exchange.

These terms are semi-secure, in that the buyer must pay bills or accept them for future payment dates, before being able to take possession of the goods. (As we will see, this is not always reliable.)

There is also the advantage to the exporter of processing bills through the well-established world banking system for bill collection.

The proceeds can be telegraphically transferred for extra speed (and cost) and the bills can be claused in various ways to protect the exporter.

When applying Documentary Bill terms, the credit manager should always try to agree with the customer on the bank to be used in the buyer's country and then stipulate that bank on the collection instructions to his own bank. If this is not done, the collecting bank will use its own correspondent bank in the buyer's country and there may be extra delays and misunderstandings due to the extra link.

The Bill is drawn by the exporter as 'drawer' and the customer is the 'drawee'. The Bill can be payable to the exporter or to a third party. If payable 'on demand', i.e. at Sight, it is called a Sight Draft. If payable 'at a fixed or determinable future time' it is called a Term Draft (sometimes referred to as a Tenor or Usance Draft).

In Chapter 3, Figure 3.9 gave an example of a Sight Draft.

DOCUMENTARY SIGHT DRAFT (DSD)

This term falls between cash in advance and full credit. The idea is for the customer to pay the value of the export as soon as the draft arrives. In practice this is allowed to be when the goods arrive, which can be later, if the documents go by air and the goods by sea.

The documentary aspect is that the document of title, the Bill of Lading, with other required documents, is attached to the Sight Draft, so the customer cannot take possession until he has paid. This only applies where there is a Bill of Lading. To obtain the same security for Air, Parcel Post, Rail or Truck deliveries, the exporter must agree beforehand with the bank to send the goods c/o the bank, who will arrange their storage if the Sight Draft is not paid on arrival of the goods. If the bank is not willing to act in this way, the exporter can consign the goods to the local agent or other friendly party.

The semi-secure aspect is that the customer may change his mind, refuse to pay the draft and ignore the goods. In this case, the exporter still has possession but must find another customer (and quickly, to avoid demurrage, storage charges or customs fines) or re-ship the goods to the UK.

Because Bills, or Drafts, incur stamp duty in some countries, buyers sometimes ask for the Sight Draft term to be changed to Cash Against Documents, or CAD. This is not quite as good for an exporter as Documentary Sight Draft and is described in more detail later.

DOCUMENTARY TERM DRAFT (D/A)

Where a period of credit is agreed, the same semi-security as above can be maintained by drawing a bill, or draft, payable at e.g. '60 days from date, documents against acceptance'. This is taken to mean 60 days from date of shipment or Bill of Lading and disputes are avoided if the exporter is careful to date his invoice with the same date.

This fixes precisely the credit period and the due date.

In many cases, the term, e.g. '60 days from sight, D/A', or '60 days from arrival, D/A' is used, to give the buyer the agreed credit period after the arrival of the goods. The problem with this is that whilst convenient for the buyer, it makes the due date uncertain for the exporter, because he does not know when taking the order, or when shipping, exactly when the goods will arrive. There is often a 'grey area' with such terms, whereby the buyer delays taking up the goods for some days or weeks, until it suits him, and still gets the agreed credit period, e.g. 60 days from then.

It is better to agree longer credit to take account of shipping time, e.g. 30 days, and convert the 60-day term to '90 days from date, D/A'. The credit period is then accurate for both parties and costs and cash flow can be planned better.

With D/A bills, the draft is 'accepted', by the customer signing across its face, to be allowed to take up the goods. When the due date arrives, the bank collects the payment, or sends the reason for any dishonour to the UK bank to pass on to the exporter.

The existence of an accepted bill is usually a matter of honour in most countries and bills are paid even if open account debts are not met. Non-payment results in various forms of adverse publicity in most countries.

Even though an accepted bill is a legal document that can be sued upon, in its own right, the exporter should not assume that a bill provides security once the goods are released. In an insolvency, the exporter has no extra preference and stands in line with other unsecured creditors.

In arranging D/A terms of payment, the exporter should notify his customer of any special clauses he intends to use, e.g. exchange or interest clauses, to avoid friction when they occur. The same point applies to the intention to protest bills for non-acceptance or non-payment.

There is a financing advantage in using bill terms, in that bills can be easily discounted by the exporter for instant cash. Figure 3.10 gives an example of a Term draft and Figure 3.11 shows the same draft, accepted by the customer.

Cash against documents (CAD)

This payment term, oddly, is misused by UK exporters although widely used and understood in W. Europe. It means the same procedure and security as a Sight Draft, without using a Draft. In other words, the documents are sent for collection through a bank and only released against payment.

Unfortunately, there is a widespread practice in the UK whereby exporters understand Sight Drafts, but take CAD to mean 'send the documents to the customer and he will then pay the cash'. In other words, no better than Open Account. Perhaps worse, because the customer, having agreed CAD terms, may be waiting for the bank to contact him about payment and this will never happen.

CAD should *always* mean documentary collection through a specified bank.

To avoid confusion altogether, it is better for exporters to add a Sight Draft (unless there are serious stamp duty problems for the customer) and process the collection through the bills system.

Most European countries prefer the use of CAD to Sight draft, if control of document release is required.

Open account

For trusted customers only. This term means an agreed period of credit, e.g. 'Open Account, 90 days from invoice date', with the documents and goods sent directly to the customer. On the due date, it is left to the customer to arrange payment so it is a good idea to arrange with each customer to remit his payment by Telegraphic Transfer (even at the exporter's expense – it is cheaper than waiting for a slow mail transfer) to the exporter's bank, quoting the bank code, full name and address and account number.

If the customer insists on a period of credit after arrival, it is better to agree instead to add a number of days and convert, say, 'Open Account, 90 days from arrival' to 'Open Account, 120 days from invoice date'.

Where customers enjoying Open Account terms get into financial difficulty, any repayment schemes involving instalments should require a series of accepted bills of exchange, to reinforce the agreement.

Consignment account

A payment term commonly in use, similar to Sale or Return, and strictly speaking a method of financing customers. When goods are sold from stock, a further payment term is needed.

These terms serve the dual role of maintaining adequate stocks of goods in the foreign country and also reducing the credit risk of the stockholder.

If goods are available in the local market, 'off the shelf' from a distributor or stockist, the end-customer will have all the comfort of a domestic purchase. Otherwise he would have to place import orders on to a supplier in the UK. The sales advantage of consignment stocks is obvious.

But to allow a good range of products to be held in stock in large quantities involves giving a credit rating to the stockholder which may be far in excess of his ability to repay on standard terms. The answer may be 'Consignment Account', whereby goods remain the exporter's property until sold.

A nominal invoice is sent with the consignment for Customs purposes but is not recorded as a sale. The exporter transfers the stock in his books from Finished Goods to Consignment Stock. The distributor/stockholder notifies sales made out of the stock every week or month or whatever is agreed, and the exporter credits his Consignment Stock, debits the distributor account and invoices him on the usual payment terms.

The problems are that goods deteriorate or are pilfered from stock; warehousing is expensive; the costs of special recording and stock-checking; the uncertainty of sales, all of which ties up capital.

The test question for deciding on Consignment Account terms must be: 'Does the consignment stock bring in sufficient extra sales we could not otherwise get, yielding extra contribution, to justify the costs incurred?'

Medium-term credit

This applies to contracts for capital goods with values above, say, £250 000 (but usually much higher) and as described in the ECGD chapter and elsewhere, there are international conventions for contracts on credit longer than the mass of normal short-term business.

Medium-term is taken to be two years or more, with five years the usual maximum. All medium-term credit is financed in some special way, usually via an ECGD Bank Guarantee and very rarely out of overdrafts.

Thus, the rules for financing schemes help to decide the precise payment terms.

If the contract requires, say, five years' credit, this usually involves:

- A down-payment with order, or before shipment.
- A percentage at time of shipment.
- The balance of each shipment at regular intervals over the five years, covered by Bills.
- Interest on the Bills.

and sometimes

- A retention of 5–20% for a stipulated period after completion until satisfactory commissioning or acceptance of a project.

A capital goods contract usually incurs early costs and risks in manufacture or pre-shipment procurement of materials or services. Thus the exporter should assess these and require the down-payment to cover them, or contribute significantly.

The payment at shipment is intended either to cover pre-shipment costs or to establish clearly the buyer's equity in the goods. There are obvious dangers in supplying high-value goods for payment several years later and it is prudent to obtain a substantial contribution from the customer by the time he obtains the goods for use. Similarly the Bills for the credit period are payable at regular intervals, to check on viability as well as for cash flow reasons.

Separate Bills should be obtained for interest charges, rather than adding interest to the Principal Bills, to allow the Principal amounts to be discounted.

Figure 5.1 shows some typical wording of payment terms on a medium-term contract.

Figure 5.1   Example of Payment Terms on a Medium-term Contract

---

(A contract for capital goods to Venezuela to be signed on 1st June 1988 for shipment in six consignments over 12 months beginning 1st March 1989, with three years' credit, total value £1 000 000.)

Payment Terms

15% of contract value, in Sterling, within seven days of contract date at Barclays Bank Ltd (+ address) for credit of XYZ Exports Ltd (+ account number).

10% of each shipment value from an Irrevocable Letter of Credit confirmed by a UK bank, to be opened and confirmed within 30 days from contract date. Payments to be made at Sight in London against presentation of: (list of documents required).

75% of each shipment value, by six equal Bills of Exchange maturing at six-monthly intervals from shipment date; up to maximum 36 months from shipment, with interest charged at 15% per annum on separate Bills. Bills for Principal and Interest to be accepted in Caracas within 14 days of each shipment.

Note: This would provide funds for XYZ Exports Ltd of:

£150 000	—1–7/6/88
£100 000	—In 6 parts between 1/3/89 and 1/3/90
£750 000	—In 6 x 6 = 36 instalments by Bills maturing between 1/9/89 and 1/3/93 (to be discounted at shipment).
15% p.a. interest	— Receivable on maturity of each bill between 1/9/89 and 1/3/93.

Countertrade

'Even at its simplest, countertrade can be a complex, expensive and uncertain mode of trading, fraught with pitfalls. In a ideal market, it would not arise. It is, however, growing and cannot be ignored. Exporters need not be deterred by countertrade but they must be prepared. With careful and imaginative planning, some exporters have been able to turn this undesirable necessity to their advantage.'

Thus, the official DTI booklet 'Countertrade' gives the view of the UK government.

Countertrade is the generic term used to describe several forms of trading in which the sale of goods to a market is made conditional, through a linked contract, to an obligation to buy goods or services from that market.

The term 'barter' is often, wrongly, used. Strictly speaking, barter is the exchange of goods for goods, e.g. 'I will give you two sheep in exchange for one pig'. The various forms of countertrade demand payment in both directions, e.g. 'I will buy your pig if you will buy my two sheep'.

Barter is an ancient form of trading which precedes the invention of money. The modern lack of money to pay for imports is the reason why it persists today, in multi-millions of Pounds equivalent. There are many bilateral deals involving goods but no money between countries within Comecon, Latin America and Africa. It is a standard feature of planned economies.

Exporters will sometimes find themselves competing for business where the foreign buyer declares that payment must be accepted in 'kind', such as cooking oil, plum jam, or the actual products of the equipment being sold. It is a very basic way for a country to pay for its imports and occurs in Eastern Europe and the developing countries. As opposed to pure barter, these proposals require linked contracts to sell and buy.

Extreme caution must be applied to such proposals because

(a)   the exporter has to dispose of the products, at a cost;
(b)   the value has to be established by an expert in that product;
(c)   there will probably be a timing difference between the contracts;
(d)   the product may not be available in the end.

Several countertrade deals have taken place successfully but it is usually necessary to involve a third-party intermediary or agent who can deal with the product being offered. Such agencies will sign a separate agreement with the exporter to take the product, offering a price leaving, say, a 20% loss on the export sale. The alternatives available at this point are:

(a)   Accept the loss for the sake of the business. (Not recommended!)
(b)   Re-negotiate the export sale price to cover the compensation loss.
(c)   Negotiate with the intermediary agency on the price being offered.
(d)   Withdraw from the business.

The lesson is to find out *at the start of a negotiation*, whether CT will be required, then to include the disposal cost, called the agio, in the export price.

It is essential, when re-selling the compensation product, to have a clause excluding consequential loss, e.g. if quality is not sampled, or the crop is late, etc.

The term countertrade covers several different ways of achieving the exchange of goods and services to conserve, or avoid an imbalance in hard currency.

Methods include:

Barter, where goods are exchanged and no money is used.
Counterpurchase, where there are linked contracts for sales by both parties who also pay each other.
Evidence accounts, like counterpurchase, but on a larger sale determined by annual protocols, and perhaps extending to triangular arrangements, e.g. a multinational may agree to have a foreign subsidiary purchase from an East European country as payment for its own sales to that country.
Offset, where one country agrees to buy a product from another country provided it contains an agreed value of its own components or labour.
Buy-Back, where a company supplies plant or know-how and agrees to buy back the product manufactured by it.

The advantages of Countertrade are mainly in keeping an export market open in times of exchange shortage with a reasonable chance of settlement. The disadvantages are that the foreign party may provide poor quality goods with no after-sales service, or have the balance of value in his favour.

The DTI booklet 'Countertrade – some guidance for exporters' is essential reading for all exporters. Not only does it clearly describe the different forms of CT, but it provides the reassurance that no exports need be lost for the lack of ability to dispose of unwanted purchases.

Performance bonds and guarantees

Tender Bonds, Bid Bonds, Advance Payment Guarantees and Performance Guarantees. Any of these is likely to be required in a capital goods project, particularly in the Middle East and Africa.

Tender and Bid Bonds are forms of guarantee requested by foreign buyers, often official or government bodies, to indicate the genuineness of a tender; so that the buyer can be recompensed if he spends time and money on the UK exporter's tender and perhaps rejects the bids of others, and is then let down when the UK firms backs out.

Of more concern to the credit manager are Advance Payment and Performance Guarantees, when a contract is actually placed. Under medium-credit contract terms an advance payment is usually required and the buyer needs to know for certain he can reclaim the advance if the exporter does not perform. Similarly a Performance Bond often carries right through to the Retention and commissioning stages of a project.

Bonds can be either:

(a)   Conditional, or
(b)   On-demand.

Conditional bonds are issued by banks and specialist surety companies, which pay out to the buyer the value of his loss only against specific proof of the exporter's default. This type of Bond is well controlled and presents no real problem to the exporter provided he performs to the contract.

The 'On-demand' Bond, has had a very chequered history. With this type, buyers have the right to claim the bond value literally on demand without having to prove default by the exporter. Surety companies do not generally agree to supply this type, but the major banks do so if requested. As they are not required to judge contract performance or check documents, banks see On-demand Bonds as fairly straightforward.

It is unfortunate that exporters agree to provide On-demand Bonds. Their problem is that tender or contract conditions require such Bonds and international competitors agree to provide them. Banks regard Bonds as part of their customers' total borrowing facilities; thus fund can be tied up for some time until the Bond is cancelled even long after the contract has been successfully performed.

Exporters who find difficulty in obtaining Bonds from the banks or surety companies may be able to do so with ECGD bond-support cover. This is available for cash or short-term credit contracts of £250 000 or more and where normal ECGD cover applies to the contract. If ECGD has to pay the bond-issuer due to a Bond being called, they do so within 30 days and have recourse on the exporter. For this reason, ECGD examines the exporter's financial condition and 'recourse-worthiness' before agreeing to cover.

The wrongful encashment of On-demand Bonds has led to the expression 'Unfair calling of bonds'. This situation arises because the bond-issuer is obliged to pay the customer at any time and without having to check performance or any documents.

The English Court of Appeal ruled in 1977 that Barclays Bank must pay out on an On-demand Bond to a Libyan buyer who had not even opened the Letter of Credit required in the contract, thus causing the exporter to refuse to deliver. It was held that the Bond was a separate agreement and that the bank was obliged to honour it as worded.

Exporters can be insured against unfair calling by either ECGD or special cover in the private market.

Most buyers require the bonds to be issued to them by a local bank who are then indemnified by the exporter's bank. This remoteness of control increases the hazard for the exporter of an unjustified pay-out. Banks perform to the wording of the bonds they have issued and do not want to be seen internationally to renege, even if this means penalizing their UK customers.

It is important for the exporter to be extremely cautious. He should try to avoid giving a Bond at all, but if the business depends upon it he should have it issued by a surety company, making it conditional and not on-demand. If the Bond has to be on-demand, it should show a completion/cancellation date in line with the contract completion and it should reduce pro-rata to work done during the period. The exporter should also insure against unfair calling.

Figure 5.2 shows the standard wording of a Tender Bond issued by National Westminster Bank. The wording is likely to be translated into the local language by the bank in the country concerned, and the bond will then be subject to the laws of that country.

Figure 5.3 shows the wording of a Performance Bond which includes an arbitration clause. It is also available without the clause.

Figure 5.2 Specimen Tender Bond

National Westminster Bank PLC ♻

International Banking Division
Bonds and Guarantees Department - Overseas Branch

OUR GUARANTEE GU(GUARANTEE NUMBER)

We understand that (APPLICANTS NAME) ("the Applicant") (APPLICANTS ADDRESS) are tendering
for the (DESCRIPTION OF GOODS) under your invitation to Tender (TENDER/CONTRACT NUMBER ETC)
and that a Bank Guarantee is required for (AGREED PERCENTAGE OF CONTRACT)% of the amount
of their tender.

We, NATIONAL WESTMINSTER BANK PLC, Overseas Branch, London HEREBY GUARANTEE the payment to
you on demand of up to (AMOUNT IN FIGURES) (say,(AMOUNT IN WORDS)) in the event of your
awarding the relative contract to the Applicant and of its failing to sign the Contract in
the terms of its tender, or in the event of the Applicant withdrawing its tender before
Expiry of this guarantee without your consent.

This guarantee shall come into force on (COMMENCEMENT DATE) being the closing date for
tenders, and will expire at close of banking hours at this office on (EXPIRY DATE) ("EXPIRY").

Our liability is limited to the sum of (AMOUNT IN FIGURES) and your claim hereunder must
be received in writing at this office before Expiry accompanied by your signed statement
that the Applicant has been awarded the relative contract and has failed to sign the contract
awarded in the terms of its tender or has withdrawn its tender before Expiry without your
consent, and such claim and statement shall be accepted as conclusive evidence that the
amount claimed is due to you under this guarantee.

Claims and statements as aforesaid must bear the confirmation of your Bankers that the
signatories thereon are authorised so to sign.

Upon Expiry this guarantee shall become null and void, whether returned to us for cancellation
or not and any claim or statement received after Expiry shall be ineffective.

This guarantee is personal to yourselves and is not transferable or assignable.

This guarantee shall be governed by and construed in accordance with the Laws of England and
shall be subject to the jurisdiction of the English Courts.

Figure 5.3 Specimen Performance Bond with Arbitration Clause

National Westminster Bank PLC ♺

International Banking Division
Bonds and Guarantees Department - Overseas Branch

OUR GUARANTEE GU(GUARANTEE NUMBER)

We understand that you have entered into a Contract (TENDER/CONTRACT NUMBER ETC)
(the Contract) with (APPLICANTS NAME)(the Applicant)(APPLICANTS ADDRESS) for the
(DESCRIPTION OF GOODS) and that under such Contract the Applicant must provide a Bank
Performance Guarantee for an amount of (AMOUNT IN FIGURES) being (AGREED PERCENTAGE OF
CONTRACT)% of the value of the Contract.

We, NATIONAL WESTMINSTER BANK PLC, Overseas Branch, London, HEREBY GUARANTEE payment to you
on demand of up to (AMOUNT IN FIGURES)(say,(AMOUNT IN WORDS)) in the event of the Applicant
failing to fulfil the Contract, provided that your claim hereunder is received in writing at
this office accompanied by:

(a) your signed statement that the Applicant has failed to fulfil the Contract,

together with either:-

(b) The signed written admission of the applicant, addressed to us, and dated not more than
     thirty days prior to the date of receipt at this office of your claim, that the applicant
     has failed to fulfill the contract.

 or

(c) a copy of an Arbitration Award in your favour, certified by a Notary Public as a true
     copy of the original of such Award expressed to be made (i) pursuant to the Contract;
     and (ii) in your favour.

and such statement together with either the written admission of the Applicant or a copy
Arbitration Award as above shall be accepted as conclusive evidence that the amount claimed
is due to you under this guarantee.

Claims and statements as aforesaid must bear the confirmation of your Bankers that the
signatories thereon are authorised so to sign.

This guarantee shall expire at close of banking hours at this office on (EXPIRY DATE)
("EXPIRY") so that any claim and statement hereunder together with the written admission of
the Applicant or copy Arbitration Award must be received at this office before Expiry in the
manner stipulated hereinabove and after expiry this guarantee shall become null and void
whether returned to us for cancellation or not and any claim and statement together with the
written admission of the Applicant or copy Arbitration Award received after Expiry shall be
ineffective.

This guarantee is personal to yourselves and is not transferable or assignable.

This guarantee shall be governed by and construed in accordance with the Laws of England and
shall be subject to the jurisdiction of the English Courts.

The major banks all have specialist departments to advise on the wording
and issue of bonds and guarantees. Of particular value is the Natwest booklet
'Foreign Bonds and Guarantees'.

Payment terms in various countries

What is normal?

Exporters wishing to fix credit terms appropriate for the buyer's market are
often faced with a confusion of opinions on 'what is usual'. The salesman
travelling the area has his own view of what is needed to get the business,
perhaps the local agent holds traditional views, the customer may demand
surprisingly long terms and trade referees approached by the exporter quote
varying terms.

Some differences are because certain goods and industries carry their own,
peculiar tradition of payment terms, e.g. foodstuffs into France on cash or very
short terms whilst machinery into France uses the standard 90 days practice.
Other differences are due to: special terms for certain contracts, where the
same firm sells other products on standard terms; support given to a customer
for seasonal business or for cash flow reasons; alternatives of net or discount,
e.g. into Germany or USA on '30 days net or 2% discount within 10 days'.

Broadly speaking, raw materials, components and quickly usable products
have terms not longer than six months; machinery, plant and fixed assets
have terms between one and five years; heavy plant, construction projects,
and major installation contracts have anything from one to seven years; at
the other extreme, food and perishable commodities are sold on very short
terms, in days or weeks.

Where long terms apply, in excess of six months, the usual basis is
instalments of six-monthly intervals, so the 'mean' credit risk period is much
reduced.

The commonsense standard which applies world-wide is that payment time
should relate to the usage or resale period of the product. It is certainly
dangerous to allow credit longer than the product's life, when the buyer's
motivation will have waned.

All standards are distorted when imports are based on foreign aid or special
bank loans which carry their own, usually very short, terms. It should not be
expected that standard sales can be made on the same terms.

Local variations in credit terms

There are many national variations of the standard. In France, where bills of exchange are used domestically as well as for imports, the practice is to add ten days to the credit terms, so '90 plus 10' would be expected.

In Italy, there is the Ricevuta Bancaria (meaning 'bank receipt') which is an instrument of collection designed to avoid the high cost of stamp tax required for bills of exchange. The RB is drawn by the seller and presented to the buyer by a collecting bank at the due date. The buyer simply has to pay it or decline to do so. There is no acceptance involved. It is not covered by the law on bills of exchange and cannot be protested for default. Its advantage over normal open account is that a bank is involved in the collection. More and more foreign exporters into Italy are now using the Ricevuta Bancaria.

In West Germany there is the 'cheque and draft' payment method, often suggested to foreign exporters by buyers. If he agrees, the exporter receives prompt payment, usually with a cash discount (normal in Germany) together with a bill of exchange for the full invoice value, maturing at say, 90 days. The exporter is expected to sign the draft, as if he had drawn it, and return it to the buyer, or drawee. The buyer can then discount the draft with his bank to obtain cheaper finance than an overdraft. Although the buyer, as drawee, has to meet the draft value at maturity, there is an obvious risk for the exporter, since the financing bank will have recourse to him if for any reason the drawee does not settle the draft.

In Belgium, the 'Escompte fournisseurs' (meaning 'suppliers' discount') is commonplace. In this case, the customer sends the exporter, at due date, a draft already accepted for a further, say 60 days. The exporter is expected to sign the draft as drawer and send it directly to the buyer's bank for discounting. The exporter then receives his expected payment at approximately the due date of the original credit period and the buyer has, in effect, a further 60 days credit from his bank. Again, there is a credit risk for the exporter, since the bank will have recourse to him in the event of default by the drawee customer.

In Turkey, the term 'Cash against Goods' is often used. It really means 'Cash against Documents with payment in local currency'. In other words the buyer is enabled to take up the documents, thus the goods, against a payment in Turkish Lira, despite the possibility of a delay in the transfer of Sterling or other hard currency by the Central Bank.

For cash flow reasons, there are the conflicting tendencies for buyers to ignore norms by pressing for longer credit and for exporters to shorten terms wherever possible.

To find out what is 'normal' needs a combination of information and experience. But it is worth the effort, so that a reliable range of terms can be established for the sales force to use.

There are dangers in a subjective approach, however, and advantages in using the regular reports of international organizations such as FCIB (Finance and Credit in International Business) of New York, or Dun and Bradstreet International, in London. The latter organization publishes a monthly digest, called 'International Risk and Payment Review' which lists, for some 105 countries, the

- Usual payment terms
- Transfer delay situation
- Risk factor (government changes, import licences, etc.)

Figure 5.4   Usual Export Payment Terms for Sales to 65 Countries

Africa

Algeria	CAD or ILC. Some CT.
Cote D'Ivoire	ILC (360 day limit)
Ghana	CILC
Kenya	Open Account possible, ILC often used.
Libya	CILC
Morocco	CILC for new accounts; 30 – 90 day drafts.
Nigeria	CILC Some CT.
South Africa	60 – 120 day drafts. Some CT.
Sudan	CILC Some CT.
Zaire	CILC using Belgian banks.
Zimbabwe	ILC on 180 days.

Middle East

Cyprus	CAD or Open Account up to 90 days.
Egypt	CILC. Some CT.
Iran	ILC 360 days (no confirmations).
Iraq	ILC 360 days (no confirmations).
Israel	All terms. ILC and up to 90 days credit common.
Kuwait	All terms. ILC common.
Saudi Arabia	All terms. Offset CT in demand.
Turkey	ILC or Drafts up to 90 days.

Western Europe

Austria	Open Account 30 or 60 days.
Belgium	All terms, 30 – 90 day drafts usual.
Denmark	30 – 60 days, all methods including ILC.
Finland	30 – 60 day drafts or ILC.
France	90 day drafts or open account.
W. Germany	30 days open account, discount for earlier.
Greece	ILC; 60 days drafts. Some CT.
Irish Republic	30 days open account (often a 90 days payment habit).
Italy	All terms. Drafts and ILC up to 120 days usual.

Netherlands	30 days open account or draft.
Norway	60 days open account or draft.
Portugal	ILC up to 60 days. Some CT.
Spain	ILC or drafts from sight to 90 days.
Sweden	30 days open account.
Switzerland	30 days open account.

Eastern Europe

Bulgaria	ILC or sight draft; pressure for CT.
Czechoslovakia	All terms 90 – 180 days; CT.
E. Germany	ILC; CT.
Hungary	All terms; ILC or Sight terms; CT.
Poland	CILC or ILC; pressure for CT.
Rumania	CILC; pressure for CT.
USSR	CAD or Drafts up to 90 days.
Yugoslavia	All terms, CT.

Asia and Pacific

Australia	All terms 30 – 60 days.
China	Usually ILC.
India	ILC; CT.
Indonesia	ILC; CT.
Japan	All terms, usually 90 days.
South Korea	CAD or 90 – 120 day ILC.
Malaysia	All terms 60 – 90 days.
New Zealand	Open account or Drafts 30 – 60 days.
Pakistan	ILC; CT.
Philippines	180 day ILC mandatory.
Singapore	All terms 30 – 90 days.
Taiwan	ILC (beware fraud on unsecured terms).

Latin America

Argentina	ILC 180 days minimum.
Brazil	CILC 180 days. Some open account for essentials.
Chile	CILC or CAD.
Colombia	All terms; CILC common.
Ecuador	ILC or CAD.
Jamaica	CILC.
Mexico	Open Account and Drafts 90 – 180 days.
Trinidad	All terms up to 90 days.
Venezuela	ILC or CILC 120 – 180 days; CT.

North America

Canada	Open Account 30 – 60 days.
USA	Open Account 30 – 60 days.

Checklist: To Improve Credit Terms
(Every credit manager should review the terms allowed to foreign customers at intervals, in the light of payment experience, and take steps to improve security and payment times wherever possible)   • *Decide* if your product range justifies standard terms.   • *Find* out the terms that are normal in each country you sell to.   • *List* customers by country, showing present terms.   • *Show* the state of compliance with terms (e.g. prompt, slow, etc.).   • *Re-negotiate* existing terms where they are not suitable.   • *Include* increased or reduced cost of credit in next price review.   • *Use* the new standards for all new customers in each market.

6 International transfers of funds

'Float time'

The credit job is not finished when the customer has paid. 'Making money flow back home is an art appreciated fully by exporters dedicated to maximising profit'. So said the magazine 'Export Direction' in 1978, when commenting on the increasing delays being experienced by exporters in receiving funds once customers had paid.

This topic is given its own space, separate from payment terms and collection techniques, because special attention is necessary by exporters to the banking processes for transferring foreign payments. Billions of Pounds, Dollars, Yen, Deutschmarks and other major currencies are constantly swilling around in the banking system, for several days, or sometimes weeks, in between the debits to customers' local bank accounts and credits to exporters' accounts. Since banks are becoming richer while industrial margins are smaller than ever in modern business history, there is a clear need for exporters to take every possible measure with banking instructions, in collaboration with customers, to speed up the process.

It is first necessary to understand the various ways that funds are transferred internationally, then examine what precision and skill can be applied to improving the flow.

SITPRO greatly assisted exporters a few years ago by producing a document 'How to Control Floating Money', a checklist to help exporters speed up their international receipts. For the first time, it gave official recognition (government and banks were on the production team) to the deteriorating situation. The expressions 'bank float time' and 'floating funds' have come to be derogatory terms rather than just descriptive. SITPRO stated that three weeks float time was not uncommon, and it calculated costs and the effects on profits. The document examines the different kinds of transfer and gives many hints on precision in instructions and documents to improve payments.

The international bank situation — some problems

The present situation has distinct historical origins. In the Middle Ages, merchants used banks to store their wealth but paid other merchants on a cash basis. After the 'Cambium Contract' document really began the international credit process, banks learned to deal across frontiers with their clients' funds. The building of empires and the incredibly rapid business growth after the Industrial Revolution encouraged a very sophisticated world banking system. Banks in every country, led by the Europeans, made correspondent relationships in other countries to settle trading accounts without actually transferring bullion. The imbalance of these international accounts created the world foreign exchange market, with its different values for currencies according to demand. The use of the Bill of Lading underpinned collection of Bills of Exchange by banks. Exports not covered by drafts were traditionally paid by letter advices (i.e. mail transfers, and later telegraphically), or by a bank's own cheque. Thus the banks of the world built their businesses by providing a magnificent money-transfer system for traders, who, having sent their valuable assets across the globe, were quickly reimbursed or notified safely of the distant customers' acceptances of tenor bills, or of their dishonour. Amazingly the services of the larger banks were just as efficient in the pre-electric days of sailing ships and horse-powered transport as in the later days of jet aircraft and electronic messaging. The reasons are a complex equation of volumes and labour costs.

Unfortunately undesirable delays and inefficiencies have seeped into banking systems, so that it is now necessary for exporters to influence events on their particular funds. Some of the adverse factors quoted by banks as causing a drop in standards are:

● Enormous increase in volume of transactions.
● Increased cost of staff to handle paperwork.
● Lower standards of education and commitment.
● Varying standards of correspondent banks.
● Reduction of bank influence over delinquent clients.
● Increase in foreign exchange controls or government interference.

The major US and European banks have addressed themselves to the volume and cost problems by developing the SWIFT system of electronic transfers, but there is a clear need for exporters to strengthen relationships with their banks and customers, to explore ways of getting back to the pre-1950 standards, and not to accept the above reasons as insoluble problems.

UK groups usually allow foreign subsidiaries or associates to run their own banking affairs, whereas US-owned corporations have a multi-national management approach that 'needs to know' about local banking costs and requires relationships with the more enterprising US banks. Comparing two manufacturing companies in, say, Italy, one with a British parent and one with an American parent, it may well be that trading efficiency brings similar profit levels, but that net 'bottom-line' profits are greater with the American company which has better organized its funding and consequent bank interest.

In Italy, cheques are debited to the payer's account, by law, from the date of the cheque, with post-dating forbidden. The payee obtains value only from the date of clearance, so that bank 'float' can be considerable. The solution to this is to arrange personal collection of significant cheques.

In France, Spain, Belgium and elsewhere on the Continent, the time taken between paying in cheques and their clearance with the issuing banks can be up to ten days, so that dates on bank statements can be wildly out from actual value dates. The solution is to make individual agreements with banks for faster value, in return for some advantage to the bank.

UK companies with foreign subsidiaries have often found that, although they may prefer a British expatriate to be in charge of finance, they employ a local expert to deal with the banks.

The risk of delay is even greater on the remittance to the UK of funds from end-customers. It is quite obvious that effective credit management of exports requires personal negotiation with banks in customers' countries to reduce the 'float' time.

Some reported examples of banking delays

A very large payment from Algeria to the UK did not arrive. A long investigation (lasting nearly three months!) revealed that the Algerian bank used a French bank in Egypt as intermediary and that bank remitted the funds to its own correspondent British bank, not the exporter's. This was a case of convenient bank inter-relationships working *against* an exporter.

A buyer in Marseilles simply asked his own bank to remit the required amount to a named exporter in the UK. The Marseilles branch sent its requirement to its Paris head office which credited as usual its London office, which paid a convenient British bank (to which it owed a large balance). The British bank had to clear the payment through the French bank's official foreign branch in London and then sent a cheque to the exporter, who paid it in to his own bank. Between the innocent Marseilles customer's payment and the mystified UK exporter's bank credit, *three weeks had elapsed* for the payment to travel 900 miles.

Many foreign buyers now pay in a third currency, such as US dollars, through dealings with European branches of US banks. If dollar cheques are sent to the UK, they have to go to New York for clearance, or if bank transfers are arranged, the US bank's involvement will add to the delays.

Instead of the exporter leaving the buyer to make payment arrangements which can suffer from a long trail of banks, it is better to agree on exactly how money will be remitted. The buyer will probably not mind since he is debited at the same time anyway, while the exporter's precise knowledge of which banks have been instructed will enable him to investigate any delay efficiently, so that no suspicion or work falls on the customer.

Some multi-national banks strive aggressively to obtain money-transfer business and, where they have UK branches, the service can be very efficient. Exporters should investigate facilities in, say, Germany, to consider opening a local bank account to receive all payments from customers in that country. The bank should then be instructed to remit funds by cable every day, or whenever is sensible, to the exporter's own bank in the UK.

Summarizing the points so far:

- Delays in foreign bank transfers have increased.
- Fund recovery needs expert management.
- SWIFT will help the banks and, eventually, exporters.
- UK groups do not manage foreign subsidiaries' banking well enough.
- In France and elsewhere, negotiate value dating.
- Ask customers to instruct their banks to remit to a specified UK bank.
- Ask all foreign payers (customers or banks) to use Telegraph Transfer or Telex Transfer.
- Open bank accounts in foreign countries to collect funds and transfer to UK in bulk by telex at agreed intervals.

Transmission methods

The ways that an exporter gets his money can be divided between:

- Cash already in UK – as in a Documentary L/C.
- Exporter originates process – as in the collection of drafts.
- Customer originates process – as in cheques, bank drafts, mail transfers and telegraphic transfers.

Documentary letters of credit

Apart from Cash in Advance terms, which are rare and even illegal for some countries, the safest way for an exporter to be paid quickly is by L/C.

The different types of L/C were described in Chapter 5 under 'Payment Terms'. There are several different ways of referring to L/Cs, e.g. Credits; L/Cs; Documentary Credits; Doc. Credits; CIL/Cs or IL/Cs; Confirmed Credits, and so on. In the interests of accuracy, the most usual types are:

- Confirmed, Irrevocable Letter of Credit   (CIL/C)
- Irrevocable Letter of Credit   (IL/C)
- Revocable Letter of Credit   (RL/C)

It is essential for exporters to realise that under Documentary Credits, banks deal in documents and *not goods*. The documents must agree precisely with the L/C requirements and the L/C is a separate contract in itself. Therefore, the exporter should:

- Check the L/C terms with his own sales contract.
- Not expect a bank to accept documentary errors.
- Not argue 'commercially' with the bank in an attempt to get paid when at fault.

The rights and obligations of banks, exporters and customers are set out in the ICC Uniform Customs and Practice for Documentary Credits (publication number 400). Exporters should familiarize themselves with these requirements.

Note:
(i)   Most L/Cs are payable on shipment by Sight Draft.
(ii)   Credit, usually up to a maximum of 180 days, can be allowed in the L/C. The exporter's draft on the advising bank can either be allowed to mature or can be discounted for cash.
(iii)   Where the L/C is payable only in country of issue, the UK advising bank will usually 'negotiate' the exporter's bill for cash, with recourse. A draft on a CIL/C can be negotiated without recourse.

It is worth quoting the Preamble to the ICC booklet U.C.P. 400 'General provisions and definitions'. These articles apply to all documentary credits, including, to the extent to which they may be applicable, standby letters of credit, and are binding on all parties thereto unless otherwise expressly agreed. They shall be incorporated into each documentary credit by wording in the credit indicating that such credit is issued subject to Uniform Customs and Practice for Documentary Credits, 1983 revision, ICC Publication n° 400.

For the purposes of these articles, the expressions 'documentary credit(s)' and 'standby letter(s) of credit' used herein (hereinafter referred to as 'credit(s)'), mean any arrangement, however named or described, whereby a bank (the issuing bank), acting at the request and on the instructions of a customer (the applicant for the credit),

(i)   is to make a payment to or to the order of a third party (the beneficiary), or is to pay or accept bills of exchange (drafts) drawn by the beneficiary,

or

(ii)   authorizes another bank to effect such payment, or to pay, accept or negotiate such bills of exchange (drafts), against stipulated documents, provided that the terms and conditions of the credit are complied with.

Credits, by their nature, are separate transactions from the sales or other contract(s) on which they may be based and banks are in no way concerned with or bound by such contract(s), even if any reference whatsoever to such contract(s) is included in the credit.

In credit operations all parties concerned deal in documents, and not in goods, services and/or other performances to which the documents may relate.

Instructions for the issuance of credits, the credits themselves, instructions for any amendments thereto and the amendments themselves must be complete and precise.

In order to guard against confusion and misunderstanding, banks should discourage any attempt to include excessive detail in the credit or in any amendment thereto.

A beneficiary can in no case avail himself of the contractual relationships existing between the banks or between the applicant for the credit and the issuing bank.

Figure 6.1 Key Stages in a L/C Transaction

(a) A contract is made between exporter and customer on L/C terms.

(b) The exporter suggests L/C specifications to the customer.

(c) Customer instructs his bank to open a L/C in favour of the exporter, specifying terms and documents required, complying with the sales contract.

(d) Issuing bank (customer's) arranges with a UK bank to advise or confirm the L/C to the exporter.

(e) Advice of the L/C is sent to the exporter, to check and subsequently use.

(f) Exporter checks that L/C conditions can be met, expiry date is adequate and that his Conditions of Sale remain intact. Asks buyer for amendment of any defects.

(g) On shipment, the exporter presents a draft to the UK bank, with the specified documents, requiring payment or acceptance for future payment, according to the terms.

(h) The UK bank checks the documents for compliance, pays or accepts draft and sends documents to issuing bank.

(i) Issuing bank checks documents against terms of credit, passes them to customer to enable goods to be taken up and debits customer's account.

(j) Bank reimbursement takes place.

Both exporter and customer know what is being purchased. It is detailed in the order. But neither may know the other's precise requirements, e.g. manufacturing time, technical coding of goods, shipping lines to be used or avoided, etc. Since L/C terms are being used to protect both parties, and L/Cs are all about *documents*, it is important that the documentary requirements match the contract details and also suit both parties.

There is a high 'failure' rate of some 60–70% of letter of credit presentations to the banks by exporters. They arise from defects between the terms of the credit – the deadline dates and the prescribed documents – and the exporters' performance as evidenced by the documents provided.

'Failed' L/C's are highly risky, since payment may never be possible.

Either at the quotation or order acknowledgement stage, a customer on L/C terms should be notified of the exporter's documentary requirements.

If the customer's order or the L/C contain unacceptable requirements, they should be rejected at once, preferably by telex communication, asking for rapid amendment of the L/C. An amendment advice should then be received from the advising bank, to complete the exercise.

In case of production or delivery delays, the requested shipment date should be proposed as one month later than the contracted shipment date.

For FOB contracts, exporters should request that the L/C permits payment against the Freight Forwarder's Receipt.

To summarize the preliminary rules for L/C business:

- Do not treat the Order as valid until an acceptable L/C is received.
- Ensure the expiry date is adequate.
- Do not accept the need for impossible documentation.

There are three vital checking stages for making L/Cs successful:

1. When asking the customer to send a L/C, specify its contents.
2. When a L/C is received, check its suitability immediately and notify all departments involved. Then telex the customer only once to arrange all amendment needed.
3. When presenting documents for payment, allow enough time before expiry to correct any last-minute errors.

Check One: Have the credit set up properly.
After experience of many unworkable credits, some exporters have developed standard letters, or printed forms, to send to customers. There is rarely a commercial objection to this practice, and on the contrary, as it is done before the banks are involved, expensive amendment fees are avoided for both parties.

A sample form is shown in Figure 6.2.

The formal procedure is for the customer to instruct his bank to open a L/C in favour of the exporter for a precise value, requiring precise documents to be presented to the bank before payment is made. The customer's bank will normally comply provided (a) the customer has sufficient borrowing power at that bank, since the L/C will normally tie up funds for at least three months, and (b) that the regulations of that country allow L/Cs for imports.

Figure 6.2 Form to Send to Customers Opening Letters of Credit

---

To: Customer ....

   Address .... (Date) ....

Ref: Your Order ....

Dear Sirs,

Documentary Letters of Credit

When opening a documentary Letter of Credit in our favour for the above order, please instruct your bank as follows:

(Exporter's correct name).
—The beneficiary is to be shown as: ....
—The Credit is to be in our possession by (date).
—The last date for shipment is to be (date).
—The last day for presentation of documents is to be (date).
—The goods are to be described as (exactly correct description that will appear on the invoice).
  Note: the word 'about' will permit us to ship + or – 10% of the quantity specified as we cannot guarantee exact quantities.)
—Shipment to be from 'any European port'.
—Part shipments allowed.
—Trans-shipments to be allowed (rarely necessary but in an emergency it may be the only way to get the goods to you).
—Only the words 'Bill of Lading' without additional words to appear.
—For FOB or C&F shipments the words 'insurance effected by buyer'.
—All bank and other charges for buyer's account.
—Documents to be presented:

  (a) Invoice (............copies).
  (b) Bills of Lading, full set of originals.
  (c) Insurance Certificate.

(Note: any other documents required under the contract will be supplied but *need not* be specified in the Credit.)

The International Chamber of Commerce (ICC), which has made such tremendous strides for world trade in standardizing bank procedures for both L/Cs and Documentary Collections, has issued a very clear guide, 'Standard Forms for Issuing Documentary Credits' (publication number 323) to help banks and importers in every country to produce uniform and effective L/Cs.

The customer's bank will send the Advice of the L/C by post or telex directly to the exporter or through a bank in the UK. Once issued, an IL/C cannot be amended or cancelled without the exporter's consent.

Check Two: Immediately the credit is received.

(a) Is it irrevocable? It should be.

(b) Is it confirmed – by a British or first class US or European bank? Preferable, but not essential, as a credit risk decision may be taken on an unconfirmed L/C.

(c) Is the exporter's name and address correct?

(d) Is the customer's name spelled correctly?

(e) Are the validity and expiry dates OK? Check that adequate time is allowed for shipping schedules and documentation.

(f) Is the value adequate for all charges?

(g) Is the description of goods correct? If not, request amendment or arrange to word invoices with identical, incorrect description plus correct version.

(h) Are the quantities correct?

(i) Is partial shipment allowed?

(j) Is the required rate of shipments OK?

(k) Is the port of shipment acceptable? Remember extra inland costs.

(l) Is the port of destination as agreed? Remember extra CIF costs otherwise.

(m) Is an export licence required by exporter?

(n) Is an import licence number quoted by customer? If required, it must be.

(o) Are any special guarantees required by customer?

(p) Can specified documents be obtained in time?

- Bill of Lading, Air Waybill, Parcel Post Receipt, etc.
- Invoices of specified forms.
- Packing List.
- Certificates of Origin, Quality, Inspection.
- Insurance Policy or Certificate.
- Others.

(q) Are there special insurance risks specified? If so, can they be covered?

(r) Are exporter's conditions of sale still intact? By meeting all the requirements of the L/C, some essential contract conditions may have been overridden.

This is the time to have discrepancies and problems sorted out; it will be too late at the time of presenting documents.

It is good practice to specify that *all* credits go to a single person in the organization immediately. That person should take several photocopies and send them to all affected departments: Sales; Production; Finance; Shipping; Technical; etc. A large rubber stamp on each should call for *immediate* checks on 'performability' and for any required amendments to be notified to the central point within 7 *days*. Then *one single* telex can be sent to the customer for several points to be changed.

Banks charge £15 – £25 for each amendment action, regardless of points.

Check Three: Before presenting the documents for payment.
The export credit function should be responsible for collecting the required documents from the other functions and for checking them for accuracy and completeness.

It should certainly be the responsibility of the export credit function to present documents to the bank for payment, since they have the incentive to obtain funds and also have the overall knowledge of L/C requirements to take care of any difficulties.

When the complete set of documents has been collected, the exporter should present them to the paying bank, together with the appropriate Bill of Exchange. A suitable standard covering letter can be produced, containing an instruction, such as: 'Proceeds to be credited immediately to (Exporter's Bank and) for the credit of (Exporter's Name) Account Number _____, under advice'.

If the L/C is payable in the buyer's country, the above letter should specify transfers by cable or Telegraphic Transfer, with charges for the customer's account (if possible).

The paying bank will compare the documents presented with those specified in the L/C and will normally credit the exporter's account without delay, advising him of the payment.

DISCREPANCIES IN DOCUMENTS PRESENTED

Despite all the checks recommended above, there will still be cases of discrepancies and, regrettably, the banks report a continual increase in the error rate. Some foreign banks in London, e.g. Indian and Pakistani banks, make very strict checks and reject discrepancies as unpayable, especially for spelling errors.

More significant discrepancies concern Bills of Lading being claused as 'stale' (out of date) or not being endorsed 'to order' or not showing 'Freight prepaid', as required by CIF contracts.

The most frequent discrepancy is presentation *after* expiry date.

Letters of Credit usually show a final date for presentation of documents following the final shipment date. Under ICC Rules, the exporter has 21 days from shipment date to present documents if no presentation date is specified.

When exporters arrange for expiry dates to be extended to match delivery delays, etc., they should be careful to arrange for UK bank confirmation to be separately extended, as this is not automatic. This rule should be *absolutely enforced* for risky market customers, since coups, bank collapses or government blockage of funds may well occur during the critical extension period when the UK confirmation no longer applies.

Discrepancies at the time of presentation can be resolved in three ways. The exporter can ask the paying bank to:

- Telex or cable the issuing bank for permission to pay despite the errors.
- Send the documents to the buyer's (issuing) bank on a collection basis.
- Pay against the exporter's Indemnity (or his bank's), giving the paying bank recourse if the issuing bank or customer eventually refuse to pay.

Cabling for permission is the cleanest solution but can still take a long time, sometimes needing an exchange between exporter and customer to explain the errors.

Sending documents on a collection basis puts the transaction on the same basis as a documentary collection without a L/C, with attendant risks.

The Indemnity technique is now widely used, and recourse rarely occurs, but exporters should resist this easy conclusion which enables inefficient export administration to be covered up by a letter of indemnity.

It is useful for exporters to consider that correct behaviour under a L/C, from originally requesting it right through to final presentation, contains most of the disciplines required to operate successfully in the export trade.

FUNDS FROM OTHER TYPES OF LETTER OF CREDIT

TRANSFERABLE LETTERS OF CREDIT
These simply provide for the beneficiary, usually the exporter, to instruct the

paying bank to pay other persons or firms. They obtain payment by presenting documents precisely as required by the beneficiary to a credit.

They are useful where the exporter is a middle-man without the resources to pay the UK manufacturers concerned. The exporter arranges for the Transferable Credit to be established in his name, permitting part shipments and authorizing the paying bank to accept instructions from the exporter to make the credit available to other beneficiaries. If the exporter does not wish his buyer to be aware of the UK suppliers, he can arrange for his name to be substituted on the transferred credit and for the shipping documents to be in the name of a third party, blank endorsed.

When the various suppliers have drawn off their funds, the middle-man (e.g. an export agent) collects his share by adding his own invoice to the documents presented.

BACK-TO-BACK CREDITS
As a less efficient alternative to the Transferable Credit scheme, the exporter without interim funds can, on receipt of a normal L/C from his customer, ask his own bank in the UK to issue a L/C in favour of one or more manufacturers or suppliers, secured by the original foreign L/C.

REVOLVING CREDITS
These are particularly used by Eastern European state buying organizations for scheduled, long-running orders.

A L/C is established in favour of the exporter, advised and payable usually through a London bank, for an overall value to suit a continuing supply or a schedule. As shipments are made and payments drawn off, the Credit is topped up either by each amount or by a monthly summary amount, allowing further shipments to be safely made.

AUTHORITIES TO PURCHASE
These are alternatives to the Documentary Credit and are sometimes used for shipment to the Far East and also Mauritius. Bills are drawn not on a bank, but on the customer, payable at sight or on a future date specified in the Authority. The exporter represents the Bill and documents to the UK bank acting on behalf of the buyer's bank. The UK bank will purchase the Bill, paying its value to the exporter. If the Authority is 'with recourse' the exporter's liability remains until it is finally paid by the buyer. Bills drawn under Authorities to Purchase carry interest from the date of the Bill until the date of final payment by the buyer. The exporter has the risk that dishonour may require payment of substantial interest in addition to repayment of the face value of the bill.

Documentary bank collections

The next most secure method of payment is by Documentary Sight Draft, whereby the document of title is only released by the bank to the buyer against payment. This is known as a D/P method of collection – Documents against Payment.

Where a period of credit is involved, the documents are released by the bank against acceptance of the tenor draft and this is known as a D/A method – Documents against Acceptance.

On both D/P and D/A collections, payment is obtained through the banking system by the exporter passing the appropriate documents plus the Bill of Exchange to his bank with instructions to collect the funds on his behalf.

Because of the well-regulated, precise nature of Bills of Exchange, we may refer to the exporter as the 'drawer' of the Bill, to the customer as the 'drawee' and to the beneficiary, usually the exporter, as the 'Payee'.

Payment on demand makes a Bill a 'Sight' Draft and payment at a future date, whether fixed, or as a number of days from date of shipment or from arrival, makes a Bill a Term Draft (also called a Tenor or Usance Draft).

The treatment of documentary collection by banks is governed by another excellent ICC publication, 'Uniform Rules for Collections' (publication number 322). Exporters should obtain this booklet and make themselves thoroughly familiar with the duties and responsibilities of the banks involved in collecting their funds.

Figure 6.3 Key Stages in a Documentary Collection Procedure

1 Exporter assembles documents on shipment, draws Sight Draft on customer.
2 Exporter completes Collection Instruction Sheet, sends it with Sight Draft plus documents to his bank.
3 Exporter's bank sends documents to a collecting bank in buyer's country.
4 Collecting bank releases documents to buyer against payment (or buyer refuses payment and does not take up goods).
5 Collecting bank remits proceeds, or advice of non-payment, to exporter's bank, who notify exporter.

STAGE 1: ASSEMBLING DOCUMENTS AND DRAWING SIGHT DRAFT

When goods are despatched, the exporter collects together the documents required by the customer as per the order, or required by local regulations. (See 'Croner's Reference Book for Exporters' for details of documentary requirements for each country.) In particular, the Bill of Lading will represent title to the goods and must not be sent directly to the customer. Where goods go by air or road/rail, there is no document of title to provide the security of a Bill of Lading, and the advice given under 'Risk Assessment' was to despatch such goods c/o the bank, who can then control their release against payment.

The exporter then draws a draft on the customer payable 'At Sight' and marked 'Sole' or 'Sola', indicating it is the only original. For really remote destinations, where Bills might get lost, exporters sometimes draw drafts in sets of two, called First and Second of Exchange, each indicating that the others are unpaid, e.g. 'First of exchange, second of same date being unpaid'.

STAGE 2: COLLECTION INSTRUCTION SHEET

The banks issue their own forms for receiving collection instructions from exporters. The document is important, as it instructs the bank to release the exporter's goods to a named buyer, against receipt of payment, with a number of supplementary instructions as to charges, method of transfer, etc. Upon completion, the exporter sends the Instruction Sheet to his bank attached to the Sight Draft and documents. The bank becomes responsible, under Article 1 of Uniform Rules, to 'act in good faith and exercise reasonable care'.

It is at the stage of completing the Instruction Form to the bank that the exporter implements several points of credit policy, as follows:

- Whether presentation to the buyer should be immediate or to await arrival of the goods. (This will depend on relationships and tradition, but the term is intended to apply to 'Sight' of the documents.)
- Whether funds should be remitted by mail or cable. (Cable is faster, but cable costs can be dearer than the interest costs of waiting about two weeks for an airmail transfer. The break-even value is about £4000 currently, i.e. £4000 $\times$ 13% $\div$ 52 $\times$ 2 = £20 = average cable cost for all countries.)
- Whether non-payment should be advised by mail or cable. (Again, this will depend on its importance. An exporter might prefer to bear cable costs to be able to get quickly after a delinquent buyer.)
- Who the bank should contact in 'Case of Need'. (How much authority will the exporter's local representative have if the bank advise him of a problem with the collection?)
- How should the goods be protected if payment is not made. (The exporter may want them re-sold, re-shipped, or dumped locally.)

- Whether to protest the bill for non-payment. (This is an effective 'hastener', but may upset a customer relationship where there is a genuine reason for non-payment.)
- Who pays the collection charges of the two banks. (If not already agreed between exporter and customer, it is usual for exporters to instruct that the customer pays. If the customer refuses, the bank charges the exporter!)

An example of a Collection Instruction Sheet is given in Figure 6.4.

STAGE 3: DOCUMENTS SENT TO FOREIGN BANKS
It is recommended that collection instructions show the name and address of the collecting bank in the buyer's country. This may be supplied by

Figure 6.4 Collection Instruction to bank (also called 'Lodgement Form', or
'Bill Instruction Form')

the customer as the bank he particularly wants to be involved, or it may be nominated by the exporter, from experience, as a particularly effective bank. If no bank is specified, the exporter's bank will use one of its own correspondent banks in the buyer's country. The collecting bank takes on full collection responsibility as agent of the UK bank. Not only will this add an extra link to the chain of banks involved, with consequent risks, but sometimes it embarrasses a customer or his bank. Therefore, exporters are urged to *arrange with buyers* the banks that will be used for collections.

STAGES 4/5: DOCUMENTS ARE RELEASED OR NOT; EXPORTER ADVISED OF FATE

There is usually a 'grey area' of delay, awaiting fate of payment or refusal of goods, caused by:

- Communication delays between banks.
- Non-arrival of goods.
- Delay in customer taking up goods.

Control over delivery of the goods is maintained by the foreign bank which is usually able to store and insure goods not taken up. The costs and extra bank charges are put to the exporter's account, unless he is able to get the customer to take them.

The exporter may be asked to allow release of the documents and goods against local currency, pending foreign exchange authorization. This needs careful judgement and reference to the country risk dossier and to ECGD if a policy-holder. The delays in obtaining Sterling can be considerable.

Eventually, the exporter receives from his bank an advice of payment or non-payment, giving a reason. Examples of payment and non-payment advices are given in Figures 6.5 and 6.6.

CASH AGAINST DOCUMENTS

As stated elsewhere, customers in many countries prefer to import on a CAD basis which is similar to Documentary Sight Draft, without using an actual draft.

The procedure is exactly the same, using a Collection Instruction form to the bank, which has the same obligations under ICC Rules and only releases the documents against payment.

The reason for CAD being preferred is usually a saving in stamp duty and bank charges by the importer, but if the exporter agrees to operate these terms, he should ensure that his Cash Book and Bill Receivable system treat CAD as if a draft had been used.

DOCUMENTARY TERM DRAFTS

The preceding drills for exporter and banks apply equally to Term Drafts, e.g. '90 days after date', except that the bank releases the documents, once

Figure 6.5 Bank Advice of Paid Bill

Midland Bank Limited

Branch address and date

To   Compact Motors Ltd   9.1.80
     Moorhead

Dear   Sir

We advise you that your   1   account has been credited today
with the following amount/s:

Details	Amount
Proceeds of FBC 0299 by order of Tatu Co., Taipei, Taiwan Rep. of China Sterling amount = £3500.00 Less our charges 6.25 3493.75	3493.75
Inv X50531	

Yours faithfully

Manager

580

an authorized official of the customer has 'accepted' the obligation to pay, by signing the draft across its face. The acceptance may show the calculated due date and/or the bank to be used for settlement, but neither is necessary under the Bills of Exchange Act.

In the period between acceptance and due date, the accepted draft is held by the foreign collecting bank, which then proceeds to collect on the due date and remit the funds to the exporter's bank as instructed, or if the Bill is dishonoured at due date, to send the advice of non-payment, giving the customer's reasons. The foregoing describes 'D/A' or Documents against Acceptance, which is the universally accepted system.

Figure 6.6 Bank Advice of Unpaid Bill

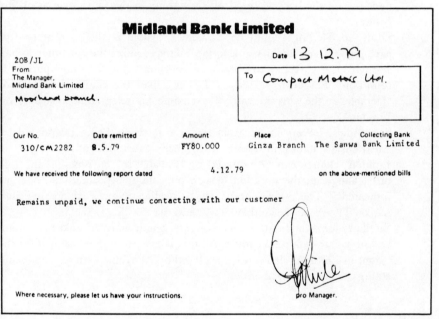

POINTS OF INTEREST ON DOCUMENTARY COLLECTIONS

- It is not necessary for an exporter to use his own bank to handle collections, although it is convenient to do so. Banks compete for this lucrative market and some are particularly well represented in certain countries. However, this puts an extra link in the chain, as when funds are received in the UK by the other bank, they must still be remitted to the exporter's bank. Nevertheless, UK exporters have the unique advantage over the rest of the world of having the sophisticated banking community in London, representing nearly all countries of the world. Exporters with significant business in particular markets should talk to London banks who specialize in those markets for advice on drafts and money transfer techniques in general.

- Similarly to the above, it is possible for an exporter to send the documents and draft *directly* to a bank in the buyer's country, or even the buyer's own bank. This system is known as 'Direct Collections' and is widely recommended by US banks around the world. One delay stage in eliminated by this method, but the exporter loses the follow-up strength of his UK bank. Exporters wishing to adopt the Direct Collection technique should obtain a supply of Collection Instruction forms from the London branches of the foreign banks concerned.

- All drafts sent for collection must be endorsed in blank, i.e. the exporter endorses on the back of the draft by signing in the same style as on the front.

- Drafts in Sterling should be claused: 'Payable at the current rate of exchange for sight drafts in London'. This requires the customer to pay enough local currency to obtain the Sterling value for the exporter. If remittance has been agreed as TT or cable, the clause should read: 'Payable at the current rate of exchange for telegraphic transfers on London'.

- Sometimes, buyers in Australasia agree to drafts being negotiated by Australasian banks in London. In these cases, the above 'sight on London' clauses can be replaced by 'Payable in* currency at the rate of exchange on the notation hereon plus stamps, postage and charges indicated'. (The asterisk indicates Australian, New Zealand or Fijian banks. The Australasian banks will add the charge particulars).

- Similarly for some South African buyers, South African banks in London will negotiate exporters' drafts. All that is needed in these cases is for the 'Sight in London' clause to be replaced by: 'Payable with exchange and stamps as per endorsement'.

Clean collections

The Clean Bill method of payment comes somewhere between documentary and non-documentary methods, in that the bills are sent through the bank collection system, but with no documents attached, as these are sent directly to the customer. If the Clean Bill is dishonoured, it has normal rights under the Bills of Exchange Act and may be used by the exporter as the basis for a legal action for recovery.

The use of Clean Bills has increased in recent years for two main reasons:

(a)   They are used domestically in several European countries and buyers tend to accept the practice for imports.

(b)   Exporters have realized that Clean Bills have more discipline than ordinary open-account terms for weaker customers.

Clean Bills can be used to obtain an acceptance *before* goods are manufactured, or shipped, where the exporter informs a risky customer that no commitment will be undertaken until a Bill is accepted.

Dishonoured Bills impose a certain adverse publicity in most countries; thus the acceptance of a Clean Bill tells the exporter his customer will *probably* meet it.

Open account – payments originated by customers

In the reducing scale of security, we now look at 'open-account' payment methods, where there is no documentary leverage on the customer to pay. These payment terms, effected by bank transfers or cheques, have become commonplace in most of the developed countries, where, statistically, most customers honour their commitments (perhaps with delays!). The terms imply a high degree of trust in the customer; thus, in the more difficult payment zones, weak currency countries and those suffering internal strife, non-documentary terms should only be operated with reliable, long-established customers.

In all cases, the exporter should agree absolutely on the period of credit, i.e. the due date of payment based on a known event, such as invoice date or Bill of Lading date, or the last day of each month.

The customer is sent the documents by the exporter, takes delivery of the goods and subsequently arranges a payment in favour of the exporter.

FOREIGN CUSTOMER'S CHEQUE

This may be in Sterling, the buyer's currency or a third currency.

Although it seems attractive that a buyer can just write a cheque in favour of the exporter, there are several disadvantages and this method of receiving settlement should be actively discouraged.

BUYER'S CURRENCY
Normally a customer's own cheque will be drawn on his own bank in his

national currency. He then sends the cheque in the post to the exporter in the UK. The disadvantages can be listed as:

(a)   If paying Sterling invoices, the customer's action is incorrect and if accepted by the exporter, could lead to a loss on exchange.

(b)   The customer may have to wait for exchange control approval or may even send a cheque without such approval.

(c)   Postal delays.

(d)   The exporter's bank will have to send the cheque back to the customer's bank to clear it, before giving value to the exporter, or will give value with recourse and charge for negotiating it.

(e)   If the cheque is eventually dishonoured, the exporter will have wasted the two to four weeks' waiting time and may even have shipped further goods to the defaulting customer.

(f)   Even if the cheque clears and has local exchange control approval, there may be no convertible market for it in London, e.g. all weak currencies.

There are two basic solutions for the exporter:

(a)   Where the customers are few, or such cheque payments are spasmodic, he should ask for a bank cable transfer or banker's draft payable in London. Systematically, each customer paying by the cheque method should be negotiated into a different payment method.

(b)   Where there are several regular customers in a market and/or significant payment values, the exporter should consider opening a bank account in that country, e.g. a D. Mark account in Frankfurt, to which all German customers billed in D. Marks would be asked to send their payments, cheque or otherwise. Customers feel more comfortable with a domestic payment system. The German bank would be required by the exporter to remit the account balance at agreed intervals with payment details telexed to the exporter daily. Also, where salesmen or others visiting customers have been in the dangerous habit of bringing back local cheques to the UK, they would be instructed to pay them into the local foreign bank account.

THIRD CURRENCY

Many foreign companies nowadays hold bank accounts in other currencies (including Sterling) but, for this section, let us say in US Dollars or Swiss Francs.

Although it may suit a customer in, say, Taiwan, to use some of his spare US Dollar account to send a cheque to the UK, the exporter is faced with both delay and risks. Wherever in the world a customer draws his Dollar cheque, it has to go to a US bank, usually in New York, to be cleared. Similarly, an Italian customer's cheque expressed in Swiss Francs drawn on a bank in Milan has to be sent by the UK bank back to Zurich or Geneva for clearance. This puts an extra stage of delay into the Sterling conversion, in addition to the same problems listed in the section above on customers' own currencies.

The solutions are for exporters either to insist on receiving cleared funds by the due date, or to negotiate with each customer to send banker's drafts payable in London.

STERLING CHEQUES

For the customer, the situation is the same as holding a US Dollar or Swiss Franc account, or any other currency foreign to him. As most exports from Uk are billed in Sterling, customers holding Sterling bank accounts abroad are naturally tempted to send Sterling cheques drawn on those accounts. In this case, although Sterling carries no exchange risk, there is still the requirement for the exporter's UK bank to send the Sterling cheque back to the customer's bank to clear. The time taken for this can vary up to about four weeks depending on the remoteness of the foreign bank and its priorities. During the waiting time, although the exporter may have marked the account as paid, there is the worry that funds may not be available later.

BANK CHEQUES

These are better known as banker's drafts. It is preferable for a customer who wishes to send a cheque in an envelope to the exporter to send a draft from his bank, either in Sterling or the required currency.

The customer's bank will issue the cheque in favour of the exporter but drawn on a bank in the UK, usually an established branch of the foreign bank, or else a major UK bank with which the foreign bank has an arrangement. An important advantage of this type of settlement is that the local bank will ensure that exchange control regulations have been met before issuing the cheque.

The exporter can pay in the cheque and receive the usual UK clearance of two to three days, from the London-based bank.

Banker's drafts can be substituted where bank transfers take a long time to come through several banks between customer and exporter. The customer can be asked to arrange a banker's draft on a UK bank with strict instructions for the funds to be telexed to the exporter's own bank on arrival.

BANK MAIL TRANSFER (MT)

This is the most commonly used form of payment for exports, and also the slowest.

The customer instructs his bank to transfer an amount of money to the bank of the exporter. The customer's bank ensures that local formalities and regulations are met and the exporter receives, *in due course,* the payment, net of any charges imposed.

Left to his own devices, a customer will probably simply ask his bank to: 'Pay £2509.63 Sterling to Exporter Ltd (+ address in UK).' His bank will debit his account and send a letter to its own head office or international branch, which in turn will send another letter to the Central Bank or FX control body, or if that is not necessary, to the bank in London with which it has a correspondent relationship. That bank, unless by coincidence the same as the exporter's bank's foreign branch, will send a letter to the international office of the exporter's bank, which in turn will advise the exporter's own branch, who will credit the exporter's account. Quite a trail! And totally dependent on individual bank staff moving pieces of paper. The whole trail of bank links may take between one and eight weeks, yet the customer was debited on day one!

This bank-to-bank method of settlement which was once highly efficient is now much criticized for delays and errors. A great deal can be done by exporters to improve the timing and accuracy of MT payments, by taking care of the following:

● Establish exactly which customers in which countries pay by the MT method.
● Ask each of the which bank they instruct to make the payment and take some sample dates.
● Look at a payment advice from the UK bank for each.
● Discuss the time lag with the UK bank.

These steps may clarify some procedural points which can be improved. Usually, the conclusion is to give the customer very precise details of the bank account to which the MT should be sent.

The example MT given earlier could have arrived much faster if the customer were asked to instruct his bank to: 'Pay by Mail Transfer £2509.63 to Midland Bank Ltd, 65 High Street, Mytown, Exshire, England, Code 40-01-99, for the credit of account 989123 Exporters Ltd, Progress Way, Mytown, Exshire, England, under advice to them.'

This contains all the required elements and leaves no room for doubt. If the payment is late or goes astray, it is the bank(s) fault and the exporter can legitimately complain.

For payments above, say £4000, the customer should instruct bank payments to be TT. If the customer refuses to pay the charges on TTs, the exporter should consider the cost-savings of doing so himself.

In the above instruction, the customer would substitute 'Cable transfer' or 'TT' and would add 'Cable/TT charges for account of payee'.

BANK CABLE OR TELEGRAPHIC TRANSFER (TT)

Bank transfers are considerably faster if instructed to go by TT or Cable. They are sent by coded inter-bank cable or telex and thus cannot go astray. We have already seen how the exporter can choose to pay TT charges rather than incur interest on slow payments. There is no difference for the customer, who is debited at the same time, whichever method is used.

UK exporters, used to the well-developed bank system in this country, with branches in every High Street achieving three-day clearances through the City, sometimes fail to realize that other countries have no such clearing arrangements. In the USA, state laws prohibit banks operating across some state borders (this has led to the lock-box system which is unnecessary in the UK), and in several European countries banks are so competitive that transactions between them can vary greatly in time and accuracy.

In many countries, especially in Spain and Italy, companies have several bank accounts and the chain can be shortened by the exporter finding out which Spanish banks are correspondent of his own bank, then asking the customer to use one of those banks for the TT.

SWIFT – the system for the future

In 1977, the major banks began to use a long-dreamed-of computer system for inter-bank transfers between countries. Optimistically named SWIFT, i.e. the Society for Worldwide Interbank Financial Telecommunications, the system is aimed at solving the enormous volume problem for the banks, by reducing paperwork handling and eliminating the risk of losing documents in the post. Memberbanks are steadily growing and the position will soon be reached where non-SWIFT banks will be virtual outsiders and will hurry to enjoy the benefits.

Connected banks communicate via computers with a high level of privacy and security, to make same-day transfers of payments where instructions are complete, and where the banks at both ends are on SWIFT.

The same defects apply as in the MT or TT chain, that out-of-town branches, not connected yet, receive normal communication methods and the SWIFT link only replaces the links of connected banks.

It is not possible or necessary for importers to specify payments to be made by SWIFT; the banks concerned are only too glad to use the system if they can. Until the network is more comprehensive, banks are neither charging extra for SWIFT payments, nor reducing standard MT or TT charges.

All the major banks produce excellent, illustrated booklets with flowcharts on Letters of Credit and Collections. Advice on direct payments by customers is less common, so we give a checklist below.

Checklist: Speeding the flow of open account receipts

1. *Work Out The Costs:*

- Apply cost of borrowing to all values received more than seven days after due date.
- Segregate cost between:

    (a) Customers late in paying
    (b) Administrative delays after the customer paid
    (c) Delays between date of transfer and date of receipt

(Surprisingly high costs of banking delays, e.g. £7500 on a total of £1 million delayed by three weeks, put the need to improve into focus).

2. *Discuss delays with Major Customers:*
- Involve them in the problem/opportunity.
- See which banks are used and the instructions given to them.
- Make a list of unacceptable delays, say, longer than seven days between the customer's debit and your credit.
- Note the cases where exchange control delays are blamed, and see whether everything has been done correctly locally.

For non-exchange control cases:

- See how many banks in the chain. Can they be reduced?
- See if the values involved affect the speed of payment

- Check whether MT or TT was instructed. Agree on TT charges.
- See if the currency of payment affected the speed of transfer.

3. *Select Better Banks*

- Discuss the effectiveness of correspondent banks with your own bank – what can they do in their markets?
- Consider opening external bank accounts in major markets, so that customers can make easy payments to those and they can transfer bulk sums to your instructions.

4. *Improve the Routing of Funds*

- Discourage customers sending their own cheques – they have to be returned for clearance, and delays! Ask such customers to switch to Bankers Drafts or TTs.
- Use the 'lock-box' system in the USA to encourage customers to pay dollars into it, and arrange bulk transfers to your instructions.
- Work on every customer using MT and convert to TT, for amounts above, say, £4000.
- Ask customers to stress to their banks the importance of using correspondents on the SWIFT system.
- For large accounts with reliable customers, suggest holding accounts in the International Branches of present banks.
  Same day transfers of large amounts can be achieved, although fees will be higher.
- Ask customers to avoid transfers over a weekend – the two days will not benefit either party. The best day for transfer instructions is Monday, especially in the Middle East, where their weekend precedes the UK's and four or five days can be lost.
- Where you have local subsidiaries or associates, consider having customers pay to them, with an inter-company adjustment in the books.

5. *Give Precise Instructions*

- Tell customers by special letter and always show clearly in invoices:
      your bank name (no address needed) and sort code
      your bank account number
      the account name if different from the invoiced one
  Example:
  '(State Terms) – payment by Telegraphic Transfer to Britbank, Moorhead (45-99-00) for account 91236407 The English Export Company reference no. 6489.'

Getting Paid for Exports

- Tell your agent, subsidiary or local representative your exact payment instructions as given to customers and ask them to help achieve precision in their area.
- Send copies of all invoices to local agents so they can check payments have been made and which banks were used in case of delay. (They can also be quicker in chasing up late payments).

6.   *Investigate Missing Payments*

- When more than 7 days elapse after a customer pays:
    get the payment details from the customer (by telex)
    ask the customer to check what his own bank did
    ask the UK bank (due to receive the funds) to check urgently
- Act on the findings to:
    complain to the offending bank
    change banks for future payment instructions
    charge interest to the bank which held the funds too long

7 Collection of export proceeds

The exporter's collection objective is: to convert sales into cash on planned dates.

The factors requiring specialist attention

The impression may have been given that if Credit Risk, Payment Terms and Remittance of Funds are properly managed, the exporter will be fully paid on time. Unfortunately, there are still problems of non-liquidity and insolvency plus excuses, errors and disputes which prevent payments from arriving on time.

In the home trade, good collections are related to effort and the frequency of follow-ups. But in export, success depends also upon documentation and the banks. There is a jungle of techniques full of pitfalls which require experience and knowledge of alternative solutions. It is fairly pointless for a company to expect a home trade clerk or accounts collector to switch to export work every now and again to 'have a go at the overdues', unless that person is trained in export techniques. He must be able to establish quickly whether non-payment is due to documentation errors or bank delays or local currency deposits or simple default and have the knowledge to apply corrective action.

Some of the risks of non-payment facing the exporter are:

- Excessive shipping delays.
- Goods not wanted on arrival.
- Drafts not accepted.
- Deliberate default at due date.
- Delays in bank transfers of funds.
- Shortage of hard currency.
- Insolvency of the buyer or his country.

Some of these risks can be insured against, via ECGD. But the objective is not to be paid through an insurance claim. The ECGD policy should only be regarded as a long-stop if all the correct drills fail.

Most of the above risks are avoided by professionally managing the significant stages:

(a)   Choosing the correct terms to suit customer and country risks.
(b)   Processing the order accurately from quotation to shipment.
(c)   Getting the documentation right first time.
(d)   Using rapid (i.e. telephone or telex) means of contact.
(e)   Involving useful aids and other resources when appropriate.

In other words, good collections require sound preparation long before an overdue account pops up, and a broader management involvement than just a collection clerk's.

Effective payment terms and good relationships with customers can avoid most crisis situations and apart from sudden blockages of transfers by foreign governments, delays mostly reflect the poor management of perfectly manageable situations.

Later sections look at techniques in detail, but at this stage, we can examine briefly some of the risks listed above:

Late shipment

The customer has his own business to run and expects his imports from the UK to arrive on time or to be given plenty of warning of delay, so that his resale or manufacture can be reorganized. Unplanned delays cause havoc for the customer, whether due to late production by the exporter or to non-availability of vessels. The customer may retaliate by not paying the account properly, or use non-payment as a leverage to get better service. Secondly, delays may invalidate letters of credit, import licences or currency authorizations.

The solutions to these collection problems certainly do not lie in chasing the customer. They exist at the UK end. There should always be a good relationship between the shipping, customer service and credit departments.

Goods not wanted on arrival

This may be caused by late shipment by which time the customer has made other arrangements and the exporter is in breach anyway, or a difficult customer may have changed his mind or have run out of funds while the goods were in transit. If it is a documentary transaction there should be a prompt notification by the bank to the export of the dishonour and the reason. If it is an open-account shipment, the customer may leave the goods on the dockside or at the airport, and not notify the exporter. So problems of storage, insurance, customs and demurrage charges may arise, as well as re-selling, re-shipping or scrapping the goods.

The solutions are to avoid late shipments and to have good local representation. A rapid notification of repudiation of goods can help achieve a solution, before local charges have made the transaction unprofitable. The worst situation is where an exporter ships to a risky customer on open-account terms without a local agent and delegates collection to a lowly clerk.

Drafts not accepted

Similar to the above, with the exporter facing a problem of distance and communication. Assuming that the bank quickly tells the exporter of the non-acceptance (and slowness and lack of bank advices is another problem requiring management attention), the customer must be contacted immediately, by telex or telephone, to establish intentions. Is the delay temporary? If not, should the customer be forced to honour the contract by threat of legal action if necessary? Can the local agent get a quick solution? Should the drafts be protested (see later on timing of this) for local publicity and as a prelude to legal action? There is no universal solution, as the facts must be carefully weighed. The usual situation on a non-acceptance is a temporary one, i.e. for various reasons, the customer delays taking up the documents for only a few days.

Deliberate default at due date

When this occurs, the exporter is faced with questions such as: Is the customer now insolvent? Has he disputed the sale and it is still not resolved? Is the default only temporary? (the commonest reason). The vital requirement is to know as soon as it happens and to identify the problem directly with the customer or with the help of the agent. The solution is to decide either to enforce the contractual due date, or to extend it to help the customer.

Delays in bank transfer

The customer may be perfectly sound and even send the exporter evidence of his local payment, but a long time elapses without the arrival of the Sterling in the UK. This can be due to documentation errors (e.g. even in a developed country like France, Sterling will not be approved unless the customs form has been produced; thus goods taken in by hand, bypassing customs, cannot be paid for) or disorganized customers may delay transfer inadvertently by not completing formalities. In the poor countries, there are lengthy processes in official requirements. Or there can be excessive delays between banks.

The solution to documentary causes is to find out quickly and send any extra documents required.

In the case of money 'lost' in the banking system, there is now a steady trend of exporters successfully claiming interest from their banks for delays between the date that the foreign bank remitted Sterling to its arrival date. That may recoup the cost of the delay, but a better solution is for the exporter to work with his bank on the selection of better banks and the instructions given.

Shortage of hard currency

There are two situations here, firstly where the customer's country is well known for its lack of foreign currency, e.g. Indonesia and Zambia, and secondly, where a sudden decree affects existing contracts. The solution with the 'well-known' countries lies in the choice of secure payment terms and ensuring that import licences are held.

The exporter who does not bother to check existing country risk or who still ships on an open basis, deserves to be caught out. In the countries where slight delays occur in the allocation of hard currency by the central banks, e.g. Dominican Republic and Jamaica, there is nothing the exporter can do with the banks, except to keep checking for payment, but he should ensure that his customers sign shortfall undertakings, i.e. that they are responsible to pay the local equivalent of the full Sterling value at the date of remittance whatever happens to the exchange rate in the delay period. Where an overnight announcement affects payment on non-secured terms, there are two steps the exporter should take. For existing debts, he should ensure with the customer that they will be paid in local currency on the due date and will do everything required officially. (Customers in such 'freeze' situations sometimes do not bother to pay the local currency and exporters wait an unknown period for transfers, then find that their debts are not in the queue anyway.)

The key document required by exporters, in transfer blockage cases, is a letter or certificate from the Central Bank authority, usually with a reference number. This proves the debt is officially in the queue.

For sales becoming due for shipment, the exporter should contact the customer to arrange alternative payment, or to re-schedule the delivery dates for when payment will be reliable, or agree to cancel the orders.

Insolvency of the buyer or country

Assuming that risk assessment has been properly managed, insolvencies should be only the very few unexpected cases. In many countries, customer insolvency results in payment moratoria or special arrangements with creditors to accept a reduced payment in final settlement to allow the customer to continue in business, e.g. in Scandinavia.

In the United States, the 'Chapter XI' insolvency rules allow a court to decide how a company can behave during insolvency, in the hope of saving it.

A knowledge of foreign insolvency procedures is useful but not essential because it is so voluminous for so few instances. It is better for the exporter to get a report on obligations and alternative actions from the local agent or auditors when a case occurs.

Country insolvencies are extremely sad. A country can be said to be insolvent when it cannot pay its way, i.e. it cannot pay for required imports and cannot raise further foreign aid.

The action for the exporter is the same as for hard-currency blockages, remembering always to work as sympathetically as possible with the innocent customers of that country to find a way of avoiding their ruin. For example, some customers faced with blocked imports have discovered external funds (commissions, Swiss bank accounts, licensing fees) to use for important contracts.

The above situations have been covered without relying on ECGD cover, to stress that correct management actions should be taken anyway. Nevertheless, the 'country/currency' type of loss is the main reason for exporters to insure with ECGD, since solutions are discussed between nations, not companies and ECGD can represent the mass of UK exporters better than any other approach.

The problems of distance, time and language

Other risks in export collections are caused by sheer distance, by time differences, and by language and attitude problems. Distance can be a problem, in that whereas a domestic credit problem can be tackled the same day with a visit to the customer or site of a project, the travel complications for an export visit and the non-availability of the customer or the agent may rule out a quick solution. Foreign visits should be well planned, with introductions or access to banks and local contacts, to give plenty of support on any difficulties met. Negotiations have to be more precise and follow-ups more thorough, to justify the expense and time involved. It is all very well to jump on the next plane from Heathrow to Madrid or Tokyo, but if the customer is in a remote area of Spain or Japan, the time required for internal travel may not be acceptable.

Time differences have to be allowed for in both travel and telephone contact. The normal UK office hours overlap only the working morning in New York, and the afternoon in Tehran. Melbourne works during the UK night. The difficulty of such limited contact applies, of course, in both directions. Some exporters with significant need for telephone contact arrange for certain staff to make and receive calls from home in the dawn hours or late at night.

The obvious communication difficulty is that of language, where few exporters are able to negotiate in the customer's language. The use of the local agent as interpreter is not really satisfactory for the sharp exchanges usually required, whether face to face or by correspondence. English has become so 'slangy' that exporters sometimes forget that the customer's school-taught English is more precise, and that colourful 'pub' language is lost on him. Similarly, crafty nuances slipped into a verbal negotiation are often totally missed by the foreigner.

Most foreign business men like to put over a competent and polite image and often say 'yes' and 'no' in what they believe are the right places. The exporter who smugly reports back on having succeeded often finds that negotiations are later re-opened due to 'misunderstandings'. A Golden Rule is never to ask a question that can be answered 'yes' or 'no'.

The differences in local practices require interpretation by a local contact, such as the agent. Correspondence from a customer can be extremely polite even when he is angry. 'Oh, that's all right then, he's accepted my explanation,' observes the English business man; but what the customer meant, very courteously, was that he *understood* the explanation but would never do business again! The classic mañana attitude is perfectly normal in the hotter countries; yet visiting UK exporters get impatient, complain of agents' laziness and customers' indifference, then are surprised when all turns out well, albeit a few days later. The tradition of arriving for dinner or for a meeting up to an hour later than agreed is the *correct* style for many countries, no 'an appalling lack of consideration by a damned foreigner' as one exporter put it.

Thus, in tackling any approach on collection matters, it is wise to accept that the English way is not the only way to do things, but it takes a lot of experience to be able to think and act internationally.

Having set the scene on the need to think differently in exporting, we next look at various ways of collecting export accounts, beginning with ledger record systems.

Export sales ledger and bills receivable system

A good export system depends on fast, accurate information from the sales ledger. Usually, bills drawn on export customers are recorded separately in some kind of bills receivable system, which is added to the sales ledger to arrive at total debtor situations.

Sometimes the sales ledger has a lowly place in a company, regarded merely as the record of debits and credits for customers and operated as a routine clerical drill. This is a pity because the sales ledger is the backbone of a company's export cash flow as a routine clerical drill. This is a pity because the sales ledger is the backbone of a company's export cash flow and is the source of a great deal of information to help both credit and sales staff.

The prime function of the sales ledger is to record for each customer, chronologically, the sales made, payments received, adjustments and the resulting balance. Thus it provides a visual record of the export receivables asset and a historical record of business with each customer and the customer's payment performance.

Arising from these basic functions, it is apparent when (a) credit management is a key task and (b) records are transferred to computer systems, the sales ledger can assist several other areas, e.g.:

- By summarizing cash flow available, now and later.
- For credit control, by comparing exposures with credit limits.
- For marketing, by analysing sales by products, area, division, etc.
- For collections, by generating reminders and listings.

For the export credit function, the prime uses of the ledger are: to help maximize sales within the credit ratings and to help collect payments promptly.

The Export Sales Ledger is operated by 'posting' invoices and credit notes to each customer's account as frequently as is economically possible (but ideally, instantly). Incoming payments are then matched to the relevant invoices, leaving outstanding balances, which at month ends are reconciled in total to a control account in the General Ledger and summarized to produce statements. The Bills Receivable Ledger records bills as debits as they are drawn on customers (simultaneous credits may be put to the customers' sales ledger accounts); it is then credited as bills are paid, leaving only unpaid bills outstanding for month-end reconciliation to the General Ledger. A separate Bills Record is useful for discounting decisions and for follow-up routines with the bank. In some Bills Receivable systems, the recording of drafts and their acceptance and payment is made quite separately from the Sales Ledger, where customer accounts are not actually credited when bills are drawn, but merely cross-referenced.

Any view of a customer's indebtedness must take in both the ledger and the ledger and the bills balance, even if the bills are discounted.

Types of sales ledger

There are three basic methods of operating a ledger: Hand-written, Machine-posted, Computerized. Whatever the type, the requirements are visibility, up-to-dateness and accuracy.

(a) *A hand-written ledger* is a permanent record, either loose-leaf or in a bound book and either hand-written or typed.

A separate page is kept for each customer and useful 'static' data and helpful notations are written down, as well as the essential entries. The advantage of a hand-written system is the economy and 'handiness' for recording relatively few accounts, say up to 100 with no more than ten invoices each per month. There are several disadvantages, however:

● Analysis is cumbersome.
● Human error occurs more frequently.
● No automatic control 'triggers' can operate.
● Monthly statements and collection reminders have to be written separately.

Figures 7.1 and 7.2 illustrate typical pages from a hand-written Sales Ledger and a Bills Receivable Ledger.

(b) *A machine-posted ledger* is produced by a person operating a special accounting machine (NCR, Burroughs, etc.) requiring skill and speed in the use of a keyboard. Invoices and credit notes are batched, for control purposes, and given to the operator to post to the individual customer accounts, maintained on stout cards. Cash payments and bills receivable are also credited to the accounts but as single payments, so that matching to individual invoices still has to be done manually. For each month's posting operation, a carbonized statement is kept over the card, so that at month's end, the statement accurately reflects the month's activity plus starting and closing balances (on the 'Brought Forward' basis). The batch totals of invoices, credits, cash, bills, etc., are posted to a Control Account which is periodically reconciled to the total of the individual accounts plus the Bills Receivable account.

Figure 7.1 Handwritten Sales Ledger Page

EXPORT SALES LEDGER Page 423

Credit Limit: £10,000 Account No. 087

Risk Category: B Customer Young Engineering Inc.,

Terms: 30 days from Invoice Address 427, WORLD Avenue

Name of Contact MRS BATES DALLAS, Texas

Telephone No. 010-1-214-57612 Country U.S.A.

Telex/Cable T. 678972

Sales Code MG 28

Currency Sterling

DATE	TRANSACTION DETAIL	DEBIT	CREDIT	BALANCE
1.1	B/Fwd			£1485.50
8.1	Payment First Nat. City Bk (MT)		1031.90	453.60
10.1	Invoice 37649	1684.30		2137.90
18.1	Credit Note CN130626		120.00	2017.90
22.1	Invoice B7790	656.70		2674.60
29.1	Payment First Nat. City Bk (MT)		453.60	2221.00
31.1	Invoice B.7861	730.00		2951.00
31.1	Balance C/F			£2951.00

Notes: (i) A typical 'brought forward' style, using one page per month. (ii) The make-up of the b/f balance £1485.50 is not known without reference to previous pages. (iii) Analysis of overdues must be manually. (iv) If bills were used, they would be credited when drawn and debited to a Bills Receivable ledger.

Figure 7.2: Handwritten Bills Receivable Ledger Page

	EXPORT BILLS RECEIVABLE						Page 264	Jan	
Date	Reference	Customer	A/C	Value	Due Date	Date Paid	Cash Received	Balance
1·1·	B/F							£72,349·60
4·1·	3643	AOC	012	1256·00	Sight			73,655·60
4·1·	3644	XYZ	044	763·50	4·3·80			74,414·10
4·1·	3625	QPR	078	3465·82	4·4·80			77,884·92
4·1·	3626	N&G	052	63·29	4·3·80			77,948·21
7·1·	Cash 3591	TNT	088				426·81	77,521·40
9·1·	Cash 3540	XYZ	044				6239·74	71,281·66
11·1·	3627	VHF	042	385·00	11·4·80			71,666·66
11·1·	3628	XXX	008	2460·30	11·3·80			74,126·96
11·1·	3629	RAC	080	751·04	11·7·80			74,877·96
11·1·	3630	GOH	036	445·50	Sight			75,373·46
31·1·	Balance C/F	—	—	29640·41	—	—	£6666·55	£75,373·46

Notes: (i) This is a simple chronological record. When a Bill is entered, the Sales Ledger is credited. (ii) Paid Bills are marked off but there is no summary per customer. (iii) Analysis of overdues is extracted from due date column.

Each customer's account card can show whatever static data are considered useful, e.g. name, address, telex number, name of contact, credit limit, marketing codes, etc.

Figure 7.3 shows a typical machine-posted sales ledger account.

(c) *Computerized accounts:* Most companies with a volume of exports now produce their customer accounts on a computer, either in-house or from a service bureau. There is either the 'batch' or 'on-line' system. In the batch system, the export invoices are collected into a batch and sent for 'punching' on to tape, which is then sent to the computer to be stored until use. Credit notes and cash are batch processed in the same way and at intervals all the punched tapes are combined with the export receivables file to produce new, updated accounts.

With on-line systems, a direct link to the computer is operated by staff using either keyboard printer terminal or a Visual Display Unit (VDU) screen terminal, who input the invoice, credit and cash details to the receivables file.

In some systems, the invoices are produced automatically as part of an integrated order-manufacture-packing note-invoice process. In this case, entry to the customer accounts is made automatically as the invoice is issued, although human editing is often necessary to produce special invoice forms and declarations and to add later charges.

Computerized accounts are always on the 'Open Item' basis whereby at each period end, only the unpaid individual transactions are printed, totalling the balance outstanding.

The obvious benefits of computer accounts is their speed and extensive capability of analysis into whatever tabulations are requested.

Figure 7.3 Machine-posted Sales Ledger Account

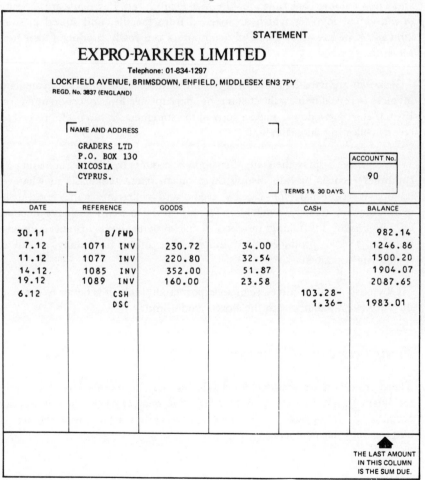

STATEMENT

EXPRO-PARKER LIMITED

Telephone: 01-834-1297

LOCKFIELD AVENUE, BRIMSDOWN, ENFIELD, MIDDLESEX EN3 7PY

REGD. No. 3837 (ENGLAND)

NAME AND ADDRESS

GRADERS LTD
P.O. BOX 130
NICOSIA
CYPRUS.

ACCOUNT No.

90

TERMS 1% 30 DAYS.

DATE	REFERENCE		GOODS		CASH	BALANCE
30.11		B/FWD				982.14
7.12	1071	INV	230.72	34.00		1246.86
11.12	1077	INV	220.80	32.54		1500.20
14.12	1085	INV	352.00	51.87		1904.07
19.12	1089	INV	160.00	23.58		2087.65
6.12		CSH			103.28-	
		DSC			1.36-	1983.01

THE LAST AMOUNT
IN THIS COLUMN
IS THE SUM DUE.

The two methods of summarizing customers' accounts are:

(a)   Brought Forward system.
(b)   Open Item system.

(a)   *The Brought Forward system* produces accounts/statements which begin with the balance brought forward from last time, and print all the individual movements in the period of posting. Payments are shown as one amount and the collector responsible for the account has to investigate previous statements to find out how the opening balance is comprised and whether any items are overdue.

(b)   *The Open Item system* (Figure 7.4) is infinitely preferable for credit work, in that it produces accounts/statements showing only those items still outstanding and a new balance each time the statement is produced. Payments are allocated to individual invoices which are deleted from the file, and stored in some kind of 'Paid Invoices' file. Only computers can really produce Open Item accounts.

Statements are used by Sales Ledger staff to allocate customers' payments to invoices to reveal items still outstanding, perhaps needing collection attention. Even if customers do not need a copy of the statement, it is a useful record for credit, collecting and sales staff.

VDU screens display the state of customer accounts by directly accessing the computer records on-line, listing them on an open item basis in whatever lay-out is requested, for use by credit and collection staff. Hard copy print-outs are usually available. The up-to-dateness of displays depends on the system for taking in data. Some systems have instant updating, showing invoices produced one minute earlier, others have daily, weekly or 'batch-run' updates.

Obviously, to maximize use of an export credit limit, it is better to compare the very latest balance with the stored credit limit.

Foreign currency sales ledger

There are two main methods for a UK company to handle sales accounting for business not expressed in Sterling. For balance sheet and end-period accounting, assets have to be converted to Sterling in a way acceptable to auditors and shareholders.

Figure 7.4 Computer-produced Open Item Statement

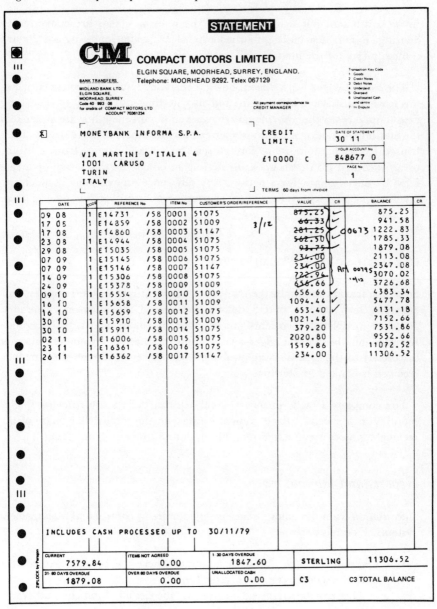

CURRENCY SALES LEDGER METHOD 1

Invoices are sent out in currency and the internal copies are converted to Sterling, either at a daily published rate of exchange, or using a standard company rate for the month.

The Sales Ledger is produced showing currency totals of invoices (because this is what customers will deal in) and also Sterling equivalents, for matching cash to invoices. When payments are received in currency they are either sold for Sterling at spot or a previously agreed forward rate, or the currency itself is used to pay for imports or foreign services via a Currency bank account, being recorded in a cash book in Sterling at either the day's rate or a rate fixed by the company for a period. Any difference on exchange between the invoice and payment values is transferred to a 'Profit or loss on exchange account'.

CURRENCY SALES LEDGER METHOD 2

Some companies maintain their sales accounts entirely in the currency. For example, they invoice in US dollars and record the sales on customers' accounts in dollars. Payments are received in dollars and actual amounts recorded on the Sales Ledger. At no time do staff or customers attempt to convert to the UK Sterling equivalent values, even though the currency received is banked in Sterling.

For company P & L purposes, total sales in dollars are converted, say, monthly at a specially fixed company rate and the total dollar value of the receivables asset is converted monthly to put on to the Balance Sheet.

Reports and tabulations

Information from the Sales Ledger is vital for credit control and management systems. Examples are:

(a)   Overlimit listing: A list of accounts where the balance exceeds the agreed exposure (i.e. the Credit Limit).
        This can be triggered to prevent the actual shipment that would take the balance into excess.
        It can also be used on a Country Limit basis, if the exporter is limiting his investment of funds in certain risky markets. Such 'exception' reports can be issued at intervals, or each morning, or, in a 'live' system, the instant a transaction excess occurs.

(b)   Future Due Dates listing: A list of all unpaid invoices or drafts, in order of due date, showing customer or account number.

      This can be used to plan cash intake, or to allocate future time to follow up, or to send to local agents or subsidiaries to give timely reminders to customers.

(c)   Aged Account Analysis: A listing of all export accounts, one line per account, analysed horizontally into columns: not yet due: 1–30 days overdue: 31–60: 61–90: 91 + : disputes: unapplied cash, etc.

      This gives a complete picture of the quality of export receivables, showing significant debts, proportions current and overdue, etc., and is often the basic tool for deciding follow-up priorities.

(d)   Customer History Analysis: A listing of all export customers showing their aged account analysis for the previous, say, 12 months plus the sales figure for each month. This shows sales and payments trends and is useful in risk assessment and market analysis.

(e)   Sales by Country.

(f)   Debts by Country.

(g)   Top 50 accounts, and so on.

Computer reports are so rapid and prolific, there must always be a rule to restrict new reports until cost-justified, followed by annual reviews of usage and cost savings.

Checklist: Sales Ledger Recommendations

- Produce by computer, to provide more management information.
- Produce statements on Open Item basis.
- Obtain maximum automatic data, to reduce manual notations.
- Have a separate Bills Receivable record, but with individual customer coding.
- Achieve fastest possible updating of accounts, to make best use of credit ratings.
- Use Sales Ledger data to help credit, collection and sales staff.

Documentation controls

We have seen how important it is for the export credit manager to check export documents for accuracy before they go to the customer or the bank.

In most companies, there are several departments involved in export and any of them may produce documents. There are two fundamental reasons why the credit department should check the assembly of documents:

- To ensure compliance with agreed payment terms. An invoicing mistake showing 90 days instead of 30 days can be expensive and upsetting. Worse, if the exporter is holding a Letter of Credit from, say, Mozambique and, due to lateness, somebody sends off the goods by air and sends the documents directly to the customer, it may be impossible to obtain payment.
- Because they are the single department in the company with the main motivation of getting paid properly. Probably five out of six other functions will do their part of the job correctly but none has the need to spot the error of the sixth.

The system recommended is for the export credit manager (ECM) to be responsible for final despatch of export documents. Thus, the shipping, transport, insurance, inspection and invoicing functions should work to the same master export order documents.

Documentary Credits, will require a precise list of documents. For Documentary Collections, there will be the standard requirements for each country plus any special ones in the customer's order. For both Letter of Credit and draft terms, the credit function should complete the job by typing the Draft and Bill Instructions to go to the bank, ensuring that all orders on those terms get the correct drafts and documents. Similarly for Open Account Terms, the credit department will ensure that the terms are correctly stated and the documents are what is needed. It is also extremely helpful on open terms if a copy invoice is *always* sent at issue to the local agent. This helps resolve disputes on the spot and gives the person more authority if he has to help collect an overdue account.

Avoiding letter of credit failures

The high failure rate in exporters' claims under Letters of Credit can be transformed into faster cash if extra attention is given to overcoming the most common errors.

Every document specified in a Credit must be complete and accurate. Not only must documents conform to the credit but they must be consistent with one another. They must not be presented later than the date specified, normally 21 days from date of shipment.

INVOICE ERRORS

Value exceeds L/C amount.

Unit prices not as indicated in L/C.

Description of goods differs from L/C.

Omission of price basis (FOB, CIF, C&F, etc.).

Inclusion of charges not specified in the L/C.

Not certified, legalized or signed as stipulated in the L/C.

The packing stated in the L/C is not the same on the invoice.

Import Licence numbers not shown, required by the L/C.

Wrong form of invoice used.

BILL OF LADING ERRORS

Not presented in full sets when requested – if a L/C calls for a set of 3, 4 or even more, then this number of signed negotiable copies must be submitted.

Not taken out in the name of the party specified in the L/C.

Alterations not authenticated by the shipping company.

Not a 'clean' bill (e.g. it bears a 'clause' that the condition and/or packing of the merchandise is defective, or 'On Deck' etc.).

L/C calls for 'Shipped on Board B/L' but 'received for shipment' Bill of Lading presented.

Not endorsed if drawn to order when L/C specifies to order and blank endorsed.

Not endorsed to bank or buyer when L/C so specifies.

Specified 'notify' parties not shown.

Not marked 'Freight Paid' or 'Freight Prepaid' in cases of CIF/C&F

shipments (the words 'Freight Payable at.......' or 'Freight to be Prepaid' not acceptable as evidence of payment of freight).

Freight amount not shown when L/C specifies this.

Dated later than the latest shipment date specified in the credit (N.B. the date of the 'on board' notation in the case of a converted 'Received for shipment' Bill of Lading).

Shipping mark not identical to that shown in other documents and/or does not include the port of discharge.

Shipment made from a port or to a destination other than that stipulated in the L/C.

Gross weights differ from those shown in other documents.

Merchandise description inconsistent with the goods description in the L/C.

Import Licence and Registration numbers, etc. not shown when L/C so specifies.

Charter Party and Forwarding Agents' bills not accepted unless expressly allowed in the L/C. However, unless not allowed in the L/C the following are acceptable:

(a)   A through Bill of Lading even though they cover several modes of transport.
(b)   A Short Form Bill of Lading.
(c)   A Bill of Lading covering cargoes on pallets or in Containers.

AIR WAYBILL ERRORS

Description of goods not consistent with that in the L/C.

Details of the number of packages with marks, weights and dimensions are incomplete.

Date of flight does not comply with the latest date of despatch stipulated in the L/C.

Not signed by the issuing carrier.

INSURANCE CERTIFICATE/POLICY ERRORS

Note: When a policy is called for under a credit, a certificate is not acceptable. However, a policy is acceptable when a certificate is called for.

Amount of cover insufficient or does not include all the risks stipulated in the L/C.

Not issued in the same currency as the L/C.

Not endorsed or signed in accordance with the L/C.

Certificate or policy dated later than date of shipment/despatch. (*Important:* cargo uninsured in this event.)

Goods not correctly described.

Alterations not authenticated.

Carrying vessel's name not shown.

Does not cover transshipment when Bill of Lading indicates that transshipment will occur.

Does not show shipping mark indicated in Bill of Lading.

Does not specifically cover 'on deck' when Bills of Lading bear the 'on deck' clause.

CERTIFICATE OF ORIGIN ERRORS

Insufficient time allowed for legalization where this is called for. (Delays in Chambers of Commerce and Consular Offices can be considerable.)

CLEAN REPORT OF FINDINGS/INSPECTION CERTIFICATE ERRORS

These documents are a common requirement for several African countries – and are normally issued by SGS or Cotecna. When shipments are planned it is important to take into account the delays in arranging inspection.

Every exporter should include these points in the final check of documents before submission to the paying bank.

Action on errors detected vary from amending documents that can be amended to cabling/telexing customers to authorize acceptance of documents which cannot be corrected.

Apart from the inability to convert, say, an Air Waybill into the specified Bill of Lading, there is often simply not enough time before expiry of the L/C to make changes. The *Golden Rule* for L/C performance is to allow a cushion of a few days before expiry, in which to get everything right.

Use of the banking system

Export account collectors should make full use of the services of the banks, which have a remarkable network of communication around the world.

Export funds come to the UK via banks except in the few cases when customers send their own cheques which are sent back through the exporter's bank for clearance in the domicile of the currency. Bankers' drafts payable at UK banks are received in the mail and do not usually present any problem. The majority of problem payments are via documentary collections or bank transfers.

Bank transfers

Bank transfers can arrive at any bank in the UK and take their time to get to the exporter. Collectors of open account debts can improve the services of the banks if they:

- Tell customers the exact name, address and code number of the bank to which payment should be made.
- Put the same details on every export invoice on open account terms.
- Ask the customers to instruct their banks to use the Telegraphic Transfer (TT) method, agreeing between them on who should pay the extra charges.
- Ask customers to notify them by telex of every payment made, quoting the bank used and reference number and date of the transfer.
- Allow two days for a TT and seven days for a Mail Transfer (MT) to arrive in their account.
- Follow up with their own bank for any late payments, quoting the foreign bank reference details.
- Establish if delays occur in UK and ask bank for interest at current borrowing rates.

After a few months of such a system, notating accounts with payment details and following up to see where slow payments have got to, the exporter may be able to improve some problem areas, e.g.:

- The customers who just do not bother to give their banks details of the exporter's bank.
- The customers who will not agree to pay for TTs or will not bother to tell their banks to send by TT.
- The customers who do not bother to notify the exporter when payments are made.
- The foreign banks who ignore their clients' requests and choose their own correspondent bank in the UK.
- The countries where delays occur before banks carry out transfer instructions.
- The UK banks who 'lose' incoming payments.

Prompt and persistent action on such bad practices should result in their being the exception rather than the rule.

It is well worth the collector developing a friendly contact at his bank who will enthusiastically pursue missing or slow payments.

Documentary collection

The UK banks usually process all collections through a few regional offices, who operate a monthly follow-up on collections requiring a response, either for acceptance or for payment. Any information advices received are passed to the exporter, but it is worth pressing for more frequent pointed follow-ups.

The collector should arrange for his Bills Receivable system to show essential dates as follows:

- Drafts are entered when they are drawn, showing date sent to the bank.
- Sight Drafts are given an artificial due date, according to distance, e.g. Europe 14 days, USA and Canada 21 days, South America, Middle East and African countries 28 days, Far East and Australasia 35 days, all from shipment.
- Term Drafts dated from arrival are allowed the same periods to be accepted and then the actual accepted due date is written in the Bill system.

- Term Drafts dated from shipment have the due date written in the Bill system as soon as they are drawn, with a space left to record that the customer has accepted.
- All Draft entries have a space to show when paid.

The system should then generate reminders, either on a diary system or by checking at intervals on any unfilled space for 'Date Accepted', 'Due Date' and 'Date Paid'. If Sight Drafts are not paid on arrival, or Term Drafts not accepted, the exporter can expect to receive an advice of fate from his bank, giving the reason. It is then relatively simple to contact the customer as required by the situation.

Unfortunately, advices of acceptance are not always received and the first information is the actual payment; or worse, the due date passes with no payment advice and the goods are rotting on a quayside, with the exporter not knowing they were never even accepted.

Checklist: Action on Overdue Drafts

- Find out the reason for non-payment as quickly as possible. If this is a genuine dispute, sort out the problem quickly using the agent. There may be a need for extended credit and the customer may accept a new bill guaranteed by the bank or other third party.

- If the customer is refusing to pay or is unable to, ensure that protest action is followed through and consider legal action to recover the debt. Involve the agent.

- If protest is not possible or wise the debt should be progressed like any open Account debt. Chase it through the agent. Also instruct the collecting bank to release the collection documents to the agent to avoid incurring bank charges. If payment does not result, employ a local debt collector or if the debt is large enough, visit the customer. Legal action is to be avoided wherever possible because of the difficulties and long timescales.

Under the Uniform Rules for Collections, article 20, the foreign collecting bank is responsible for sending prompt advices of payment or non-payment, acceptance or non-acceptance to the UK banks. But *the UK bank has no obligation at all to send reminders to the foreign bank if it sends no advice*, except that under article 1, the UK bank must 'exercise reasonable care'. So, as foreign correspondent banks are often delinquent in advising the fate of bills, the exporter should take the initiative. The follow-ups from the Bills system should be:

(a)   A request to the exporter's bank for advice of fate and simultaneously.

(b)   A telex or cable to the apparently delinquent customer.

It is prudent also for the exporter to tackle his customer. Although his bank is supposed to be handling the collection for him, bank follow-ups are too infrequent to satisfy most collectors. Not only may it move the customer, but if he has already accepted the reminder may stir him to speak to his delinquent bank about the non-communication.

Interest charges

Compared with the UK, where charging interest to customers often offends, many countries accept interest for credit or late payments as a standard practice.

Exporters should consider three types of interest recovery:

(a)   Charged to customers at standard rates for the basic credit period.

(b)   Charged to customers at penal rates for late payments.

(c)   Charged to banks for transfer delays.

The intention to charge interest to customers should always be notified in advance and the right to do so written into contract conditions.

Interest for the basic credit period should be charged at the rate applying in the buyer's country (rates are obtainable from banks and export publications). It is easy to apply the drafts, where a clause should be printed on the face of the drafts and not just put into the instructions to the collecting bank.

A typical interest clause on a draft might read:

> 'Plus Interest at the rate of 8% per annum from the date of draft until date of remittance to London.'

The collecting bank becomes responsible for collection of the total value, under article 21 of the Uniform Rules. In fact, such a clause removes the draft from the protection of the Bills of Exchange Act, because the total amount is no longer 'certain', but it is still used frequently and effectively.

On open account transactions, interest can be charged either openly on the invoice or consolidated in the price charged for the goods. In this case, it can only be hoped that the buyer will pay on the due date as there is no mechanism (such as a collecting bank) to enforce payment at the time.

Penalty interest for late payment

The interest rates charged for credit are not usually high enough to deter slow payers, who may even be willing to pay for extra credit at such reasonable rates. This is not to be encouraged by exporters, who need cash on agreed dates.

Interest for lateness should be at penal rates which should be stated in conditions of sale, specially printed on order acknowledgements. A suitable penalty rate for most countries would be 2% per month from due date to date of receipt of payment.

Companies in Italy borrowing at 18% per annum and in France at 14% per annum would find it cheaper to borrow from their bank to avoid a 24% charge, but the same charge would not deter a Brazilian company borrowing locally at 40 to 60% per annum. The penalty rate should be geared to be about one and a half times local borrowing rates, if possible.

Exporters should be careful not to hoist the rate too high, or it would be rejected by a court as usurious. Also, exporters to the Middle East countries should check with their banks on whether it is possible to charge interest to customers *at all*, as religious influence in some countries absolutely forbid it, and business may suffer it the authorities are insulted.

Interest from banks for transfer delays

This was discussed earlier, under 'use of banking services'. It is important to present the bank with proof of payment before claiming interest for delays. The rate to charge should be the exporter's own cost of money, since that is the cost of the bank's error.

Protest of bills

A technique to encourage bills to be accepted and paid on time is to notify customers that any dishonoured bills will be 'protested'.

This will involve a local notary public calling on the customer to demand acceptance or payment, failing which he will record the refusal and reasons in a deed of protest, which is a necessary prelude to legal action in many countries.

The effect of protest may be to damage a customer's local business reputation and is sometimes an act of bankruptcy. As any protest action has to be taken within 24 or 48 hours in most countries, the exporter must give his bank instructions to protest or not when originally sending the bill for collection, in the space provided on the bank form.

As some bills are dishonoured for perfectly genuine reasons, exporters should be careful in selecting customers for protest action. If the risk category system is used, then 'C' category customers might be candidates for protest, whereas A's and possibly B's would be given the benefit of the doubt whilst dishonoured bills were investigated. ECGD policy-holders are required to protest wills wherever it is possible to do so, to preserve ECGD's right to take legal action later if necessary.

Advantages

1. The knowledge that you will protest is an incentive for the customer to pay your bills promptly on maturity.
2. A protested bill can be actioned in court, without having to go through the procedure of proving the contract, or delivery, etc.

Disadvantages

1. The protest is published in an official gazette. This bad publicity can damage the customer's reputation and cause creditors to go for bankruptcy.
2. The debt is normally frozen in local currency equivalent value. If the local currency is weak, by the time you are paid, you may get substantially less than the invoice value.
3. Time is limited in which to protest. There may be another time limit within which legal action may be taken.
4. There is a fee for protesting a bill.

Checklist: Protest action on Drafts
• Check on countries where protest action is required.
• Decide on which customers you are prepared to upset on default.
• Note records on selected customers to instruct bank to protest for dishonour.
• Instruct bank not to protest on all other bills.

Collection tools

By taking good care of documentation and bank instructions, the exporter can help himself to be paid on time. But there are customers who do not pay because:

- They do not have the funds to pay.
- Or they are inefficient and overlook payments.
- Or they have a dispute or grievance of some kind.

The normal range of collection tools is designed to prevent these risks, or to tackle them quickly when they occur.

Order acknowledgement

Good collections begin at the acknowledgement stage, in the sales office, when the exporter should:

(a)   Examine the buyer's order and note the details precisely.
(b)   Identify any unacceptable conditions and negotiate out of them (this avoids disputes later).
(c)   Apply his own conditions of sale and special clauses.
(d)   Stress the payment terms and the need to pay by TT.
(e)   Notify which bank to be used.
(f)   Emphasize the price basis, e.g. CIF or C and F.
(g)   Explain the procedure for returns and disputes.
(h)   Tell the customer who the local agent is.
(i)   Where L/C terms apply, notify the requirements.

Possibly on receipt of the order acknowledgement, the buyer will react and argue. Fine! This is the time to resolve differences, rather than book the order hurriedly to get the month's sales target, keep quiet and then have an uncollectable debt later.

Invoice

The prime purpose of an invoice is to obtain payment. As a collection tool, a well-designed, effective export invoice will abolish the whole area of dispute caused when an invoice is unclear, not acceptable to the customs or the bank or not received at all due to bad addressing.

Many exporters still use home trade invoices for exports, simply adding the extra 'bits' considered necessary. At the other extreme, experienced exporters carry stocks of invoice with headings and clauses, in French, German, Italian, Spanish, Arabic, etc., so that the typist or computer can insert all the readily understood data in standard spaces.

Customers appreciate, above all, the thoughtfulness of a clear, effective invoice, which they can use to check the goods and pass for foreign payment.

Export credit managers should always participate in the design of invoices, and ensure that unnecessary technical clutter does not disguise the elements essential for the customer to generate payment, or to meet L/C requirements. The invoice is not the place for technical data or promotional advertising. Those belong elsewhere, such as on advice notes. The invoice is used by financial people.

Copy invoices should *always* be sent to the local agent or subsidiary company to help solve disputes or to collect payment and simply to keep him fully informed of what is happening in his territory.

'Croner's Reference Book for Exporters' gives the essential requirements for invoices for every country of the world.

Statement of account

These have limited value as collection tools in export. The usual UK habit of sending monthly statements listing all the transactions in a month as a routine summary is not followed in most other countries (except the UK-influenced Commonwealth). Where statements are used, e.g. in Germany, Norway and Sweden, they are sent as specific collection reminders at due date. The reason for the difference from UK is the peculiar English habit of 'net monthly account', whereby all invoices for a month are settled at the end of the next month. In most other countries, particularly the USA, Germany and Switzerland, invoices are payable X days from invoice date and collection systems demand payment on the 8th, 17th, 25th or whatever the due date is.

Export credit managers should not automatically use Statements as collection reminders, but should:

● Ask customers if they need Statements as summaries of trading and, if so, send them as a customer service.
● Use Statements internally for follow-up but generate reminders by other means.

On no account should Statements of Commission Accounts be sent to agents without their prior, precise instructions. In many countries, agents do not wish tax authorities or state officials to detect their foreign earnings. This is not to say that UK exporters should collaborate in breaking a foreign law, but an agent's request as to Statements should be respected. It may even be his wife he is hiding his earnings from!

Drafts and special clauses

Drafts and Bills of Exchange are excellent methods of collection through an established banking system.

The use of a 'Clean Bill' is recommended as a direct collection tool for some countries, e.g. Spain, France and Belgium. It is used where the terms of open account lead to delays in settlement by bank transfers. The exporter draws a Bill, without documents, on the agreed credit terms, and sends it for acceptance by the customer who notes it with the name and address of the bank to be used for payment at due date. The Clean Bill is sent for collection through the exporter's own bank with all the usual instructions and is more likely to be honoured at due date than an open account transaction.

Some foreign customers on open account terms may send the exporter Promissory Notes. These are not strictly Bills of Exchange, as they are drawn by the payer, promising to pay the exporter, but they are useful as unconditional orders to pay, and have been described as legal, international IOUs. Promissory Notes which can be discounted for immediate cash and collected through normal bank collection systems are included with Bills of Exchange in the ICC Uniform Rules for Collection.

In most European countries, banks will guarantee payment of Bills of Exchange by adding their name to the Bill, or 'avalizing' it. Some companies, particularly in France, have standing arrangements with their banks to 'aval' Bills. In other cases, exporters may ask their customers to arrange this, agreeing on who should bear the small charge. Such 'Bank Bills' can be discounted more readily and at finer rates than ordinary Bills of Exchange.

There are several useful ways in which Bills can be claused to aid collection.

In all cases, clausing should be agreed beforehand with the customers:

- 'Payable' at the banker's selling rate for demand drafts on London.' This is used on Bills drawn in Sterling, to indicate that the customer must pay at the exchange rate quoted by the collecting bank. Foreign charges may be deducted, but if the Bill is claused:
- 'Payable at the banker's selling rate for demand drafts on London together with all bank charges,' the exporter will receive the face value of the Bill.
- 'Exchange as per endorsement.'
  This clause is used on Bills on South and East African customers. It allows the exporter to be paid in full in Sterling and the customer to pay in his own currency. The exporter negotiates such Bills in London, then the bank calculates the exchange required to be paid by the customer at due date, plus the bank's charges.

LOCAL CURRENCY RELEASE

Documents on Sight Drafts in Sterling or hard currency are normally released by banks against payment by the customer in his own currency, who has completed his obligation. ICC Uniform Rules only allow this if the remittance is to be made immediately, but it is common in some countries with foreign exchange shortages to experience delays in transfer of the Sterling or hard currency equivalent, sometimes for months. If the local currency devalues during the delay period, which is likely by the very nature of the problem, the exporter will be short-paid. Credit managers should take care to instruct the bank to release the documents only against a 'shortfall undertaking', whereby the customer must pay enough local currency at remittance date, to buy the full face value of the bill.

Letters

A golden rule for export collections is *not* to use letters. Letters should be written to customers to discuss problems and to provide information. For collection reminders, they are too slow, may not be understood and, if not answered, it is not known whether they even arrived. In collection work, *immediacy is essential* and for the long distances of export, this means telephone, telex, cable, or if it is a really serious and large problem, a personal visit.

If despite these views, exporters can afford to collect overdues by letter, they should at least:

● Avoid English jargon, keeping each point very brief.
● Address the letter to an individual.
● Be extremely polite, however firm, and observe courtesies.
● Best of all, correspond in the buyer's language.

Gower Publishing have published a useful book entitled 'Debt Collection Letters in Ten Languages' which gives sample letters in the main European languages. Using these increases the chances of a reply, but understanding the reply requires a different level of linguistics.

Export debts are too individual to warrant the UK system of a series of reminders, from a polite Number 1 to the threatening Numbers 4 or 5, at defined intervals.

The objective of a collection letter is to evoke a reponse. If not a response by payment, the need is for an explanation of non-payment. Any such explanation requires an individual pursuit of a solution. If no reply at all is received to a reminder letter, enough time will have been lost already, so it is important to make immediate contact by telephone or by use of a local source.

Telexes and cables

The exporter's customer file should always show the telex number, if he has one. If not, a cable must be used, but as cables are charged per word and are generally expensive, they should only be used for high value debts and the wording should be carefully worked out for maximum effect.

Example of a Cable Reminder

OSEAGRAM TAIKOK SINGAPORE FOR WON LEE ACCOUNTANT STOP NOTIFY URGENTLY PAYMENT DATE AND BANK USED FOR OVERDUE INVOICES 62734/5/6 VALUES POUNDS 42718 ORDER T 1434/79 STOP YARWOOD XYZ LTD MANCHESTER STOP

This wording carefully implies that payment has probably already been made of the apparently overdue invoices and that the exporter is trying to trace the funds. If so, the customer will probably send details, or get his bank to do so. If not paid, it may remind a forgetful or slightly delinquent customer to get on with it.

The cost of a cable is far less than the interest cost of late payments.

The same approach applies to telexes, except that being cheaper, more variations and a less abrupt style can be used.

Apart from specific technical matters that sometimes have to be included in collection messages, exporters usually find that all their skilful wordings come down in the end to three or four essential varieties. This being so, it is well worth having these few wordings translated into the languages of the main buying countries.

Several commercial translation bureaux in UK undertake to provide such translations at a relatively cheap cost.

It then only remains to add personal names and debt details to the standard messages.

Telexes should always be aimed at individuals for both effectiveness and politeness, so it follows that exporters should take the prior trouble to find out (on visits, from agents, sales staff or the customers directly) the names of financial decision-makers. The names should be carefully stored in the customer file for use when needed.

Telephone

Making rapid contact by telephone to collect accounts can be much more efficient and cost-effective than waiting for a reply to a letter or telex. Customers are usually polite enough, or impressed enough, by long-distance telephone calls, to be 'available' to talk. It can be very rewarding to renew an old contact by telephone for a few minutes and even more rewarding to establish a new business friendship.

There are problems and disadvantages:

- The time difference means careful pre-planning.
- The customer's accountant may not speak English and an English-speaking member of staff will probably have to take a message and call back (or not!).

- Copy documents cannot be displayed – although the use of FAX reduces this problem where customers have FAX facilities.
- There may be excessive connection delays.

Foreign calls need extra-special planning, to avoid wasted expense. The account, customer dossier and full details of the problem should be in front of the caller. The intended questions should be noted down.

Many towns abroad can now be dialled direct; but otherwise, the number should be booked 'person-to-person' naming the person required. The cost is then only charged when the named person picks up the phone.

When talking to foreigners, collectors should always have a sympathetic ear. Avoid dominating the conversation and allow the foreigner to explain. He is probably struggling under the double handicap of finding the right words in English and trying to obtain more details. Because it is easy and relatively polite to say 'yes' or 'no', foreigners often say these words to answer questions they do not quite understand. It is therefore important always to avoid asking 'Yes/No' questions.

For example, instead of asking 'Have you paid our September invoice for steel rods?', it is far better to ask 'What date was your payment for ..., etc.?' This forces the customer to supply information of some kind, whereas a straight yes or no shows he has not understood.

The call should conclude either with details of the payment made or with a promise to pay a particular amount by a particular date. All international calls should be confirmed by a letter or telex summarizing any agreements made.

Personal visits

Collection visits are rarely justified on cost grounds but are undoubtedly the most effective way to resolve problems and to arrange payments.

The cost of airfares and a hotel can be economical if the debt problem is large or serious enough, but usually it is better for a credit manager either to:

- Combine a debt collection visit with one for other purposes, e.g. contract conditions, customer investigation, etc.
- Or arrange several customer visits on one trip.

Sometimes it is possible to accompany a sales person who can help with introductions and any local agent or subsidiary can help set up the visit and be present in meetings to help with translations or technical difficulties.

There are great advantages in the export credit manager 'doing the rounds' of foreign customers whenever the chance occurs. It is still unusual in most countries to receive a financial visitor and extremely friendly hospitality is often shown by staff who are normally starved of personal contact with their foreign suppliers. The overall objective of personal meetings is to establish strong contacts for quick action on problems and preference in payments.

In Eastern Europe, in particular, where the state-controlled businesses are usually swamped with visiting salesmen, the neglected financial staff welcome the luxury of a business discussion.

Another useful purpose of a credit visit is to go with the customer to his bank to discuss transfer delays or to explain precisely how payment should be worded.

VISIT REPORT

On return to base, a Visit Report should always be made for circulation to interested parties and for the file. The Visit Report should be the basis for writing to the persons met abroad to thank them for assistance and hospitality and to confirm detailed agreements made.

A Visit Report should be simplified under these headings:

Visited: (name of customer)   Date:

Met: (person and job title)

Purpose: a
              b   (brief summary of problems or other purposes)
              c

Results: a
               b   (linked to stated purposes plus note of
               c   agreements made, for subsequent follow-up).

Follow-up systems

Export accounts and bills receivable should be organized into systems for follow-up, in case the payment terms are exceeded for any reason.

For open-account terms, the ledger should be analysed at intervals, e.g. fortnghtly, to extract due dates that have passed, and the accounts listed for action.

Whether this is done manually or automatically by computer, enough data should be extracted to allow efficient follow-up. Here is a suggested system:

(a)   Fortnightly, list accounts overdue.
(b)   Telex the agent or local contact in each country concerned, with a list. Ask for follow-up and telexed reply within two days.
(c)   If the local friend fails, arrange direct follow-up, e.g.:

   ●   Below £5000 overdue, telex the customer. If no telex, send a letter. Cable if the customer is risky, otherwise send a letter.
   ●   Above £5001 overdue, telephone the customer.

(d)   Copy list and actions to Sales Department. Ask for comment.
(e)   If responses unsatisfactory or promises not kept, follow up more strongly and insist on help of agent, subsidiary and/or Sales Department.
(f)   Aim to achieve payment or acceptable reason for non-payment within one month of due date.
(g)   Failure after one month requires special action per account (e.g. visit, or change of terms, or use of collection agency, or legal action).

This does *not* mean rushing into legal action one month after a debt is due. It is hard enough to win export business without losing it through rigid collection action. But it is important that all standard approaches are completed within one month, so that appropriate special actions can be based on true delinquency.

Bills Receivable systems should be followed up in a similar way, except that the bank should also be pressed to obtain payments or answers.

Involvement of sales staff

The large amount of contact with customers by sales staff and the generally good relationships should not be neglected when collection problems occur.

In some companies, sales staff insist on being the only people to contact customers. In such organizations, they have a heavy responsibility to collect efficiently and not relegate the task because of its difficulty or unpopularity.

Sales staff should feed in to credit people every scrap of customer information that affects risk or payment. In return, credit staff should keep sales people informed of collection actions taken with customers, either by lists or copies of letters and telexes.

When export sales staff are about to travel abroad, the credit manager should supply them with details of all overdue accounts for the territory being visited. It would be quite wrong, and even embarrassing, for an export salesman to wine and dine a customer to win an order when that same customer is seriously delinquent in paying a previous order. Although the salesman may not want to ruin his chances by doing battle, he should carefully make it clear to the customer that he knows about the debt, so that the customer knows he is dealing with a combined sales/finance force.

Even in his UK office, the export salesman can be asked to telephone or telex his friends within a delinquent customer company to organize a payment.

Use of agents and associates

Collection of overdue accounts should be an essential part of agent's agreement. Normally, export commission should be credited on a sale, but not paid until the funds are received. This system correctly completes the agency relationship, and, as a by-product, strengthens it, increasing the contact between agent and exporter.

There are still many cases where the appointed agent is just a name and address in a remote country, to whom credit notes are issued on a territory basis for orders received direct from customers. It is far better to make the agent earn his commission by obtaining credit information, reporting on customer finance problems and directly collecting overdues.

On bill instructions to the bank, the agent should always be shown as 'case of need', either 'for information only' or for the bank 'to follow their instructions without reserve'. In the latter case, the exporter must be confident he can trust the agent to take any action, or incur any expense.

On Open Account transactions, the agent should always be sent a copy invoice at time of shipment, so that no time is lost in obtaining details of debts when called upon to collect.

As recommended earlier, the agent should be given regular lists of overdues in his territory, preferably by telex, to report back customer payments or excuses within two days for further action.

Where the exporter has associated companies or subsidiaries abroad, he should arrange a mandatory system for local assistance on unpaid accounts or bills of exchange. Such local companies should be even better equipped than agents, perhaps with even a credit manager, to make efficient collection calls in the customer's language and to report results back through inter-company channels.

Use of external collection agents

Figure 7.5 gives a list of just some of the agencies that undertake foreign debt collection.

Figure 7.5   Some Collection Agencies Handling Foreign Debts

Dun and Bradstreet International,
Holmers Farm Way,
High Wycombe,
Bucks., HP12 4UL.

The British Mercantile Agency Limited, (part of Legal and Trade Group)
Sidcup House,
12–18 Station Road,
Sidcup,
Kent, DA15 7EH.

Graydon-ATP International,
Hyde House,
Edgeware Road,
London, NW9 6LW.

Commercial Credit Consultants,
Unicredit House,
2, Cotton Street,
Liverpool, L3 7DY.

Note: Commercial Officers in British Embassies and Consulates in all countries will supply names of local collection agencies where they exist. ECGD also maintain a list of some.

Most agencies operate a 'no collection – no fee' basis with charges of between 10% and 50% on amounts collected. Extra charges are made if legal action becomes necessary.

Some agencies operate out of UK by letter, telex or telephone, and arrange visits by local associates when required. Others are actually based in several European countries and USA and elsewhere.

ECGD and other national credit insurance companies sometimes employ collection agencies for debt handling after claims have been paid to exporters. If they recommend their use by the exporter before a claim is paid, ECGD bear 90% of the collection charges.

Well-organized exporters with good credit managers may still find it economic to use external agencies for certain debts. Unfortunately, although agencies will be more useful to badly organized exporters, these are the very ones who dither at their collection activity and usually leave it far too long before placing in the hands of the experts, by which time it may be uncollectable.

Exporters should have thorough discussions with agencies before appointment, to check on:

- Which countries they cover most effectively.
- Whether recoveries are paid net of charges and when.

Legal action

The widely held view is that foreign legal action for debt recovery is expensive, slow to mature and to be avoided.

Certainly legal action must never be regarded as a routine 'next step'. It should be considered only after all other approaches have failed and even then only for really significant debts. It is often better to compromise on a percentage settlement or write off a smaller debt, than risk incurring irrecoverable charges.

A case was reported recently where a UK firm was still waiting six years after beginning proceedings in El Salvador. The lawyer's fees had reached 80% of the debt value and his latest *surface mail* letter had asked for further copies of invoices!

Those depressing views are probably accurate for lone exporters operating from long distance. Obviously, every country has its simple debt procedures, with the equivalents of summonses and writs being adjudged all the time. The requirement for a UK exporter is strong local representation which can:

- Review the file on a UK export debt.
- Assess the chances of recovery, by local standards.
- Instruct an in-house legal man or appoint a suitable lawyer in the town.
- Follow through and cease proceedings if chances recede.

Dishonoured Bills of Exchange should be protested to facilitate legal action and ECGD require policy-holders to take legal action as directed when claims are admitted, with ECGD normally bearing 90% of costs.

The BOTB are always willing to advise exporters on legal action and all British Embassies and Consulates provide help in finding local lawyers.

Factoring

The subject of Factoring export debts is dealt with fully in the Export Finance section, as the facility is seen by most exporters as an enhanced form of finance.

However, collection of receivables is a prime activity in the factoring 'package' and they are extremely good at it. All the major export factoring companies are subsidiaries of banks and have excellent foreign representation. Their service offers a package of risk assessment, taking invoices and ledgering them, collecting the debts, and of course, advancing the value at shipment. Their service fee of 2–3% of turnover has to be compared with an exporter's cost of doing all those things in-house.

Exchange controls abroad

It is usual for most governments to apply varying degrees of control over the inward and outward flow of foreign currencies.

Exporters usually only invoice customers in certain hard currencies. Invoicing in, say, Brazilian cruzadas would, because of devaluation, involve considerable exchange loss over the period of credit.

For most customers the currency on the exporter's invoices is not the national currency, and the customer must buy the invoiced currency to pay the exporter. Buying and selling of foreign currencies is rigidly controlled by the customer's Exchange Control authority in most countries.

Governments resort to a variety of methods virtually anywhere at any time!

(i)   Occasional Delays.
        Customers have to 'queue' for exchange. Supply and demand determines the delay and customers are normally required to deposit local funds when applying, so that the Central Bank has the use of the exporter's money.

(ii)   Statutory Delays.
         Countries with serious deficits of FX impose a statutory waiting period
         between application and allocation. The customer has to deposit local
         currency and the Central Bank again has the use of the money.

(iii)   Two-tier rates of Exchange.
         In a dual rate of exchange system the normal, free-market rate is for
         all transactions other than the import of specified goods which have
         an artificial, static rate, less favourable for the importer, to encourage
         him to buy locally rather than import.
            In some serious exchange situations an artificial rate may be set for
         priority imports, more favourable than the free market, although the
         importer may have to wait for allocation.

(iv)   All imports to be settled by Letter of Credit.
         This is imposed to monitor exchange and register the debt centrally.
            The government may require bills of exchange to bear a heavy stamp
         duty. This provides revenue and makes importing less attractive.

(v)   Prior Deposits.
         The customer has to deposit a percentage of his import licence,
         according to the importance of the goods to the national ecconomy,
         ranging from 10% to 1000% in various markets.
            The funds remain with the authorities for, say, 6 months, without
         earning interest and are a very costly deterrent to importing. If business
         is highly profitable, the exporter might loan the deposit to the customer.
         Repayment as well as payment for the goods may then be delayed.

(vi)   Documentation Errors.
         Most governments permit FX remittances only on presentation of
         import licences and various other specified documents. Irregularity
         in documentation can delay payment until rectified.

(vii)   Deduction of Agent's Commissions.
         Collecting banks have to ensure in some markets that commissions are
         properly received. They are paid by the bank to the agent, with the
         exporter receiving a net remittance.

(viii)   Moratorium and Debt Rescheduling.
         A country in serious financial difficulties may temporarily stop all
         FX outflow, whilst it plans what to do. The moratorium is usually
         followed by debts to foreign countries being consolidated and repaid
         by installments over a period with interest at an agreed rate.

Action required by exporters:

(i), (ii), (iii), (iv), (v), (vi)
Check that customers pay local currency at due date and present documents required to support FX applications.

(i), (ii), (v)
Check customers remain liable for the exchange risk until granted hard currency.

(i), (ii), (iii), (v), (viii)
Check that Sales staff are informed of delays and adjust their prices accordingly.

(i), (iii), (v)
The queue for exchange is on a 'first come, first served' basis. Control may be delegated to commercial banks and it may be worth your agent pressing the bank for priority.

(i), (ii), (iii)
Look into the possibility of interest from the banks since they have the use of the money during the 'waiting' period. (Even though you are unlikely to succeed, it may encourage some priority when allocating exchange.)

(i), (ii), (iii)
Obtain occasional estimates of the exchange delays in the future. Tell all interested parties.

(iii)
Check that bank collection instructions specify that a deposit in local currency will be acceptable pending allocation of the hard currency.

(iv)
Check every order is covered by a L/C.

(iv)
Explore whether the customer can be persuaded to bear the stamp tax. Accept lower security by the documents being delivered to the customer against simple receipt?

(vi)
Follow up with local Agents any documentation errors.

(vii)
Check that no affected credit notes are paid out separately.

(viii)
Make an official claim as soon as the moratorium is announced. Provide lists of outstanding invoices and all copy documentation should be readily available.

If the scheme includes the option of investing locally, consider that against the long-term prospect of repayment. Evaluate offers from companies to discount your debts for immediate payment, e.g. 50% now in return for all the blocked currency.

Checklist: To improve export collections

- Acknowledge every order stating terms; bank sort code and account number; L/C requirements.
- Check creditworthiness of customer for value and terms.
- Ensure good local representation in every market.
- Obtain L/C before shipment – and check suitability.
- Verify import licence exists, if necessary.
- Check creditworthiness again at date of shipment.
- Credit Department check documents to banks/customers.
- Send copy invoices to local agents, for Open Account items.
- Use best banks for bill collections?
- Instruct banks on Protest, Interest, Exchange and Case of Need.
- Chase banks for prompt advices of dishonoured bills.
- Ensure all funds remitted by TT or Cable.
- Arrange good account information to flag problems.
- Contact overdue customers locally, or by urgent means such as fax, telex, phone or visit.
- Have enough time for competent coverage and follow-up.
- Arrange local pressure (collection agents, lawyers) for substantial debts.
- Avoid expensive litigation wherever possible.

8 Export credit insurance

The case for insuring export debts

The fundamental risk in exporting is that of not getting paid – in full, on time, or at all!

The reasons can be many, including errors by the exporter or by the agencies working for him. These are within the control of the exporter.

But what of the events outside his control? Even after the exporter has prudently checked the creditworthiness of his buyer, the buyer may default at due date. He may even be insolvent. He may reject the goods on arrival despite having contracted to purchase them and without any defect in the goods. The buyer's country may delay or prevent transfer of Sterling or other hard currency to the UK, or may issue a decree or law to cancel import licences or restrict imports already approved. There are many kinds of governmental actions, even by the UK government, which can frustrate a perfectly good contract, leaving a loss for the exporter. There are also various states of war and civil disorder which can prevent a sale being completed.

Credit insurance provides peace of mind about payments and confidence in market strategy. Indirectly it helps the exporter obtain better or cheaper finance, as well as credit information, and it usually encourages a more disciplined approach to credit granting.

There is a direct cost involved, the insurance premium; and an indirect cost, that of administering the policy to preserve its benefits.

The main risk today is the transfer delay from countries with inadequate foreign currency reserves. This ranges from a few weeks in, say Greece, to a few months in, say, Jamaica, up to 4 years in Zambia. Premium rates reflect this and it is hard to get cover at all for some markets, e.g. Poland and Mozambique.

Thus, a good guide to credit risk, especially country risk, is the *availability* of credit insurance cover, as well as its *cost* and its *special conditions*.

It is a dangerous mistake for exporters *without* CI cover to ignore the experience of the insurers (visible in their conditions) and it is unwise for exporters *with* CI cover to rest on that alone and not take positive steps to obtain faster cash and better customers wherever possible.

The best possible management of export receivables occurs where there is company-wide attention to credit and collections in partnership with well-negotiated credit insurance protection.

So, credit insurance underpins credit management to protect an exporter's cash flow and profits from bad debts and slow payments in overseas markets.

There are other advantages in credit insurance besides the prompt payment of claims whenever insured customers or markets fail.

- A supplier can identify and avoid 'high risk' business, or potentially weak markets.
- A more adventurous use can be made of credit terms to generate increased sales volume and profit.
- Access to finance becomes easier.

The providers of insurance cover

There are several providers of credit insurance premium, each specializing in some features but providing, in all, a wide range of selectivity in cover. A few specialist broker companies exist who, free of charge to the exporter, can help find the right kind of cover at the best cost.

There are two main types of credit insurance company:

(a)   Government-backed, e.g. ECGD in UK and its counterparts in other major countries, which exist to support national exports.
(b)   Commercial, e.g. Lloyd's of London and Trade Indemnity Co which cover exporters anywhere.

In the UK, the Export Credits Guarantee Department (ECGD) is the governmental department responsible for providing UK exporters with insurance cover against commercial (customer) and political (country) risks. About 30% of short-term exports are insured and about 95% of medium-term (over 2 years). Every OECD country has its equivalent credit insurance body.

The standard Guarantee is issued annually to cover total turnover. Markets can be excluded within reason, but not individual buyers. Credit Limits are agreed for all accounts and claims are met for 90% of commercial losses and 95% of political ones, within the limits sets.

In addition, ECGD issue guarantees to banks who provide finance.

All the OECD governmental agencies have suffered large cash flow deficits in recent years due to massive claims for transfer losses from debt-ridden countries. As a result they have restricted cover for many markets and increased premium rates.

The private market offers selective cover for single contracts, buyers or markets at much higher premium rates. Some cover only commercial risks, some only political, and some both. Each insurer has a different angle. Specialist brokers shop around on behalf of exporters (at no cost) to find cover for contracts regarded as risky. Private insurers include Lloyd's, AIG, Black Sea and Baltic, Pan Financial and Trade Indemnity. With no national loyalty, they cover sales from anywhere.

Types of credit risk

Credit insurance companies like to classify risks into types, and it is good practice for exporters to think on similar lines when exercising controls. The risks can be categorized as:

Commercial (Buyer) Risks
- Insolvency of the buyer.
- Failure to pay within six months of due date.
- Failure to take up goods properly despatched.

Political (Country) Risks
- Government actions outside UK which prevent or delay transfer of payments.
- Moratoria on external debt decreed by paying country.
- Government actions which prevent performance of the contract.
- Cancellation of licences by either government.

These are the well established risks for which exporters seek protection. There are some other 'political' risks which are less obvious but which cause increasing concern these days as so many foreign governments run short of foreign exchange.

- Contract non-ratification: where a public buyer does not meet the 'conditions precedent' in a major contract, e.g. fails to take the steps needed (deposits, signatures, certificates, etc) to make a deal effective.
- Unfair calling of bonds: where the exporter has performed properly but the public buyer still demands payment under a performance, advance payment, retention or other bond.
- Confiscation, expropriations: where plants or assets abroad are seized without adequate conditions.
- Contract repudiation by a public buyer: where a public buyer does this without reasonable cause and the exporter is powerless to act in reality.

ECGD - its purpose and services

How is ECGD constituted?

The Export Credits Guarantee Department is a separate department of the Government, formed in 1919, and accountable to the same minister as the Department of Trade and Industry. It has its headquarters in London and regional offices around the country, serving exporters in those areas.

ECGD's power currently comes from the Export Guarantees and Overseas Investment Act of 1978. Section 1 of the Act deals with normal credit insurance activity; Section 2 covers business which cannot be justified by normal standards but is necessary in the 'national interest'; Section 3 makes the preferential bank finance schemes possible; Section 4 deals with foreign aid loans; and Section 5 empowers ECGD to operate cost escalation cover for capital goods, discontinued at present.

ECGD is required to operate at no net cost to the public purse, therefore it seeks to balance its books of claims and administration expense by obtaining adequate premiums over a short period of years. Unfortunately the massive claims experience on places such as Mexico, Brazil and Nigeria in the 1980s has stretched the balancing period to its longest ever, and ECGD have the classic marketing dilemma that raising prices may cause customers to go elsewhere.

What does ECGD do?

It assists UK exporters of goods and services in two extremely important ways. It provides direct insurance cover against commercial and political risks and by guaranteeing banks indirectly makes finance available at preferential interest rates.

Even with sound credit management, the export market is beset with 'political' risks, such as the overnight *coup d'état*, the lack of Sterling for transfer, the cancellation of import licences and so on, and the sheer difficulty of long-distance control makes foreign debt insurance attractive to many firms.

ECGD's own reasons, given in its booklet 'ECGD Services', are: 'In insuring exporters against the risks of non-payment, it enables them to pursue a bolder marketing policy – taking on new buyers and breaking into new markets without fear of crippling loss. Secondly, ECGD's support for export finance, by enhancing exporters' liquidity, can help exporters offer competitive terms and win contracts they might otherwise lose.'

Probably the main reason why ECGD is always in demand is that the world market has changed from a sellers' to a buyers' market, with terms of payment stretching to longer credit periods. This has created greater risks and also the need to finance the waiting period at the least expensive available rates of interest.

ECGD stress that credit insurance is not a substitute for sound credit management. Companies that buy an ECGD policy then abandon normal credit checking and collection follow-up, find that difficulties and losses occur because they lose touch with their customers' financial situation. On the contrary, operating an ECGD policy produces self-disciplines of good export practice which actually aid sales.

What kinds of policies does ECGD issue?

Full details follow, but broadly, cover for standard, repetitive business is given on a 'comprehensive' basis, for which all exports must be insured, good or bad risks, for at least a year at a time.

Cover for non-repetitive, large value contracts, usually for longer-than-standard credit terms, is given on 'Specific' policies, for which premium is calculated individually.

Specific insurance can be for either 'supplier credit' or 'buyer credit'. With supplier credit, the exporter finances the credit period he is granting and thus requires ECGD cover. With 'buyer' credit, the exporter is paid at or about shipment and the customer has a loan from a UK bank with ECGD guaranteeing repayment by the customer to the bank.

Comprehensive short-term guarantee (CST)

This is the normal policy for UK exporters, selling on terms up to six months. There is a flat premium rate, charged per £100 of export sales, requiring the policy-holder's whole export turnover or a good slice of it to be included, thus giving ECGD an acceptable spread of risks.

ECGD may agree to issue a policy for a selected range of markets, instead of whole turnover, but in this case the volume of selected turnover must be substantial and, of course, a higher rate of premium is charged because of the greater risk of loss.

The CST Guarantee is reviewable annually and is available to all kinds of exporters, whether manufacturers, merchants or confirming houses, on the basis that goods or services are exported from UK to an overseas country under a contract made with a buyer outside the UK.

Exporters not yet insuring with ECGD are advised to read
(a)   'ECGD Services', the extremely informative ECGD booklet, and
(b)   a Specimen Policy for CST cover, to see the precise definitions involved.

There is also a series of very practicable ECGD booklets which deal in question and answer format with getting started, obtaining credit limits, making claims, and so on.

PRE-CREDIT RISK

In addition to the credit risk, exporters can also be covered for the Pre-Credit Risk, which applies to the period between date of order and shipment date, provided that the goods are shipped within twelve months of order date. An additional premium is applied to contract cover, which is particularly attractive to exporters of non-standard goods or services; but the cover can only be applied to total insured turnover, i.e. no selection of contracts can be made.

RISKS COVERED

(a)   Insolvency of the buyer.
(b)   The buyer's failure to pay within six months of due date for goods which he has accepted.
(c)   The buyer's failure to accept goods despatched to him (where such

failure is not due to the exporter's actions and where ECGD decides against legal proceedings).

(d)　　A general moratorium on external debt decreed by the government of the buyer's country or of a third country through which payment must be made.

(e)　　Any other action by the government of the buyer's country which prevents performance of the contract.

(f)　　Political events, economic difficulties, legislative or administrative measures arising outside the UK which prevent or delay the transfer of payments or deposits made in respect of the contract.

(g)　　Legal discharge of a debt (not being legal discharge under the proper law of the contract) in a foreign currency which results in a shortfall at the date of transfer.

(h)　　War and certain other events preventing preformance of the contract provided that the event is not normally insurable with commercial insurers.

(i)　　Cancellation or non-renewal of a UK export licence or the prohibition or restriction on export of goods from the UK by law (this risk is covered only where the Pre-Credit Risk section of the guarantee applies).

Also, ECGD covers the failure of 'public buyers', i.e. central, regional, provincial and local government buyers and allied bodies, to perform the contract, provided the default cannot be attributed to any fault of the policy-holder.

PERCENTAGE OF COVER

Exporters are required to bear a percentage of any loss themselves, as an incentive to act prudently in granting credit and managing difficult situations.

For losses arising out of risks (a) and (b) above, ECGD will pay 90% of any loss.

Under risk (c), 20% of the original sales value is deducted from the loss, to be borne by the exporter, then ECGD pays 90% of the balance.

For the risks (d) to (i), ECGD pays 95% of the loss, except where it arises before shipment, i.e. under Pre-Credit Risk cover, when ECGD pays 90%.

With the 'public buyer' cover, ECGD pays 95% of any loss arising after shipment and 90% of pre-shipment losses.

Figure 8.1 Types of loss covered by ECGD (reproduced by kind permission of National Westminster Bank)

Cause of Loss	Percentage of Cover	
	Before Despatch Pre-Credit Risk	After Despatch
Insolvency of Buyer	90%	90%
Buyer's failure to pay for goods he has accepted within six months of due date	N/A	90%
Prevention of payment caused by general moratorium on external debt declared by buyer's country or a third country through which payment is to be made	90%	95%
Other action by the Government of buyer's country which prevents performance of the contract	90%	95%
Political events, economic difficulties etc., outside the UK which impede the transfer of payments in respect of the contract	90%	95%
Cancellation or non-renewal of UK export licence	90%	95%
War and certain other events, preventing performance of the contract provided that the event is not one normally insured with commercial insurers	90%	95%
Buyer's failure to take up goods despatched to him not caused by breach of contract on the part of exporter where ECGD determines that legal action would not be worthwhile.	N/A	Exporter bears a first loss of 20% of full original price and ECGD bears 90% of balance

PAYMENT OF CLAIMS

Risk (a):	Insolvency of buyer; paid immediately on proof of insolvency.
Risk (b):	Protracted default; paid six months after due date.
Risk (c):	Failure to take up goods; paid one month after resale.
Risks (f) and (g):	Delay in transfer or shortfall in legal discharge of debt in local currency; paid four months after due date or four months after completion of transfer formalities, whichever is the later.

All others risks: Paid four months after the event which causes loss, or immediately after loss is sustained, whichever is the later.

For some markets where there is an existing, continuing delay in transfers, ECGD have applied 'claim waiting periods', which have the effect of sharing the real delay between ECGD and the exporter.

PAYMENT OF PREMIUMS

Premium is paid on CST Guarantees in two parts. A non-refundable premium is paid at the start of each year of the policy and the amount is fixed individually for each policy, according to the volume of export turnover, and also the use made of the ECGD credit limit service.

Also, premium is paid monthly on export shipments, at a flat rate fixed each year for each policy.

Exporters who cover the Pre-Credit Risk also pay premium each month on export contracts declared at a separate flat rate.

CREDIT LIMITS

Exporters have a great deal of discretionary power under a CST Guarantee. ECGD does not require details of individual contracts or shipments and usually only acquires this knowledge when a claim is made.

However, all export customers must have a Credit Limit which represents the maximum ECGD liability under each policy. These Credit Limits are fixed at different levels, i.e.

- For a first order up to £250 with a new buyer, the exporter can deal freely, provided he has no adverse information on the buyer.
- For a debt balance up to £5000 (usually, but specified anyway in the policy) the exporter can deal freely, provided he holds one satisfactory

credit report on the buyer from a bank or credit reporting agency. Also, previous trading experience can be used to establish a discretionary Credit Limit.
- Credit Limits above the specified discretionary limit are approved individually by ECGD upon application. These Credit Limits remain valid until varied or cancelled by ECGD.

Credit Limits are never cancelled retrospectively by ECGD, so contracts accepted under Pre-Credit Risk cover or shipments made up to the date of cancellation of cover are safely insured, if properly declared with all conditions met.

CREDIT TERMS

Although CST Guarantees apply in general to credit terms up to six months, terms are restricted for some foreign markets, either by local decree or as a matter of prudence in credit assessment of the market.

Policy-holders receive a list of markets where restrictions apply to terms available. Similarly when individual Credit Limit applications are made, restrictive conditions may be applied, in the interests of obtaining safe payments.

It is obvious that the shorter the credit terms, the more insured sales are possible under a particular Credit Limit.

COVER FOR RE-EXPORTS

The standard CST Guarantee covers goods exported from the UK but cover can also be given for goods imported into UK and re-exported. No cover is available, however, for a special list of products which directly compete with goods available from UK manufacturers.

CONTRACTS IN OTHER CURRENCIES

A list of currencies other than Sterling can be shown in a schedule to the Guarantee and normal cover can apply to contracts in these currencies. Contracts made in various other currencies can also be covered by special agreement with ECGD.

CURRENCY EXCHANGE LOSSES

ECGD will issue a Foreign Currency Contracts Endorsement to exporters who wish to invoice in foreign currency and cover the receipts in the forward exchange market or with a currency loan. In the event of a valid claim for the normal risks, ECGD will pay up to 10% extra if the exporter can demonstrate an extra loss through the currency cover taken out.

EXTENSIONS TO STANDARD COVER

Cover can be added to the standard policy for:

(a)   Export contracts made with a UK merchant or confirming house.
(b)   Sales made to an overseas subsidiary or associated company.
(c)   Sales made ex-stock of UK goods held overseas following trial and demonstration or after exhibiting at an overseas trade fair.
(d)   External trade, i.e. where goods are moving from their country of origin to the buyer's country without coming into the UK. As with the re-export cover situation, there is a short list of sensitive goods directly competitive with UK products, and no cover can be given for these.

Supplemental extended terms guarantee (CXT)

Holders of the basic CST Guarantee engaged in certain types of business where credit periods in excess of 180 days are necessary, can obtain the CXT Guarantee.

This is available for credit periods between 180 days and five years, where the delivery is within two years of the contract date. It is also available for the basic guarantee business of up to 180 days credit where the delivery period is more than 12 months from contract date and pre-delivery risk cover is required.

A special premium rate is quoted for each customer approval based on the grading of the market and the risk period.

Subsidiaries guarantee

This is a separate guarantee along the lines of the standard CST Guarantee, to cover sales made by an overseas subsidiary of goods supplied by a UK parent or associate company. ECGD would normally insist upon covering the exports to the subsidiary before covering sales made by that subsidiary.

Supplementary stocks guarantee

This guarantee can be given to CST Guarantee policy-holders who have cover for sales made from overseas stocks.

It covers the goods while held in stock against certain risks of loss, such as:

- War between UK and the country where stocks are held.
- Requisition or confiscation of goods by the foreign government where the goods are held or where in transit to stock.
- Actions preventing the re-export of goods from the holding country.

At the commencement of cover, ECGD agrees a 'stock limit' for each country concerned and premium is paid at a flat rate percentage of these stock limits. Cover ceases 18 months after the date of shipment from UK.

Specific guarantee – medium-term credit

Individual guarantees can be arranged to cover capital goods contracts or large projects which would not be suitable for comprehensive-type cover. Specific Guarantees can run from shipment or contract date, but are generally taken for contract cover in view of the individual nature of the goods or the risks in the longer manufacturing period.

Risks covered are as for CST Guarantees except that no cover is given for failure of private buyers to take up goods shipped. Cover is limited to 90% for all risks.

ECGD covers default by government buyers at any stage of the transaction, thus replacing the insolvency and protracted default risks of commercial transactions. Erection costs can be included in the policy.

Cover for up to five years' credit is available. Longer periods can be considered if the UK content of the contract exceeds £2 millions or if foreign credit insurers are covering competitive offers for longer credit periods, unless the competitor's terms are part of his national aid programme.

Premium rates are higher than on CST Guarantees and are payable when the offer of cover is accepted.

It is important that exporters negotiate Specific Guarantees with ECGD as early as possible in the contract negotiation, so that cover availability for that market can be confirmed and premium costs can be indicated and included in contract costings. ECGD will also indicate at the early stage whether the proposed credit terms are in order and whether any cross-guarantees are required.

Foreign currency cover is available on Specific Guarantees.

Constructional works guarantee

A constructional works contract provides for the execution of specified works; accordingly the overseas client is known as an 'employer'. A feature of such contracts is that both the supply of goods and materials and the performance of services are undertaken under one contract. Payment is normally made against the presentation of an engineer's certificate or through periodic invoices to the employer. The ECGD Specific Constructional Works Guarantee provides cover against non-payment for both the goods and services elements of constructional works contracts.

COVER

During the period before a certificate or invoice is presented (the 'pre-credit risk' period) cover relates to costs incurred by the contractor. After presentation of a certificate or invoice, cover relates to sums owed by the employer.

RISKS COVERED

The risks covered under the Specific Constructional Works Guarantee are as follows:

(i)   Insolvency of the employer.
(ii)   The employer's failure to pay within six months of due date sums due under the terms of the contract.
(iii)   A general moratorium on external debt decreed by the government of the employer's country or of a third country through which payment must be made.
(iv)   Any other action by the government of the employer's country which prevents performance of the contract in whole or in part.
(v)   Political events, economic difficulties, legislative or administrative

measures arising outside the UK which prevent or delay the transfer of payments or deposits made in respect of the contract.

(vi) Legal discharge of a debt (not being legal discharge under the proper law of the contract) in a foreign currency, which results in a shortfall at the date of transfer.

(vii) War and certain other events preventing performance of the contract, provided that the event is not one normally insured with commercial insurers.

(viii) Cancellation or non-renewal of a UK export licence or the prohibition or restriction on export of goods from the UK by law (this risk is covered only where the pre-credit risk section of the guarantee applies).

In the case of public employers, ECGD covers failure or refusal of the employer to perform under the contract.

The guarantee gives cover against 90% of loss on all risks.

EXTRA COVER

Because construction contracts are not normally for a fixed price and a contractor often has a contingent liability to provide extra work, ECGD is able to give a commitment to provide cover for these contingencies within certain limits. Premium is charged for this cover: 10% of the additional premium (non-returnable) is payable when basis cover is taken out. The balance becomes payable as and when the contractor makes use of the additional cover.

Services policies

ECGD can guarantee exporters of services against loss of earnings, provided the services are performed abroad or the benefit of the services performed in the UK is enjoyed overseas by the buyer.

Examples of services covered are:

- Technical or professional assistance.
- Refits, conversions, overhauls, or repairs to ships or aircraft.
- Leasing or hiring.
- Supply of technical 'know-how' under licence or royalty.

If services are as a continuous business and take less than 12 months, with payment terms up to six months, basic comprehensive cover is available and whole turnover must be insured.

The Comprehensive Services Guarantees provides cover against losses due to:

(i)   insolvency of the principal;

(ii)   the principal's failure to pay within six months of due date for services performed for which invoices have been submitted to him;

(iii)   a general moratorium on external debt by the government of the principal's country or a third country through which payment must be made;

(iv)   any other action of the government of a foreign country which wholly or partly prevents performance of the contract;

(v)   political events, economic difficulties, legislative or administrative measures occurring outside the UK which prevent or delay transfer of payments;

(vi)   legal discharge of the debt in the principal's country, notwithstanding that due to exchange rate fluctuations the amount transferred is less than the debt;

(vii)   war, revolution, civil disturbance or specified natural disasters outside the UK preventing performance of the contract, provided that the cause of loss is not normally commercially insured;

(viii) cancellation or non-renewal of an export licence or the imposition of fresh export licensing restrictions (if cover is held from date of contract);

(ix)   where ECGD has confirmed in writing that the principal or guarantor for the principal is a public principal or national government authority, the failure or refusal of that principal to fulfil any of the terms of the contract.

The policy covers 90% of loss on the first two risks and of any loss occurring in the pre-credit period (before invoices are sent) and 95% on the others. It does not cover loss due to events preventing completion of a contract in circumstances which could free the client from his obligations to make payment under the contract.

For services where there is no continuing pattern of business or for which comprehensive-type cover is otherwise not appropriate – for example, a consulting engineer's services in connection with a major constructional project – a further form of services cover related to the specific policies is available. This is the Specific Services Guarantee which covers all earnings under the individual service contract.

Bond support cover

Where a large contract requires the exporter to provide a guarantee or bond against non-performance ECGD will arrange support in the form of an indemnity to the bank or bonding company.

This can be arranged for Bid Bonds, Advance Payment or Progress Payment Bonds, Performance Bonds and Release of Retentions Bonds.

If ECGD has to make payment to the bondholder it reclaims the amount from the exporter under a related recourse agreement, but the payment is refunded if the exporter is not at fault in the contract.

Unfair calling of bonds cover

ECGD will cover exporters 100% for any loss due to the unjustified calling of a bond, i.e. where the exporter was not in default in performance. The exporter must hold basic ECGD cover for the contract itself.

Because the form of the bond and the buying country must be approved by ECGD, it is advisable for exporters to make arrangements for cover early in their negotiations and certainly before they commit themselves.

Tender to contract cover

Exporters who tender for project contracts in foreign currency can obtain ECGD cover against losses due to exchange rate movements occurring between date of tender and date of contract. Limits of between 3% and 25% of the contract price are applied and tendering periods of three to nine months are eligible. Normally cover only applies to US Dollar and Deutschmark tenders for contracts being insured or financed under ECGD policies.

Before this scheme was introduced, when exporters had to quote the foreign currency, they had to guess the equivalent in the currency of the sterling that they hoped to receive. If they sought cover in the forward exchange market but did not then win the contract, they would have risked loss in closing out their forward contracts. If they did not cover forward but did win the contract and sterling had appreciated, their tender price would earn less sterling than anticipated.

Under the ECGD scheme the exporter, when preparing his bid price, gives ECGD an estimate of the sterling he expects to receive and the overall payment period. Using current market rates ECGD gives the exporter a list of guaranteed forward exchange rates covering this payment period. ECGD guarantees that the sterling realized from currency payments will be no less than the list of guaranteed rates. Cover is for tender periods up to two years, with the rates being re-set every nine months if the supply contract is still being pursued.

If the supply contract is won the exporter enters into forward exchange contracts in the normal way and declares to ECGD the sterling sums which they produce. If these fall short of the sums guaranteed, ECGD pays the shortfall to the exporter up to a maximum of 25%; if they exceed the guaranteed value the excess is paid to ECGD.

ECGD premium consists of an initial charge which is not returnable, plus – if the contract is won – a further charge according to the time between cover and the award of contract. Additional premium is charged if cover is required in more than one currency and if the guaranteed rates are re-set at the nine-month points.

Guarantees to banks for export finance

ECGD support for export finance includes a willingness to agree to the assignment of an exporter's rights under the CST policy to a bank, in order to obtain a loan or increased overdraft.

Many financial institutions are guaranteed directly by ECGD in order to take on all or part of the risks in financing exports.

Since the ending in 1987 of the Comprehensive Bank Guarantee (CBG) to provide 100% finance for short-term export credit at only 5/8% over base rate, no short-term cover is directly available to exporters' banks. A variety of banking innovations have been brought to market in its place, although the cover is less and the cost more than before.

ECGD guarantees to banks now consist of:

- Specific Guarantees, to match Specific Guarantees and Supplemental Extended Terms Guarantees to exporters.
- Foreign Currency Specific Bank Guarantees, for two years credit or more in currency over £1 million.
- Buyer Credits, for bank loans to foreign borrowers on contracts over £1 million.
- Conditional Buyer Credits, a simpler version of Buyer Credits.
- Lines of Credit cover, for financing multiple contracts.
- FINCOBE and ABE guarantees for finance houses.

SPECIFIC BANK GUARANTEES

ECGD will issue this to a financing bank where the exporter is negotiating a contract on terms of two years or more with Specific Guarantee cover or a Supplemental Extended Terms Guarantee.

This Guarantee enables the bank to provide finance to the exporter at special interest rates determined case by case according to the credit period and the buyer's country, with a present minimum rate of $7^1/4\%$.

ECGD guarantees to pay the bank, unconditionally, 100% of the value of bills or notes, three months after due date, for contracts for capital goods, production goods, constructional works or services.

ECGD has recourse to the exporter for amounts advanced outside the underlying insurance cover.

Premium is charged on a scale according to the length of credit and the country concerned.

FOREIGN CURRENCY SPECIFIC BANK GUARANTEES

These apply to simple contract financing, where the terms exceed two years and the value is £1 million equivalent or more. The guaranteed finance can be in US dollars, Deutschmarks, Yen or certain other major currencies.

BUYER CREDIT GUARANTEES

These are now fairly unusual, in view of the reduction in major construction projects since the debt crisis. They originated in the early 1960s, when ECGD agreed to guarantee UK banks who were willing to finance large capital projects abroad, by lending directly to the customer or his bank, so that the exporter/contractor could be paid at shipment without recourse.

The advantages of Buyer Credit over the more common supplier credit are:

- The buyer obtains longer credit than the exporter can usually allow.
- Work in progress can be paid for and manufacturing costs recovered earlier.
- Lightly capitalized exporters can take contracts where normal recourse would not be available for ECGD on supplier credit.

With a Buyer Credit facility, the buyer must pay the exporter 15 to 20% of the contract value on signing the contract. The balance of 80 to 85% is paid to the exporter by a UK bank out of a loan made to the buyer by the bank which is guaranteed 100% by ECGD for capital and interest.

The contract must usually be for £1 million or more. Foreign goods and services may be included but the UK bank loan will be for an amount lower than the UK content, so that the down-payment plus payment from the loan will see the exporter paid in full, usually quite early in the contract period. There remains for the UK bank the collection of the guaranteed loan repayments from the foreign buyer or ECGD.

Obviously the exporter faced with a contract opportunity for Buyer Credit should establish that the buyer is willing to consider a UK bank loan instead of supplier credit. When a bank has indicated its interest in the project, an early approach should be made to ECGD to discuss terms and cover.

Four separate legal agreements are required in each case:

(a)   The Supply contract between the UK exporter and the foreign buyer.
(b)   The Loan Agreement between the UK bank and the foreign borrower.
(c)   The Guarantee from ECGD to the UK bank for the loan repayment.
(d)   The Premium Agreement between ECGD and the exporter.

The only contractual agreement between the exporter and ECGD is the Premium Agreement, by which the exporter pays the cost of ECGD premium for the guarantee to the bank. Note: Although the bank is the guaranteed lender, the premium is payable by the exporter, who is considered the real beneficiary.

Premium costs are similar to Specific Guarantee costs and should be established early on, to ensure correct costing and pricing of the contract.

CONDITIONAL BUYER CREDIT GUARANTEE

ECGD's buyer credit guarantee in this case depends on the bank having done the essential legal work on the validity of contracts and in the UK and the buyer's and borrower's country. It is an ideal format when speed is needed and it leaves the bank free to negotiate and sign without step-by-step ECGD permission. In the event of a claim, the bank's diligence would then have to be checked.

Figure 8.2   Guide to Establishing a Single Project Buyer Credit

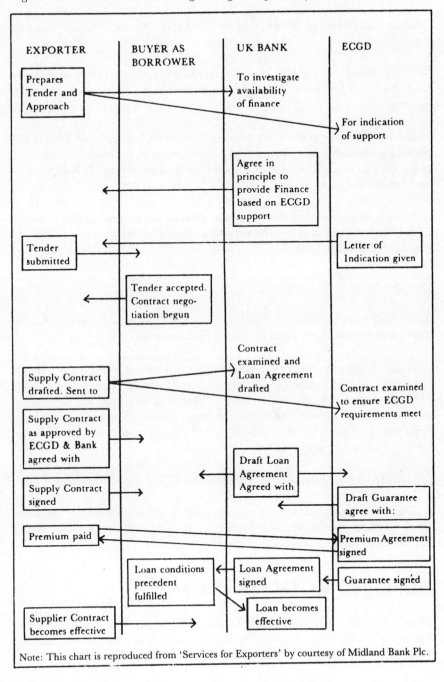

EXPORTER	BUYER AS BORROWER	UK BANK	ECGD
Prepares Tender and Approach		To investigate availability of finance	
			For indication of support
		Agree in principle to provide Finance based on ECGD support	
Tender submitted			Letter of Indication given
	Tender accepted. Contract nego-tiation begun		
Supply Contract drafted. Sent to		Contract examined and Loan Agreement drafted	Contract examined to ensure ECGD requirements meet
Supply Contract as approved by ECGD & Bank agreed with			
		Draft Loan Agreement Agreed with	
Supply Contract signed			Draft Guarantee agree with:
Premium paid			Premium Agreement signed
	Loan conditions precedent fulfilled	Loan Agreement signed	Guarantee signed
		Loan becomes effective	
Supplier Contract becomes effective			

Note: This chart is reproduced from 'Services for Exporters' by courtesy of Midland Bank Plc.

LINE OF CREDIT GUARANTEE

This kind of financing is described in the Export Finance chapter in some detail.

ECGD guarantee the UK bank lending to a foreign borrower on a buyer credit basis, to finance a variety of contracts over a period, usually, twelve months.

The ECGD cover is for 85%, since each exporter has to obtain 15% of his particular contract paid before delivery. He also has to persuade the customer to get the contract included in the line of credit, and in turn, ECGD have to approve the inclusion.

As with a single project Buyer Credit, there is no contractual link between ECGD and the exporter, so the premium is paid by the exporter to ECGD through the lending bank.

FINCOBE AND ABE GUARANTEE

These well-known acronyms stand for: Finance Contracts (Overseas Banks) Endorsement and; Associated Borrower Endorsement.

Major financing banks are increasingly arranging loans with foreign borrowers, usually banks, to operate in a very similar fashion to the lines of Credit above, for general purposes. There normally does not have to be any connection between the various contracts financed by a loan, and the definition of 'capital or semi-capital' goods can be stretched to include the wishes of all parties on occasions.

The FINCOBE is the normal guarantee by ECGD for such loans.

The ABE is used where there is a very close relationship between the banks involved. Since that closeness reduces the risk of default, only political risk is covered, and the premium rate is lower.

Managed ECGD policies

There are at least two companies, Unexis and Cadex, who offer a service of operating ECGD cover on behalf of small to medium size companies, through umbrella policies.

The advantages include, for a cost-effective fee, the policy administration, especially useful for companies with no experience at all of working with ECGD. In addition, the managers ensure that claims are not jeopardized through bad documentation, and they tend to bring through, very quickly, one of the indirect benefits of cover well known to experienced policy-holders, viz. the disciplines needed to maintain cover, which in turn tend to improve the credit and collection performance.

The private market of credit insurance

Reasons for using non-governmental organizations

Exporters considering credit insurance normally think of ECGD and indeed, for many years it was said that only the government could ever afford to cover multi-millions of transfer risks.

However, the non-government market has been in place for many years and has developed new insurance products in the 1980s, due mainly to the need for political risk cover on a selective basis.

Although ECGD now also operate on a selective basis, their international agreements and self-imposed restrictions allow scope for the complementary role of other insurers.

In particular, Trade Indemnity has become prominent among commercial insurers, through their existing home trade client base, their excellent publicity and their underwriting expertise in exports.

Some reasons given for exporters using the private market are:

● Cover is required only on single contracts or buyers.
● 'Catastrophe' cover is all that is needed, i.e. the exporter is willing to take losses up to a high level himself.
● Although the percentage of premium rate is higher than ECGD, the cost in pounds is less because the 'safe' business can be excluded.
● ECGD cover is restricted for the required markets.
● Does not want all the commitment and administration of a continuing policy.
● The origin of goods and destination of payments does not suit ECGD conditions.

Who are the private market insurers?

TRADE INDEMNITY PLC

Established in 1918. Shareholders include several famous insurance companies. Separate export policies were issued in 1980 for customer risks only, then political risk was added in 1985. TI insure on a 'whole turnover' basis but allow various exclusions. Their standard indemnity is 85% of a similar range of risks to those covered by ECGD except that repudiation of the goods by the buyer is not covered. Premium is charged as a single flat rate percentage on sales and is payable in advance.

Cover is from shipment on credit terms up to 180 days and there is a discretionary credit limit, usually £10 000, above which clearance has to be obtained from TI. Goods can be of any origin.

The obligations for the exporter include early notification of overdues and quarterly declarations of sales by country.

No guarantees are issued by TI to banks for financing purposes, but TI agree to policy assignments in most cases. And Exfinco (described under 'Export Finance') stipulate that clients may hold either ECGD or TI cover.

TI does not provide support for the issue of bonds, nor does it cover their unfair calling.

It is said by specialist brokers that exporters selling standard goods mainly to established customers in rich countries would benefit from TI cover rather than ECGD, who are better at covering contract risks on sales to difficult markets.

TI also make available policies based on the 'aggregate first loss' and the 'catastrophe' basis. With the first loss system, the exporter agrees to take the losses up to an annual maximum and TI pay out on any losses above the agreed level. Premium rates are lower than in the standard policy, because the losses for the underwriter are expected to be less. In such a policy, the exporter's standard of credit risk management is not a prime condition.

With 'catastrophe' cover, TI need to satisfy themselves as to the controls being exercised in the exporter's credit management system. A level of loss is again agreed for the exporter, with TI paying out 100% of losses above that level up to a stated maximum, e.g. losses covered above £100 000 to £1 million. The premium is calculated on the amount of exposure for the insurer rather than on sales. Catastrophe cover appeals to exporters with excellent credit management, large turnover and individually huge customer debts.

TI also offer Specific Account Policies for sales to specified customers and Special Policies which are tailored to suit single risks, such as orders which are well above the average 'worry level' for an exporter.

For those exporting less than £1 million per year, there is the Smaller Exporters Policy. Cover is from 70% to 85% of agreed discretionary or approved credit limits and whole turnover is expected to be insured. The chore-work of declarations is very much reduced on these policies.

PANFINANCIAL INSURANCE CO. LTD

PF were formed in 1982 and operate in London on behalf of US, Swedish and Japanese shareholders. Their policies are strictly based on the catastrophe principle and they have two important pre-conditions of cover:

- the exporter must have good credit controls.
- the buyer's market must have sound insolvency laws.

Cover is for insolvency only, not default, plus political risk as agreed. Indemnity is 100% on the exposure between the annual aggregate and the maximum liability.

Any origin of goods can be covered and pre-delivery risk can be added to cover by agreement.

PF also cover specific risks in a policy called 'Contract Completion', which applies to the major political risks only; also the unfair calling of bonds in 'Wrongful Calling of On-Demand Guarantee Insurance', and 'Non-honouring of Letters of Credit' cover, where a state-owned bank does not meet a properly complied with letter of credit.

AMERICAN INTERNATIONAL UNDERWRITERS (UK) LTD

AIU is part of the AIG company of New York, established in 1919. Its standard product is for comprehensive whole turnover. Indemnity is 90% for insolvency, default and the usual range of political risks. The premium basis is unusual, in that it varies by market and is charged quarterly on outstanding balances.

The credit period can be up to 360 days and any origin of goods is permitted. Limits are agreed for both customers and countries. Pre-delivery risk of insolvency and political events can be added to cover if products are subject to such loss effects.

AIU is particularly active in covering political risk on selected orders, including unfair calling of bonds. Its US ownership prevents it from insuring business in certain communist countries.

LLOYD'S OF LONDON

Lloyd's is not a single company, but a place of business for hundreds of separate sydicates, of which only a handful offer credit insurance policies. By its own rules, Lloyd's is not allowed to cover commercial risks. Political risks are covered for individual contracts and a great deal of choice is open to the exporter. Premium is charged on a selected amount of exposure, whether the profit element or all or part of the sales proceeds. Indemnity is usually 90%.

BLACK SEA AND BALTIC

This company operates in London and Vienna and is owned by the Russian government. It specializes in covering state buyers in the Comecon countries, although it takes a jaundiced view of some of them.

ASSURANCES DE CREDIT

Known colloquially as 'Namur', this company operates from Croydon with headquarters in Belgium. It offers commercial risk cover only and claims a flexible approach and a fast response to requests from exporters. Whole turnover is expected.

CREDIT AND GUARANTEE INSURANCE COMPANY LTD

This company in Tonbridge, Kent specializes in covering customer default only on contracts over £100 000 in West European countries. 'C&G's' trademark is its willingness to examine the wording on complex contracts, giving an exporter exposure well in excess of normal levels. Having taken that trouble, their indemnity is 100%.

International organizations

The two principal organizations for credit insurance companies are the Berne Union, the popular name for the International Union of Credit and Investment Insurers, and the ICIA, the International Credit Insurance Association.

The Berne Union was formed in 1934 with ECGD as a founder member, and it now has 40 member insurers from 32 countries. Its official purpose is 'to work for the international acceptance of sound principles of export credit and investment insurance and the establishment and maintenance of discipline in the terms of credit for international trade'. In simpler parlance, the members work together to prevent an international credit race.

The standards for credit terms are applied by all members, so that exceptional terms, if they are to be insured, have to be referred and agreed. In practice, this means that export negotiators can relax in the knowledge that their competitors from, say, France or Italy cannot offer more attractive credit terms without ECGD or Trade Indemnity knowing. (Note: it has sometimes proved difficult to check allegations of 'bending' the rules in time to win contracts.)

The ICIA also brings its members together for consultation and agreement on standards and exclusions. It was formed in 1926 and has 44 members from 28 countries. Its four stated activities are:

- Regular exchange of views on economic conditions.
- Exchange of information on individual risks.
- Co-operation in collections and recoveries.
- Co-operation in reinsurance arrangements.

Trade Indemnity is a leading ICIA member and a vigorous user of the information exchange facility. Whereas for many years, members agree to cover the exports only of companies in their own country, the loosening of national barriers now means that exporters in any member country can approach any insurer they believe gives the best cover.

The OECD (Organization for Economic Co-operation and Development) is a busy organization of 22 countries, which amongst other trade matters, influences export credit insurance in two respects: the 'Consensus' and the rescheduling of debts.

The Consensus (officially the 'International Arrangement of Official Export Credit') issues guidelines each year on four major areas:

- Categorization of all the countries of the world into Rich, Intermediate or Poor according to per capita income.
- Minimum pre-delivery payments on medium-term credit.
- Maximum credit periods (i.e. longer for poor countries than for rich ones).
- Minimum interest rates on medium-term credit, so that government subsidies do not play a part in international competition.

Each year a list of countries is published, showing those in each of the I, II, or III categories. A table is then produced, as shown in Figure 8.3.

Figure 8.3   International Consensus Guidelines.

	Relatively Rich	*Inter- mediate*	*Relatively Poor*
	I	II	III
Minimum payment by delivery	15%	15%	15%
Minimum interest rates for credit between two and five years	?%	?%	?%
Minimum interest rates for credit over five years	?%	?%	?%
Maximum credit periods	5–8^1/2 yrs	8^1/2 yrs	10 yrs

Note: The interest rates vary each year whereas the other factors have remained static for some time, although the markets to which they apply vary according to changes in category.

The OECD also form the Paris Club of creditor countries to meet governments of countries who need to reschedule their foreign debt situations. Credit insurers are at the forefront of creditors in such cases, and rescheduling affects a nation's ability to obtain further export credit.

Use of credit insurance brokers

It is always worth considering the use of specialist credit insurance brokers. They cost the exporter nothing, as their commission or brokerage is paid by the insurers. Most private market insurers, e.g. Lloyds, will only deal through brokers.

The use of brokers expanded in the 1950s when Trade Indemnity Company Ltd and ECGD increased their sales promotions. Credit insurance brokerage became a specialist activity within the wider business of insurance broker companies and the UK Credit Insurance Brokers' Committee was formed in the City of London (a list of members appears at the end of this chapter in Figure 8.4).

A broker is squarely placed between exporter and insurer. His first task is to assess the exporter's needs and the detailed mechanics of his export credit and then approach the insurer to obtain the most suitable facilities. He is finally left with the task of proving the cost-effectiveness of the proposed policy to the exporter. Once the insurance policy is issued, the broker's services are available on a 'demand' basis for servicing the exporter's needs.

From the insurer's point of view, the broker is useful for:

- Obtaining and expanding business.
- 'Training' clients in correct procedures.
- Keeping clients informed of developments and new facilities.

From the exporter's point of view, the advantages of using a broker are:

- Considerable assistance at the outset, to interpret wording, explain conditions and procedures.
- Availability at any time to consult on tactics or alternative facilities.
- Joint approaches, by letter or visit, to underwriters for cover or claims negotiations.
- Discussions on improving office systems based on broker's knowledge of systems of other exporters.

Figure 8.4   Members of the UK Credit Insurance Brokers' Committee (UKCIBC)

Alexander Stenhouse
Norman Insurance House
Kings Road
Reading
Berkshire RG1 4LW
Telephone 0734 61100

Bain Clarkson Credit Ltd
Alpha House
Suffolk Street
Queensway
Birmingham B1 1LS
Telephone 021 632 4211

CT Bowring and Co. Insurance Ltd
PO Box 145
The Bowring Building
Tower Place
London EC3P 3BE
Telephone 01-283 3100

The Credit Insurance Association Ltd
Lloyds Chambers
1 Portsoken Street
London E1 8DF
Telephone 01-235 3550

Credit Insurance Services Ltd
89 High Road
South Woodford
London E18 2RH
Telephone 01-505 3333

Finance Risk Managers Ltd
St Michael's Rectory
St Michael's Alley
London EC3V 9DS
Telephone 01-283 7345

Jardine Credit Insurance Ltd
Jardine House
6 Crutched Friars
London EC3N 2HT
Telephone 01-528-4444

Lowndes Lambert UK Ltd
Aspen House
Temple Street
Swindon
Wilts SN1 1SH
Telephone 0793 26252

John Reynolds & Co. (Credit Insurance) Ltd
Byrom House
21 Quay Street
Manchester M3 3JA
Telephone 061 832 9022

Risk Administration Ltd
Walsingham House
35 Seething Lane
London EC3N 4AH
Telephone 01-488 3288

Sedgwick Credit Ltd
Sedgwick House
The Sedgwick Centre
London E1 8DX
Telephone 01-377 3456

Willis Wrightson Ltd
10, Trinity Square
London EC3P 3AX
Telephone 01-488 8111

9 Finance for exports

Overview – the lazy overdraft versus the alternatives

The UK, and the City of London in particular, has an embarrassment of riches in banks offering to finance export credit in various ways – trade finance schemes, forfaiting, factoring, leasing, discounting and so on.

It seems odd, then, that some 75% of UK exports are simply financed out of overdraft. Exporters allow credit and just borrow against their ordinary bank facility until customers pay.

Some of the available financing methods are designed to provide bulk money for all or part of an exporter's debts, but the impression given by bank publicity is that the banks will use their expertise and flair in any way needed to help win orders.

The most common reason for exporters leaning on their overdrafts is that they sell first and only consider special funding if their overdraft is at a limit or if they become especially aware of an attractive scheme. It is probably true that while overdraft money is available, most exporters see it as 'less bother' than the 'fancy finance' schemes they see advertised, if indeed they do see them.

There certainly appears to be scope for better marketing by the banks, both in terms of publicity and of matching exporters' risk and delay at the right price.

The recent evolution of UK export finance

A significant event occurred in 1986 when the government ended its 100% guarantee to banks, through ECGD's Comprehensive Bank Guarantee

(CBG), for providing money to exporters at only 5/8% over base rate. The obvious subsidy on the interest rate was causing a major annual bill for the tax-payer, but exporters were assured by government that the banking system was ready with alternative financing schemes. In fact, it was some time before the major banks announced any standard packages for general exports and, without subsidy or 100% guarantees against foreign default, it followed that they required recourse on the exporter and charged higher fees than before.

The scene changed also for medium-term credit for capital goods, where the 'Consensus' of OECD credit insurance agencies had traditionally agreed to subsidized fixed interest rates for the three categories of market. While it made some economic sense to charge low rates of interest to the growing list of 'Relatively Poor' countries, at a large cost of subsidy, it made increasingly less sense to give subsidies to the 'Relatively Rich' countries and from 1988, the Consensus rates no longer applied to the category I nations, such as USA, Canada and the EEC.

The length of credit required by a buyer may well be longer than a bank is willing to finance, so either the exporter or his bank has to work hard at a tailored deal for money to match the credit terms.

Whereas buyers have always preferred prices in their own currencies, so many currencies are now 'soft' or unacceptable to exporters, that bank finance either has to match the contract currency or offer a reasonable conversion to Sterling. For example, the Exfinco FSA scheme (see later) guarantees that the exchange rate given to exporters to quote, will be used in converting invoices for cash at shipment.

The risk of non-payment has increased enormously since the debt crises of so many countries since 1982, with the transfer and exchange losses more usual than customer insolvency losses. Thus, the case for off-loading the risk to a credit insurer has increased, whether the cover is taken by the exporter or by the financing institution. Either way, the cost of protection has to go into prices or be absorbed to reduce margins.

The problem of passing on the extra costs of finance and credit insurance can certainly affect competitiveness in specific cases. In some markets, especially the poorer ones, 'total' prices are taken apart by buyers or their governments to find out interest costs and other add-ons. Careful management can sometimes find out whether the buyer is sensitive to price, currency, interest-rate or financing charges, then rearrange the unattractive elements so that the total recovery by the exporter is the same but the sensitive items are made acceptable.

In a sense, the Exfinco story typifies the national inertia when it comes to innovative finance meeting the expressed need of the market. There has been a very limited take up, despite Exfinco having surveyed carefully what exporters needed instead of overdraft money for exports. They confirmed that the few giants who account for most of the UK total exports already had access to ample funding. But the thousands of ordinary exporters (not necessarily small firms) signalled a desire for a package which gave:

- cash at shipment;
- protection against non-payment;
- fixed interest costs;
- no exchange risk.

So Exfinco offered to meet these needs, subject to a few exclusions. Provided exporters have their own ECGD or Trade Indemnity cover, Exfinco will buy the goods from them at shipment, as 'undisclosed principals' and offer guaranteed currency rates for non-Sterling deals.

One reason for the lack of take up may be that so many exporters go ahead without adequate credit insurance protection, thus not qualifying for Exfinco's finance, nor that of some banks, such as Barclays who also offer to 'buy' the goods at shipment.

Other banks simply buy the debts without recourse or with limited recourse, in the forfaiting style, while other schemes offer an element of marketing assistance, as in Confirming House operations, or risk assessment and ledger work as in Factoring. And some of the more recent trade finance schemes offered by the banks combine elements of all these features.

The available array is considerable but underused.

Credit management and export finance

'Time is money.' 'Exports are being paid more slowly.' These popular aphorisms of exporting surely indicate that the use of shareholders funds and interest-bearing loans, until money comes in from customers, is an active task for senior management, not a passive or delegated role.

The need for interim finance is obviously linked with sales decisions to grant credit in the first place and with how much tolerance is then allowed on late payments. So credit management has a role in planning the amount and timing of finance.

The treasury function in major corporations normally has the task of arranging short and long-term general funding to match the life and size of assets, if properly done.

However, most companies do not have the resources to employ specialists in treasury work, or elevate the credit management role to an effective level. Thus it falls to top management to ensure somehow that conscious decisions are taken on when to allow credit and how to finance the delay, without relying on the lazy trough of overdraft money with its uncertain future cost.

The obvious connection between credit and treasury management is that granting credit sensibly and collecting revenue promptly can drastically reduce the need for expensive extra funds. Thus it is odd that, in most large firms, graduate high-flyers are funnelled into treasury jobs, to cultivate and be cultivated by the banks, in order to borrow extra millions at fractionally cheaper rates. The same brain-power could be used to collect the company's own slow revenue instead, and reduce the need for external funds. The balance sheet would certainly sparkle more brightly.

Why special finance is necessary

Almost every company that exports also sells in the home trade. It is usually difficult to establish export profitability because of shared costs but it would be reasonable to suppose that if a company made the national average of 4% Net Profit before tax, and had Total Debtors equivalent to 72 days of sales, the split might be:

	NPBT	DSO
Home	6%	65
Export	1%	95
Total	4%	72

The export margin is undoubtedly depressed by the cost of waiting longer for debts to be paid, as well as by extra costs.

The Export Debtors asset is more complex than the Home version, due to the variety of payment terms and delays, and it is salutory for an exporter to compare his estimate of how long exports take to get paid with the actual DSO (Days Sales Outstanding) ratio. It is invariably underestimated because we think of the main credit terms, rather than the total time taken.

The actual DSO is easily calculated in either short or long form.

- Short-form DSO = $\dfrac{\text{Total Debtors at month end} \times 365}{\text{Total Sales for preceding 12 months}}$

- Long-form DSO
  Deduct actual total sales for each month from Total Debtors until the Total Debtors figure is exhausted. It is more accurate than the annual average approach of the short method, because the most recent sales are more relevant.

Thus an exporter with a mixture of methods from Letter of Credit to Open Account and Drafts, and credit periods up to 120 days, selling to rich and poor markets, could experience month-end Debtors in excess of 100 days of sales value.

Allowance must be made for the four time effects after invoicing:

- the transport period;
- the credit term;
- late payment by customer or country;
- transmission of funds by the banks.

Consider a typical sale on 60 days terms which takes 2 weeks to reach the customer. The customer could be strong or weak; his country could be rich or poor.

The following matrix shows how long the total payment time could be:

A = Strong customer, rich market
B = Strong customer, poor market
C = Weak customer, rich market
D = Weak customer, poor market

	A	B	C	D
Shipment time, up to arrival	14	14	14	14
Credit term	60	60	6	60
Payment delay (say)	–	–	30	30
Transfer delay (say)	–	90	–	90
Bank 'float' time	14	14	14	14
Total Period (days)	88	178	118	208
Cost of waiting, at 12% p.a.	3%	6%	4%	7%

So, the best situation on the supposed 60 days credit could be 88 days, and the worst (depending on the actual default periods) 208. Action to reduce the delays, and ways of covering the cost in prices are dealt with elsewhere, but here we are concerned with the exporter being out of funds for so long.

The choice available

In view of the erratic and uncertain nature of export payments it is extraordinary that some 75% of UK exports are financed out of the main company overdraft, i.e. companies just keep on writing cheques regardless of when sales are collected. Whereas the few remaining blue chip giants can afford the overdraft route since they get the finest interest rates from banks queuing up to lend them more, the majority of exporters have limits on how much they can borrow and pay from 1% to 4% over base rate.

The government, through the Bank of England, presses the banks to provide export money more easily and cheaply, yet it is not clear how hard-up exporters use this fact in their overdraft negotiations. It is said that many small exporters never even discuss their sales ledgers with their banks. What is certain is that the banks have produced a large range of trade finance schemes and hope exporters will talk to them even if they are not the exporter's normal clearer.

The sources vary according to their preference for countries, i.e. the sovereign risk, and the nature of the sale, capital or semi-capital goods requiring repayment over periods up to 10 years, to ordinary products on credit maturing up to 6 months. Most trade finance depends on ECGD default protection for bank or exporter and this condition prevents money being available for off-cover markets. But the banks proclaim their wish to satisfy exporters with rapid replies to proposals and tailored packages at acceptable prices. This in turn has required ECGD to be more flexible in providing cover to match.

Every exporter should occasionally take an objective look at his sales debt portfolio, together with a view of forthcoming business. The profile tends to change within fairly short time-scales, as to the size of debts, credit terms and the mix of market and customer risks.

A review, as a prelude to considering financing, should include:

- Sales value per annum, in total and by market.
- Number of different markets and customers.
- Market risk (coded say, I, II, III per OECD Guidelines).
- Sales value analysed by credit terms (e.g. 30, 60, 90 days, etc.).
- Existence of credit insurance cover (for actual accounts).

Figure 9.1   Finance for Export Sales – Initial Decision Path

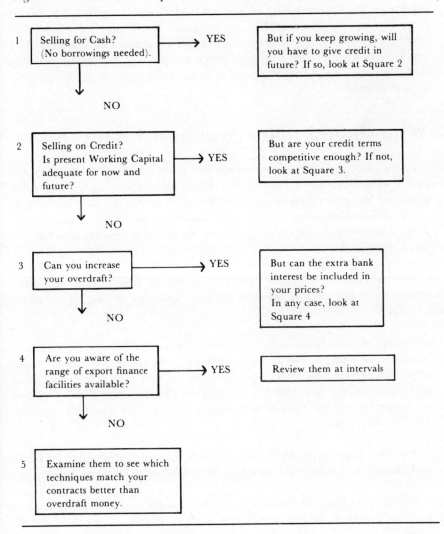

1 | Selling for Cash? (No borrowings needed). → YES → But if you keep growing, will you have to give credit in future? If so, look at Square 2

NO

2 | Selling on Credit? Is present Working Capital adequate for now and future? → YES → But are your credit terms competitive enough? If not, look at Square 3.

NO

3 | Can you increase your overdraft? → YES → But can the extra bank interest be included in your prices? In any case, look at Square 4

NO

4 | Are you aware of the range of export finance facilities available? → YES → Review them at intervals

NO

5 | Examine them to see which techniques match your contracts better than overdraft money.

In return for cost-savings, better risk management and faster cash, exporters have to accept the need to arrange and monitor a mixture of financing. For example, instead of just the Sales Ledger and Bank Overdraft, there may be for the same total sales, the Sales Ledger and Bank Overdraft (both reduced), two banks forfaiting debts that can be avalized, three banks buying goods or debts without recourse to certain markets, the discounting of all bills of exchange not otherwise financed, and an Acceptance Credit for bulk borrowing against any other unpledged debts!

Some bank brochures refer to 'tailored finance to suit each exporter', which sounds ideal, but the reality of the size and bureaucracy of banks makes it uneconomic to do other than try to fit any one exporter's debtors into 'modular' products. There are certainly cases of specialist bank staff helping exporters to win significant orders through constructing exceptional packages for buyers, but for everyday exports, it is up to the exporter to find the right kind of finance.

Who should manage export finance?

The impression given by institutional and bank booklets is that the banks can be entrusted with arranging the right kind of financing for exporters. Exporters know that there is a considerable gap between the daily hurly-burly in an industrial company's export office and the availability of bank finance. It is clearly for each exporter to take the initiative, no matter how busy or under-resourced he is.

The skills of a corporate specialist in export finance can contribute significantly, not only to minimizing costs but also to helping to satisfy customers.

The duties of credit controllers in various firms range from simply collecting whatever the ledger throws up each month right through to the complete range of planning receivables, checking credit risks, collecting funds and purchasing external services such as insurance and finance. In matters of detail, decisions on export finance are probably more closely related to the credit management function than any other.

The very large corporations have separate managers responsible for credit and finance, and enough information and collaboration to do the right things.

The greatest need for financing expertise is in the vast number of small to medium size firms, where usually:

- the credit control function is reactive, because it is too low in the hierarchy, despite having the essential information on the credit to be financed.
- the sales function is busy with customers and does not get involved in technical financial devices which might seem unnecessary or frustrate the order-getting.
- the accounting staff keep the books and, apart from an occasional long-term loan, manage cash flow through a combination of overdraft and manipulation of out-going payments.

So, how should they be organized to take advantage of specialist trade finance?

While it is never easy for overstretched managements to ensure there is occasional specialist attention to needs, every board of directors should (a) recognize the basic signals from their export business and (b) make a senior person responsible for managing export finance as and when called for.

The basic signals for most exporters are:

- Export cash flow is slower than the home trade and probably slower than it was five years ago.
- The cost of waiting between initial expense and final payment is larger than is ever estimated.
- Dependence on overdraft is lazy and throws costs and profits into uncertainty because interest rates fluctuate with no warning.
- Some forms of finance save costs in other areas such as risk assessment, collection and marketing information.

The senior person given responsibility for export finance needs the occasional time but the permanent authority to:

- analyse existing and future business by market, customer, size, credit term, and actual DSO.
- keep a 'fix' on interest cost and currency exposure.
- evaluate topically the various financing schemes available.
- cultivate helpful relationships in several different banks, e.g. two clearers, a merchant bank, two foreign banks in London, people in forfaiting and factoring, (and a specialist credit insurance broker is also a valuable ally).
- monitor actual direct savings and indirect benefits against those originally intended.

The alternative types of finance can be divided among:

- Short-term
- Medium or long-term
- Foreign Currency

We now examine these facilities. Any combination is possible for a business and traditional facilities should be objectively reviewed at intervals for cost-effectiveness.

Short-term finance

Overdrafts

Most businesses maintain an overdraft facility with a UK bank. Export sales, along with other transactions, can be financed on a simple turnover basis, without any specific arrangements, by drawing cash needed during the purchasing and manufacturing periods and replenishing the bank account on receipt of the sale proceeds.

If the overdraft limit is reached, it should be possible to negotiate an increase by discussing with the bank manager, in more detail than he might otherwise be aware of, the contracts for which the extra money is needed.

It is also possible to obtain increased overdraft money by simply assigning security such as the ECGD policy to the bank. An attraction of this is that such assignment does not need registration at Companies House under the Companies Act.

Overdrafts incur interest charges, from 1% above Base Rate for prime borrowers to 4% above Base Rate for smaller, newer companies.

Even if overdraft money is available, the interest rates charged may be higher than the rates on other facilities.

Bills of exchange are valuable in obtaining funds prior to customers' payment, for two reasons: banks compete to handle bill collections, and each bill is easy to distinguish as a financing instrument, compared, say, to open account invoices. The two standard types of finance against bills are 'Advances' for clean, non-documentary collections and 'Negotiations' for documentary bills.

Advances against bills

The exporter can obtain an advance of a percentage of the face value of 'clean' bills from the bank which is entrusted with their collection. The balance is paid when the customer has paid, but in the event of non-payment, the bank has recourse to the exporter for the original advance.

The cost of the advance is usually the same as overdraft rate.

Negotiation of bills

This is an extremely useful and simple way of raising export finance.

Banks will normally agree to purchase exporters' foreign Bills when originally submitted for collection. Even shipping documents without Bills may be treated in this way, e.g. CAD transactions going through the same bank. The exporter is paid at the time of negotiation, the bank sends the Bills for normal collection and obtains reimbursement when the foreign customer settles. If payment is not received, the bank has recourse to the exporter, charging his account with the amount advanced plus interest for the period since the advance.

There is no difference in the collection method when a Bill is negotiated and neither the customer nor the foreign bank involved can tell the difference between a negotiated Bill already paid to the exporter and a normal Bill sent for collection.

The cost of negotiation to the exporter is normally the usual overdraft rate for him, charged on the period between the advance and the bank receiving settlement.

Exporters should note that when a Bill has been negotiated, the bank becomes 'a holder in due course' and has the right of action in the event of the buyer's default, unless the Bill carries Protest instructions.

Bills drawn in currencies other than Sterling can be negotiated in the same way as Sterling Bills, when either currency or Sterling can be advanced. It may be useful to negotiate a currency bill in order to pay for an import liability in the same currency. However, the exchange liability remains until payment date, when any loss incurred by the bank if Sterling has strengthened will be charged to the exporter. Similarly, if currency has been advanced and the Bill is unpaid, the exporter will have to buy currency to repay the bank, using the current spot rate, which may have moved against the £ Sterling. Therefore, the likely exchange rate movement during the period of credit must be considered by the exporter before negotiating a foreign currency Bill.

Clean acceptance credits

Some exporters prefer to obtain bulk financing of exports, regardless of individual sales and open account or draft terms. An Acceptance Credit facility, issued for an agreed total, gives the exporter the right to obtain funds by drawing a single bill on the financing bank itself, for a term of usually 90 or 180 days, provided there are underlying unpaid exports for the value not pledged in any other way. Drawings are usually for a minimum of £100 000.

The bank accepts the bill and discounts it in the London Discount Market at very fine rates, simultaneously paying the face value to the exporter, less an acceptance commission and discount interest.

When the bill reaches maturity, the exporter may either repay the sum or simply renew the loan with a fresh bill for a further period. This 'revolving' finance may continue for the period of the agreement and drawings can be adjusted to requirements.

The most obvious benefit is that the attractive rate of interest is fixed for the term of the bill, so the facility can be used tactically by drawing on it when overdraft rates are expected to rise.

Acceptance Credits are provided by the 16 leading merchant banks, as members of the Accepting Houses Committee, plus a few major banks.

The following description is quoted from a booklet issued by Hill, Samuel and Co. Ltd, one of the merchant banks specializing in Acceptance Credits. They are members of the Accepting Houses Committee.

'Acceptance Credits are an extremely simple and highly competitive means by which a company, irrespective of size, can finance its working capital requirements. They add flexibility to a company's short-term borrowings and can be complementary to an overdraft provided either by ourselves or a clearing bank.

They apply to domestic business, exports, imports or shipments between overseas countries.

As with any banking facility, we shall wish to satisfy ourselves as to the financial stability of the company and we shall ask the details of the facility required, i.e. amount, purpose, duration, etc.

Once the terms of a facility have been agreed, we will issue a letter confirming the arrangement in detail and permitting you to draw Bills on us.

Security is not necessarily required, but this depends upon the financial position of the company, the nature of the transaction and the security given for the company's other short-term borrowings.'

The services of Confirming Houses in the UK provide rapid payment as an alternative to allowing credit to foreign buyers.

Confirming houses

These are companies established in the UK, acting as agents for overseas buyers. They place or confirm orders on UK firms as principals and are fully responsible for payment, usually on cash or very short terms, say, 14 days, for a cash discount of perhaps $2^1/2\%$.

The confirming house grants credit of up to 180 days to the overseas buyer, on a separate fee basis.

Thus the exporting UK firm has no foreign credit risk and the service is particularly useful to companies which do not wish to grant export credit terms yet are not able to obtain a L/C from their buyer.

In some cases, a confirming house will also arrange shipment or will act for the buyer in controlling shipping dates from the UK.

Some confirming houses have an on-going relationship, or even a trading agreement, with overseas buyers to seek out suitable products and negotiate purchase details.

A special type of confirming house is the 'stores buyer' firm which undertakes purchasing of UK products for overseas department stores and thus provides a valuable contact point for UK firms marketing relevant products.

Factoring

An exporter can sell his export debts to a factoring company and thus relieve himself of the tasks of credit checking, ledgering, some documentation and collection as well as (usually) eliminating any risk of bad debt or currency loss.

The worries for the exporter of creditworthiness of buyers, the stability of the buyer's country and the mystiques of foreign collections can be taken on by the factor, in return for a service fee of between $3/4\%$ and $2^1/2\%$ of the sales value. In addition, the collections can be advanced at an agreed percentage over Base Rate.

Usually a factoring agreement is signed between the exporter and the factoring company the outset, whereby the factor agrees to purchase without recourse the exporter's debts as they are invoiced, on terms up to 180 days, and to pay a proportion, e.g. 75% of the invoice value to the exporter immediately.

The finance charge for the advance is based on the exporter's previous average collection period, e.g. 82 days.

If the exporter chooses not to draw off the advance percentage, the factor will pay 100% at the agreed average maturity date.

The factor investigates the creditworthiness of customers and establishes Credit Limits. The exporter sells within the Credit Limits and delivers and invoices to customers in the usual way, but sends a copy invoice to the factor.

This enables payment to be advanced to the exporter and also begins the sales ledger operation of the factor, who produces statements and reminders up to the point of payment by the customer.

If the exporter sells above the Credit Limit, the factor may allow this but then has recourse to the exporter in the event of non-payment by the customer.

Invoices in foreign currency are usually converted to Sterling at the rate on the date of receipt by the factor, so that exchange risk is eliminated.

Customers are asked to pay direct to the factor.

The advantages to an exporter of factoring are:

(a)　　Only one debtor – the factor.
(b)　　No sales ledgering necessary.
(c)　　No need to credit check or credit insure.
(d)　　Non-recourse finance available.
(e)　　Regular cash flow.
(f)　　No foreign currency risk.
(g)　　Substantial savings in staff and collection systems.

The disadvantages to be considered are:

(a)　　The service charge may be greater than the cost of employing own staff and systems.
(b)　　Contact with customers is reduced or eliminated.
(c)　　As the business grows and the factor's charge becomes unacceptable, the exporter will have developed no in-house expertise.

Some factors provide another service – Invoice Discounting. Under this scheme, the exporter retains his sales ledger and collection responsibility but still sells his invoices to the factor, at a discount, and is paid a high percentage in advance.

Payments are made by customers to the exporter and customers are usually not aware of the invoice discounting facility with the factor.

For both schemes, factors apply selective criteria to both clients and end-customers. Service charges are decided by country risks, volume and specific difficulties, and finance charges are usually the same or slightly higher than normal bank borrowing rates.

As most factors are owned by the large banks, it may be advantageous for an exporter to deal with the factor owned by his regular bank.

The Association of British Factors, established in 1976, embraces most of the principal factoring companies. It has, as one of its major aims, the promotion of the highest possible standards of professionalism within the industry.

Figure 9.2   The Major UK Factoring Companies

Company	Principal shareholders
Alex. Lawrie Factors Ltd	Lloyds & Scottish Group
Anglo Factoring Services Ltd	Security Pacific Eurofinance Inc
Arbuthnot Factors Ltd	Arbuthnot Latham Bank Ltd Yorkshire Bank plc
Century Factors Ltd	Close Brothers Ltd
Credit Factoring International Ltd	Wholly owned by National Westminster Bank
Griffin Factors Ltd	Forward Trust Group Ltd, a member of Midland Bank Group
H. & H. Factors Ltd	Fuji Bank Hambros Bank plc
International Factors Ltd	Lloyds & Scottish Group

Factors Chain International (FCI) is a huge worldwide association started in 1964. It has 65 member companies in 27 countries, with Arbuthnot's from the UK. The code of reciprocal conduct allows rapid credit checking and collection of accounts in the countries of other members.

Exfinco (the export finance company)

Were established by the former head of a leading factoring company, in 1985, to provide exporters with a 'one-stop' solution to export finance, i.e. to support them with finance from order-taking through to payment including foreign currency transactions.

The Exfinco service is based on the 'undisclosed principal' concept, with a standing offer to buy a client's products for cash at date of shipment, then appoint the exporter as agent for the sale of the products.

The exporter only has to send Exfinco copy invoices and receives the credit insured value, usually 90%, without recourse. ECGD or Trade Indemnity cover must be held by the exporter. Currency invoices are converted at best spot rates if sterling is required. If customers default, the exporter claims from his credit insurance policy on behalf of Exfinco.

Exfinco's excellent FSA (Forward Sale Agreement) facility allows exporters to quote confidently in currency and be paid at shipment at the agreed rate, with all credit and currency risk for Exfinco.

Procedure:

1. Exporter requests a Forward Sale Agreement.
2. On receipt of an order, exporter calls for Exfinco to establish a currency rate to obtain the required Sterling.
3. Invoice is sent to Exfinco referenced to the FSA.
4. Exfinco pay exporter 90% of sterling value 3 days later. The balance of 10% is paid at the customer DSO average date.

Exfinco's charge, of an all-in fee at a percentage above base rate for the credit period, is deducted from the cash payment at shipment. The rate is similar to normal overdraft rate but the comprehensive services included, at no extra charge, make the rate very economical.

For small exporters, defined as having sales less than £500,000 per year, there is the FINFOREX service, a variation of the standard facility. It encourages new and small exporters to be more competitive by selling in customers' currencies, with all the benefits of a big-company treasury operation behind them.

Trade finance from clearing banks

From the 60s to the mid-80s, the most exports that were not financed out of overdraft, depended on the ECGD Comprehensive Bank Guarantee (CBG) which provided 100% finance through the banks at 5/8% over base rate, for sales with basic ECGD cover. Obviously the interest rate was heavily subsidized by the government and when the scheme was finally withdrawn in 1986 the clearing banks acted in various ways to provide alternatives.

The two problems for the banks were how to provide 100% of cash if they themselves were not guaranteed by ECGD any more, and how much to charge for taking over the credit risk.

Barclays Bank offer the 'Tradeline' scheme for exporters with an ECGD policy and 'Tradeflow' for those without, and for the Smaller Exporters Scheme members. Both agreements allow for debt purchase or goods purchase as undisclosed principals, and payment can be in sterling or currency, except that SES payments can only be in sterling. The cost of the schemes vary slightly, with a flat charge added to the interest charge for Tradeflow, to cover ECGD premium paid by Barclays.

Lloyds Bank have their Finance for Exports scheme for companies exporting over £1 million per year. Like Barclays, Lloyds have their own policy with ECGD, but unlike Barclays, clients become joint policy-holders with Lloyds, even if they have their own ECGD policy. Lloyds require an acceptable spread of risks, all of which must be insured, then pay out 90% on both bills and open account, without recourse, and in either sterling or currency.

National Westminster Bank's scheme is called 'Export Ease' in three varieties. The Joint Policy Plan is for prime corporate customers with exports over £1 million and it finances individual transactions over £10 000. 90% is provided without recourse on the back of the exporter's own ECGD policy, but accepted drafts are preferred to open account business. (Note: over 60% of exports from UK are on open account terms and likely to increase in the northern part of the single European market post-1992.) Fees are charged as negotiable interest rates on credit periods plus handling charges for drafts.

The Insured Export Scheme is for established customers of the bank with exports over £250 000 and individually over £10 000. The bank has its own ECGD policy and requires ECGD's approval of the exporter's suitability to join the scheme. Again 90% is financed for either bills or open account. A flat charge is made based on volume and credit terms, plus an annual facility fee.

The Confirming Finance Scheme is for bills business of large corporates exporting over £1 million per year with individual transactions above £50 000. 100% is provided, without recourse, on the bank's own ECGD policy.

There is a scheme for Smaller Exporters defined as 'small business customers of the bank' exporting up to £250 000 per year and individual deals up to £10 000. Only drafts and promissory notes are financed at 90% without recourse, and clients must not have their own ECGD cover. An annual facility fee is charged plus a flat charge for 12 months according to volume and credit terms. There is an ECGD premium surcharge for foreign currency sales and a charge for each buyer credit limit approved.

The Royal Bank of Scotland also have three schemes. Two of them are similar to those above, but one is a variant of confirming house business. Each foreign buyer signs a contract with the bank's confirming house subsidiary and receives a revolving line of credit. The exporter receives 100% at shipment, without recourse, with charges paid by the customer (in view of the credit period they receive from the bank.)

Midland Bank's scheme, called MIDFES, was the first of the clearing bank schemes to replace the CBG. It provides 90% finance without recourse, to exporters selling more than £1 million per year. Exporters have to become joint ECGD policy holders with Midland, who take care of administration of the policy. Fees are quoted individually, according to risk as well as the credit period and value.

In all the above trade finance schemes operated by the banks, the exclusion conditions and non-insured markets, plus the time taken to respond to applications for finance, are all reasons given by exporters for adverse comparisons with the former CBG scheme.

Forfaiting

This fast developing form of non-recourse finance now takes many forms, including some of the trade finance schemes above. It has existed for many years as an alternative to credit-insured finance for medium-term credit in excess of one year but forfaiting is now available on credit terms down to 90 days. The principles and procedure are fully described in the Medium-Term finance section that follows.

Medium-term finance

Where the buyer's obligation to pay extends over a long period, no exporter can afford just to wait and hope. Even for a fully creditworthy customer and market, a long credit period can see a change in circumstances. This is why some 95% of medium-term credit is insured by ECGD or the private market. And the same time-effect causes exporters to want their money with certainty at the outset. Whereas most banks will advance money as long as they can claim it back if the customer doesn't pay, the 'certainty' required by exporters means that some organization has to be asked to take over the risk, and relevant charge will arise. Thus medium-term finance can be wholly or partly without recourse to the exporter and any risk can be carried, by the exporter, the financing bank, or a credit insurer. It follows that an exporter will pay more for 'non-recourse' than 'with recourse' money.

There is also a choice between finance for supplier credit or buyer credit: supplier credit is the most usual form, where the exporter, as supplier, gives credit to the customer, but is repaid eventually by the customer. In buyer credit, a bank makes a loan to the buyer or his bank, and pays the exporter cash at shipment, then the borrower repays the bank, not the exporter.

ECGD specific bank guarantee (SBG)

The government, through its agency ECGD, guarantees a bank for 100% of the value it finances on a contract for two years credit or longer. Medium-term credit usually calls for 15% to be paid by the buyer before shipment, leaving 85% to be paid in installments (usually equal and 6-monthly), covered by bills of exchange accepted by the buyer in favour of the exporter, or promissory notes drawn by the buyer in favour of the exporter.

To qualify for the bank finance, the exporter must have ECGD cover for the contract itself.

The installment bills are sent for acceptance and then purchased by the bank from the exporter without recourse. In the event of non-payment, the bank will claim from ECGD under the SBG, and ECGD will have recourse to the exporter for the self-retention percentage of the basic contract cover, usually 5% or 10%.

The interest rate is that currently in force for the category of market, I, II, or III, under the Consensus Guidelines and has the great benefit, for all concerned, of being fixed for the total period of credit. (Note: from 1988, EEC contracts do not qualify for the subsidized, fixed interest rates.)

It is estimated that fewer than 200 UK exporters are seriously competitive in the capital goods field, and the standard ECGD product is very well understood by all of them. They know that it is necessary to speak to both ECGD and a financing bank very early in the negotiations for business, to ensure that:

(a)   cover will be indicated as available for the contract; and

(b)   the bank, if guaranteed by ECGD, is willing to advance the funds at the agreed rates.

The bank will charge a commitment fee for tying up the funds in advance and prudent exporters establish all the financing and administration costs before prices are agreed with buyers.

In certain rare cases, ECGD agree to guarantee banks who finance pre-shipment expenses for production, where such money is essential to the UK company bidding for orders above 1 million.

ECGD comprehensive extended terms banker's guarantee (CXBG)

This is available where an exporter is a regular user of the Specific Bank Guarantee scheme for contracts insured under a Supplemental Extended Terms Guarantee. The CXBG covers a 12-month period during which the exporter sends details of each extended terms approval to the bank and applies for financing. The bank issues a contract approval and confirms that advances will be made available against Bills or Promissory Notes. The CXBG will not roll liabilities forward from one year to the next but will concertina into one guarantee all the Specific Bank Guarantees for one year. The same procedure for recourse to the exporter applies as in the SBG facility.

ECGD buyer credit – single contract cover

Whereas an exporter normally gives credit to his buyer, on short or medium terms, and finances this credit from his own borrowing resources, it is possible on major contracts to arrange 'Buyer Credit', where a UK bank makes a loan to the foreign buyer and pays the exporter cash at shipment.

Single contract cover from ECGD can make Consensus-rate finance available on capital goods contracts with a value of £1 million or more, where medium-term credit (i.e. up to five years) or long-term credit (i.e. over five years) is required. (See 'Lines of Credit Cover' below for details of similar finance for small-value contracts.)

The exporter should approach ECGD and his bank very early in the contract negotiations because of the rather complex requirements of the specific agreements involved.

Buyer Credit finance requires four separate agreements:

(a)   *The supply contract* between exporter and buyer.
(b)   *The loan agreement* between UK bank and buyer/borrower.
(c)   *The guarantee agreement* between ECGD and the UK bank.
(d)   *The premium agreement* between ECGD and the exporter.

A bank loan under Buyer Credit cover will normally be limited to 85% of the contract price. By international agreement, the buyer must pay 15% by the delivery date and this proportion must be financed by non-ECGD backed sources.

The bank, which is 100% guaranteed by ECGD, pays the exporter in the UK at the stipulated contract stages. As each payment is made, the bank's loan to the foreign buyer is increase, but this is between the bank and the buyer and is of no direct concern to the exporter who has been paid without recourse. However, contractual and commercial responsibilities between exporter and buyer are not reduced in any way by the ECGD guarantee to the UK bank.

Premium rates are similar to those for Specific policies although the total premium costs are generally higher because credit periods are generally longer in Buyer Credit than in Supplier Credit.

In direct contrast to Specific Credit finance, all bank fees are payable by the foreign borrower.

The advantages of Buyer Credit financing are considerable for the exporter:

(a)   Construction and pre-shipment costs can be paid for, if such payments are specified in the supply contract.
(b)   There is no recourse claim on the exporter if the buyer defaults. Therefore, there is no contingent liability to be noted in the exporter's Balance Sheet.
(c)   The contract, although probably complex commercially, can be regarded as an export cash contract.

The disadvantages of taking a Buyer Credit approach to financing a contract can be summarized as:

(a)   Negotiating difficulties in putting together a supply contract that suits ECGD *before* it will agree to guarantee the UK bank.
(b)   The buyer may prefer a more straightforward Supplier Credit deal involving, say ten half-yearly Bills of Exchange over five years.

(c)   There may be political difficulties in a foreign buyer taking a long-term loan from a British bank.

ECGD lines of credit

In addition to Buyer Credit finance for single major contracts, ECGD issues guarantees to UK banks for lines of credit made available to foreign banks or financial bodies.

Under these lines of credit, capital goods contracts can be negotiated for relatively small values. Exactly the same requirements apply as in single contract cover above, except that ECGD approval of the supply contract conditions is not so stringent.

There are basically two types of line of credit cover:

(a)   Project Line of Credit, where several individual UK contracts might be awarded to tie in with a major foreign activity, such as an oil exploration project.
(b)   General Purpose Lines of Credit sometimes called 'shopping-basket credits', where a foreign buying institution places several small contracts for capital goods and related services, usually for several different projects or purposes, up to the total value of the line of credits.

Exporters should keep themselves constantly updated on lines of credit available to them. Several are under-utilized at any one time and there is room for initiative in getting contracts included by the particular foreign government or buyer.

The Department of Trade and Industry publishes details quarterly, in the 'British Business' magazine, listing:

● Foreign country and borrowing body.
● UK bank (or syndicate of banks).
● Decription of eligible contracts and values.
● Loan value.
● Closing dates.

Alternatively, exporters can enquire through ECGD.

Forfaiting

This provides 100% non-recourse finance for short or medium-term credit, by means of the purchase by a specialist bank of bills of exchange or promissory notes which have been guaranteed by a major bank in the buyer's country.

Neither the bank nor the exporter needs credit insurance cover, since the debt is regarded no longer as a trade credit risk, but rather as sovereign risk. The non-recourse to the exporter also means there is no risk from transfer delay at the due date.

The tremendous benefit of knowing that payment is rapid and safe, and from a forfaiting bank in London, is however subject to a difficult requirement – that of obtaining the 'aval' or guarantee on the bills of a major bank. In the case of poorer countries, this would almost certainly be the Central Bank.

The facility lends itself to exports to government or ministry customers, or to local suppliers of those end-users, or simply for products which are so important to the market that official payment guarantees are willingly given.

Whereas up to the 1970s, forfaiting was a skill practised by banks mainly in Switzerland, the market then moved to London, where there are now many banks, both specialist and divisions of major banks.

The National Westminster Bank's specialist unit quotes the benefits of forfaiting as:

- The balance sheet and cash flow effects of converting debtors to cash.
- Foreign exchange risk removed.
- Fixed rate finance at rates quoted before contract prices are committed.
- Finance available in all major currencies.
- Credit periods financed from 90 days to 5 years or more.
- No country risks.
- No source restriction on goods (e.g. do not have to be UK origin).
- No need for credit insurance cover.

The cost to the exporter is made up of three elements:

- Interest rate, for the credit period.
- Bank margin, for the risk and work involved.
- Commitment fee, for committing funds up to purchase of bills, or cancellation date if applicable.

The total cost is expressed as a single fee charged as a percentage of the transaction value, and deducted at the time the bank purchases the bills.

The banks issue guideline tariffs showing, for indication purposes only, the rates applying to various markets for various currencies.

There are considerable benefits in forfaiting bills in currencies such as Yen, Swiss Francs and D. Marks, where the interest rates are invariably lower than sterling. The single fee of forfaiting, say, Swiss Franc bills drawn on a customer in a risky market such as Brazil, can be less than any other combined finance plus protection.

The terminology of forfaiting is easily demystified: the word forfaiting is from the French 'a forfait', meaning the forfeiting of one's rights, in this case to a debt; the need to have bills 'avalized' is an anglicization of the French 'aval', meaning guarantee.

The essential guarantee can take one of three forms:

- The 'per aval' guarantee and signature of the major bank across the face of the bill of exchange accepted by the customer, or across the face of his promissory note
  or
- A letter of guarantee from the major bank, referring indisputably to the debt being forfaited
  or
- A special agreement by letter, between the major bank and the forfaiting bank.

It is vital in every case that the exporter approaches a forfaiting bank in advance, to establish:

(a)　　their willingness to undertake the forfaiting.
(b)　　the cost (usually to go into pricing).

Leasing

An exporter considering a leasing agreement with a foreign customer will usually sell the equipment to a UK leasing company which then provides a leasing facility to the customer. In this way, the exporter has cash or secure payment for his product.

The major banks and many leasing companies in the UK are able to help exporters, particularly of capital goods, by introducing them or their products to leasing companies in their customers' countries.

Thus the exporter generally has a choice of selling his product to a UK leasing company or to a foreign leasing company which will make local leasing arrangements for the buyer.

There are two broad ranges of lease agreements:

(a)   *Operational Leases:* where foreign earnings are produced on the assets which remain the property of the UK company.

(b)   *Full-Payout Leases:* where the full value of the product is recovered during the lease period, plus a profit margin and interest costs. At the end of the lease period, the foreign lessee can either purchase the equipment outright or continue the lease at a nominal fee.

The exporter should receive at least 15% of the total rent by the date of shipment, and the lease agreement stipulate payment of the balance at no greater than six-monthly installments.

Tax advantages in leasing vary in different countries, but the principal motivation for a leasing company is the tax allowance on purchasing capital equipment.

The advantages of leasing are normally taken to be:

● Balance sheet benefit of lower fixed assets and capital.
● Much reduced initial expense in obtaining assets.
● Repayments can be matched with earnings from asset.
● Lease period is normally longer than standard credit period.
● Repayments are allowed for tax as expenses.

Foreign currency finance

Traditionally, UK firms have borrowed their own currency, sterling, when financing exports. It is now becoming more popular for companies with regular and substantial foreign activity to obtain financing in the currencies of their customer markets.

Currency borrowings fall into three categories:

(a)   Amounts borrowed for up to six months to be repaid by sales receipts in the same currencies.

(b)   Loans for capital expenditure or overseas investment, with repayment over a period of years out of currency income.

(c)   Fixed-interest-rate loans to finance large contracts for the export of capital goods.

The currencies available are those in which there is trading in the Euro-currency market at any particular time. The two advantages of currency loans over sterling borrowings are:

- interest rates are usually lower.
- exchange risk is avoided by repaying loans with trade receipts or earnings in the same currencies.

Loans in advance of short-term receipts

On sales made in foreign currencies, there is normally a risk of exchange loss arising if the currency concerned has become weaker than the pound between invoice date and payment date. In other words, the customer's payment in currency may not produce the full sterling value required.

Exporters may therefore prefer to borrow foreign currencies against the value of exports in the same currencies, on terms up to six months.

The amount of currency borrowed can be converted to sterling immediately by the exporter's bank and the exchange risk is eliminated by repayment of the loan from the currency received from the foreign customer.

The risk is this type of finance is that the foreign customer does not pay at maturity. The exporter must then buy currency at spot rate, possibly suffering a loss, to repay the loan.

If the exporter borrows in this way, he cannot also sell forward his expected currency receipts, as they are required to repay the loan. Thus, any premium available cannot be taken.

The interest rate on a Euro-currency loan is decided by the domestic interest rate of the foreign country concerned. Since the forward premium on selling the currency forward is based on the difference between UK interest rates and those of the other country, there is normally little or no difference in cost between taking a loan or selling forward.

Eurocurrency loans

There are three main types of Euro-currency loan:

(a)   Fixed-rate loans.
(b)   Floating-rate loans.
(c)   Stand-by credits.

FIXED-RATE LOANS

A straightforward fixed-interest basis for up to five years repayment, where the exporter can easily fix his costs and arrange suitable repayment. The disadvantage is that market interest rates on other finance may reduce considerably during the period of the loan and early repayment may not be possible.

FLOATING-RATE LOANS

On floating rate Euro-currency loans for up to five years, interest is usually chargeable with six-monthly rate changes. This is because the underlying inter-bank loans are reviewed on a six-monthly basis.

Some floating-rate loans have a multi-currency clause, which gives the exporter the opportunity to switch repayment into a weaker currency so that it will cost less to repay at maturity.

The advantage of floating-rate currency loans versus other types of funding must be carefully assessed by the exporter with his bank and will depend upon the reliability and frequency of foreign income receipts.

STAND-BY CREDITS

When related to Euro-currency loans, a stand-by credit is simply a commitment given by a bank to provide an exporter with a currency loan at an agreed interest rate. A commitment fee is charged, usually at 1% per annum on unused funds, and the commitment is reviewed at regular intervals.

Large project loans

Foreign currency loans from UK banks to foreign buyers/borrowers can be arranged to finance contracts approved by ECGD under Buyer Credit facilities.

Currently, for Buyer Credit projects up to £5 millions, the exporter can decide between financing in sterling or currency, but can only finance in currency for contracts above £5 millions, except in EEC countries where the option applies to all values.

International aid

There are many reasons for funds to be provided as 'aid', some of them politically expedient in origin, but the fundamental need of some countries for assistance in paying for essential imports is not disputed. The basic cause is the imbalance in wealth between nations, especially on a per capita income measurement, and the imbalance is caused in turn by a combination of population growth and slow industrial development in the poorer countries (i.e. net 'demand' status) versus stable populations and mature industrialization in the richer ones (i.e. net 'supply' status).

It has been estimated that 150 of the world's 208 countries are net importers on a continuing basis, which appears to be an insoluble problem. How can they ever afford to pay for supplies to feed and shelter their increasing millions?

Until success is achieved with the various development programmes intended to reduce import needs and increase export earnings, there are several agencies, bilateral and multilateral, which supply money for immediate needs and also for longer-term infrastructure projects.

There are two different views on international aid:

- it should be 'tied', because
  money would be more plentiful if donor countries could be sure it would be spent on their exports

or

- it should not be tied, because
  poor countries can spend their rare aid more sensibly if it is not restricted to contracts with the donor countries.

Most exporting firms never become involved in aid-funded contracts, as most aid is spent on large projects which appeal only to capital goods contractors. But all companies should be aware of the facilities and their mechanisms, in case of need for occasional business. For example, exporters who risk-categorize their markets according to their ability to generate hard currency – so that the exporters do not waste marketing expense – have policies such as 'CILC only for high-risk markets, except for aid-funded opportunity orders'.

World bank

Probably the most famous aid agency. It is based in Washington and has close ties with various committees and pressure groups in the United Nations. The World Bank concentrates on aid for developing countries and has three operating units:

- International Bank for Reconstruction and Development (IBRD).
- International Development Agency (IDA).
- International Finance Corporation (IFC).

The stated aims of the IBRD and IDA are 'to promote economic progress in developing countries by providing financial and technical assistance in both the public and private sectors'. The IDA works with the most poor countries.

The IFC is different in that it works to arrange capital funding to stimulate growth in the private sector.

The organizations were set up after WW2 alongside the International Monetary Fund (the IMF) which was intended to stabilize international currencies. The Comecon countries chose not to join either body and the IBRD is now 'owned' by some 140 countries who subscribe capital for its redistribution.

The IBRD lends funds for up to 20 years to government-backed projects, while the IDA will go to 60 years. Given the parlous state of foreign debt repayment by the same beneficiary countries, the status of the IBRD and IDA loans can be considered more akin to grants.

World Bank projects are publicized in various business bulletins, but principally in the UN fortnightly called 'Development Business'. All projects must be open to international tender but the task for exporters is to get involved early enough in the planning stage of a funded project to stand a chance of competing effectively in the tendering.

World Bank payments are made reliably on completion of contracts, or at agreed contractual stages, and usually in US dollars.

European development fund (EDF)

The European Community undertakes its own many and varied aid programmes according to resolutions of its parliament from time to time.

However, the major EC activity is based on the Lome Conventions, of which the 'Third' one is currently in process, whereby EC members supply aid to 66 'ACP' countries (Africa, Caribbean and Pacific).

Some £5 billion has been allocated to projects in agriculture, transport and industrialization. The money is provided for approved business in the form of grants for 80% and soft loans, i.e. very low interest rates fixed for long periods, for the balance.

The process for funding begins when an ACP country applies for aid for a specific purpose. Aid officials visit to verify the scope and justification of the project and it is at this stage of prior publicity and feasibility study that exporters have the opportunity to get involved with end-users.

The EC monthly publication 'ACP – EEC Courier' gives details of current and planned projects.

The Lome Conventions are not just to facilitate aid programmes. In return for projects guaranteed to be placed with EC exporters, the ACP states have free access to EC markets for agricultural produce without any tariff restrictions.

Other European Community aid

Annual programmes for EC aid and co-operation in trade are agreed with other groups of nations:

- Asia and Latin America (the ALA group).
- the Maghreb (Morocco, Algeria, Tunisia).
- the Mashraq (Egypt, Syria, Jordan, Lebanon).
- the Mediterranean Group (Cyprus, Malta, Israel).

Arab development agencies

There are several agencies which came into being after the dramatic increases in oil prices in the 1970s, to try to redistribute revenue within Arab countries in order to speed up development. The best known is the OPEC Fund for International Development. The Islamic Development Bank operates strictly to Islamic law and principles, mainly distinguished by its participation in projects rather than charging interest on loans.

Other development banks

All regions of the world have accepted the concept of sharing out to poorer countries an annual amount of funding supplied by richer ones. There is the

Asian Development Bank, based in Manila; the African Development Bank in the Ivory Coast; the Inter-American Development Bank in Washington; and the Caribbean Development Bank in Barbados.

Tenders are published internationally, but opportunities are few and total funding is smaller than the World Bank schemes.

Bilateral schemes

Every major country makes its own arrangements for aid to individual countries, in addition to its commitments to multi-nation groupings. The USA has its agency for international aid known as USAID; Germany has its KFW and the UK operates through the government's Overseas Development Agency (ODA), part of the Projects and Export Policy Division (PEP) of the Department of Trade and Industry.

In 1979 the Government decided that a portion of Overseas Aid should be directed to be of commercial advantage to UK exports. This small part is aimed at supporting major projects that meet specific economic criteria. The Overseas Development Agency will process applications for contract-linked aid in two months and will award aid so as to:

(i)   match the aid element of foreign competitors' bids supported by 'mixed credits';
(ii)   help entry into difficult markets which offer substantial opportunities;
(iii)   provide up to 100% of the cost of feasibility studies that will improve chances of winning major contracts.

Information on aid

The two principal ways for exporters to maximize the opportunities afforded by aid-funded business are to use specialist consultants who will work on their behalf to obtain exact details and documentation, or to make direct contact at intervals with the agencies mentioned. In the latter case, time can be saved by approaching the World Aid Section of the Department of Trade and Industry in London, who attempt to keep accurate records of the state of play of projects funded by development aid.

As ever, in the highly competitive world of exporting, the onus is on exporters to be well-placed, in their markets of interest, to find out about forthcoming contract opportunities, whether as main contractors or, in the case of smaller firms, as suppliers into larger firms.

10　Foreign currency

Overview of currency situations

This chapter deals with the practical applications of foreign currency in exporting – pricing in currency to help with orders and increase profits; negotiating with banks to obtain rates of exchange; and day to day procedures to handle the risks involved. Examples and calculations are given, to explain the terminology. However, there is no substitute for practical experience and every export credit manager should develop the skills needed to deal with banks, foreign customers and sales staff.

A good way for an exporter to test his grasp of theory and practical ability to be to feel confident enough to:

● Explain the structure and terminology of the FX market.
● Identify the factors which influence exchange rates.
● Describe the steps involved in pricing quotations and invoices in foreign currencies to achieve planned sterling values.
● Calculate the sterling equivalent of currency receipts and unpaid billings.
● Select the appropriate method to offset risks of exchange losses.

Sterling is an alien currency for every export customer. They have to worry about the cost of buying sterling with their own currencies, to settle the UK exporter's invoices. Because exchange rates change unpredictably from day to day, foreign customers face an uncertain cost at future dates.

If the exporter helps his customers by invoicing them in their own currencies, then he takes on the problem instead, because he does not know how much sterling he will get when he banks the customers' currency payments.

So, in every export transaction, either exporter or customer must cope with a foreign currency. And if the sale is in a third currency, say US dollars for a UK export to Brazil, then both parties have to deal with an alien currency.

It may help win an order from a customer in France to price and invoice in

French Francs or an American in US dollars. Customers feel more comfortable comparing prices in their own currency.

An exporter who invoices in a foreign currency, runs two different kinds of risk:

● the exchange risk : that when funds are received, the rate of exchange produces less sterling than expected.
● the soft currency risk : that funds may not be convertible to sterling because there is no demand for them in the banking system.

Fortunately, London has the world's most extensive FX market, with expert advice readily available for exporters, so that neither the exchange risk nor the soft currency problem should be a barrier to competitive export marketing.

The day-to-day problem is the irregular and unpredictable fluctuations in exchange rates. In this century, up to World War II, major currencies remained unchanged for very long periods. Stability was reinforced by strong trade agreements between powerful nations and by the imperial influences of major powers such as Britain and France. Because prices and volumes of trade were largely controlled, the values of currencies against one another had little reason to change.

WW2 was followed by the break up of empires, the loosening of trade agreements and independent viability of many countries. The volatile import and export performance of most countries plus excessive government borrowings in recent years have caused fluctuations in demand for individual currencies.

Another vital ingredient in the currency mix is exchange control regulations. In 1972, the IMF (International Monetary Fund) persuaded the UK to fix the value of the £ Sterling at 2.6 US dollars. This was meant to achieve stability by giving a reliable base of the two leading currencies.

The agreement required the UK government strictly to control export and import payments. Whenever poor UK export performance (= low demand for sterling) caused the exchange rate to drop below $2.6, the government had to intervene by selling reserves to buy sterling. Before long, reserves were massively depleted, so that sterling had to be allowed to 'float' again, to find its own value without government action. Rates of exchange remain as unpredictable as ever.

This is what makes business pricing difficult and there are no forecasters with a constantly accurate track record on predicting exchange rates.

Risks in foreign exchange

- The currency of the sale may not be freely convertible in the London FX market – this can be checked in advance.
- A fully convertible hard currency is subject to fluctuations in its rate of exchange to the £.
- Payment delays increase the exchange rate risk.
- The customer's country may impose controls which restrict, delay or completely ban expected payments.

The risk of volatile exchange rates has to be seen against the waiting period. Although rates can become more favourable as well as less, a good business rule is that the shorter the credit period for the sale, the less the currency risk.

So, time is a major element in currency risk. For example, the exchange rate will almost certainly change between issuing a price list and receiving the currency for a sale, producing either a windfall profit or an unplanned loss for the exporter.

Any amount lost due to exchange rates must be related to the projected profit on the transaction. In a severe case, the entire profit can be lost.

Example: In a £10 000 sale, your planned net profit is 8% or £800. Your invoice is priced at $20 000 using a rate of $2.00 to the £. When you receive the $20 000 payment two months later, the exchange rate is $2.2 and you receive only £9090 from the bank. The exchange loss exceeds your sale profit. But if the rate had moved instead to $1.9 you would have received £10 526, an unexpected exchange profit of £526 on top of the transaction profit.

It is easy to think of risks to prices and receipts; but other exporting decisions are affected by currency rates:

- Planning future sales values.
- Sales and profit forecasts.
- Personal negotiations and quotations.
  (Haggling in currency, where to drop your local currency price to a point where the exchange rate could produce a loss on the sale!)

There may also be late payment by the customer (remember, the longer the wait, the greater the risk), or a complete non-payment because of insolvency. Or the need to repay currency loans or other obligations, which depend on receipt of customers' payments.

An increasing problem these days is that more and more countries cannot cope with their foreign debt burdens. This reduces their scope for importing the goods they need, and delays their ability to pay even for the reduced import values. Imagine a rather poor, less developed country and the following possible effects of their foreign currency crisis.

(a)   Reduced FX reserves mean fewer planned imports.

(b)   Imports are classified as either priority or luxury goods.

(c)   Import licences are essential for all imports, and it is difficult for importers to justify licences for luxury goods.

(d)   Foreign currency can only be allocated to licensed imports.

(e)   A minimum of six months credit is required for all imports.

(f)   A ban on all foreign payments for two years, or the offer of 40% settlement on existing debts.

(g)   A tight reclassification of all unused import licences.

As well as the non-availability of currency from some countries, there is the risk of non-convertibility, that is, the FX market in London is not willing to exchange them for pounds or other hard currency. Examples might be Zambian Kwachas, Egyptian Pounds, Chilean Pesos, and so on. It is important to avoid this risk by not contracting to take payment in 'soft' currencies, i.e. by contracting in an acceptable hard currency. However, for exporters faced with owning soft currencies, usually 'blocked' in the buyer's country, there are usually quasi-bank schemes for local disposal of the funds at a large discount, perhaps as high as 50%.

In case it all seems too hazardous to bother with, remember that the alternative of insisting on sterling prices and payments, transfers the problem to customers, which then impacts competitiveness.

The foreign exchange market

The FX market is not a particular place like the Stock Exchange or the Metal Exchange. It is a mixture of individuals and banks linked by telephone, telex and computer screen. The dealers in the market are:

- the major British banks
- some of the foreign banks in London
- some merchant banks
- major banks in major foreign business centres (Frankfurt, Hong Kong, New York, West Coast USA, Tokyo, etc.)
- brokers dealing between the dealers.

Up to the 1920s, FX dealers did meet in a particular place, the London

Figure 10.1   World Value of the Pound (by Permission of the Financial Times)

FT GUIDE TO WORLD CURRENCIES

The table below gives the latest available rates of exchange (rounded) against four key currencies on Monday, June 19, 1989. In some cases the rate is nominal. Market rates are the average of buying and selling rates except where they are shown to be otherwise. In some cases market rates have been calculated from those of foreign currencies to which they are tied.

COUNTRY	£ STG.	US $	D-MARK	YEN (X 100)
Afghanistan (Afghani)	99.25	64.0735	32.4877	44.3575
Albania (Lek)	10.1908	6.5789	3.3357	4.5545
Algeria (Dinar)	11.7126	7.5613	3.8339	5.2346
Andorra (F Fr)	10.3700	6.6946	3.3944	4.6346
Andorra (Sp Peseta)	193.15	124.6933	63.2242	86.3240
Angola (Kwanza)	47.587	30.7211	15.5767	21.2679
Antigua (E Carr $)	32.526	20.9806	10.6393	14.5553
Argentina (Austral)	322.526	207.0406	105.4237	143.9553
Aruba (Florin)	2.7530	1.7772	0.9011	1.2303
Australia (Aus $)	2.0452	1.3203	0.6694	0.9140
Austria (Schilling)	21.535	13.9025	7.0490	9.6245
Azores (Port Escudo)	256.20	165.3970	83.8625	114.5027
Bahamas (Bahama $)	1.5490		0.5070	0.6922
Bahrain (Dinar)	0.5770	0.3724	0.1888	0.2578
Balteric Is (Sp Peseta)	193.15	124.6933	63.2242	86.3240
Bangladesh (Taka)	47.80	30.8586	15.6464	21.3631
Barbados (Barb $)	3.0934	1.9970	1.0125	1.3825
Belgium (Belg Fr)	64.05c / 64.50g	41.3492 / 41.6397	20.9656 / 21.1129	28.6256 / 28.8268
Belize (B $)	3.0760	1.9857	1.0068	1.3747
Benin (CFA Fr)	518.50	334.7320	169.7217	231.7318
Bermuda (Bermudian $)	1.5490		0.5070	0.6922
Bhutan (Ngultrum)	25.00	16.1394	8.1833	11.1731
Bolivia (Boliviano)	4.0296	2.6014	1.3190	1.8009
Botswana (Pula)	2.7917	1.8023	0.9140	1.2478
Brazil (Cruzado)	1.5490	1.566	0.5864	0.8002
British Virgin Is (US $)	1.5490		0.5070	0.6922
Brunei (Brunei $)	3.029	1.9554	0.9914	1.3537
Bulgaria (Lev)	1.3560	0.8766	0.4445	0.6069
Burkina Faso (CFA Fr)	518.50	334.7320	169.7217	231.7318
Burma (Kyat)	12.1868	7.8644	3.9448	5.3818?
Burundi (Burundi Fr)	254.55	164.3318	83.3224	113.7653
Cameroon (CFA Fr)	518.50	334.7320	169.7217	231.7318
Canada (Canadian $)	1.8540	1.1969	0.6068	0.8286
Canary Is (Sp Peseta)	193.15	124.6933	63.2242	86.3240
Cp. Verde Is (CV Escudo)	125.3701	80.9361	41.0376	56.0313
Cayman Is	1.2578			
Cent. Afr. Rep (CFA Fr)	518.50	334.7320	169.7217	231.7318
Chad (CFA Fr)	518.50	334.7320	169.7217	231.7318
Chile (Chilean Peso)	394.381	254.1381	128.8576	175.9374
China (Renminbi Yuan)	5.7525	3.713b	1.8829	2.5709
Colombia (Col Peso)	579.32	373.996i	189.6301	258.9139
Comoro Is (CFA Fr)	518.50	334.7320	169.7217	231.7318
Congo (Brazz) (CFA Fr)	518.50	334.7320	169.7217	231.7318
Costa Rica (Colon)	124.578	80.4247	40.7783	55.6773
Cuba (Cuban Peso)	1.1713	0.7561	0.3834	0.5234
Cyprus (Cyprus £)	0.7880	0.5087	0.2579	0.3521
Czechoslovakia (Koruna)	24.35c / 15.78i	15.798 / 10.1872	7.9705 / 5.1653	10.8826 / 7.0525

COUNTRY	£ STG	US $	D-MARK	YEN (X 100)
Greenland (Danish Krone)	11.8925	7.6775	3.8927	5.3150
Grenada (E Carr $)	4.1526	2.6808	1.3592	1.8559
Guadaloupe (Loc Fr)	10.3700	6.6946	3.3944	4.6346
Guam (US $)	1.5490		0.5070	0.6922
Guatemala (Quetzal)	4.2300	2.7307	1.3846	1.8905
Guinea (Fr)	461.40	297.8695	151.0310	206.2122
Guinea-Bissau (Peso)	999.70	645.3840	327.2340	20.7016
Guyana (Guyanese $)	46.32	29.9031	15.1620	20.7016
Haiti (Gourde)	7.690	4.9644	2.5171	3.4368
Honduras (Lempira)	3.0607	1.9888	1.0084	1.3768
Hong Kong (HK $)	12.0122	7.7548	3.9319	5.3685
Hungary (Forint)	96.0764	62.0247	31.4489	42.9391
Iceland (Icelandic Krona)	89.75	57.9406	29.3780	40.1117
India (Indian Rupee)	25.00	16.1394	8.1833	11.1731
Indonesia (Rupiah)	2733.215	1764.5029	894.6693	1221.5486
Iran (Rial)	114.75	74.0800	37.5613	51.2889
Iraq (Iraqi Dinar)	0.4793	0.3094	0.1568	0.2142
Irish Rep (Punt)	1.1475	0.7408	0.3756	0.5128
Israel (Shekel)	2.9575	1.9098	0.9776	1.3301
Italy (Lira)	2217.75	1431.7301	725.9410	991.1731
Ivory Coast (CFA Fr)	518.50	334.7320	169.7217	231.7318
Jamaica (Jamaican $)	8.3839	5.4124	2.7443	3.7469
Japan (Yen)	223.75	144.4480	73.2405	100
Jordan (Jordanian Dinar)	0.8730	0.5635	0.2857	0.3901
Kampuchea (Riel)	154.90	100	50.7037	69.2290
Kenya (Kenya Shilling)	32.65	21.0781	10.6873	14.5921
Kiribati (Australian $)	2.0452	1.3203	0.6694	0.9140
Korea North (Won)	1.4919	0.9631	0.4883	0.6667
Korea South (Won)	1025.35	661.9431	335.6301	458.2569
Kuwait (Kuwaiti Dinar)	0.4584	0.2959	0.1500	0.2048
Laos (New Kip)	845.90	546.0942	276.8903	378.0558
Lebanon (Lebanese $)	779.77	503.4021	255.2438	348.5005
Lesotho (Maluti)	4.3182	2.7877	1.4134	1.9299
Liberia (Liberian $)	1.5490		0.5070	0.6922
Libya (Libyan Dinar)	0.4569	0.2600?	0.1494	0.2040
Liechtenstein (Swiss Fr)	2.6600	1.7043	0.8641	1.1798
Luxembourg (Lux Fr)	64.05	41.3492	20.9656	28.6256

COUNTRY	£ STG	US $	D-MARK	YEN (X 100)
Peru (Inti)	4593.68a	2965.5777	1503.6505	2053.0413
Philippines (Peso)	31.90	20.5939	10.4418	14.2569
Pitcairn Is (£ Sterling)	1.00	0.6455	0.3273	0.4469
Pitcairn Is (NZ $)	2.7025	1.7446	0.8846	1.2078
Poland (Zloty)	1293.8	835.2485	423.5024	578.2346
Portugal (Escudo)	256.20	165.3970	83.8625	114.5027
Puerto Rico (US $)	1.5490		0.5070	0.6922
Qatar (Riyal)	5.5780	3.6010	1.8258	2.4929
Reunion Is. de la (F/Fr)	10.3700	6.6946	3.3944	4.6346
Romania (Leu)	14.78i	9.5416	4.8379	6.6055
Rwanda (Fr)	129.15	83.3763	42.2749	57.7206
St Christopher (E Carr $)	4.1526	2.6808	1.3592	1.8559
St Helena (£)	1.00	0.6455	0.3273	0.4469
St Lucia (E Carr $)	4.1526	2.6808	1.3592	1.8559
St Pierre (French Fr)	10.3700	6.6946	3.3944	4.6346
St Vincent (E Carr $)	4.1526	2.6808	1.3592	1.8559
San Marino (Italian Lira)	2217.75	1431.7301	725.9410	991.1731
Sao Tome (Dobra)	168.8173	108.1112	54.8953	72.7675
Saudi Arabia (Riyal)	5.7981	3.7420	725.9410	231.7318
Senegal (CFA Fr)	518.50	334.7320	169.7217	231.7318
Seychelles (Rupee)	8.89	5.7391	2.9099	3.9731
Sierra Leone (Leone)	97.2405	62.7763	31.8299	43.4594
Singapore ($)	3.029	1.9554	0.9914	1.3537
Solomon Is ($)	3.5793	2.3107	1.171b	1.596
Somali Rep (Shilling)	630.58	407.0684	206.4091	281.8234
South Africa (Rand)	4.3182c / 6.2370g	2.877 / 4.0264	1.4134 / 2.0415	1.9299 / 2.7874
Spain (Peseta)	193.15	124.6933	63.2242	86.3240
Spanish Ports in N Africa (Sp Peseta)	193.15	124.6933	63.2242	86.3240
Sri Lanka (Rupee)	52.00	33.5700	17.0212	23.2402
Sudan Rep	6.921	4.4680	2.2654	3.0931
Surinam (Guilder)	2.7453	1.7723	0.8986	1.2269
Swaziland (Lilangeni)	4.3182	2.7877	1.4134	1.9299
Sweden (Krona)	10.3325	6.6704	3.3821	4.6178
Switzerland (Swiss Fr)	2.600	1.7043	0.8641	1.1798
Syria (£)	32.298	20.8508	10.5721	14.4348

Exchange rate table (left block):

Currency				
Denmark (Danish Kroner)	11.8925	7.6775	3.8927	5.3150
Djibouti Rep (Djib Fr)	270.55	174.6610	88.5597	120.9162
Dominica (E Carib $)	4.1526	6.8808	3.3592	1.8559
Dominican Rep (D Peso)	9.8586	6.3644	3.3270	4.4060
Ecuador (Sucre)	783.42o / 847.00a	505.7585 / 546.8043	256.4386 / 277.2504	350.1318 / 378.5474
Egypt (Egyptian £)	3.8526	2.4871	1.2610	1.7218
El Salvador (Colon)	7.70	4.9709	2.5204	3.4413
Equat Guinea (CFA Fr)	518.50	334.7320	169.7217	231.7318
Ethiopia (Ethiopian Birr)	3.1592	2.0395	1.0341	1.4119
Falkland Is (Falk £)	1.00	0.6455	0.3273	0.4469
Faroe Is (Danish Kroner)	11.8925	7.6775	3.8927	5.3150
Fiji (Fiji $)	2.8853	1.8598	0.9427	1.0660
Finland (Markka)	6.337	4.4138	2.2879	3.0556
France (Fr)	10.3700	6.6946	3.3944	4.6346
Fr Cty/Africa (CFA Fr)	518.50	334.7320	169.7217	231.7318
Fr Guiana (Local Fr)	10.3700	6.6946	3.3944	4.6346
Fr Pacific (CFP Fr)	187.00	120.7230	61.2111	83.5754
Gabon (CFA Fr)	518.50	334.7320	169.7217	231.7318
Gambia (Dalasi)	6.2353	3.1615		4.3166
Germany East (Ostmark)	3.0550	1.9722	1	1.3653
Germany West (DMark)	3.0550	1.9722	1	1.3653
Ghana (Cedi)	410.844	265.2317	134.4824	183.6174
Gibraltar (Gib £)	1.00	0.6455	0.3273	0.4469
Greece (Drachma)	262.25	169.3027	85.8428	117.2067

Exchange rate table (right block):

Currency							
Macao (Pataca)	12.3724	7.9873	4.0498	5.5295	25.9522	13.1587	19.9664
Madeira (Port Escudo)	256.20	165.3970	83.8625	114.5027	136.6042	69.2635	94.5698
Malagasy Rep (MG Fr)	2398.18	1541.7559	781.3283	1067.3430	33.3066	12.8314	17.5395
Malawi (Kwacha)	4.3695	2.8208	1.4302	1.9528	34.7120	16.9717	23.1718
Malaysia (Ringgit)	4.1817	2.6996	1.3688	1.8689	1.3203	0.6694	0.9140
Maldive Is (Rufiya)	12.9346	8.3502	4.2339	5.7808	4.2198	2.1396	2.9213
Mali Rep (CFA Fr)	518.50	334.7320	169.7217	231.7318	0.9789	0.4963	0.6777
Malta (Maltese £)	0.5589	0.3608	0.1829	0.2497	2070.7488	1049.9476	1433.5597
Martinique (Local Fr)	10.3700	6.6946	3.3944	4.6346	1.5490	0.5070	0.6922
Mauritania (Ouguiya)	115.5649	74.6473	37.8477	51.5530	2.0452	0.5070	0.9140
Mauritius (Maur Rupee)	24.0786	15.5446	7.8817	10.7613	1.3203	0.6694	
Mexico (Mexican Peso)	3830.77a / 3553.49d	2473.0600 / 2423.1697	1253.9345 / 1228.6382	1712.0759 / 1677.5374	198.1447 / 567.2369	100.468 / 287.6104	137.177i / 392.6c27
Miquelon (Local Fr)	10.3700	6.6946	3.3944	4.6346	3.6575	1.8545	2.532f
Monaco (French Fr)	10.3700	6.6946	3.3944	4.6346	0.6455	0.3273	0.4465
Mongolia (Tugrik)	5.1608	3.3316	1.6992	2.3065	1.5490	0.5070	0.6922
Montserrat (E Carr $)	4.1526	2.6808	1.3592	1.8559	878.65		
Morocco (Dirham)	13.45	8.6830	4.4026	6.0111	0.6515	0.3303	0.4511
Mozambique (Metical)	1130.86	730.0581	370.1669	505.4122	115.6294 / 1431.7301	58.6284 / 725.9410	80.0c31 / 991.i731
Namibia (S A Rand)	4.3182	2.7877	1.4134	1.9299	37.9255	19.2296	26.255d
Nauru Is (Australian $)	2.2482	1.3203	0.6694	0.9140			
Nepal (Nepalese Rupee)	36.912	23.8295	12.0824	16.4969	4468.0438	2265.4464	3093.1.43
Netherlands (Guilder)	3.4425	2.2224	1.1268	1.5385	1	0.5070	0.6922
N'nd Antilles (A/Guilder)	2.7684	1.7872	0.9061	1.2372	1	0.5070	0.6922
New Zealand (NZ $)	2.7025	1.7446	0.8846	1.2078	2.3434	1.1882	1.6223
Nicaragua (Cordoba)	11403.35	7361.7495	3732.6841	5096.4692			
Niger Rep (CFA Fr)	518.50	334.7320	169.7217	231.7318	9.6191	4.8772	6.6592
Nigeria (Naira)	11.3812	7.34747	3.72547	5.0865	0.3405	0.1726	0.2357
Norway (Nor Krone)	11.1100	7.1723	3.6366	4.9653	15624.3124	7922.1145	10816.5631
Oman (Rial Omani)	0.5895	0.3805	0.1929	0.2634	373.6281	189.4436	258.6592
Pakistan (Pak Rupee)	31.50	20.3357	10.3109	14.0782	111.6520	56.6009	77.2533
Panama (Balboa)	1.5490	1	0.5070	0.6922	2.1287	1.0793	1.4737
Papua New Guinea (Kina)	1.3489	0.8708	0.4415	0.6028			
Paraguay (Guarani)	1730.55	1117.2046	566.4648	773.4301			

Top-right block (additional countries):

Currency	($)			
Taiwan	40.20			
Tanzania (Shilling)	211.60			
Thailand (Baht)	39.20			
Togo Rep (CFA Fr)	518.50			
Tuvalu (Pa Ang)	2.0452			
Tunisia	6.5365			
Turkey (Dinar)	1.5164			
Turks & Caicos (Lira)	3207.59			
Tuvalu (US $)	1.5490			
(Australian $)	2.0452			
Uganda (New Shilling)	306.9262			
U A E (Dirham)	5.6655			
United Kingdom	1.00			
United States (US $)	1.5490			
Uruguay (Peso)	878.65			
USSR (Rouble)	1.0092			
Vanuatu (Vatu)	179.11			
Vatican (Lira)	2217.75			
Venezuela (Bolivar)	58.7466			
Vietnam (Dong)	6921.00			
Virgin Is-British (US $)	1.5490			
Virgin Is-US (US $)	1.5490			
Western Samoa (Tala)	3.63			
Yemen (Rial)	14.90			
Yemen PDR (Dinar)	0.5275			
Yugoslavia (Dinar)	24202.06			
Zaire Rep (Zaire)	578.75			
Zambia (Kwacha)	16.50			
Zimbabwe ($)	3.2975			

Special Drawing Rights June 16 1989 United Kingdom £1 24387 United States $1 22939 Germany West D Mark 2 46431 Japan Yen178 262 European Currency Unit Rates June 19 1989
United Kingdom £1 47720 United States $1 04163 Germany West D Mark 2 07076 Japan Yen151 505

Abbreviations: (a) Free rate; (b) Banknote rate; (c) Commercial rate; (d) Controlled rate; (e) Essential Imports; (g) Financial rate; (h) Exports; (i) Non commercial rate; (j) Business rate; (k) Buying rate; (l) Luxury goods; (m) Market rate; (o) Official rate; (p) preferential rate; (q) convertible rate; (r) parallel rate; (s) Selling rate; (t) Tourist rate; Some data supplied by Bank of America, Economics Department, London Trading Centre. Enquiries: 01 834 4360/5.
Monday, June 19, 1989.

Royal Exchange. When sterling declined and other currencies became traded from their own countries, the telephone and teleprinter made it possible for rapid links between dealers without having to meet. Electronic aids now communicate rate movements to all dealers almost simultaneously.

International time differences have created zonal markets for FX. Currency can be bought or sold at any time of day or night somewhere in the world. Normally, however, FX trading tends to follow national business hours using local banks.

The FX market consists of some 600 authorized banks and secondary banks, with private lines to FX brokers, who save the banks having constantly to contact each other.

A FX dealing room appears to be a hectic chaos of people, telephone in hand, shouting across the room to others and watching VDU screens. The reality is that each person is a specialist and trained to work under pressure on particular currencies only.

Agencies such as Reuter's and Dow Jones supply dealers' VDUs with news items which may help to influence rates during each day.

Foreign exchange terminology

The 'Financial Times' provides an excellent daily display of currency information and each month also publishes the 'World Value of the Pound', a chart which shows 200 countries, the names of each currency and its rate of exchange for £1 sterling (See Figure 10.1.) The code letters show that the currencies of some countries are controlled in some way, which means they are not freely traded and their rates are not their probable free market values.

Figure 10.2 is a daily list of the 16 major trading currencies. The 'Other Markets' currencies listed in Figure 10.2 are fairly tradeable and can be accepted from customers, although there may be difficulty in arranging 'forward' contracts for them.

The date: in the top left-hand corner. This example shows August 19. The rates are at the close of business in London on that date. Remember that trading continues in other world centres.

Day's spread: This shows the range of rates traded. The first figure is always the bank's rate for selling a currency and the second figure its rate for buying. So taking the example of the US dollar shown as 1.6960 – 1.7045, this means that, at some point during the day, the banks would sell you $1.6960 for £1 and would give £1 for every $1.7045 offered by you.

Figure 10.2 Foreign Currency Rates v Sterling.

POUND SPOT- FORWARD AGAINST THE POUND

Aug.19	Day's spread	Close	One month	% p.a.	Three months	% p.a.
US	1.6960 - 1.7045	1.7015 - 1.7025	0.36-0.35cpm	2.50	1.14-1.09pm	2.62
Canada	2.0790 - 2.0915	2.0900 - 2.0910	0.24-0.17cpm	1.18	0.74-0.62pm	1.30
Netherlands	3.63 - 3.64	3.63 - 3.64	1¾-1⅝cpm	5.57	5¾-5⅛pm	5.98
Belgium	67.35 - 67.75	67.45 - 67.55	30-15cpm	4.00	80-61pm	4.18
Denmark	12.31¼ - 12.34¾	12.31¼ - 12.32¼	3¼-2½orepm	0.68	9¾-8¾pm	3.00
Ireland	1.1985 - 1.2025	1.2000 - 1.2010	0.37-0.32ppm	3.45	1.23-1.08pm	3.85
W. Germany	3.21¾ - 3.22¾	3.21¾ - 3.22¼	1⅝-1½pfpm	5.82	5-4¾pm	6.06
Portugal	261.20 - 262.55	261.45 - 262.45	23-69cdis	-2.11	79-172dis	-1.92
Spain	210.45 - 211.70	210.50 - 210.80	33-13cpm	1.31	72-50pm	1.16
Italy	2384 - 2390	2385¼ - 2386¼	3-parlirepm	0.75	6-parpm	0.50
Norway	11.72½ - 11.78	11.76¾ - 11.77¾	1½-2oredis	-1.78	5⅜-6dis	-1.93
France	10.91¼ - 10.93½	10.91¼ - 10.92¼	3⅜-3cpm	3.50	9⅝-8⅞pm	3.39
Sweden	11.02 - 11.04	11.02¾ - 11.03¾	¾-⅜orepm	0.67	2⅞-2⅛pm	1.00
Japan	226½ - 227¾	226¾ - 227¾	1⅜-1¼ypm	6.93	3⅞-3⅝pm	6.60
Austria	22.58 - 22 67	22.64 - 22.67	11½-10⅝gropm	5.86	34-31⅜pm	5.77
Switzerland	2.70¼ - 2.71¼	2.70¼ - 2.71¼	1⅞-1⅝cpm	7.76	5¼-5pm	7.57

Belgian rate is convertible francs. Financial franc 68.45-68.55 . Six-month forward dollar 1.97-1.92cpm 12 months 3.35-3.25cpm

Close: This is the most important column. It shows the spot rate for each currency at the close of the business day. The US dollar shows at $1.7015–1.7025. So, although it had stood at $1.6960 at some point, by the close it had weakened, so the £1 could purchase $1.7015. The closing rate for cashing dollar receipts into pounds was $1.7025.

The Spot Rate is the rate a bank will use 'on the spot' to convert a currency. It changes frequently during the day but for a rough idea each morning the newspaper shows the closing spot rates of the previous day.

Golden Rule No. 1:
The *first* figure is the bank's *selling* rate, the *second*, or right-hand figure, is the bank's *buying* rate.

One month: This shows an amount of each currency as either *premium* (pm) or *discount* (dis), or par.

For example: the US dollar is 0.36–0.35c pm
the Portuguese escudo is 23–69c dis

These are the amounts a bank would add to or deduct from the spot rate in agreeing today to sell or buy currency one month later – in this case on 19th September.

Golden Rule No. 2:
Forward *premiums are deducted* from both selling and buying rates; forward *discounts are added*.

So, the rates the banks would have agreed on August 19th to sell or buy on September 19th would have been, e.g.

	Spot Rate	*One month pm/dis*		*Forward Rate*
US	1.7015–1.7025	less 0.36–35c pm	=	1.6979–1.6990
Portugal	261.45–262.45	plus 23–69c dis	=	261.68–263.14

% p.a.: The percentages per annum shown are simply the annual rate of the one month premiums or discounts against the spot rate.

Three months: This shows the forward premium or discount for delivery of a currency three months after the spot date of the chart.

% p.a.: This reflects the three month premium or discount at an annual percentage of the spot rate.

Figure 10.3   'Other Currencies' *v.* £ Sterling

OTHER CURRENCIES

Aug.19	£	$
Argentina	20.2555 - 20.4000	11.9200 - 12.000
Australia	2.0840 - 2.0870	1.2285 - 1.2295
Brazil	459.10 - 461.55	270.15 - 271.50
Finland	7.6030 - 7.6245	4.4740 - 4.4760
Greece	256.05 - 260.60	150.40 - 152.90
Hong Kong	13.2415 - 13.2575	7.8020 - 7.8040
Iran	121.70	70.50
Korea(Sth)	1222.60 - 1232.45	719.80 - 725.60
Kuwait	0.48370 - 0.48480	0.28275 - 0.28325
Luxembourg	67.45 - 67.55	39.60 - 39.70
Malaysia	4.5005 - 4.5120	2.6520 - 2.6540
Mexico	3876.10 - 3879.40	2281.00 - 2290.00
N. Zealand	2.6360 - 2.6430	1.5540 - 1.5560
Saudi Ar.	6.3745 - 6.3795	3.7495 - 3.7505
Singapore	3.4595 - 3.4650	2.0360 - 2.0380
S. Af (Cm)	4.1660 - 4.1770	2.4550 - 2.4570
S. Af (Fn)	5.7580 - 5.9085	3.3900 - 3.4785
Taiwan	48.55 - 48.75	28.55 - 28.65
U.A.E	6.2435 - 6.2485	3.6725 - 3.6735

Selling rate

There are also *cross-rates*, which are expressions of one foreign currency against another. Example: (fictitious rates used)

Market rate for £ sterling   = $\dfrac{US \$}{\$1.5}$ $\dfrac{F.Franc}{FF10.00}$

Cross Rate: $1 = FF6.66
              FF1 = £0.15

This could be stated as FF10 = $1.5 = £1 (there may be times in export negotiations when you need to convert directly from one currency to another without reverting into sterling).

The daily financial press, such as the Financial Times, prints a chart of cross-rates for the major currencies. See Figure 10.4.

Figure 10.4   Major Currency Cross Rates

EXCHANGE CROSS RATES

Aug 19	£	$	DM	Yen	F. Fr.	S. Fr.	H. Fl.	Lira	C$	B. Fr.
£	1	1.702	3.220	227.3	10.92	2.708	3.635	2386	2.091	67.50
$	0.588	1	1.892	133.5	6.416	1.591	2.136	1402	1.229	39.66
DM	0.311	0.529	1	78.59	3.391	0.841	1.129	741.0	0.649	20.96
YEN	4.399	7.488	14.17	1000	48.04	11.91	15.99	10497	9.199	297.0
F. Fr.	0.916	1.559	2.949	208.2	10.	2.480	3.329	2185	1.915	61.81
S. Fr.	0.369	0.629	1.189	83.94	4.032	1	1.342	881.1	0.772	24.93
H. Fl.	0.275	0.468	0.886	62.53	3.004	0.745	1	656.4	0.575	18.57
Lira	0.419	0.713	1.350	95.26	4.577	1.135	1.523	1000	0.876	28.29
C$	0.478	0.814	1.540	108.7	5.222	1.295	1.738	1141	1	32.28
B. Fr.	1.481	2.521	4.770	336.7	16.18	4.012	5.385	3535	3.098	100.

Yen per 1.000 French Fr. per 10: Lira per 1.000 Belgian Fr. per 100.

How the exchange rate is established

A rate of exchange is the price of one currency against another. But who decides what the rate should be?

Firstly, there is no real decision maker, because market forces create supply and demand for currencies, and therefore relative values. The price is adjusted from minute to minute during the working day by banks doing actual deals.

Rates are basically determined by:

(a)   Large money movements between countries, consistency of trade settlements, investments, governmental payments, bank settlements and speculative dealing;

(b)   Confidence in national economies, industrial performance;

(c)   Market opinions on short-term rate effects.

When forming opinions about a country's currency, always remember that for the market is dealing in both sides, e.g. the Italian lire and sterling, and it is the balance of opinion and money movement that influences the price, or rate.

There is also the strong influence of the US dollar on all currencies. Whereas you may form an opinion for your company on say, the French franc, based on your intimate knowledge of the French economy and your UK economic expertise, the bank dealer takes all currencies through the US dollar rate, i.e. how many francs to the dollar, then applies the dollar/sterling conversion rate. Thus the strength of the US dollar has a direct bearing on another currency's rate to sterling.

And there is the effect of interest rates, whereby high interest rates available for deposits in a country will drag worldwide currencies into that country. For example, US interest rates were deliberately kept high in the 1980s, to attract foreign money into the USA. Because the other currencies had been sold to buy dollars, the demand for dollars kept its rate of exchange at a high level, not related to the US balance of trade.

Bank quotations

It is important to know how a rate is quoted by a bank – mistakes can be costly. Fortunately in the UK, the banks are consistent in quoting a number of foreign units for £1.

Banks usually quote a *pair of rates*, e.g. US $1.6910–1.6920 to the pound. The first figure, for the bank selling the currency to you, would be useful if you were importing. To make a profit, a bank will give fewer units of a currency when selling it than it requires when buying. The second rate shown, $1.6920, is the number of dollars the bank will need for £1.

The difference between the two rates is the spread, of vital interest to a bank. For a very high currency value, say above one million dollars, the spread will be tiny, whereas for ordinary trade transactions the difference will be large to compensate the bank for the work in many small deals before it 'goes into the market' to dispose of or buy a worthwhile volume of currency.

Spot rates are quoted for immediate delivery, although in practice, two days are allowed for accounts to be created. This is the *value date*.

Forward rates are quoted by banks for settlement, e.g. for delivery of your dollar receipts to the bank and the credit of sterling to the account, on future dates. From a bank's point of view, the forward margin is important, i.e. the premium or discount, the difference between their cost of buying and selling currencies. An exporter is interested in the outright forward rates – the combination of the spot rate and the forward margin.

Example

You ask the bank (probably by telephone) for the dollar exchange rate, at spot and for one month's time. You do not have to say whether you are buying or selling, but don't blame the bank for asking you! The bank quotes:

	Bank Selling		Bank Buying	
Spot Rate	$1.7015	–	$1.7025	= £1 sterling
One month forward margin	0.0036	–	0.0035	premium
Outright price for one month's time =	$1.6979	–	$1.6990	= £1 sterling

The forward *premium* means that dollars are more expensive in the future. Dollar receipts will convert into more pounds – it is worth remembering that if a currency is at a premium to sterling, it can make more profit (see later).

Supposing the bank quotes a forward *discount* for a currency – from our chart let us say Portuguese Escudos for three month's time.

The forward *discount* means that the currency is weaker than sterling – a given number of Escudos will produce less sterling in the future.

	Bank Selling		Bank Buying	
Spot Rate	Esc.261.45	–	Esc.262.45	= £1 sterling
Three month's forward margin	0.79	–	1.72	= discount
Outright price for three month's time	Esc.262.14	–	Esc.264.17	= £1 sterling

We have just looked at examples of *fixed forward rates,* which are not a good idea for most exporters, because customers' payments are not as reliable as that. For this reason, banks also offer 'option' forward dates for settlement.

Option Forward contracts give the choice of delivering the currency between two agreed dates, perhaps two weeks apart. To compensate the bank for its uncertain date of receipt, the forward margin will be less favourable than in a fixed date contract.

The contract with the bank can be made by telephone or in writing. The key features of a FX contract are:

- to buy or sell
- a specific amount
- of a named currency
- for delivery on an agreed date
- or between two agreed dates
- in exchange for another currency
- at a specific rate of exchange.

Remember, a contract is legally binding and must be completed exactly by due dates. There is no leeway.

Close outs and extensions

Supposing the customer doesn't pay. The bank deal is a real contract, and the exporter must find the currency to deliver to the bank on the agreed future date.

Perhaps they have currency payments coming in from elsewhere. If not, they must 'close out' or 'extend' the forward contract. To do this the bank will sell them currency at spot on the future date to settle the contract.

When the customer's payment eventually arrives, there is no longer a forward contract to apply it to and it must be sold at spot.

Alternatively, the original forward contract can just be extended, if, for example the exporter is fairly certain that the payment will arrive one month later.

The bank calculates a 'close out' rate, then applies the new spot rate for the extra month.

Example

Forward sale $175,000 @ 1.7650	=	£99 150
Spot close out purchase @ 1.8400	=	(£95 108)
Extended forward sale @ 1.8500	=	£94 595
Final receipt total	=	£98 637

Forward rates and future actual rates

There is no connection whatsoever between a quoted forward rate and the eventual spot rate when that date arrives.

The forward margin is calculated by taking:

(a)   the spot rate today;
    and applying
(b)   the differential in interest rates in the two countries.

In simple terms, currencies of countries with interest rates lower than the UK normally are at a forward premium to sterling, while currencies with higher interest rates would be at a discount.

Example
If the cost of borrowing US dollars were 9% per annum, and sterling cost 12% p.a., the difference of 3% would mean a 1.5% premium for the six month forward dollar rate. If the spot rate were $1.5 to the £, the 1.5% premium would be 2.25 cents, or so.

From this, you may think that a good grasp of likely interest rate movements is the best indicator of future exchange rates. Well, the task has always defeated governments, economists and FX experts.

It is nevertheless natural to try to forecast future rates. For that useful order, today, for US $20,000 due for payment in three months' time, the bank offers a rate of $1.6920 less a forward premium of 0.65 cents, producing £11 866 at $1.6855. Supposing the opinion of your company's economic expert is that the dollar will drop to $1.60, you could decide to wait instead to sell at spot, to produce perhaps £12,500.

Which would be right course of action? This is a classic 'bird in the hand' dilemma: guarantee receipt of £11 866, or back the hunch that would produce an extra £634? Company policies vary on this subject, but remember that the dollar could strengthen, or the pound weaken considerably during the credit period, giving you less than the forward rate quoted by the bank, not more.

So you always have a choice – play safe and contract today with the bank for a guaranteed rate; or back your view of future exchange rate movements and just wait, with the chance of extra profit or loss.

Eurocurrencies, the EMS and the ECU

The EEC member countries believe in developing the economic strength of a market of 350 million people, both within Europe and to face world competition. The banking community has flourished through lending the currencies of other countries, known as Eurocurrencies. Some degree of exchange rate stability has been achieved through the European Monetary System framework of control. The ideal of a common EEC currency has advanced through the use of the ECU, the European Currency Unit.

All these items have a bearing on the worldwide foreign currency market and on pricing exports.

Eurocurrencies

There is a mystique about the word Eurocurrency that is quite undeserved. The prefix 'Euro' simply refers to the market, outside its own country, where a currency is lent or borrowed. So, banks in Europe, lending US dollars refer to them as Eurodollars, whereas banks in Hong Kong lending US dollars call them Asian dollars.

The currencies themselves are no different, whether pounds, dollars, francs, marks or whatever. The tremendous increase in Eurocurrency loans in recent years demonstrate that banks and companies have learned the advantages of *borrowing* currency at low interest rates when they have the confidence of repaying loans with currency receipts.

Eurocurrencies can only be lent or borrowed, i.e. they require repayment at a certain date. They cannot be bought or sold – that would be the job of the regular foreign exchange market.

The Eurodollar was the first Eurocurrency and remains the most heavily lent. Eurocurrencies really took off in the mid 1950s, when surplus US dollars were available at a time that the US government fixed low interest rates on domestic US deposits. US banks found a ready market in Europe at interest rates higher than those available in the US and borrowers keen to borrow at rates much lower than their own national ones. When sterling rates were at 16% in UK, Eurodollars were available at 12% in London, whereas US dollars in USA were lent domestically at 11% pa.

Figure 10.5 Interest rates for Eurocurrencies

EURO-CURRENCY INTEREST RATES

Aug.19	Short term	7 Days notice	One Month	Three Months	Six Months	One Year
Sterling	$9\frac{7}{8}-9\frac{3}{4}$	$10\frac{1}{8}-10$	$10\frac{15}{16}-10\frac{13}{16}$	$11\frac{1}{2}-11\frac{3}{8}$	$11\frac{1}{2}-11\frac{3}{8}$	$11\frac{1}{2}-11\frac{3}{8}$
US Dollar	$7\frac{15}{16}-7\frac{13}{16}$	$8\frac{3}{16}-8\frac{1}{16}$	$8\frac{3}{8}-8\frac{1}{4}$	$8\frac{11}{16}-8\frac{9}{16}$	$9-8\frac{7}{8}$	$9\frac{1}{4}-9\frac{1}{8}$
Can. Dollar	$9-8\frac{3}{4}$	$9-8\frac{3}{4}$	$9\frac{3}{8}-9\frac{1}{8}$	$9\frac{7}{8}-9\frac{5}{8}$	$10\frac{1}{4}-10$	$10\frac{5}{8}-10\frac{3}{8}$
D. Guilder	$5\frac{3}{8}-5\frac{1}{8}$	$5\frac{3}{8}-5\frac{1}{8}$	$5\frac{1}{2}-5\frac{3}{8}$	$5\frac{5}{8}-5\frac{1}{2}$	$5\frac{3}{4}-5\frac{5}{8}$	$5\frac{7}{8}-5\frac{3}{4}$
Sw. Franc	$2\frac{3}{4}-2\frac{1}{2}$	$3-2\frac{3}{4}$	$3\frac{3}{16}-3\frac{1}{16}$	$3\frac{13}{16}-3\frac{11}{16}$	$4\frac{1}{8}-4$	$4\frac{3}{16}-4\frac{1}{16}$
Deutschmark	$4\frac{7}{8}-4\frac{3}{4}$	$4\frac{7}{8}-4\frac{3}{4}$	$5-4\frac{7}{8}$	$5\frac{5}{16}-5\frac{3}{16}$	$5\frac{5}{8}-5\frac{1}{2}$	$5\frac{11}{16}-5\frac{9}{16}$
Fr. Franc	$7\frac{3}{8}-7\frac{1}{4}$	$7\frac{3}{8}-7\frac{1}{4}$	$7\frac{1}{2}-7\frac{3}{8}$	$8-7\frac{7}{8}$	$8\frac{3}{8}-8\frac{1}{4}$	$8\frac{9}{16}-8\frac{7}{16}$
Italian Lire	$11-9$	$10\frac{1}{4}-9\frac{1}{4}$	$10\frac{3}{8}-9\frac{7}{8}$	$11\frac{1}{4}-10\frac{3}{4}$	$11\frac{1}{2}-11\frac{1}{8}$	$11\frac{3}{4}-11\frac{3}{8}$
B. Fr. (Fin)	$6\frac{3}{8}-6\frac{1}{4}$	$6\frac{7}{16}-6\frac{5}{16}$	$6\frac{15}{16}-6\frac{13}{16}$	$7\frac{5}{16}-7\frac{3}{16}$	$7\frac{3}{4}-7\frac{5}{8}$	$7\frac{7}{8}-7\frac{3}{4}$
B. Fr. (Con.)	$6\frac{1}{2}-6\frac{1}{8}$	$6\frac{1}{2}-6\frac{1}{4}$	$7-6\frac{3}{4}$	$7\frac{1}{2}-7\frac{1}{8}$	$7\frac{7}{8}-7\frac{1}{2}$	$8-7\frac{5}{8}$
Yen	$4\frac{5}{8}-4\frac{1}{2}$	$4\frac{5}{8}-4\frac{1}{2}$	$4\frac{5}{8}-4\frac{1}{2}$	$4\frac{15}{16}-4\frac{13}{16}$	$5\frac{1}{16}-4\frac{15}{16}$	$5\frac{1}{16}-4\frac{15}{16}$
D. Krone	$8-7\frac{3}{4}$	$8\frac{1}{3}-7\frac{7}{8}$	$8\frac{3}{8}-8\frac{1}{8}$	$8\frac{5}{8}-8\frac{3}{8}$	$9-8\frac{3}{4}$	$9\frac{1}{4}-9$
Asian $Sing	$8-7\frac{7}{8}$	$8\frac{1}{4}-8\frac{1}{8}$	$8\frac{3}{8}-8\frac{1}{4}$	$8\frac{3}{4}-8\frac{5}{8}$	$9-8\frac{7}{8}$	$9\frac{5}{16}-9\frac{3}{16}$

Long term Eurodollars: two years $8\frac{5}{8}-8\frac{1}{2}$ per cent: three years $8\frac{11}{16}-8\frac{9}{16}$ per cent: four years $9\frac{5}{8}-9\frac{3}{8}$ per cent: five years $10-9\frac{3}{4}$ per cent nominal. Short term rates are call for US Dollars and Japanese Yen; others, two days' notice

The European Monetary System (EMS)

The European Monetary System (or EMS) began in 1979 within the EEC as a means of establishing a 'zone of monetary stability'. Businessmen like to have a fair idea of future exchange rates when planning, but until 1979 were frustrated by the unpredicatable fluctuations of free markets.

Following a period in the 1970s when European banks tried various ways of co-operating to achieve more stable exchange rates, the creation of the formal EMS meant that the member governments agreed to keep their exchange rates within a fixed band of each other – about a maximum of 2% either way. Occasionally, some weaker members, such as the Italian Lire, the Danish Kroner and the Irish Punt are allowed a greater divergence, while the German Mark remains the strongest and least changing member and therefore the dominating yardstick. The nickname 'the snake' describes the swerves of the various currency rates against each other.

At August 1989, the UK was not a member of the EMS as sterling is a major world oil currency and its changing fortunes could cause too many adjustments to the 'snake' rates of the others.

The EMS is being created in stages:

- Firstly, the exchange rate framework.

- Next, some pooling of national reserves under the European Monetary Co-operation Fund.
- Then, a formal European Monetary Fund to control policy.
- And the creation, and widespread use of a common currency, and European Currency Unit (the ECU) as a means of reserves and a real currency for settling international debts.

The belief of the European governments is that the EMS will create monetary stability within Europe for long periods and encourage sound growth of businesses.

Figure 10.6 shows the agreed EMS rates at mid-1988.

Figure 10.6   EMS Currency Rates

EMS EUROPEAN CURRENCY UNIT RATES

	Ecu central rates	Currency amounts against Ecu Aug.19	% change from central rate	% change adjusted for divergence	Divergence limit %
Belgian Franc	42.4582	43.6650	+2.84	+1.06	±1.5344
Danish Krone	7.85212	7.97208	+1.53	-0.25	±1.5404
German D-Mark	2.05853	2.08286	+1.18	-0.60	±1.0981
French Franc	6.90403	7.05985	+2.26	+0.48	±1.3674
Dutch Guilder	2.31943	2.35149	+1.38	-0.40	±1.5012
Irish Punt	0.768411	0.776387	+1.04	-0.74	±1.6684
Italian Lira	1483.58	1541.63	+3.91	+2.81	±4.0752

Changes are for Ecu, therefore positive change denotes a weak currency
Adjustment calculated by Financial Times.

The European Currency Unit (ECU)

The European Currency Unit, or ECU is the early version of a common European currency. Here is an extract from a speech by the Chairman of Barclays Bank in October 1985: 'Europe's new international currency, the ECU was introduced in 1979 ... subsequently used by the private sector to minimise the risks created by fluctuating exchange rates. Use has not been uniform. Italians have been using the ECU far longer than most and almost 50 percent of Italian exports are invoiced in ECUs but British companies have been slow to use the new currency ...'

The ECU is a cocktail of each of the EEC member states' currencies (including sterling, despite not being an EMS member) mixed in proportion to the member's economy. Each is weighted according to its strength against the others.

In mid-1989 one ECU was equivalent to:

68	pence Sterling
1.04	US dollars
2.06	W. German marks
1.78	Swiss Francs

If exports are priced in ECU, customers can now purchase ECU to settle invoices.

The ECU is a typical *basket currency*, that is, it is a composite of several others. Its price fluctuations are therefore twofold:

- Daily movements in its member currencies rates.
- Changes in the official weightings, which are reviewed whenever a currency strengthens or weakens really significantly.

Functions of the ECU:

- As a means of settlements between EEC member governments.
- As a yardstick (in French, 'numeraire') of exchange variations within the EMS.
- As part of the official reserves of each EEC government, but most importantly for exporters.
- As a separate foreign exchange currency for trade debts, for loans and for investments.

To quote further from the search mentioned earlier: '... the ECU will become one of the top three currencies by the end of the century ...'

Marketing aspects of currency v. sterling

About 70% of UK exports are invoiced in sterling. In a highly competitive world market place, it seems a little odd that we set out to create such a significant barrier to selling.

An exporter in a very strong selling position, as a sole source of supply to a customer, or a trade monopoly, could do business on his own terms, including deciding the currency as sterling. But few have a seller's market. Even if they do they should consider future relationships in case buyers' positions strengthen.

Over 60% of world trade is conducted in US dollars. The less developed countries depend on World Bank or IMF (International Monetary Fund) loans which are all made in US dollars.

It is nearly always better export marketing strategy to talk to the buyer in his own money langugage or at least in a money language he can understand readily, that is, US dollars.

For example, an order from Holland for £20 000 was converted to Dutch guilders at spot rate of 3.775 = £1, total guilders 75 500. Delivery time was two months and payment terms one month, so the guilders were sold to the bank for three months forward, at an outright rate of 3.71 (3.775 – 0.075 pm), yielding £20 350. The customer was happy to do business at prices he could understand, and the exporter was happy with the extra £350 profit (1.75%).

In another case a British textile company obtained a £4 million order from Saudi Arabia, which both sides agreed should be invoiced in US dollars, the world currency of oil. The exporter converted the contract value to $5.6 million, deliveries were spread over one year, and three months' credit allowed for each shipment. With scheduled dates, the exporter was able to sell forward, at a premium of about 5%, adding a further £200 000 to his margin.

For maximum marketing edge, every export negotiator should know what scope there is in currency – and how it affects prices, profits and risk.

In the case of several sales of small values, the forward market for each order would be fiddly and take a lot of time, so instead it would be better to have loans in the currencies, convert the loans to sterling to use in the business, and let the customers' payments flow back to the lending bank to repay the loans. No exchange risk is involved and there is the use of the money meanwhile. The interest rate of the foreign currency loan is usually cheaper than sterling!

Exporting in currency might be a bad idea:

(1)   If the currency is very weak, so there is no forward market for it or possibly no means of changing it to sterling.
       or
(2)   Some currencies have a forward market, but are at a discount to sterling so no future profit is available from selling forward.
       or
(3)   The customer might know all about the scope for forward premiums so might demand a share of it in some way.
       or
(4)   Some customers in strong currency countries, such as Germany, actually demand sterling prices, since they know they will have to find fewer units of their own money to pay sterling invoices.

Let's look at each of the 'bad news' items in turn. On point 1, currency invoicing should only apply to hard currencies. So you would not even consider markets whose currencies were not freely tradeable. In point 2, with hard currencies trading at a future discount, forward contracts would produce less than current spot rates, but the exchange value is at least fixed. It may be possible to recover any shortfall in pricing. The marketing advantage of having a happy customer can be preserved but take full account of an income flow at a discount.

Point 3. At least you have a customer and an extra income from the forward sale which can be shared, if you so negotiate, as a price reduction or in longer credit terms or some other benefit. So, not exactly a bad idea.

Point 4 is not really in the same category as the others. You may find that you would like to sell in currency but your customer reverses the situation by demanding sterling invoices. He knows that he can save money by buying sterling forward at a discount or waiting until due date to buy sterling forward at a discount or waiting until due date to buy sterling at spot. Your desire to obtain a currency premium then depends on your negotiating weapons, of which a share of the currency premium is one.

There is usually a fine choice for marketing men, i.e.:

- Will customers in countries with currencies stronger than sterling prefer to pay in sterling because it will cost them less of their own currency to do so, at due date?
  or
- Will they prefer to be invoiced in their own currency because it is easier to understand and because the price can be haggled down by the percentage of the forward premium?
  or
- If the customer is not price-sensitive or the competition not very strong, can you invoice in the customer's strong currency and make an extra profit by selling it forward?

The marketing approach might successfully be:

(1) Find out how the customer would like to be billed.
(2) Try to find out what the competition are doing.
(3) Decide if the customer's currency is stronger or weaker than sterling in the period up to due date.

Your strategy for strong and weak currencies might be:

- try to sell in currency at full price;

- if necessary to compete, quote a currency price reduced by the forward premium;
- agree to quote in sterling if the customer insists and if more business is available that way.

For currencies weaker than sterling:

- price in sterling;
  or
- price in currency, inflated by percentage of the forward discount.

Pricing and invoicing

Basic considerations

When converting product prices into currency, never lose sight of the required sterling price.

There are probably three main kinds of pricing situations:

- The standard price list, either for in-house use or to issue to agents, distributors and customers.
- Pricing individual orders, enquiries and quotations.
- Equipping a person for a selling visit with alternative currency prices for different time periods.

Whichever situation you are addressing, consider:

- The currency itself – is there a market and a forward rate?
- The premium or discount effect – will the future bring more, or less, sterling?
- The time element – how long to allow in pricing, from today through production, delivery and credit periods up to final expected payment date?

But whatever you do: *recover your full intended sterling price.*

There is always commercial judgement as to whether the market will pay your currency price – the same consideration that applies to your sterling prices.

Pricing policies for currency

(A)   'Company' rates of exchange, which somebody in the company decrees for all main currencies against the £ or $, usually revises each month and issues to all user departments.

or

(B)   'Market' rates of exchange, calculated by relevant users in the company from bank quotations, each time there is a need.

CALCULATING CURRENCY PRICES

Quotations to customers probably allow for a variety of delivery dates, possibly from 1 week to 3 months or more. You almost certainly allow customers periods of credit for their payments – probably different in various markets, and you have seen how expected currency proceeds can be sold forward at an agreed rate. You should not convert your price into currency at today's spot rate – rather, you should use the forward rate for the end date of the likely credit period. As well as being more accurate, this basis will be justifiable in any discussion with the customer.

This is called the competitive pricing method. It is called that because you are passing the total gain from the forward premium to the customer.

Example: An enquiry from the USA for delivery in 2 months at 30 days credit.

Event	Date	Sterling	US$ Rate	US$ Currency Price
Enquiry received	1.6.	£1000.00	1.60 spot	1600
Delivery date	1.8.		(0.01 pm)	
Payment due	1.9.		(0.0005pm)	
		£1000.00	$1.585 =	$1585

Example: An order from Norway for immediate delivery at 30 days credit

Event	Date	Sterling	N.Kr Rate	N.Kr Currency Price
Order received	1.6.	£1000.00	11.40 spot	11 400
Delivery date	1.6.		–	
Payment due	1.7.		0.04 dis	
		£1000.00	11.44	= N.Kr 11 440

Figure 10.7   Two examples of benefiting from currency premiums

1. *Forward Sale of Receipts:*   Order value Swiss francs 246,250
                                                      (£100,000)
                                          Payment due in three months

Order value sold forward at   2.46250   (Spot)
                                       – 0.03125   (3 months premium)
                  Forward rate   2.43125

Swiss francs 246 250 @ 2.43125   =   £101 285 guaranteed
Intended Sterling price   =   £100 000
                            gain   =   £   1 285

The gain can be used as: profit   £   1 285
or, to be competitive: price reduction up to   £   1 285
or: terms increase up to   40 days (at 12%)

2. *Borrow in Currency of Sale:*   Order value Swiss francs 246,250
                                          Payment due in three months

Waiting 3 months for £100 000 would cost (at 12%)   £3000
Instead,
Borrow the sale value Sw. Fr. 246 250 today
Convert (at Spot) @ 2.4625
        = £100 000 cash *today*

Interest on Swiss franc loan @ 5% pa. for 3 months
        = Sw. Fr. 3078, charged @ 2.4524   = £1255
          Interest saved   = £1745

The saving is available as profit, price reduction or terms increase.

Funds are available three months earlier.

Loan is repaid on receipt of customer's payment of Sw. Fr. 246 250.

Currency and tender bids

Because of the dominance of the US dollar, most tenders for capital projects, e.g. in the LDCs, are expected to be in dollars. The problem for the tendering exporter is how to offset the exchange risk if the tender is successful.

If the tender is rejected, there is no cost or problem. But if it is accepted, a long time will elapse before revenue flows, with all the uncertainty of the exchange rate at that future date.

If the contract value is sold forward when the tender is submitted, and the tender is rejected, the exporter has to find the dollars from somewhere (possibly buy them at an unknown future spot rate) to honour the forward contract.

If the contract value is not sold forward when tendering, but the exporter waits until his bid is accepted and then decides to sell forward, the exchange rate could have deteriorated in the period of tender evaluation, possibly three or six months, and he is stuck with a dollar price which may produce a loss.

One solution is to build in a price 'hedge' related to the timing of the whole transaction, and hope that this is not uncompetitive. Assume, for example, a dollar price tendered on Day 1, then acceptance on Day 90, performance by Day 270, then payment in dollars. If the forward margin for nine months is 3%, that could be put into the original price without actually selling forward, which would only be done when the bid was accepted.

Another solution is to purchase Currency Traded Options. In return for a non-refundable premium, an exporter can purchase an option for the right to purchase an amount of sterling for dollars at a guaranteed rate, up to a particular date. The premium varies from day to day in the market and also between banks. The premium will be the exporter's only cost but he could gain from an advantageous exchange rate at maturity.

If sterling strengthens by the time the customer pays, the rate guaranteed in the option is taken up, and the only cost is the premium already paid at the outset.

But if sterling weakens, by the time the customer pays, to a rate below the option rate, the exporter can just ignore the option and sell the receipts at spot, to make an exchange gain.

The Traded Option facility allows the exporter to avoid the exchange risk at the cost of an 'up-front' premium which can usually be built into the tender price.

Example
UK export tender to Saudi Arabia: £100 000 @ $1.70 = $170 000
Tender decision in 3 months, payment 3 months later
Risk: if sterling rises to $1.71 or above, receipts will be less than £100 000.
Solution: buy 8 Call Options of £12 500 @ $1.70 each for 6 months
Cost: $2500 (non-refundable, and amount varies with market view of sterling
v. dollar in six months' time)
Result: £100 000 guaranteed if £ rises above $1.70
                 Extra profit guaranteed if £ falls below $1.70
                 Cost fully known in advance
                 No need for selling receipts forward.

Checklist: Hedging Against Currency Losses

- Sell forward, preferably on fixed contract basis, but if the customer payment date is uncertain, make it an option forward contract.
- Borrow in the currency for the credit period; repay with the customer's payment.
- Use receipts to pay liabilities in the same currency.
- Net off receipts and payments between subsidiaries.
- Traded Options for tenders and major uncertainties.
- Stay in Sterling – simple, but not very competitive.

Glossary of foreign exchange terms

Broker	– one who brings dealers who are buyers and sellers of foreign currency together, charging a brokerage for the service.
Cross Rate	– the price of one foreign currency against another.
Dealer	– one authorized to deal on the foreign exchange market.
Discount	– the forward margin of a currency which is added to the spot rate to give a forward rate.
Fixed Forward	– a forward market where the date for delivery is fixed precisely.
Margin	– the difference between the spot and forward price of a currency. If the forward price of the currency is greater than the spot price, the margin is said to be a premium; if less, a 'discount'. Where there is no margin, the forward value is referred to as 'par'.
Option	– a deal where delivery may be made at any time between

Forward	two named dates.
Par	– when the forward rate of exchange is the same as the spot rate of exchange.
Pip, or Point	– one hundredth part of a unit of currency.
Premium	– the forward margin of currency which is deducted from the spot rate to give a forward rate.
Rate of Exchange	– the price of one currency against another.
Spot	– the exchange must be made within two working days from the date of the deal.
Spread	– the difference between a quoted buying and selling rate.
ECU	– European Currency Unit.
EMS	– European Monetary System.
Eurocurrency	– any currency lent or borrowed outside its own country.

11   Training in export credit and finance

Overview – the need for expert staff

Some exporters hire staff 'with experience' and therefore believe no training is necessary. Sometimes, new starters are sat 'next to Joe' to learn what to do. In most companies, there is some degree of intentional training, whether just material to read, internal training programmes arranged by the Personnel or Training Department outside courses, evening classes, or correspondence courses and examination work.

Highly motivated individuals will seek out information for themselves anyway, to do their job better in order to 'get on', but as a result, may take their skills elsewhere, leaving the exporter with the lesser performers.

Managers have a duty to organize regular training of staff and themselves, to refresh memories on existing procedures, to implement new drills and to learn about useful developments. There is never time to do this properly, so precious training time must be organized objectively.

The questions that export management should ask itself are:

- Are customers satisfied with our accuracy and timing?
- How much money do we lose on errors and delays?
- Do we fail to keep new starters?
- Do we have any weak links in our staffing?
and primarily
- Do we all think and act as world-traders?

The well-rounded, qualified, export credit person should strive to achieve 'MICM, MIEx' after his name, indicating to all concerned that he has taken the trouble to study and pass the qualifying examinations of the Institute of Credit Management and the Institute of Export.

But there is a wide selection of motivation and training available for staff and this section looks at:

- In-house training, including a Credit Manual.
- Sales/Credit collaboration.
- Industry credit meetings.
- Export Forums.
- Seminars, Conferences and Courses.
- Books.
- Correspondence courses, and Distance Learning.
- Examination studies.

In-house training

Training, like charity, begins at home. Staff are influenced all the time by what to do and what they see around them, whether good or bad practices.

In-house training is usually a mixture of formal and informal. Sometimes, well-laid plans for regular sessions fizzle out after a while, so the planning of training should follow three points in sequence:

(a)   What are our company's policies and procedures?
(b)   Do our staff understand and operate them?
(c)   Can staff contribute a better way than ours to do it?

The sequence is important, otherwise all kinds of wild ideas on better methods flood in without properly knowing existing drills. The manager should keep a simple file which shows:

- A manual, or document of the company's credit drills, bank procedures, agencies used, etc.
- A list of staff and dates of when the drills were read and/or discussed.
- Notes of problems, weaknesses, suggestions, etc., to be actioned.

Whether new starters are sat next to Joe to pick up what they can, or more sophisticated systems send people round the company for weeks or on external courses at several hundred pounds a time, there is still a need, *at least annually*, to go through the credit departmental drills with everybody, for a valuable hour, or day, or however long it takes to be satisfied.

It is useful for staff to write their own part of a credit procedure manual, e.g. collection methods or bank documents used. Firstly, this helps straighten out their thinking into sequential disciplines. Secondly, it helps fill in gaps of knowledge which they have to seek to complete sequences.

It is also useful to ask staff to stand up in staff meetings to explain to the others what they do and why they do it. This usually induces preparation, which itself is an excellent self-training device.

Figure 11.1 shows a complex list of possible contents for a Credit Manual. From this list, exporters may like to select the appropriate items for their own operations.

While there is no substitute for departmental managers ensuring that the company's procedures are understood, the training can be reinforced by:

- identifying weak or unsatisfactory activities
- using external training experts to deal with them

The weakness of relying solely on in-house training is that staff are not made aware of successful techniques in use elsewhere. External trainers can repair that defect and also present 'how others have solved it' sessions.

Where large numbers of staff are involved, it can be cheaper per head to bring the trainer to the firm rather than sending individuals off to public training events.

Figure 11.1   Suggested Contents of an Export Credit Manual

---

1   OBJECTIVES AND POLICY
  (a)   Statement of export credit objectives
  (b)   Statement of export credit assessment policy
  (c)   Statement of export collection policy
  (d)   Factors considered in policy setting
        (i)   Sales requirements
        (ii)   Company funding
        (iii)   Industry and competitors
        (iv)   Product needs
        (v)   Economic/political risks
  (e)   Method of review and update

2   ORGANIZATION
  (a)   Company organization chart (showing credit department links)
  (b)   Credit department organization chart (jobs, titles, report responsibilities)
  (c)   Job Descriptions (duties, responsibilities)
  (d)   Qualifications/requirements for jobs (education, experience, personal)
  (e)   Training (programmes, types, reviews)
  (f)   Performance reviews (methods, records)

3   CREDIT PLANNING
  (a)   Investment available
  (b)   Credit/sales requirements
  (c)   Budget items
  (d)   Reports – monthly, special

4 WORKING PROCEDURES
   (a) Credit Assessment
        (i)   How information is used from:
                Credit agencies Trade associations
                Banks   Reference books
                Customers   ECGD
                Visit Reports   Others
        (ii)   Methods of deciding limits/categories
        (iii)   Procedures for Balance Sheet analysis:
                Ratios used
                Analysis techniques
        (iv)   Securities from:
                Guarantees   Letters of Credit
                Banks   Others
        (v)   Procedures for Documentary Collections
        (vi)   Credit Insurance procedures
                Credit limits
                Records
                Claims
   (b) Payment Terms
        (i)   Approval levels
        (ii)   Methods of deciding
        (iii)   Discounts
        (iv)   Interest charges
        (v)   Reasons for withdrawal of credit
   (c) Order Approval
        (i)   Delegated level
        (ii)   Central referral levels
        (iii)   Use of credit limits
        (iv)   Stop of supply
        (v)   Credit committee decisions
   (d) Collections
        (i)   Invoicing
        (ii)   Checking of export documents
        (iii)   Follow-up timetable
        (iv)   Rules for statements
                Documentation
                Letters   Agencies
                Telexes/cables Legal
                Telephone visits Sales help
        (v)   Sample documents
        (vi)   Follow-up after write-off
        (vii)   Bank collection procedures
        (viii) Consignment accounts
        (ix)   Contract retentions
        (x)   Bonds and guarantees
        (xi)   Dispute solving
        (xii)   Claims committee
        (xiii) Bad Debt Reserves
        (xiv) Penalty interest
        (xv)   Dealing with Lawyers/Liquidators

5 REPORTING
   (a) Forms and definitions
   (b) Variance analysis of Budget or previous periods
   (c) Special reports
   (d) Computer requirements

6 Documentation Samples

7 Use of Export Credit Manual
   (a) Circulation
   (b) Review/amendments

Sales/credit collaboration

Exporters are missing readily available training if they allow sales and credit departments to operate separately with little contract. The credit department wants to know all about customers and sales plans. Sales people want to sell to good risks who will still be there next year. Both departments build up valuable skill and knowledge which should be shared as often as possible for the company benefit.

Methods of training credit staff in the sales operation:

(a) Put credit staff into the export sales office for a while.
(b) Arrange for export sales staff to talk about their activities at credit meetings.
(c) Invite credit staff to export sales meetings.
(d) Ensure that visiting customers or agents are introduced to the export credit staff.
(e) Copy export bulletins to credit staff.
(f) Copy export correspondence on any financial matter to credit staff.
(g) Hold problem-solving meetings between credit and export staff, tabling claims, disputes and potential problems.
(h) On return from selling trips, export salesman to explain to credit staff the list of customers seen, commenting on size, reputation, financial state, etc.

At a more senior management level, collaboration training can take place in 'export workshops' where credit and export sales executives explore areas to achieve more effective cooperation. The following are typical subjects for discussion:

● How does the export department determine which customers to approach?
● Are there minimum marketing or financial standards which a prospective customer must meet before appointed a distributor or given territorial rights? What are those standards? How rigorously are they enforced?
● How can the credit department help in these processes?
● Under what circumstances is an account dropped or put on such strict terms that it is effectively discontinued?

● Should marginal customers receive special credit or sales services such as long-term or capital financing, working-capital financing beyond normal terms, or general management assistance? If so, how should export and credit departments coordinate such activities?

The entire area of customer confidence in an exporter can be improved by a united sales/credit image which always shows a thoroughly professional approach to finding ways of meeting the customer's needs. Top managements of exporting companies can profit by overcoming passive resistance to inter-departmental training and collaboration by giving special assignments on these matters to marketing and credit staff. The results in profit awareness are well worth the extra time required.

Industry credit meetings

Many UK industries, e.g. oil, plastics, electronics, pharmaceuticals, etc., organize regular meetings between credit managers to exchange information. The practice of swapping techniques and procedures is even more useful to credit staff, so training seminars are arranged, some annually, some more frequently. The usual practice is to gather staff from different companies in the same industry and for the training to be shared between their managers, with case studies and syndicate work for the delegates. Typical subjects covered include: 'How to target for export collections', 'Assessment of country risks' and 'Dealing with banks on bills'.

These training seminars are more beneficial than external seminars as they are confined to a single industry. Some benefits are:

(a)   Direct acquisition of knowledge.
(b)   Indirectly obtaining explanations in syndicate group work.
(c)   Discovering relative strength by comparison with competitors.
(d)   Making new acquaintances for subsequent contact.

Export forums

Export credit forums are an excellent form of training, as they accommodate the needs of both experienced practitioners and new staff. In a large assembly, delegates may pose general problems or specific questions, volunteer answers, offer to contact later, or merely listen and make notes. The wealth of knowledge in a roomful of 100 export credit staff means that a delegate's problem is nearly always answered on the spot. Forums have a Chairman to interpret questions and tease out answers from those who should know and it is usual to have a panel of experts, from industry, the government, banks and ECGD, to provide exceptional information when required. Questions are invited from delegates when booking and time is also allowed on the day for impromptu subjects.

The Institute of Credit Management's London Branch has such an event for export credit men giving the opportunity of live discussion of unusual problems, for example: Performance Bonds; Terms for French customers; Devaluation currency risks; available publications on foreign balance sheets; Direct Collections through foreign banks; payment delays from Zaire and Turkey; how to collect faster from Italy and Portugal; members' experiences on terms and speed of payment with Bahrain, Ghana, Nigeria, Korea, Taiwan, Singapore, Japan, Hong Kong, Columbia, Ethiopia, Lebanon, Venezuela, Nicaragua and Chile, and many others.

The American credit management association, NACM, recognized years ago the need to get export credit men together and formed FCIB, with its own European branch, which organizes a Credit Forum three times a year in different European capitals, on the same lines as the ICM event in UK. Its delegates from fifteen or so different countries mostly have worldwide or European credit responsibilities. Credit problems are the same for all exporters, and subjects from a recent FCIB meeting were:

- Protesting drafts in Eastern Europe.
- Incoterms interpretation.
- Arab boycott – Israeli origins.
- Payment by commissions of third-party debts.
- Expansion of credit business with China.
- Shortage of hard currency in Poland and Romania.

and several others, the mass of contributions being in terms and payments experience for 26 difficult countries.

Seminars, conferences and courses

Training seminars and conferences in export credit are organized by several bodies in different parts of the UK. As profit-making ventures, they generally are aimed at a wide catchment area, which makes subject treatment difficult, e.g. the basics of Bills of Exchange will not appeal to the experienced contractor of building works who wants to know the legal situation on foreign Bonds and Retentions. Exporters should study the variety of brochures that come their way by post and see where the material offered might be useful to their particular staff needs. No public seminars are 100% useful, because of the mismatch of delegates and subjects, but the benefits come from a mixture of knowledge, definitions and working hints, plus the motivation effect on staff selected for such training.

In looking for suitable courses, managers should be careful not to depend totally on academic lecturers, who may well be out of touch with topical solutions. A good programme will probably have four or five topics in one day, with a good ratio of practising credit men to academics. There should always be time allowed for questions from the floor and always notes issued to delegates to reinforce the verbal material.

Dun and Bradstreet International run frequent and excellent courses for 1 or 3 days. One-day topics include 'Export Credit and Payments', 'Letters of Credit', 'Documentary Bills of Exchange' and others, while the three-day residential course 'The Complete Export Credit Manager' is comprehensive and allows time for useful group discussion of experiences and techniques. Details of all current courses are available from the Courses Manager at D & B in High Wycombe.

The Institute of Credit Management, through its Seminar Committee, organizes training seminars in export subjects, usually in London hotels covering topics such as: 'collection techniques', 'the differences in export from home trade', 'Export clauses in contracts', etc. Full details of forthcoming export training can always be obtained from the Secretary of the ICM at Easton House, Easton-on-the-Hill, Stamford, Lincs PE9 3NH, UK.

The Institute of Export runs occasional public seminars on export credit topics and its magazine 'Export Today' carries advertisements also for commercial firms performing training work. In addition, the Institute's regional branches have monthly meetings which are sometimes devoted to credit and finance topics, particularly on matters of documentation. Details of all I of Ex training activities are available from the Director of Education at Export House, 64, Clifton Street, EC2A 4HB.

The Chambers of Commerce around the country, particularly in Birmingham and Manchester, include export credit and finance in their range of courses for business people. The courses are usually run in partnership with commercial organizations who obtain specialist speakers to meet the Chambers' requirements. Members should contact their local Chamber for details of forthcoming courses. Such requests, particularly for specific topics, help Chambers to formulate future staff training courses.

Full-scale conferences on export credit subjects tend to be single events attracting audiences to hotel venues on subjects of topical business interest. Conferences are for listening to expert speakers, and do not have the learning benefit available to participative delegates at seminars. Useful conferences tend to be advertised in the financial press and in export magazines, such as 'Export Times' and 'Euromoney'.

Books

Training at all levels can be enhanced by the selective use of books and booklets, which:

● increase actual knowledge;
● provide reference data when needed;
● help in preparation for examinations.

Complete books on export credit and finance are rare, but there are relevant sections of other books, and a large number of booklets from official bodies and the banks. It is often said that exporters are smothered in official advice, but the real need is for time to extract the particular advice each practitioner needs. In recent years, the clearing banks and National Westminster Bank in particular have produced some first-class A4-size booklets on all the major export finance topics. They are free of charge and provide excellent training material for staff, with clear layouts, definitions and flowcharts.

The following list is but a handful of recommended material:

On general export topics

Into Active Exporting	BOTB	(free)
How To Start Exporting	Dept of Employment	(free)
Exporting For The Smaller Firm	BOTB	(free)
Exporter and Forwarder	Institute of Freight Forwarders	
Croners Reference Book For Exporters	Croner Publications	

On export credit

Credit Management Handbook	Edwards (Gower Publishing)
International C M Handbook	Clarke (Gower Publishing)
Credit Management	Bass (Business Books)

On export finance

Banking on Exports	BOTB
Trade Finance Report	Euromoney Magazine
Trade Finance Review	Export Times
Finance of International Trade	Watson (Institute of Bankers)

On payment terms and risks

International Risk and Payment Review	Dun and Bradstreet

On export law

The Export Trade	Schmitthoff (Stevens and Sons)

On credit insurance

Credit Insurance	Edwards (Woodhead Faulkner Pub.)	
Market Review	Credit Insurance Assoc.	(free)
ECGD Services	ECGD	(free)

On foreign exchange

Foreign Exchange for Export/Import	Barclays Bank	(free)
Foreign Exchange	Natwest Bank	(free)

On countertrade

Countertrade	DTI	(free)
The Countertrade Handbook	Francis (Woodhead Faulkner Pub)	

On performance bonds

Foreign Bonds and Guarantees	NatWest Bank	(free)

On documentary credits/collections

Guide to Documentary Credit Operations	ICC London	
Documentary Credits	NatWest Bank	(free)
The Documentary Credits Handbook	Davis (Woodhead Faulkner Pub)	

On international trade conventions

Guide to Incoterms	ICC London
Uniform Rules For Collections, 322	ICC London
Uniform Customs and Practice for Documentary Credits, 400	ICC London

Note: The Midland Bank free booklet 'Services for Exporters' is an excellent all-round document for training credit staff and for daily reference use. It gives concise, accurate descriptions of all the most usual export credit and collection activities from a bank's point of view.

Correspondence courses and examinations

The expressions 'Distance Learning' and 'Open Learning' have replaced the older term 'Correspondence Course'. Distance learning simply means the study at a distance from the tutor, but nowadays with the inclusion of lessons on audio and sometimes video and computer floppy disk. Good distance learning courses are very effective, including as they do a variety of pace and text style, and requiring a number of self-test exercises at intervals. Open learning means there is no need for pre-qualification, i.e. courses are open to anybody.

Company staff often study topics in detail in random fashion, for general interest or job progression, but may not think of formalizing their study to obtain qualifications to prove their skills to others. It is now very common for employers to encourage staff to study by paying their tuition costs and examination fees.

We look here at examination study provided by:

● the Institute of Credit Management;
● the Institute of Export;
● Dun and Bradstreet International.

The ICM syllabus is largely based on home trade credit but requires members to cover export within the total all-round approach.

The Institute of Export syllabus deals largely with marketing and shipping but has essential sections on trade finance matters.

Institute of credit management

Entry is by student membership, with examinations held twice per year leading to the designation MICM (Grad). The subjects are:

Intermediate
(a)   Business Environment
(b)   Accountancy
(c)   Business Law
(d)   Credit Management I

Final
(a)   Credit Management II – Advanced Studies
(b)   Credit Management III – Case Studies and Essay
(c)   Law of Credit Management
(d)   Legal Proceedings and Insolvency

Details of ICM membership and examinations are available from the Education Secretary at the ICM. Tuition is by private study, or attendance at evening classes at a number of national colleges, or through the correspondence course offered by Rapid Results College for the Intermediate subjects, or the Institute's own Distance Learning course for the Finals.

The institute of export

Examinations lead to the qualification MIEx (Grad) and tuition is provided by colleges, correspondence courses from Wolsey Hall and private study. The examination is in two parts, the first aligning with the Foundation Course in Overseas Trade, which is operated by the Institute together with the Institute of Freight Forwarders. It covers:

(a)   Marketing
(b)   Principles of Law relating to Overseas Trade
(c)   International trade and Payments
(d)   Transportation and Documentation

Part Two covers:

(a)   Export Distribution
(b)   Export Markets, Selection, Research, Statistics
(c)   Principles of Management in Export

Details of IEx membership and examinations are available from the Director of Education.

Note: a combination of MICM (Grad) and MIEx (Grad) qualifications is powerful evidence of a good grounding in export credit matters and related topics.

Dun and Bradstreet International

D & B run a distance learning course called 'Credit and Financial Analysis' which includes export credit. It can be studied for information only or Test answers can be submitted for marking, leading to a Diploma. The course is recognized by the ICM who allow diploma holders exemption from the Credit Management I exam. subject.

12 Useful information and sources

'There is no need for exporters to struggle alone' – is the message of cheer for all those who beaver away in dark corners, despairing of ever pleasing the customer or getting paid and wondering all the while how other exporters cope. Never before has there been so much information available nor so many organizations offering advice. Some, for a fee, will even take over the tasks of selling, shipping, finance, collections and the rest. Much of the information is free.

The data that follows describes helpful services and information, split between organizations and reference material.

External organizations

Some useful bodies outside the company which the export credit person can call upon for information are grouped into:

- Professional: ICM; FCIB; Institute of Export.
- Official: BOTB; DTI; SITPRO; ICC.
- Banking: UK and foreign banks.

ICM – the Institute of Credit Management Ltd

Easton House,
Easton-on-the-Hill,
Stamford,
Lincs PE9 3NH.
Telephone: 0780 56777.

This is the professional body for staff in credit management and includes the retail, commercial and export sectors of business. There are four classes of membership: Student Member, Ordinary Member (MICM), Member by Examination (MICM (Grad) and Fellow (FICM).)

The ICM, whose President is Sir Kenneth Cork, is controlled by a Council of members mostly employed in senior credit jobs, who meet monthly to direct the affairs of sub-committees and national branches. There are offices abroad and affiliations in several Commonwealth countries. The ICM's publicity leaflet lists the following benefits:

- The monthly 'Credit Management' magazine, with articles on every aspect of modern credit and a special monthly 'Export' feature.
- Educational courses and training events.
- Seminars.
- The National Conference, the prestige event of the year.
- Job Bureau.
- Technical Advisory Committee, dealing with questions of credit, insolvency, job functions, export, debt collection and reporting.
- Regional branches, for convivial gatherings of like minds.
- Consultation with government on matters of credit legislation.
- Special facilities such as occasional Salary Surveys.
- Bookshop.

Of particular value are the twice per year Export Credit Forums organized by the London Branch.

FCIB – Finance and Credit in International Business

FCIB/NACM Corporation,
520 Eighth Avenue,
New York, NY 10018-6571,
USA.
Telephone: 212-947-5070.

Institute of Export

64 Clifton Street,
London EC2A 4HB.
Telephone: 01-247 9812.

This is the professional body for exporters. Its prime interest is education and training and its first-class examination structure, now linked to the Foundation Course in Overseas Trade, is respected everywhere. The Institute has several regional branches where members meet to exchange views and listen to speakers experienced in specialist export subjects.

The advantage for export credit managers in qualifying for the Institute is in acquiring knowledge of all the practical marketing and shipping activities that affect credit and finance abroad.

DTI – the Department of Trade and Industry

1 Victoria Street,
London SW1H 0ET.
Telephone: 01-215 7877.

The DTI is responsible to government for:

- Overseas Trade. International trade policy including the promotion of UK interests in the European Community, GATT, OECD, UNCTAD, etc.
- Export Promotion. Through the BOTB, the promotion of exports and assistance to exporters; bilateral trade relations.
- Industrial Policy and Assistance. Policy for industry generally and certain industries in particular (ship-building, steel, telecoms, etc.).

The Department of Trade and Industry provides services for exporters in close association with the Foreign and Commonwealth Office (responsible for overseas Embassies, Consulates, High Commissions) and with ECGD (separately responsible to the Secretary of State).

BOTB – British Overseas Trade Board

1 Victoria Street,
London, SW1H 0ET.
Telephone: 01-215 5365.

The BOTB is responsible with the DTI mainly for coordinating and directing the Government's export promotion services. Its duties are listed as:

(a)   Advising the Government on strategy for overseas trade.
(b)   Developing Government export promotion services.
(c)   Encouraging and supporting industry and commerce in overseas trade with the aid of appropriate official and private organizations.
(d)   Contributing to the exchange of views between Government and industry to help solve problems for exporters.

It is managed by a Board drawn from industry and the City, Chambers of

Commerce, the CBI, the TUC and various export-orientated Government departments.

The BOTB's services are still under-used and probably not even known by many exporters. All export credit men should at least get hold of the annual reports, which show how vigorous the BOTB has become and how it can help exporters.

Some of the services provided are summarized here:

- Overseas tariffs and import regulations – a data bank on tariffs and other Government regulations.
- Market assessments – these help to find the best prospects overseas.
- Overseas visitors – assembles background information before the exporter arrives in the market.
- Export intelligence service – provides subscribing firms with details of specific export opportunities and other information matched by computer to subscribers' individual needs.
- Agency finding service – enquiries into the prospects for selling an exporter's products in an overseas market and attempt to interest suitable agents.
- Overseas traders' list – short lists of business contacts in overseas markets for most products.
- Status reports – information on the standing of overseas firms (excluding credit).
- Manufacture under licence (sale of know-how) – information about overseas regulations and advice on where to go for help.
- Export marketing research scheme – advice on the methodology of export marketing research and its relevance to a firm's export plans.
- Tackling large-scale projects – early warnings about overseas project opportunities, free background information and advice about projects including those financed by the World Bank and other lending agencies.
- Market statistics – trade and economic data on foreign countries, with foreign telephone and other directories of interest to exporters.
- Overseas seminars and symposia – financial support for participants.
- Overseas trade fairs and exhibitions – organizes shows of British products overseas. Space is sold at very attractive rates and, outside Western Europe, assistance given towards travel costs.
- Overseas missions and promotions – assistance is given.
- Market entry guarantee scheme – offers firms underwriting assistance for certain eligible costs in a new venture.
- The BOTB's regional network (outside London) – services and counselling.
- The Overseas Posts of the Foreign and Commonwealth Office –

Embassies, High Commissions and Consulates – liaise with the CRE and seek out information and early warnings of openings for UK exports. They notify changes in tariff and import regulations, provide market appraisals and help UK firms find suitable agents, representatives, distributors and associates for joint venture partnerships, give UK business visitors assistance and advice, and arrange introductions.

- The Central Office of Information – the production centre of the Government's world-wide publicity network.

SITPRO

The Simplification of International Trade Procedures Board is an independent body established in 1970 and sponsored by the DTI. Its terms of reference are to help in rationalizing international trade procedures, especially documentation, and to help improve export performance generally.

SITPRO made its name originally through its standardization of export documents by a process which aligned a single master with all other required documents. This was later taken onto computer systems such as SPEX.

SITPRO has also produced several excellent guideline documents, some in conjunction with the banks, such as checklists for processing letters of credit, and the brochure 'How To Control Floating Money'.

SITPRO has its executive and staff at: 26/28 King Street, London, SW1Y 6QW (telephone 01-930 0537), and is assisted by a number of Policy, Working and Advisory Groups made up of people from industry, banking, official bodies and government.

Its publicity literature is well worthwhile for keeping in touch with progress on good practices in many areas of export credit.

ICC

The International Chamber of Commerce is not a chamber of commerce in the usual sense. It is based in Paris, with an active London office, and represents some 7000 companies through working committees in some 58 countries. The ICC promotes free trade and self-regulation by business and is famous for its development of internationally agreed standards, such as Incoterms and the Uniform Customs and Practice for Documentary Credits. It is frequently consulted by the United Nations, the EEC and the OECD.

In the UK, the ICC is controlled by a Council of active members and advised by senior industrialists. It ensures that British views are fully represented in worldwide ICC activity and has direct access to government.

The specialist ICC Commissions develop codes of conduct, operating guidelines and international standards in many areas, particularly in banking techniques and trade practices.

Apart from its well known publications for exporters, the ICC operates an effective Arbitration Court to resolve contractual disputes, and is combatting maritime fraud through its International Maritime Bureau.

Details of all activities and publications can be obtained from: The Director, ICC, UK, Centre Point Building, London WC1A 1QB (telephone 01-240 5558).

UK and foreign banks

The major UK banks provide a useful range of financial and information services for exporters, as covered extensively in previous chapters. It is worth mentioning that their publications are free, and some particularly useful for training and reference purposes are:

'Services for Exporters'	Midland Bank
'Exporters Bulletin'	National Westminister Bank
Country Reports	Barclays Bank (on behalf of Abecor group of European Banks)

The latter give interesting economic news and statistics on individual country sheets but also, as a quick guide to country risk, they show the cover for imports out of foreign currency reserves with comments on payment performance as 'not problems', 'variable delays' and so on.

Exporters should not just rely on their own friendly clearing bank for information, they should see what the banking market has to offer for their particular territories and products. It is worth repeating – *all* the major UK banks produce excellent booklets for exporters, free of charge.

The role of foreign banks in the UK is less well known. They are here to represent their country or their foreign Head Office and can be divided between the long-established type and the recent arrivals in the City.

One main activity of the long-established foreign banks is advising documentary credits to UK exporters on behalf of their national customers, and exporters must remember that the credits are only as good as the issuing banks' countries, even when sent from the prosperous-looking chrome and glass branch edifice in the City of London. They are also generally cooperative in obtaining reports and reference on national companies. The European banks in London, particularly Swiss and German, are extremely sound on foreign exchange forecasts and advice.

The foreign banks that flooded into the City in the 60s and 70s were mainly US and Middle Eastern. The American banks were restricted by expansion laws in the USA and saw London as the base for growth in Europe, particularly with Euro-dollar loans. Many UK companies have been 'hard sold' by politely aggressive US banks to borrow money or for total 'money-management' schemes. Direct Collections for example whereby UK documentary collections are sent to, say, Bank of America in Bombay, can be remitted rapidly, upon payment by telex to Bank of America in London. One of the most useful services of the US banks in London is foreign exchange dealing, and exporters are certainly recommended to get a mix of advice on forward currency rates, etc., from a UK clearer, a merchant bank and a US bank.

Reference data

From the mass of export information available from the press, magazines, libraries and trade associations, we have selected data on the following topics:

- Terms and expressions, in dictionary style.
- Useful business vocabulary, in English, French and German.
- Foreign balance sheet expressions, with English translations.
- Foreign company structures and availability of accounts.
- Foreign chambers of commerce in London.
- Major international organizations, with addresses.
- Foreign travel data (Time zones; distances; jet-lag effects; country information; etc.).
- International groups providing aid and loans.
- Useful publications for export credit and finance staff.

Glossary of export terms

Acceptance or Accepted Draft	A bill of exchange signed by the party upon whom it is drawn, i.e. the drawee.
Advance Payment Bond	A Bond from a bank or a surety company on behalf of an exporter

guaranteeing the refund to a buyer of his advance payment if the exporter does not complete the contract.

Advising Bank	The bank which advises the terms of a letter of credit to a seller (beneficiary).
Agent	One who acts with the authority of another person, who is then the Principal.
Air Waybill	Document of carriage for air freight.
Arbitration	Submission of disputed matter to a third person for decision.
Arrangement	Agreement between debtor and his creditors to reschedule debt repayments over a longer period.
At Sight	Payable on demand.
Aval	The joint and several guarantee of a Bill of Exchange usually given by a bank.
Average	Damage or loss at sea. Used in insurance documents as either partial loss (with particular average), or total loss (free of particular average).
AWB	*See* Air Waybill.
Back-To-Back Credit	A Letter of Credit funded by another letter of credit.
Banker's Draft	The cheque of a bank's own account.
Bid Bond	Same as a Tender Bond.
Bill of Exchange (B/E)	A legally defined payment demand issued by a seller/creditor to a buyer/debtor.
Bill of Lading (B/L)	Receipt given by ship owner or agent for goods received on board a vessel for carriage to a stated destination. It is also evidence of the contract of carriage and a document of title to the goods.
Blank Endorsement	Signature on back of a B/E or B/L, without any qualifying instructions, enabling the value to be transferred to a party not yet named.
BOTB	British Overseas Trade Board, part of the Department of Trade and Industry, responsible for helping exporters and government on export matters.
C and F	Cost and freight. Same as CIF but excluding insurance.

Case of Need	A representative or agent of the exporter in the buyer's country.
Cash Against Documents (CAD)	Shipping documents sent to bank with instructions to be handed over to consignee only in exchange for the sum due.
Caveat Emptor	Literally – 'let the buyer beware'. Unless warranty is offered, the buyer is at risk.
Certificate of Origin	A document to prove place of origin of goods specified.
Certified Invoice	An invoice certified by an authorized Chamber of Commerce, usually as to origin and value.
Charter Party	Contract for a vessel leased for a specific period of voyage.
CIF	Cost, insurance, freight. Cost of goods plus freight and insurance to named port of destination.
Clause	An additional condition in a document.
Clean Collection/Clean Bill	Bill of exchange without shipping documents attached, collected through the banking system.
CMR	Road consignment transport document.
COD	Cash on delivery.
Collecting Bank	Bank authorized to collect from a customer.
Commercial Paper	A banking term for negotiable bills of exchange.
Confirmed Irrevocable L/C	L/C issued irrevocably by one bank and confirmed (guaranteed) by another bank.
Confirming Bank	A bank which adds its guarantee to a Letter of Credit issued by another bank.
Consideration	Act or promise or price for which agreement is entered into.
Consignment Account	An account for goods stocked locally, usually where buyer is not a good credit risk. Seller retains ownership of goods until sold.
Consular Invoice	Invoice prepared on special form and legalized by consul of importing country to confirm details and origin.
Convertible Currency	Currency freely exchangeable for other main currencies.

Correspondent Bank	Bank in formal relationship with another bank in a particular transaction.
Credit	Has many variations:
	• The trust given by a seller to a buyer to pay at a future date.
	• A letter of credit.
	• Period within which a debtor should pay.
Credit Insurance	Protection against the risk of non-payment by a buyer or country.
Credit References	Information obtained to describe the status and payment record of a buyer.
Credit Risk	Risk of customer insolvency or non-payment.
Credit Terms	Method and period allowed for payment.
Currency Permit	Authority to buyer from his government to pay in foreign currency.
Customs Entry Form	Declaration by exporter to customs before export.
D/A	Documents against Acceptance.
DDP	Delivered Duty Paid. The exporter is responsible for all costs and risks as far as the customer's premises.
Dangerous Goods Note	Certificate issued by exporter declaring to carrier that goods are hazardous.
Debtors	The amounts owning to a seller from customers.
Demurrage	Charge made for delay in unloading ships.
Direct Collection	A documentary bill of exchange sent directly to the collecting bank by the exporter.
Discrepancy	Mistake or omission in documentary requirements.
Dishonour	To refuse to accept or pay a cheque or a bill of exchange.
Documentary Credit, or Documentary Letter of Credit	A document issued by a bank on behalf of a buyer in favour of a seller through another bank which makes payment to the seller against stipulated documents.
Documentary Collection	Generic term for collections made through banks against documents with

	or without bills of exchange attached.
Documentary Sight Draft	A Bill of Exchange payable at Sight, to which documents of title are attached for release against payment.
Documents Against Acceptance	Shipping documents attached to draft due at a future date for a bank to present to drawee who, upon acceptance of draft, obtains release of the goods.
D/P	Documents against Payment.
ECU	European Currency Unit.
EEC	European Economic Community (Common Market).
EFTA	European Free Trade Area.
EMS	European Monetary System (The 'snake').
Endorsee	Person to whom bill of exchange is transferred by endorsement of third party.
Endorser	One who endorses a bill, and accepts liability.
Escrow	Delivery to a third person usually a bank, of funds to be held until performance of some event.
Ex Works	Net cost of goods at manufacturer's works with buyer responsible for all subsequent costs.
Exchange Rate	Value of one currency against another.
Exchange Risk	Risk because of difference between rate of foreign exchange at time commitment is undertaken and rate at time of discharge.
Export Licence	Issued by a government to an exporter to permit the export of particular goods or services.
External Account	A bank account held in another country or in another currency.
FAS	Free alongside ship. Cost of goods plus all charges until placed alongside a vessel at a named port.
First of Exchange	First or principal copy of a bill of exchange to be presented and honoured, the other copies then being automatically cancelled.
FOB	Free on Board. Cost of goods plus all

	charges until placed on board vessel at named port.
FOR	Free on Rail. Cost of goods plus all charges until placed on rail at a named railway station.
Forward Exchange Contract	Contract whereby bank agrees with client the future rate of exchange that will be used in buying or selling currency.
Free of Particular Average	Insurance clause covering total loss only, except when vessel has been sunk, stranded or burnt, when partial loss is paid.
Freight Forwarder's Receipt	Receipt for goods prior to actual shipment.
Front-end Finance	Finance for the portion of a supply contract not covered by credit terms, i.e. the down payment.
GATT	General Agreement on Tariffs and Trade.
General Average	Contribution made by each exporter in proportion to the value of his goods, towards a loss incurred at sea by act of sacrifice for the general good.
Gross Weight	Total of goods and packing.
Groupage Bill of Lading	B/L including goods consolidated with others.
House Airbill	Special air waybill used for consolidated air shipments, i.e. those of different exporters grouped together.
ICC	International Chamber of Commerce.
IMF	International Monetary Fund.
Import Duty Drawback	Reclaim by importer of duty paid (normally because goods to be re-exported).
Import Entry Form	Application by buyer to his customs to import goods.
Import Licence (I/L)	Licence issued by buyer's government to buyer to authorize import.
Incoterms	The internationally standard definitions of delivery terms issued by the ICC.
Indemnity	Security to prevent person (often a bank) from being harmed by act which he does at request of another.

Indent	Order given by an overseas buyer to supplier, confirming house or export merchant for goods to be purchased.
Insolvency	The inability to meet liabilities from assets.
Inspection Report (of clean findings)	Certificate issued by inspector acting in exporter's country on behalf of buyers.
Instruction Schedule	List of instructions to a bank relating to a draft to be collected.
Insurable Interest	Monetary interest in property essential to obtain insurance cover.
Irrevocable Letter of Credit (ILC)	L/C which cannot be cancelled or amended once issued without consent of all parties.
Issuing Bank	The bank which issues a letter of credit on behalf of a buyer.
L/C	Letter of Credit.
Lien	Right by which person can claim charge against property of debtor as security.
Local Currency	The currency of the buyer's country.
Mail Transfer	Transmission of payment between banks, either by airmail or surface mail communication.
Marine Risks	In insurance, events which could cause losses in sea shipments.
Mate's Receipt	Receipt given by the mate of vessel for goods later exchanged for Bill of Lading.
Moratorium	An agreement between a debtor and his creditors to a postpone payment obligations for a specific period. Alternatively a unilateral declaration of postponement by a country.
National Standard Shipping Note	Form completed when delivering goods to receiving authority at British freight terminal.
Negotiable	Capable of transferring rights to another party, e.g. on a payment, documents or a bill of lading.
Net Weight	Weight of goods only, without any wrapper or container.
Nostro Account	The amount held by a bank in another bank overseas.
Notary Public	Public official who authenticates a written statement.

OECD	Organization for Economic Co-operation and Development.
Open Account	Payment term indicating direct exchange of goods/services for payment from buyer to seller.
Order	A request from a potential buyer to be supplied by a potential seller. It becomes a contract when accepted.
Packing List	Detailed list of goods in a package, giving weights and sizes.
Parcel Post Receipt	Receipt issued by Post Office for goods exported by post.
Part Shipment	An agreed delivery of part of a total order.
Particular Average	Partial loss of insured goods.
Performance Guarantee	A Bond from a bank or surety company on behalf of an exporter guaranteeing the buyer that the contract terms will be met.
Political Risk	Risk of government action preventing payment.
Port Mark	Port of destination, stencilled on packages for export.
Presenting Bank	Bank presenting documents to a drawee for acceptance or payment.
Principal	Main party to a contract.
Pro Forma	Specimen (e.g. Pro Forma Invoice).
Promissory Note	An unconditional promise in writing made by a debtor to pay a fixed sum to a creditor on a specified date.
Protest	Legal procedure recording the refusal of a drawee to accept or pay a Draft – a prelude to legal action.
Rail Consignment Note	Transport document for goods sent by rail.
Receivables	(or Accounts Receivable) The amounts owing to a seller by customers.
Recourse	The right to recover funds paid if certain events occur.
Remitting Bank	The bank processing a collection on behalf of a seller.
Revocable Letter of Credit	L/C which can be cancelled before payment.

Revolving L/C	L/C which is restored to full value after use up to a certain date.
Roll on – roll off	Ferry vessel allowing lorries to drive on and off without having to unload.
Roll-over	The extension of a financial commitment at due date.
Sales Contract	A contract between a buyer and a seller for the supply of goods or services.
Second of Exchange	Second copy of a bill of exchange to be presented and honoured when the first copy is not available.
Shipping Note	*See* National Standard Shipping Note.
Shortfall Undertaking	A written agreement by a foreign buyer to be responsible for payment of any additional sum required in local currency to meet an invoiced value.
Shortpayment	Payment of less than the full amount of a debt.
Single Administrative Document	The form which has combined transport and customs requirements in the EC since 1988.
SITPRO	Simplification of International Trade Procedures Board.
Sola	Indicates only one copy of Bill of Exchange is in use.
Spot Rate	Rate applied when foreign currency is required for immediate delivery.
SWIFT	Society for Worldwide International Funds Transfer. A modern system of electronic computer transfer of funds between banks in different countries.
Tare	Actual weight of packing only, without goods.
Telegraphic Transfer	Transmission of funds between banks, using cable, telex or telegram.
Tender Bond	A financial guarantee from a bank or surety company in favour of a potential buyer assuring him of the genuine intent of the exporter submitting a tender.
Tenor Draft	Same as Term Draft.
Term Draft	A Bill of Exchange requiring acceptance by the drawee for payment at a future date.
Title	The right to own goods.

TIR	Transport International Routier. The symbol on road freight transport to indicate customs – sealed loads moving between member countries of the EEC.
Transfer Risk	Risk of inability of buyer's country to remit hard currency.
Transferable L/C	L/C whose benefits can be given to a named other party.
Underwriter	Insurance decision maker who acts for an insurance syndicate or company.
Uniform Customs and Practice (UCP)	Set of standard rules issued by the ICC governing the responsibilities of parties in documentary letters of credit operations.
Uniform Rules for Collections (URC)	Set of standard rules for banks handling foreign documentary collections.
Usance Draft	Same as Term Draft.
Validity Date	Date up to which a L/C may be used.
Value Received	The consideration, or value, in a transaction.
Vostro Account	The account held by an overseas bank in a UK bank.
War Risks	In insurance, risks of loss due to war events.
Weight List	Certificate of weights of exported goods.
Works Requisition Note	Exporter's own document requesting work or goods within his organization.

Business vocabulary in English, French and German

(This is intended to help export credit managers with a basic knowledge of French and/or German who need to use detailed financial expressions in correspondence.)

English	*French*	*German*
Account	Compte	Konto
Accountant	Comptable	Rechnungsprüfer
Advertising	Publicité	Werbung
Agreement	Accord	Abkommen, Vertrag
Appreciation	Appréciation, plus-value	Wertsteigerung
Associate	Associé	Teihaber

Automation	Automation	Automatisierung
Balance	Balance	Saldo
Balance of Payments	Balance de paiements	Zahlungsbilanz
Balance Sheet	Bilan	Bilanz
Bank	Banque	Aktienbank
Central bank	Banque Centrale	Zentralbank
Clearing bank	Banque de Clearing	Cleringbank
Commercial bank	Banque Commerciale	Handelsbank
Merchant bank	Banque d'affaires	Remboursbank
Bank Rate	Taux Officiel	Diskontsatz
Bid – takeover	Faillite	Konkurs, Bankrott
Bid – takover	Offre Publique d'achat	Übernahmeangebot
Bill of Lading	Connaissement	Seefrachtbrief
Board of Directors	Conseil d'admini-stration	Vorstand
Bond	Obligation	Schuldverschreibung
Bonded Warehouse	Entrepôt hors douane	Zollniederlage
Budget	Budget	Budget, Voranschlag
Business	Affaires	Geschäft
Capital Goods	Biens d'équipement	Investititionsgüter
Cargo Handling	Manutention	Güterumschlag
Cheap	Bon Marché	Billig
CIF (cost, insurance, freight)	CAF (coût, assurance, frêt)	CIF (Kosten, Versicherung, Fracht)
Claim	Réclamation	Anspruch
COD (Cash on delivery)	Livraison contre remboursement	Zahlbar bei Lieferung
Collateral	Collatéral	Deckung, Sicherheit
Commission	Commission	Provision
Company	Société	Gesellschaft
Associate Company	Société affilée	Nahestehende Gesellschaft
Holding Company	Société holding	Holdinggesell-schaft
Limited Liability company	Société à responsa-bilité Limitée Société anonyme	Gesellschaft mit beschränkter Haftung
Parent Company	Société-mère	Muttergesell-schaft
Partnership	Société en commandité	Partnerschafts-gesellschaft

Subsidiary	Filiale	Tochtergesell-schaft
Competition	Concurrence	Wettbewerb
Component	Composant	Bestandteil
Computer	Ordinateur	Computer
Consumer Goods	Biens de consomma-tion	Verbrauchsgüter
Containerization	Containeurisation	Umstellung auf Container
Contract	Contrat	Vertrag, Kontrakt
Control System	Système de contrôle	Kontrollsystem
Cooperative Society	Société en co-opérative	(Konzern-) Genossen-schaft
Cost	Coût	Kosten
Cost of living	Coût de la vie	Lebenshaltungs-kosten
Credit	Crédit	Kredit, Gutschrift
Credit balance	Solde créditeur	Kreditsaldo
Credit squeeze	Reserrement du crédit	Kreditbeschrän-kung
Creditor	Créancier	Gläubiger
Currency	Monnaie	Währung
Convertible currency	Monnaie convertible	Konvertible Wäh-rung
Hard currency	Monnaie forte	Harte Währung
Soft currency	Monnaie faible	Weiche Währung
Customs duties	Droit de douane	Zoll
Data processing	Informatique	Datenverarbeitung
Debt	Dette	Schuld
Debtor	Débiteur	Schuldner
Delivery	Livraison	Lieferung
Developing Country	Pays en voie de développement	Entwicklungsland
Director	Administrateur	Vorstandsmitglied
Managing Director	Directeur général	Direktor General
Discount, rebate	Escompte	Diskont, Rabatt
Dumping	Dumping	Schleduderausfuhr
Durables	Biens d'équipment	Langlebige Ver-brauchsgüter
Duty	Taxe, Douane	Zoll
Customs duty	Droit de douane	Einfuhrzoll
Stamp duty	Droit de timbre	Stempelsteuer
Economy	Economie	Wirtschaft, Ekonomie

Economy of scale	Économie de masse	Kostenminderung durch grosse Serien
EEC (European Economic Community)	CEE (Communauté Économique Européenne)	EWG (Europäische Wirtschaftsgemein-schaft)
EFTA (European Free Trade Association)	AELE (Association Européene de Libre) Échange)	EFTA (Europäische Freihandelszone)
Embassy	Ambassade	Botschaft
Employee	Employé	Angestellter, Arbeitnehmer
Equity	Actions	Aktienkapital
Estimate	Évaluation	Schätzung, Voranschlag
Exchange	Bourse, Bureau de Change	Börse, Wechseln
Foreign exchange	Change	Devisen
Exchange control	Contrôle des Changes	Devisenkontrolle
Exchange rate	Taux de Change	Devisenkurs, Wechselkurs
Floating exchange rate	Taux de Change flottant	Gleitender Wechselkurs
Executive	Exécutif	Leitender Angesteller
Factoring	Factoring	Debitorenverkauf
Factory	Usine	Fabrik, Werk
Financial Year	Exercice	Finanzjahr, Geschäftsjahr
Forecast	Prévisions	Voraussage
Freight	Frêt	Fracht
Goodwill	Droit à la Clientèle	Firmenwert
Gross	Brut	Brutto
Hire Purchase	Vente à tempérament	Abzahlungsgeschäft
Import Licence	Licence d'importation	Einfurlizenz
Import Quota	Contingent d'importation	Einfuhrquote
Income Tax	Impôt sur le revenu	Einkommensteuer
Indemnity	Indemnité	Entschädigung, Haftpflicht
Insurance	Assurance	Versicherung

Interest	Intérêt	Zinsen
Majority interest	Majorité	Mehrheitsanteil
Interest rate	Taux d'intérêt	Zinsfuss
Inventory	Stock	Inventar, Bestand
Invoice	Facture	Faktura
IOU	Doit	Schuldschein
Lease	Bail	Pacht
Liability	Obligation	Verbindlichkeit
Current liability	Passif exigible à court terme	Laufende Verbindlichkeit
Deferred liability	Passif à long terme	Rückstellung
Long-term	à long terme	Langfristig
Losses	Pertes	Verluste
Management	Gestion	Geschäftsleitung
Manager	Directeur	Manager, Geschäftsleiter
Manufacturing	Fabrication	Hersellung
Margin	Marge	Spanne
Profit margin	Marge bénéficiaire	Gweinnspanne
Market	Marché	Markt
Market Research	Recherche des Marchés	Marktforschung
Market Share	Part du Marché	Marktanteil
Marketing	Marketing	Vermarkten
Maturity	Échéance (date d')	Fälligkeit
Medium-term	à moyen terme	Mittelfristig
Merger	Fusion	Fusion, Zusammenschluss
Money	Monnaie	Geld
Mortgage	Hypothèque	Hypothek
Nationalization	Nationalisation	Verstaatlichung
Net Assets	Valeurs Nettes	Netto Aktiva
Obsolescence	Désuétude	Veraltung
Order	Commande	Auftrag
Overdraft	Découvert	Kontoüberziehung
Overheads	Frais Généraux	Betriebskosten
Packaging	Emballage	Verpackung
Par	Pair, Parité	Pari, Nennwert
Power of Attorney	Procuration	Vollmacht
Premium	Prime	Aufgeld, Agio

Price	Prix	Preis
Profit Margin	Marge Bénéficiaire	Gweinnspanne
Profitability	Rentabilité	Rentabilität
Proxy (Person)	Fonde de pouvoir	Stellvertreter, Bevollmächtigter
(Document)	Procuration	Vollmachtsurkunde
Public Corporation	Régie	Öffentliche-rechtliche Körperschaft
Quotation	Cotation	Preisangabe
Rate (Exchange)	Cours	Wechselkurs
(Interest)	Taux	Zinfuss
Bank rate	Taux Officiel (d'escompte)	Diskontsatz
Exchange rate	Taux de Change	Devisenkurs, Wechselkurs
Raw Materials	Matières Brutes	Rohstoffe, Grundmaterialen
Rebate, discount	Remise, escompte	Rabatt
Receipt	Recu	Quittung
Risk	Risque	Risko
Royalty	Droits d'auteur, redevance	Tantieme, Lizengebühr
Salary	Traitement	Gehalt
Sale	Vente	Verkauf
Salvage (money)	Prime de Sauvetage	Bergegeld
Savings Bank	Caisse d'épargne	Sparkasse
Securities	Titres	Wertpapiere
Share	Action, Titre, Valeur	Aktie
Share Certificate	Certificat d'action	Aktienzertifikat
Short-term	à court terme	Kurzfristig
Solvent	Solvable	Solvent, zahlungsfähig
Spot	Comptant	Kassa, sofort, zahlbar
Stamp Duty	Droit de Timbre	Stempelsteuer
Standing Order	Ordre Ouvert	Ständiger Auftrag
Stock (Inventory)	Stock	Inventar
(Share Capital)	Valeurs, capital	Stamm-Kapital
Stock Control	Gestion de Stocks	Lagerkontrolle
Strike	Grève	Streik
Subsidy	Subvention	Subvention
Subsidiary	Filiale	Tochtergesellschaft

| Suppliers | Fournisseur | Lieferant |
| Surcharge | Surtaxe | Aufgeld |

Tax	Impôt	Steuer
Corporation tax	Impôt sur les sociétés	Körperschaftssteuer
Future tax reserve	Réserve pour impôts futurs	Rückstellung fur zukünftigte Steuerbelastung
Income tax	Impôt sur le revenue	Einkommensteuer
VAT	Taxe à valeur adjoutée (TVA)	Mehrwertsteuer
Trade	Commerce	Handel
Free Trade	Libre Échange	Freihandel
Trade Union	Syndicat	Gewerkschaft
Trading Profits	Bénéfices d'exploitation	Handelsgewinne
Turnover	Chiffre d'affaires	Umsatz

Underwriter	Assureur	Versicherer
Unemployment	Chômage	Arbeitslosigkeit
Unsecured	Sans Garantie	Ungesichert

| Value | Valeur | Vermïgenswerte, Werte |
| Viable | Viable | Lebensfähig |

Wage	Salaire	Lohn
Wholesale	en Gros	Grosshandel
Work-in-progress	en Cours de Fabrication	im Arbeitsprozess
Working Capital	Fonds du roulement, Capital d'exploitation	Betriebskapital

Foreign balance sheet terms and English equivalents

FRENCH

| Bilan | Balance Sheet |
| Actif | Assets |

| Amortissements | Depreciation |
| Autres valeurs immobilisées | Other Non-Current Assets |

| Banques et cheques posteaux | Cash at Bank |

Caisses	Cash in Hand
Clients	Receivables
Comptes d'Associés	Associate Company Receivables
Constructions	Buildings
Effets à recevoir	Bills Receivable
Immobilisations	Fixed Assets
Immobilisations incorporelles	Intangibles
Matériel et outillage	Machinery and Tools
Matériel de transport	Vehicles
Matières premières et fournitures	Raw Materials and Supplies
Mobilier et matériel de bureau	Furniture and Fittings
Montant brut	Total Gross
Montant net	Total Net
Produits finis	Finished Goods
Produits semi-ouvrés	Work-in-Progress
Titres de Participation	Investments
Valeurs d'exploitation	Inventories
Valeurs Realisables à Court Terme on Disponibles	Current Assets
Passif	Liabilities
Banques	Bank Loans
Capital Social ou Personnel	Capital
Capitaux Propres et Reserves	Capital and Reserves
Dettes à Court Terme	Current Liabilities
Effets à Payer	Bills Payable
Fournisseurs	Creditors
Compte de Pertes et Profits	Profit and Loss Account
Achats	Purchases
Chiffre d'Affaires	Turnover
Compte d'exploitation generale	Trading Account
Dotation	Depreciation
Frais de Personnel	Salaries
Frais Divers de Gestion	Administrative Expenses
Frais Financiers	Interest Charges
Impôts sur les Bénéfices	Tax on Profits
Ristournes, Rabais et Remises obtenus	Discounts and Allowances
Stock au début de l'exercice	Opening Stock
Stocks à la fin de l'exercice	Closing Stock
Travaux, Fournitures et Services exterieurs	Supplies and Services
Ventes	Sales

GERMAN

Aktiva	Assets

Abschreibungen	Depreciation
Anlagen in Bau und Anzahlungen auf Anlagen	Fixed Assets in Buildings less Advance Payments
Anlagevermögen	Fixed Assets
Ausleihungen	Loans
Beteiligungen	Investments
Betriebs and Geschäftausstattung	Factory and Office Equipment
Finanzanlagen	Financial Assets
Forderungen	Receivables
Forderungen an Verbundene Unternehmen	Amounts Due from Associate Companies
Geleistete Anzahlungen	Prepayments to Suppliers
Geschäftswert	Goodwill
Grundstücke und Grundstückgleiche – Rechte mit Geschäftsfabrik und anderen Bauten	Land and Property and Rights with Buildings
Grundstücke und Grundstückgleiche Rechte ohne Bauten	Land, Property and Rights, without Buildings
Kassenbestand, Banken und Postscheckguthaben	Cash in Hand and Bank
Konzessionen, Gewerbliche Schutzrechte und Ahnliche Rechte	Intangible Assets (royalities, concessions, etc.)
Maschinen und Maschinelle Anlagen	Machinery and Plant
Rechnungsabgrenzungsposten	Pre-paid Expenses
Roh, Hilfs, und Betriebstoffe	Raw Material and Supplies
Schecks	Cheques
Umlaufvermögen	Current Assets
Unfertige Erzeugnisse	Work-in-Progress
Erzeugnisse und Waren	Finished Goods
Vorräte	Stocks (inventories)
Wechsel	Bills Receivable
Werkzeuge	Tools
Passiva	Liabilities
Anleihen	Loans
Bilanzgewinn	Retained Earnings
Freie Rücklagen	Voluntary Reserves
Wertberichtigungen	Provisions
Gesetzliche Rücklage	Legal Reserves
Grundkapital	Share Capital
Kurzfristige Verbindlichkeiten	Current Liabilities
Lastensausgleichs Vermögensabgabe	Tax Reserve
Offene Rücklagen	Capital Reserves
Rückstellungen	Accrued Liabilities
Sonstige Verbindlichkeiten	Other Liabilities
Steuern	Taxes

Verbindlichkeiten aus Lieferungen und Leis-tungen	Trade Creditors
Verbindlichkeiten Gegenüber Kreditinstituten	Liabilities to Banks
Verbindlichkeiten Gegenüber Kreditinstituten davon durch Grundpfan drechte gesichert	Bank Liabilities – Secured by Charge
Verbindlichkeiten gegenüber verbundenen Unternehmen	Liabilities to Associate Companies
Wechselverbindlichkeiten	Bills Payable
Aufwendung fur Roh Hilfs und Betriebstoffe	Cost of Goods Sold
Gesamtleistung	Total Revenue
Jahresüberschuss	Profit for Year
Jahresverlust	Loss for Year
Löhne und Gehälter	Salaries
Rohertrag (Rohaufwand)	Gross Profit (Loss)
Sonstige Aufwendungen	Other Expenses
Sonstige Erträge	Other Income
Umsatzerlöse	Turnover
Zinsen und Ahnliche Aufwendungen	Interest and Financial Charges

SPANISH

Activo	Assets
Activo Circulante	Current Assets
Almacenes	Stocks
Anticipos en Compras	Advance Payments to Suppliers
Caja y Bancos	Cash and Bank
Cartera de Valores	Securities
Cuentas Corrientes o Deudores	Receivables
Effectos a Cobrar	Bills Receivable
Fabricacion Existencia	Finished Goods
Immovilizado	Fixed Assets
Inmuebles	Property
Inversiones	Investments
Maquinaria	Machinery
Materia Prima	Raw Material
Terreno	Land
Trabajos en Curso	Work-in-Progress
Utiles	Tools
Pasivo	Liabilities
Amortizaciones	Depreciation
Capital Social	Share Capital
Creditos Bancarios	Bank Loans
Dividendo	Dividend
Efectos a Pagar	Bills Payable
Exigible a Corto Plazo	Current Liabilities
Exigible a Medio y Largo Plaza	Medium and Long-Term Liabilities
Fondos Propios	Shareholders' Funds
Impuestos	Tax

Reserva	Reserve
Saldos Acreedores	Creditors
Cuenta Perdidas y Ganancias	Profit and Loss Account
Beneficio	Profit
Gastos Financieros	Financial Expenses
Ingresos de Explotacion	Gross Income
Previsiones	Provisions
Remanentee jericicio Anterior	Balance Brought Forward
Resultado Bruto	Gross Profit

Foreign company structures and financial accounts

EUROPE

Austria

AG (Aktiengesellschaft) = Limited Company.
GmbH (Gesellschaft mit beschrankter Haftung) = Partnership with Limited Liability.
OHG (Offene Handelsgesellschaft) = Joint and Several Partnership.
GmbH & Co. KG = A Partnership with a GmbH wholly liable.

Only the AG companies have to publish certified balance sheets. They appear in the official 'Wiener Zeitung' as soon as published and annually in the book 'Finanz-Compass'.

Addresses for copies

Weiner Zeitung (Bilanzabteilung),
Rennweg 16,
A1030, Vienna.

Compass-Verlag (Abteilung Finanz-Compass),
Wipplingerstrasse 32,
A1013, Vienna.

Belgium

SA/NV = Limited Company.
SCA = Limited Partnership.
SC = Cooperative Company.

Balance Sheets are published in French or Flemish (hence the 'SA/NV') for all the above types and copies are available from:

Banque Nationale de Belgique SA,
5 Boulevard de Berlaimont,
B1000, Belgium

or, the local Greffe du Tribunal de Commerce.

Denmark

A/S = Limited Company, minimum issued capital DKr 100 000.

ApS = Limited Company, minimum issued capital DKr 30 000.
I/S = Limited Partnership.
KA/S = Partnership Limited to Shares.

Only A/S and ApS companies have to file Balance Sheets and ApS companies can be exempted.

Published Balance Sheets can be obtained from:

Aktieselskabregistret,
Nygade 4,
1164, Copenhagen K.

Finland
Companies with net worth exceeding Fmk 2 million have to file Balance Sheets at the central registry at:

Patentti-ja Rekisterihallitns,
Kaupperekisteri,
Bulevardi 21,
00120 Helsinki 12.

The language of the Balance Sheet may be Finnish, Swedish or German.

France
SA (Société Anonyme) = Limited Company.
SARL (Société à responsibilité limitée) = Partnership with Limited Liability.
SNC (Société en nom collectif) = Joint and Several Partnership.
SCS (Société en commandité simple) = Partnership Limited to Shares.

Only the SA has to file Balance Sheets and in the French tradition of business secrecy, does not have to disclose shareholders and shareholdings. Quoted SA companies require a minimum capital issued of F500 000 and non-quoted SA companies F100 000. An SARL must have a minimum of F20 000.

Copy Balance Sheets must be filed at the local Court Registry and companies with assets above F10 million must publish their accounts in the BALO (Bulletin des Annonces Légales Obligatoires). There is considerable delay in filing accounts in France.

For companies based in Paris, the Registry address is:

Greffe du Tribunal de Commerce de Paris,
Bureau 6,
1 Quai de Corse,
75004 Paris.

West Germany
AG
GmbH
OHG   } As defined for Austria above.
GmbH & Co. KG

An AG must have a minimum capital of DM 100 000 and a GmbH DM 20 000.

In Germany, the banks take equity in companies and thus control many of them.

It is said that German banks are investment trusts. Surprisingly for the disciplined German business system, there are fairly loose controls on filing Balance Sheets.

AG and large GmbH companies have to file Balance Sheets but there are no public rights to inspection. Publication is made in the official

> Bundesanzeiger Verlagsgesellschaft mbH,
> Postfach 108006,
> D5000, Cologne 1.

Greece
AE ⎫
EPE ⎬ Limited Company

Balance Sheet results have to be published in the Government Gazette plus two newspapers. Exporters are advised to obtain Balance Sheets from any of the major Greek banks or credit agencies.

Italy
SpA (Societa per Azioni) = Limited Company.
SRL (Societa a Responsibilita Limitada) = Partnership with Limited Liability.
SNC (Societa in nome collettivo) = Collective Partnership.
SAS (Societa Accomandia Semplice) = Special Limited Partnership.
SCRL (Societa Cooperativa a Responsibilita Limitada) = Cooperative.

SpA companies must have a minimum share capital of Lit 1 million and SRL companies Lit 50 000.

Italian accounting conventions are unclear and it is difficult to relate assets to trading activity or to see how the declared profit figure is calculated.

Only SpA companies have to file Balance Sheets, at the local Registry for the area in which they are based.

Luxembourg
SA ⎫
SARL ⎬ As for France

All companies are registered at the Company Registry and publish their Balance Sheets in the Luxembourg Gazette. The limited information provided by SA companies is available from:

> Le Greffier en Chef,
> Tribunal d'Arondissement,
> Boite Postale 15,
> Luxembourg.

Netherlands
NV (Naamloze Vennootschap) = Limited Company.
BV (Besloten Vennootschap) = Private Limited Company.
VOF (Vennootschap Onder Firma) = General Partnership.
CV (Commanditaire Vennootschap) = Limited Partnership.

Only NV companies and BV companies with assets above Dfl 8 million have to file Balance Sheets at the Commercial Register held by the Chamber of Commerce in their area.

Norway
A/S (Aksjeselkap) = Limited Company (Min. Capital Nkr. 50 000).
K/S (Kommanditselskap) = Limited Partnership.
Ansvarlig Handelsselskap = Trading Partnership.

Only A/S companies have to file Balance Sheets at the local Business Register and some are exempted from doing so by the Government.

Available from the Handelsregisteret for the area of the company.

Spain
SA (Sociedad Anonima) = Limited Company.
SRL (Sociedad de Responsibilidad Limitada) = Partnership with Limited Liability.

Only publicly owned SA companies have to publish Balance Sheets, at the company registry for the province concerned.

A high proportion of companies is owned by the major banks, thus financial stability is provided even if Balance Sheet data are unreliable or missing.

Portugal
SARL = Limited Company.
EP = Nationalized Company.

Both types have to publish publicly their Balance Sheets in the Official Gazette, available up to 12 months later from:

> Diario da Republica,
> Imprensa Nacional - Casa de Moeda,
> Avenida Dr Antonio Jose de Almeida,
> Lisbon 1.

Sweden
AB (Aktiebolag) = Joint Stock Company. Min. Capital Skr. 50 000.
HB (Handelsbolag) = General Partnership.
KB (Kommanditbolag) = Limited Partnership.

Only AB companies have to file accounts for public inspection. The central office address is:

> Kungl Patent och Registerings Verket,
> Bologsbryan,
> Box 6151,
> 102-33 Stockholm.

Switzerland
AG = As per Germany (minimum capital Sfr. 50 000).
SA = As per France (minimum capital Sfr. 50 000).
GmbH/SARL (minimum capital Sfr. 20 000).

All firms are registered in the Commercial Register and new firms are published in the Official Gazette. There is considerable protection for companies in not having to reveal accounts for inspection, and there is no central office. Accounts of major companies are available only to shareholders.

USA

Incorporated companies normally make their audited Balance Sheet available for inspection, either directly to an enquirer, through a bank, or (most easily) through a credit reporting agency. Considerable data is provided, e.g. previous history, notes on products, extensive personal notes on directors plus voluminous accounting detail.

Commonwealth Countries

Many of the former colonies and all of the industrialized nations such as Canada and Australia have a high standard of accounting conventions and good disciplines for publishing Balance Sheets. A succession of regimes in some African countries has effectively reduced the standard of company accounts where disclosures of assets and profits became unwise. As general advice, the exporter should find out from experience, with the aid of a local agent, which countries produce reliable accounts, worth analysis.

Australia
NEW SOUTH WALES
Commissioner for Corporate Affairs, 175 Castlereagh Street, Sydney NSW 2000.
QUEENSLAND
Office of Registrar of Companies and Commercial Acts, State Government Bldg, Anzac Square, Brisbane, Queensland 4000.
SOUTH AUSTRALIA
Registrar of Companies, State Bank Building, 51 Pirie Street, Adelaide, SA 5001.
TASMANIA
Companies Registry, Public Buildings, Macquarie Street, Hobart, Tasmania 6000.
VICTORIA
The Companies Office, 451 La Trobe Street, Melbourne, Victoria 3000.
WESTERN AUSTRALIA
Registrar of Companies, Companies Registered Office, Public Trust Building, 565 Hay Street, Perth, WA 6000.

Canada
Office of Registrar General, Department of Consumer and Corporate Affairs, Ottawa, Ontario K1A OC9.

Hong Kong
The Companies Register, Kayamally Building, Queens Road Central, Hong Kong.

New Zealand
Companies Registry, 175 The Terrace 1, Wellington.

Foreign Chambers of Commerce in London

ARAB-BRITISH CHAMBER OF COMMERCE
42 Berkeley Sq, W1A 4BL. Telephone 01-629 1249. Telex 22171
(This office houses the Secretary-General, Administrative and Financial Staff.)

ARAB-BRITISH CHAMBER OF
  COMMERCE,
26A Albemarle St, W1A 4BL. Telephone 01-499-3400.
(This office deals only with Certification, Documentation, Liaison and Business Information.)

AUSTRALIA
Australian-British Trade Assn, 6th Floor Dorland Hse, 18–20 Lower Regent St, SW1Y 4PW. Telephone 01-930 2524. Telex 8954430.

AUSTRIA
Austrian Commercial Delegate in Great Britain, 1 Hyde Park Gate, SW7 5ER. Telephone 01-584-6218. Telex 25668.

BELGIUM
Belgo-Luxembourg Chamber of Commerce in Great Britain (Inc), 36–37 Piccadilly, W1V 0PL. Telephone 01-434 1815. Telex 8953411.

BRAZIL
Brazilian Chamber of Commerce in Great Britain, 35 Dover St, W1X 3RA. Telephone 01-499 0186.

CANADA
Canada-United Kingdom Chamber of Commerce, 3 Regent St, SW1Y 4NZ. Telephone 01-930 2794.

CHINA
Sino-British Trade Council, 25, Queen Anne's Gate, SW1H 9BU. Telephone 01-222 8785.

COMMONWEALTH
Federation of Commonwealth Chambers of Commerce, 69 Cannon St, EC4N 5AB. Telephone 01-248 4444. Telex 888941.

FRANCE
French Chamber of Commerce in Great Britain, 54 Conduit St, W1R 9SD. Telephone 01-439 1735. Telex 269132.

EAST GERMANY, GDR
Chamber of Foreign Trade of the DDR, 124/128 Broadway, NW9 7BS. Telephone 01-202 3844. Telex 27337.

WEST GERMANY, GFR
German Chamber of Industry and Commerce, 12/13 Suffolk St, SW1Y 4HG. Telephone 01-930 7251.

HONG KONG
Hong Kong Trade Development Council, 14-16 Cockspur St, SW1Y 5DP. Telephone 01-930 7955. Telex 916923.

INDIA
Indian Chamber of Commerce in Great Britain, 7 Artillery Lane, E1 7LP. Telephone 01-247 8078.

INDONESIA
Indonesia Assn Inc, Cereal Hse, 58 Mark Lane, EC3 7RE. Telephone 01-480 5493.

ISRAEL
Anglo-Israel Chamber of Commerce, 126/134 Baker St, W1M 1SH. Telephone 01-487 5908.

ITALY
Italian Chamber of Commerce for Great Britain in London, Heathcoat Hse, 20 Savile
Row, W1X 2DQ. Telephone 01-734 2411. Telex 24870.

JAPAN
c/o Mitsubishi Corporation, Bow Bells Hse, Bread St, EC4M 9BQ. Telephone 01-
236 2060.

LUXEMBOURG
Belgo-Luxembourg Chamber of Commerce in Great Britain (Inc), 36–37 Piccadilly,
W1V 0PL. Telephone 01-434 1815. Telex 8953411.

NETHERLANDS
Netherlands-British Chamber of Commerce, Dutch Hse, 307/8 High Holborn, WC1V
7LS. Telephone 01-405 1358. Telex 23211.

NEW ZEALAND
New Zealand Chamber of Commerce, Dorland Hse, 18–20 Lower Regent St, SW1Y
4PW. Telephone 01-930 2524.

NORWAY
Norwegian Chamber of Commerce, London, Inc, Norway Hse, 21/24 Cockspur St,
SW1Y 5BN. Telephone 01-930 0181.

PORTUGAL
Portuguese Trade Dept, Portland Hse, Stag Pl, SW1E 5BH. Telephone 01-834 3903.
Telex 918089.

SPAIN
Spanish Chamber of Commerce, 5 Cavendish Sq, W1M 0DP. Telephone 01-637
9061. Telex 8811583.

SRI LANKA
Ceylon Assn in London, 133 Old Brompton Rd, SW7.

SWEDEN
Swedish Trade Commission, 73 Welbeck St, W1M 8AN. Telephone 01-935 9601.
Telex 22620.

USSR
British-Soviet Chamber of Commerce, 2 Lowndes St, SW1X 9ET. Telephone 01-235
2423.

USA
American Chamber of Commerce (UK) 75 Brook Street, W1Y 2EB. Telephone 01-
493 0381.

YUGOSLAVIA
Yugoslav Economic Chamber, Crown Hse, 143/147 Regent St, W1R 7LB. Telephone
01-734 2581. Telex 27552.

These are able to provide extensive data to UK business men on products,
industries and sometimes on particular firms.

Foreign embassies in London

AUSTRIA
18 Belgrave Mews West, London SW1X 8HU. Telephone 01-235 3731

AUSTRALIA
Australia House, Strand, London WC2B 4LA. Telephone 01-438 8000

BANGLADESH
28 Queen's Gate, London SW7 5JA. Telephone 01-584 0081.

BELGIUM
103 Eaton Square, London SW1W 9AB. Telephone 01-235 5422.

BRAZIL
32 Green Street, London W1Y 3FD. Telephone 01-499 0877.

BULGARIA
186/188 Queen's Gate, London SW7 5HL. Telephone 01-584 9400.

CANADA
Macdonald House, 1 Grosvenor Sq, London W1X 0AB. Telephone 01-629 9492.

CHILE
12 Devonshire Street, London W1N 1FS. Telephone 01-580 6392.

CZECHOSLOVAKIA
25 Kensington Palace Gardens, London W8 4QY. Telephone 01-229 1255.

DENMARK
55 Sloane Street, London SW1X 9SR. Telephone 01 235 1255.

EGYPT
26 South Street, London W1Y 5PJ. Telephone 01-499 2401.

ETHIOPIA
17 Prince's Gate, London SW7 1PT. Telephone 01-589 7212.

FINLAND
38 Chesham Place, London SW1X 8HW. Telephone 01-235 9531.

FRANCE
21–24 Grosvenor Place, London SW1X 7HU. Telephone 01-235 7080.

GERMANY, DR
34 Belgrave Square, London, SW1X 8PZ. Telephone 01-235 9941.

GERMANY, FR
23 Belgrave Square, London SW1X 8PZ. Telephone 01-235 5033.

GREECE
1A Holland Park, London W11 3TP. Telephone 01-727 8040.

HUNGARY
35 Eaton Place, London SW1. Telephone 01-235 4048.

INDIA
India House, Aldwych, London WC2B 4NA. Telephone 01-836 8484.

INDONESIA
38 Grosvenor Square, London W1X 9AD. Telephone 01-499 7661.

IRAN
27 Princes Gate, London SW7 5JG. Telephone 01-584 8101.

IRAQ
21 Queen's Gate, London SW7 5JG. Telephone 01-584 7141.

IRELAND, REP.
17 Grosvenor Place, London SW1X 7HR. Telephone 01-235 2171.

ISRAEL
2 Palace Green, London W8 4QB. Telephone 01-937 8050.

ITALY
14 Three Kings Yard, Davies St, London W1Y 2EX. Telephone 01-629 8200.

JAPAN
43–46 Grosvenor Street, London W1X 0BA. Telephone 01-493 6030

LUXEMBOURG
27 Wilton Crescent, London SW1X 8SD. Telephone 01-235 6961

NETHERLANDS
38 Hyde Park Gate, London SW7 5DP. Telephone 01 584 5040

NEW ZEALAND
New Zealand House, Haymarket, London SW1Y 4TQ. Telephone 01 930 8422.

NORWAY
25 Belgrave Square, London SW1X 8QD. Telephone 01–235 7151

PAKISTAN
35 Lowndes Square, London SW1X 9JN. Telephone 01-235 2044

POLAND
47 Portland Place, London W1N 3AG. Telephone 01-580 4324

PORTUGAL
11 Belgrave Square, London SW1X 8PP. Telephone 01-235 5331

SPAIN
24 Belgrave Square, London SW1X 8QA. Telephone 01-235 5555

SWEDEN
11 Montagu Place, London W1H 2AL. Telephone 01-724 2101

SWITZERLAND
16–18 Montagu Place, London W1H 2BQ. Telephone 01-723 0701

USA
24 Grosvenor Square, London W1A 1AE Telephone 01-499 9000

USSR
13 Kensington Palace Gardens, London W8 4QX Telephone 01-229 3628

YUGOSLAVIA
7 Lexham Gardens, London W8 5JU Telephone 01-370 6105

Whereas Chambers of Commerce can provide trade information and contacts, the UK business man should contact the embassy, or High Commission of the country concerned for information on visas, official regulations and government department contacts.

Major international organizations

ADB ASIAN DEVELOPMENT BANK
2330 Paseo de Roxas, POB 789, Pasay City, Philippines. Telephone 80 72 51

AfDB AFRICAN DEVELOPMENT BANK
BP 1387, Abidjan, Ivory Coast. Telephone 32 07 11. Telex 717 498

THE ARAB LEAGUE
Midan Al Tahrir, Cairo, Egypt

ASEAN ASSOCIATION OF SOUTH EAST ASIAN NATIONS
Jalan Taman, Pejambon 6, Djakarta, Indonesia

BADEA ARAB BANK FOR ECONOMIC DEVELOPMENT IN AFRICA
Sharaa el Baladia, POB 2640, Khartoum, Sudan

BIS BANK FOR INTERNATIONAL SETTLEMENTS
7 Centralbahnstrasse, CP 262, CH 4002 Basel, Switzerland. Telephone 23 30 33
Telex 62487

CENTO CENTRAL TREATY ORGANISATION
Secretariat: Eski Büjük Millet Meclisi Binasi, Ankara, Turkey

CMEA (COMECON) COUNCIL FOR MUTUAL ECONOMIC ASSISTANCE
Prospekt Kalinina 56, Moscow, USSR. Telephone 290 91 11. Telex 141

THE COLOMBO PLAN
12 Melbourne Ave, POB 596, Colombo 4, Sri Lanka. Telephone 81813

THE COMMONWEALTH
Marlborough Hse, Pall Mall, London SW1Y 5HX, England. Telephone 01-839 3411

THE COUNCIL OF EUROPE
Ave de l'Europe, F-67006 Strasbourg CEDEX, France. Telephone (88) 61 49 61
Telex 870943

ECOWAS ECONOMIC COMMUNITY OF WEST AFRICAN STATES
6 King George V Rd, Lagos, Nigeria

EFTA EUROPEAN FREE TRADE ASSOCIATION
9–11 rue de Varembé, CH-1211 Geneva 20, Switzerland. Telephone 34 90 00. Telex
22660

IBEC INTERNATIONAL BANK FOR ECONOMIC CO-OPERATION
15 Kuznetskiy Most, 103031, Moscow K-31, USSR. Telephone 295 16 88

IBRD INTERNATIONAL BANK FOR RECONSTRUCTION
AND DEVELOPMENT
1818 H St, NW, Washington, DC 20433, USA. Telephone (202) 477 1234

ICA INTERNATIONAL CO-OPERATIVE ALLIANCE
11 Upper Grosvenor St, London W1X 9PA, England. Telephone 01-499 5991

ICC INTERNATIONAL CHAMBER OF COMMERCE
38 Cours Albert 1er, 75008 Paris, France. Telephone 359 05 92. Telex 650770

ICFTU INTERNATIONAL CONFEDERATION OF FREE TRADE UNIONS
37–41 rue Montagne aux Herbes Potagères, B–1000 Brussels, Belgium. Telephone
217 80 85. Telex 26785

IDA INTERNATIONAL DEVELOPMENT ASSOCIATION
1818 H St, NW, Washington, DC 20433, USA. Telephone (202) 477 1234

IDB INTER-AMERICAN DEVELOPMENT BANK
808 17th St, NW, Washington DC 20577, USA. Telephone 393 4171

IEA INTERNATIONAL ENERGY AGENCY
2 rue André-Pascal, 75775, Paris Cedex 16, France

IFAD INTERNATIONAL FUND FOR AGRICULTURAL DEVELOPMENT
Prov. Hqtrs: Via del Serafico 107, EUR, Rome, Italy

IFC INTERNATIONAL FINANCE CORPORATION
1818 H St, NW, Washington, DC 20433, USA Telephone (202) 477 1234

ILO INTERNATIONAL LABOUR ORGANIZATION
4 Route des Morillons, 1211 Geneva 22, Switzerland. Telephone 99 61 11

IMF INTERNATIONAL MONETARY FUND
19th and H Sts, NW, Washington, DC 20431, USA. Telephone (202) 393 6362

IOC INTERNATIONAL OLYMPIC COMMITTEE
Château de Vidy, CH–1007 Lausanne, Switzerland. Telephone 25 32 71. Telex
24024

LAFTA LATIN AMERICAN FREE TRADE ASSOCIATION
Cebollati 1461, Casilla de Correo 577, Montevideo, Uruguay. Telephone 40 11 21

NATO NORTH ATLANTIC TREATY ORGANISATION
B-1110 Brussels, Belgium. Telephone 241 00 40. Telex 23-867

OAPEC ORGANISATION OF ARAB PETROLEUM
EXPORTING COUNTRIES
POB 20501, Kuwait City, Kuwait. Telephone 44 8200 Telex 2166

OAS ORGANISATION OF AMERICAN STATES
Pan Amercian Union Bldg, 17th St and Constitution Ave, NW, Washington DC
20006, USA. Telephone 331 1010

OAU ORGANISATION OF AFRICAN UNITY
POB 3243, Addis Abab, Ethiopia. Telephone 157700. Telex 21046

OECD ORGANISATION FOR ECONOMIC CO-OPERATION
AND DEVELOPMENT
2 rue André-Pascal, F-75775 Paris Cedex 16, France. Telephone 524 82 00. Telex
620160

OIC ORGANISATION OF THE ISLAMIC CONFERENCE
Kilo 6, Mecca Rd, POB 178, Jeddah, Saudi Arabia. Telephone 23880

OPEC ORGANISATION OF THE PETROLEUM EXPORTING COUNTRIES
Obere-Donaustrasse 93, A-1020 Vienna, Austria. Telephone 26 55 11. Telex 7-4474

THE WARSAW PACT
Hdqtrs of the Joint Command: Moscow, USSR

UNCTAD UNITED NATIONS CONFERENCE ON TRADE
AND DEVELOPMENT
Palais des Nations, 1211 Geneva 10, Switzerland. Telephone 34 60 11

EUROPEAN COMMUNITIES COMMISSION

Situated at the EEC Headquarters
200 Rue de la Loi, B-1049 Brussels. Telephone 735 00 40

Secretariat General
Legal Service
Customs Union Service
Environment and Consumer Protection Service
Joint Research Centre
Euratom Supply Agency
Security Office
Special Assignments Office

EUROPEAN ATOMIC ENERGY COMMISSION
200 Rue de la Loi, B-1049 Brussels, Belgium. Telephone 735 80 40

EUROPEAN COAL AND STEEL COMMUNITY
200 Rue de la Loi, B-1040 Brussels, Belgium. Telephone 735 00 40

EUROPEAN ECONOMIC COMMUNITY
200 Rue de la Loi, B-1049 Brussels, Belgium. Telephone 735 00 40. Telex 21877
COMEU B

EUROPEAN PARLIAMENT
Centre Européen, Kirchberg, POB 1601, Luxembourg. Telephone 477 11. Telex 494
PARLEURO 1

EUROPEAN COURT OF JUSTICE
Centre Européen, Plateau de Kirchberg, POB 1406, Luxembourg. Telephone 476
21. Telex CURIALUX 510

EUROPEAN COUNCIL OF MINISTERS
170 Rue de la Loi, B-1049 Brussels, Belgium. Telephone 736 79 00

EUROPEAN INVESTMENT BANK
Place de Metz 2, BP 2005 Luxembourg. Telephone 43 50 11. Telex 3530
BANKEULU

Foreign travel data

Time zone differences, distances between capitals, miles and kilometres,
Bucharest or Budapest? how much currency to the £– these types of problem
beset the credit man setting out to negotiate face to face. The following data
may help.

The DTI's 'Hints to Businessmen' booklets for each country of the world
provide a great deal of information for the business traveller.

PUBLIC HOLIDAYS

Most countries are closed for business on more days than the UK, and
in strongly Catholic countries small businesses and partnerships also close
for various Saints' days. Please check proposed visit dates *before* expense is
incurred.

FLYING DISTANCES

The chart in Figure 12.3 shows the distances between principal airports,
although there may not be direct flights in all cases. To estimate flying times,
divide distances by an assumed average speed of 550 mph.

TIME-ZONES

The world is divided into 24 time-zones, each representing one hour. Dividing
24 into 360° means that each one-hour zone is 15° longitude. As the sun
rises in the east and travels west, world time follows it. With London fixed
at Greenwich Mean Time (GMT), countries to the east of London are ahead
of GMT and those to the west are behind it.

Approximate time calculations can be made from this system using map
longitudes but some countries, e.g. China, apply the same time across all their
time-zones while other countries have their own daylight saving systems, e.g
British Summer (GMT + 1) and DST in the USA (local time + 1). Figure
12.1 shows the time-zones on a world map.

Credit Managers planning to telephone abroad and unable to work from
time-zones may find the list useful in Figure 12.2 showing times in foreign
cities when noon (GMT) in UK.

Figure 12.1   Time Zones on a World Map

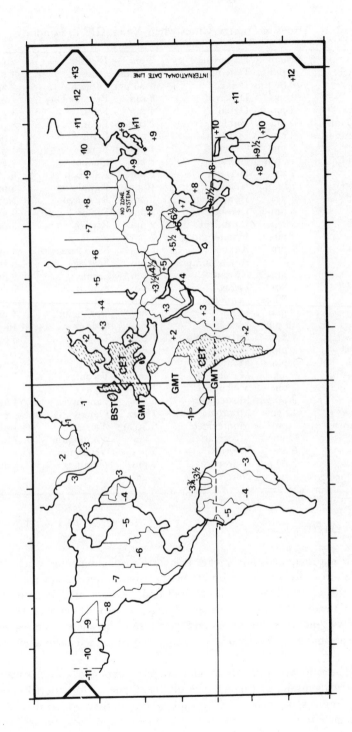

Getting Paid for Exports

Figure 12.2   Times in Foreign Cities when Noon (GMT) London

Accra	Noon	Damascus	2 pm	Nicosia	2 pm
Abu Dhabi	4 pm	Darwin	9.30 pm	Oslo	1 pm
Adelaide	9.30 pm	Delhi	5.30 pm	Ottawa	7 am
Algiers	1 pm	Djakarta	8 pm	Panama City	7 am
Amman	2 pm	Dubai	4 pm	Paris	1 pm
Amsterdam	1 pm	Dublin	Noon	Peking	8 pm
Ankara	2 pm	Frankfurt	1 pm	Perth	8 pm
Athens	2 pm	Geneva	1 pm	Prague	1 pm
Auckland	12 pm	Gibraltar	1 pm	Quebec	7 am
Athens	2 pm	Helsinki	2 pm	Rangoon	6.30 pm
Auckland	12 pm	Hobart	10 pm	Rawalpindi	5 pm
Baghdad	3 pm	Hong Kong	8 pm	Reykjavik	Noon
Bahrain	3 pm	Istanbul	2 pm	Rio de Janeiro	9 am
Bangkok	7 pm	Jerusalem	2 pm	Riyadh	3 pm
Beirut	2 pm	Johannesburg	2 pm	Rome	1 pm
Belgrade	1 pm	Karachi	5 pm	San Francisco	4 am
Berlin	1 pm	Kuala Lumpur	8 pm	Santiago	8 am
Berne	1 pm	Kuwait	3 pm	Seoul	9 pm
Bogota	8 am	Lagos	1 pm	Singapore	7.30 pm
Bombay	5.30 pm	Leningrad	3 pm	Sofia	2 pm
Bonn	1 pm	Lima	7 am	Stockholm	1 pm
Brisbane	10 pm	Lisbon	1 pm	Sydney	10 pm
Brussels	1 pm	Luxembourg	1 pm	Taipei	8 pm
Bucharest	1 pm	Madras	5.30 pm	Tehran	3.30 pm
Budapest	1 pm	Madrid	1 pm	Tokyo	9 pm
Buenos Aires	9 am	Manila	8 pm	Toronto	7 am
Cairo	2 pm	Melbourne	10 pm	Tunis	1 pm
Calcutta	5.30 pm	Mexico City	6 am	Vancouver	4 am
Canberra	10 pm	Monrovia	11 am	Vienna	1 pm
Cape Town	2 pm	Montevideo	8.30 am	Warsaw	1 pm
Caracas	8 am	Montreal	7 am	Washington	7 am
Chicago	6 am	Moscow	3 pm	Wellington	12 pm
Colombo	5.30 pm	Nairobi	3 pm	Winnipeg	6 am
Copenhagen	1 pm	New York	7 am		

JET-LAG EFFECT

Jet-lag is not imagined, nor a joke. It is a travel phenomenon which doctors recognize as a disease which upsets bodily rhythm and causes the brain to be less efficient than usual. The human body has got used to doing things within a steady 24-hour time-cycle. Flying east to west, or vice versa, the body crosses different time-zones and, as a result, digestion, sleep, excretion, heart-beats and so on take varying times to return to their normal patterns.

There are no pre-medications and no post-cures available, so travellers should try to minimize time-change effects. Some multi-national company 'kings' simply stay on head office time wherever they go, so that all their minions have to eat, sleep and meet at odd local hours. Some more ordinary

Figure 12.3 Distances between Principal Airports

Intercontinental distances

	Auckland	Bahrain	Bangkok	Bombay	Hong Kong	London	Moscow	New York	Paris	Rome	Singapore	Sydney	Tehran	Tokyo
Amsterdam	12225	3126	6058	4606	7102	209	1399	3639	261	809	6955	10882	2880	7935
Auckland		9113	5950	7629	5682	11404	11268	8828	14452	11443	5226	1341	9331	5472
Bahrain			3331	1500	3970	3162	2155	6596	3001	2418	3927	7770	652	5141
Bangkok				1869	1064	5929	4392	8644	7810	5494	896	4684	3392	2846
Bombay					2670	4478	3136	7781	4353	3847	2430	6308	1741	4182
Hong Kong						5989	4441	8050	8493	5777	1605	4582	3843	1786
London							1557	3440	227	896	6754	10568	2741	5955
Moscow								4646	1533	1490	5242	9925	1545	4653
New York									3628	4263	9525	9944	6113	6754
Paris										688	6752	10667	2610	6200
Rome											6238	10147	2129	6143
Singapore												3912	4110	3294
Sydney													8021	4854
Tehran														4770

European distances

	Athens	Berlin	Brussels	Copenhagen	Frankfurt	Glasgow	Lisbon	London	Madrid	Manchester	Moscow	Paris	Rome	Stockholm	Vienna
Amsterdam	1350	364	98	393	228	444	1149	231	909	304	1399	261	809	710	595
Athens		1240	1300	1331	1122	1795	1772	1500	1467	1634	1429	1304	657	1555	793
Berlin			398	220	270	888	1434	591	1154	668	992	544	750	516	333
Brussels				469	191	542	1068	217	818	332	1384	170	734	802	574
Copenhagen					422	668	1537	608	1281	618	957	637	955	332	545
Frankfurt						672	1165	406	884	517	1255	289	595	754	385
Glasgow							1315	349	1114	185	1625	558	1241	1000	1039
Lisbon								971	319	1130	2418	902	1152	1865	1351
London									774	164	1557	215	907	898	790
Madrid										929	2121	649	836	1612	932
Manchester											1575	372	1056	950	899
Moscow												1533	1476	760	1026
Paris													688	963	649
Rome														1266	482
Stockholm															848

UK business men try the trick of keeping their watch set to London time and arrange meetings to allow eating and sleeping at their usual UK times, however odd they may seem locally.

Other ways of reducing jet-lag effects are to:

- Keep calm before and during the flight – avoid delays and panics.
- Fly in daytime, to manage sleep at normal UK times.
- On a very long flight, or series of long flights, try to adjust to the local sleeping times by sleeping in-flight at prearranged times.
- Reduce smoking and drinking alcohol in-flight (alcohol plus jet-lag induces an extra hangover effect).
- Drink more soft, non-fizzy drinks to combat dehydration in-flight.

If possible, avoid major meetings or contract signings for at least one day after arrival, preferably having a de-lagging weekend locally before the important work begins.

Figure 12.4 gives the ICAO formual to calculate how long jet-lag will last.

Figure 12.4　　A Formula for Jet-Lag

ICAO calculate the number of days of rest needed to overcome jet-lag as:

$$\frac{T/2 + (Z\text{-}4) + C_d + C_a}{10}$$

T = hours in transit
Z = number of time zones crossed
C_d and C_a are the departure and arrival coefficients listed in the table below.

Time of day		Departure coefficient	Arrival coefficient
0800	1159	0 = good	4 = bad
1200	1759	1 = fair	2 = fair
1800	2159	3 = poor	0 = good
2200	0059	4 = bad	1 = fair
0100	0759	3 = poor	3 = poor

EXAMPLE
A traveller leaves Montreal at 1800 hours local time (C_d = 3), spends nine hours travelling, and arrives in Paris at 0800 hours (C_a = 4) having crossed five times zones. The number of day's rest he needs is:

$$\frac{9/2 + 1 + 3 + 4}{10} = 1.25 \text{ days}$$

Rounded up to the nearest half-day = 1.5 days.

COUNTRY INFORMATION

Figure 12.5 tables 40 frequently visited countries, giving their key data.

Figure 12.5   Key Data on 40 frequently Visited Countries

Country	Population (millions	Capital	Area (square miles)	Language
Australia	13.64	Canberra	2 967 909	English
Austria	7.51	Vienna	32 366	German
Belgium	9.89	Brussels	11 800	French in S, Flemish
Brazil	109.18	Brasilia	3 286 000	Portuguese
Bulgaria	8.76	Sofia	43 796	Bulgarian
Canada	23.14	Ottawa	3 560 238	Eng/French
Czechoslovakia	14.91	Prague	49 000	Czech/Slovak
Denmark	5.07	Copenhagen	16 629	Danish
Eire	3.16	Dublin	26 599	Eng/Irish
Finland	4.73	Helsinki	130 100	Finnish/Swedish
France	52.92	Paris	212 729	French
East Germany (GDR)	16.79	Berlin (East)	41 768	German
West Germany (GFR)	61.50	Bonn	95 975	German
Greece	9.17	Athens	50 930	Greek
Hong Kong	4.38	Victoria	404	Eng/Chinese
Hungary	10.60	Budapest	36 000	Hungarian
Iran	33.40	Teheran	634 000	Persian/Farsi
Iraq	11.12	Baghdad	167 925	Arabic
Israel	3.47	Jerusalem	7 993	Hebrew
Italy	56.19	Rome	116 237	Italian
Japan	112.77	Tokyo	143 000	Japanese
Luxembourg	0.36	Luxembourg City	999	French/German
Netherlands	13.71	Amsterdam	15 892	Dutch
New Zealand	3.14	Wellington	103 735	English
Nigeria	64.75	Lagos	356 669	English/Ibo/Yoruba
Norway	4.03	Oslo	125 053	Norwegian
Poland	34.36	Warsaw	120 700	Polish
Portugal	9.45	Lisbon	34 700	Portuguese
Romania	21.45	Bucharest	91 671	Romanian
Saudi Arabia	9.24	Riyadh	927 000	Arabic
South Africa	26.13	Pretoria	471 445	Afrikaans
Spain	35.97	Madrid	194 833	Spanish
Sweden	8.22	Stockholm	173 603	Swedish
Switzerland	6.35	Berne	15 937	Ger/French/Italian
Turkey	34.37	Ankara	301,380	Turkish
United Arab Emirates	0.66	Abu Dhabi Town	12 355	Arabic
UK	54.97	London	94 222	English
USA	215.12	Washington DC	3 614 254	English
USSR	256.67	Moscow	8 650 000	Russian
Yugoslavia	21.56	Belgrade	98 766	Serbo-Croat

Economic aid groups

Exporters come across many names or initials of official organizations representing groups of nations and financial institutions. These bodies influence export business, in terms of project finance, restrictions or preference on imports, or in some way the planning of foreign governments.

The responsibilities and activities of some of these are examined here:

STERLING AREA (OR SCHEDULED TERRITORIES)

This now consists of only the UK, Channel Islands, Isle of Man, and Gibraltar.

FRENCH MONETARY AREA (FRANC ZONE)

Several countries continue to link their currency to the French Franc which remains their reserve currency. The member countries are: Benin, Cameroon, Central African Empire, Chad, Comoros, Congo People's Republic, Gabon, Ivory Coast, Mali, Niger, Senegal, Togo, Upper Volta. The French Franc itself is used in Metropolitan France, the Overseas Departments of Guadeloupe, French Guinea, Martinique, Reunion, the Overseas Territory of St Pierre and Miquelon and Mayotte.

INTERNATIONAL MONETARY FUND (IMF)

This was created in 1945 as a result of the 1944 Bretton Woods Conference. It exists to encourage monetary cooperation and currency stability and to assist in removing exchange restrictions. It also attempts to boost world trade in order to maintain high levels of employment and to develop the resources of its member nations. The IMF has been active in recent years in actually providing millions of dollars to poor nations to find their imports, backed by teams of experts who impose financial disciplines in an attempt to solve the poor nations' underlying defects.

INTERNATIONAL BANK FOR RECONSTRUCTION AND DEVELOPMENT (IBRD)

A year after the IMF, the IBRD was also begun as a result of the Bretton Woods Conference. Its funds come from subscriptions from member countries who are also members of the IMF. The purpose of the IBRD is to provide long-term (up to 25 years) finance to nations to increase production and raise living standards, raising the money by the issue of its own bonds. As well as loans, the IBRD finances resource surveys and feasibility studies prior to development proposals.

GENERAL AGREEMENT ON TARIFFS AND TRADE (GATT)

Over 150 nations conducting over 80% of world trade have contracted to this multilateral agreement, which began in 1948. It provides a common code for international trade conduct, regular consultation on trade problems between nations and the facilities for negotiating reductions or tariffs and trade barriers.

ORGANIZATION FOR ECONOMIC COOPERATION AND DEVELOPMENT (OECD)

Twenty-four nations comprise this body which succeeded the Marshall Plan in 1960 to promote policies to achieve the highest sustainable economic growth, employment and standard of living in member countries, compatible with financial stability. Also, it sets out to coordinate bilateral and to the third world and to expand world trade on a non-discriminatory basis.

EUROPEAN ECONOMIC COMMUNITY (EEC) - THE COMMON MARKET

Formed by the Treaty of Rome, 1957, and began in 1958, with the aims of: a customs union and a common external tariff (now a fact), a full economic union, free movement of labour and capital, harmonized economic and social policies, common policies for agriculture, transport, competition, energy and foreign trade.

The original *six* were: France, W. Germany, Italy, and the three Benelux countries (Belgium, Netherlands and Luxembourg). In 1973, the six became nine when Denmark, UK and Eire joined. Then in the 1980s, Spain and Portugal came along, and Greece made it *twelve*.

The EEC nations are linked in several other specific ways, with the European Parliament's members now becoming more influential and the Court of Justice's judges pronouncing on major national issues. The Council of Ministers and the executive EEC Commission are both headquartered in Brussels and in addition to masterminding the EEC, also direct the activities of the ESCS (The European Coal and Steel Community) and Euratom (The European Atomic Energy Community).

The nations of Turkey, Faroes, Rumania and Yugoslavia have associated membership of the EEC, providing full customs union. There are Association Agreements on specific trade matters between EEC and Algeria, Cyprus, Egypt, Israel, Jordan, Lebanon, Malta, Morocco, Syria and Tunisia, as well as the Lomé Convention of 58 nations and with other developing countries.

EUROPEAN FREE TRADE AREA (EFTA)

Following the EEC formation in 1958, seven major nations, who did not relish the thought of its political union, signed the Stockholm Convention in 1960 to form EFTA. Its purpose is to remove trade tariffs between members and to encourage freer world trade.

The members are now: Austria, Iceland, Norway, Sweden and Switzerland. The original seven included Portugal, Denmark and UK who left to join the EEC and Iceland came into the group. Finland has a very close associate status.

The detailed removal of tariffs were achieved much earlier than planned. Reduced duties on exports between members requires a certificate of origin and there is no EEC-like common external tariff.

EFTA is governed by a Council of Representatives in Geneva, with a Secretariat and specialist working parties and committees.

There is considerable attraction to the EFTA approach to free trade without political union. Many Europe watchers believe EFTA will grow in size in the near future.

COUNCIL FOR MUTUAL ECONOMIC ASSISTANCE (CMEA) - COMECON

The Comecon system was begun in 1949 in Moscow to coordinate the trade and economic policies of member countries and to provide 'mutual aid' and technical assistance. The Comecon members are: USSR, Bulgaria, Cuba, Czechoslovakia, East Germany, Hungary, Mongolia, Poland and Rumania. Observer status is allowed to: Angola, Laos, North Korea, Vietnam and Yugoslavia.

LATIN AMERICAN FREE TRADE ASSOCIATION (LAFTA)

Began in 1960 with headquarters in Montevideo, Uruguay, with the object of removing trade restrictions and tariffs between members plus harmonization of external trade and coordination of assistance and development within its area, all by this year. Members are: Argentina, Brazil, Chile, Colombia, Ecuador, Mexico, Paraquay, Peru, Uruguay and Venezula.

The Andean Group is a sub-division of LAFTA with its own timed programme. Its members are: Bolivia, Chile, Colombia, Ecuador and Peru.

CARIBBEAN COMMUNITY (CARICOM)

This was formed in 1973 to achieve economic cooperation, common essential services and coordination of foreign policies. Members are: Antigua, Barbados, Belize, Dominica, Grenada, Guyana, Jamaica, Montserrat, St Kitts/Nevis, St Lucia, St Vincent, Trinidad and Tobago.

Useful publications

It is easy to suffer a surplus of information, by storing books and magazines 'just in case'. After taking care of special industry or product requirements, the export credit manager will probably find the following sufficient to have at his elbow:

- Daily, the 'Financial Times'.
- Weekly, the 'Economist'.
- Weekly, 'British Business' (DTI).
- 'Croner's Reference Book for Exporters'.
- 'ECGD Services'.
- Various bank reviews.
- "International Risk and Payment Review" – Dun and Bradstreet.

The 'Financial Times' carries commercial world news, analyses of countries, masses of information on currencies and interest rates, and is a most pleasurable daily way of keeping in step with the world of export.

The 'Economist' has a good balance of political, economic and financial news stories and statistics and provides substantial background for foreign risk assessment.

'British Business' covers domestic matters as well as foreign, and a recent volume selected at random included the following items of interest to the export credit manager:

- Short summary of key business news items, e.g.
  end of exchange controls
  export shipbuilding loan scheme.

- Economic indicators at a glance, e.g.
    GDP, price indices, company liquidities, exchange rates.
- Review of new publications.
- Technology news and new products.
- EEC news, e.g.
    sales to Japan, new legislation.
- Overseas trade news, e.g.
    embassies being closed, ECGD loan to Nigeria, conference on Egypt, register of companies collaborating to sell to third world, white paper on GATT, some SITPRO experiences, export training.
- Market reports, e.g.
    Israel, Arab boycott, Mexico, Venezuela.
- Export services, e.g.
    telephoning Tanzania and Morocco.
- Country data, e.g.
    situation in Sudan import bans in Peru.
- Official Statistics (considerable data and analysis).

'Croner's Reference Book for Exporters' is published by Croner Publications Limited, 46–50 Coombe Road, New Malden, Surrey, KT3 4QL. Telephone: 01-942 9615. It is loose-leaf in a ring-binder, with monthly amendments, and is divided into two sections, Information and Countries.

INFORMATION SECTION

- Export Terms, explanation of abbreviations and terms.
- BOTB, a clear description of its services.
- Export Controls, Prohibition List, Customs Procedures.
- Export Finance, explanation of payment terms and methods.
- EGD, description of insurance facilities.
- Marine Insurance, Postal Information, Certificates of Origin, Bills of Lading, Special Invoice Forms, Carnets, etc.

COUNTRY SECTION

Separate pages for every country, in alphabetical order, showing:

- Political description, capital, population, language, etc.
- Currency units and exchange rate to the £.
- Direct Dialling Codes and Time Differences.
- Public Holidays.
- Embassy and Chamber of Commerce abroad.

- Import restrictions and exchange controls.
- Bills of Lading, Consular Invoices, Certificates of Origin, Commercial Invoices, EEC or other forms needed.
- Consular fees, Duties imposed.
- Special certificates, e.g. for food, livestock, etc.
- Marking of goods and samples.
- Packing material regulations.
- Shipping, Air Freight and Postal arrangements.
- Banks (principal only).
- UK regulations, e.g. export licences, re-exports, etc.

At the end is a list of principal ports and airports in alphabetical order, referenced to their countries.

'International Risk and Payment Review' is published by Dun and Bradstreet International in London and has the effect of telling the exporter what others are doing about payment terms, transfer delays and other risk factors which affect selling and getting paid. It is a monthly production on an annual subscription. Some 105 countries are included, classified alphabetically within world regions, and for each there are three columns of data – Usual Payment Terms; Transfer Situation; and Risk Factors.

Other Recommended Books and Publications:

Cash By Express	SITPRO
Credit Management Handbook	Gower Publishing
International Credit Management Handbook	Gower Publishing
Credit Insurance	Woodhead Faulkner
Documentry Credits	Woodhead Faulkner
The Countertrade Handbook	Woodhead Faulkner
Credit Management	Business Books
Finance of International Trade	Institute of Bankers
The Export Trade	Stevens & Sons
Hints to Businessmen	BOTB
Guide to Incoterms	ICC
Systematic Export Documentation	SITPRO
Credit Management (Journal)	Institute of Credit Management
Services for Exporters	Midland Bank
UCP 400	ICC
URC 322	ICC
Trade Finance Review	Export Times
Countertrade	DTI
Euromoney Trade Finance Report	Euromoney Publications
Exporters Bulletin	NatWest Bank

Guide to export terms and information

(The Institute of Credit Management have kindly agreed to the publication below of their guide to export credit procedures.)

Guidelines for sales/marketing and credit department

The aim must always be to set the shortest payment terms commercially possible, because:

(i)   Time costs money and extended credit reduces profit margins.
(ii)   The longer the period of credit, the great the risk of non-payment.
(iii)   A short credit period facilitates a greater volume of business within a credit limit.

To achieve the required volume of export sales, it is necessary sometimes to agree extended credit, depending on the demands of the market and the policy of the competition. 'Extended Credit' is here defined as up to 180 days.

The job of the Credit Department is firstly to assess the risk and secondly to recommend payment terms which enable sales to be made without excessive risk or cost.

Terms of payment available

There is a choice between two basic types:

(i)   Documentary, where there are doubts about creditworthiness.
(ii)   Open Account, where the customer is fully trusted.

Documentary terms mean using a Bill of Exchange, payable at sight or at a future date such as 30, 60 or 90 days from date of Bill of Lading.

The document of title, the Bill of Lading, which enables the buyer to take possession of the goods, is sent through the banking system with the Bill of Exchange and only released to the buyer against payment (Sight Draft) or acceptance (Time Draft).

A documentary bill gives semi-security in that the release of the goods is controlled. Security can be improved by obtaining a Letter of Credit, preferably confirmed by a UK bank.

Open Account means sending the Bill of Lading direct to the customer with the goods (or by airmail) and trusting him to pay on the agreed date. In some markets it is the practice to cover open account payment by a Bill, known as a clean Bill, to distinguish it from a Documentary Bill. Use of open account terms is normally restricted to buyers of high standing.

Which terms to use

Apart from assessing ordinary 'commercial' risk, i.e. how much credit can be justified on the known facts, the choice of payment terms may be dictated by outside forces such as:

(i)   Transfer Risk, where there is the prospect of long delays because the buyer's country is short of Sterling as in Brazil in 1982.
(ii)   Political Risk, where there is the possibility of commerce between the UK and the buyer's country being interrupted by war, revolution, etc. as in Argentina in 1982.

Where these risks exist to a serious degree, business should only be undertaken on an Irrevocable Letter of Credit confirmed by UK bank. (The term 'UK bank' includes foreign banks in the UK whose standing is undoubted.) An ECGD policy would enable business to be conducted on less secure terms, subject to special conditions imposed by ECGD.

The choice of terms may also be affected by:

(i)   Special regulations in the buyer's country,
        e.g. importers wishing to buy on L/C terms must deposit 200% of the FOB value with the Central Bank.
(ii)   Policy of the competition.
(iii)   Normal commercial practice in the buyer's country, e.g. German buyers may expect a cash discount.

To summarize, payment terms may be affected by a combination of the following:

- Transfer Risk.
- Political Risk.
- Government Regulations in the buyer's country.
- Competitor's activity.
- Local market practice.

Sources of information

(i) Bank Reports
Generally more helpful than domestic UK bank reports, especially from US banks.
(ii) Credit Agency Reports
There are several first class agencies available.
(iii) Agents
A basic part of an agent's job should be to provide information, especially on new buyers.
(iv) Embassies, Consulates, etc.
These are more useful in markets outside Europe.
(v) Credit Contacts
A valuable source of contact is FCIB, an organization concerned with export credit and finance, based in Brussels.

Credit agencies

Different agents should be used for different markets, according to the quality, speed and cost.

Principal features to look for in a credit report are:

(i) A very recent date of search and/or updating.
(ii) A summary of the financial structure of the company, plus an extract from the latest Accounts.
(iii) A brief résumé of the company's operations and current reputation.
(iv) Details of associations, through shareholdings of owners/directors, with other companies.
(v) The company's payment reputation and the level of credit normally given by suppliers.
(vi) Details of any charges, liens or debentures (affecting assets available.
(vii) Name and address of Bankers.

The disclosure of financial information varies considerably from market to market and also depending on the legal form of the company.

Whilst many UK agencies offer a world wide reporting service, it is worthwhile checking on the cost and availability of local agencies, particularly in France and Germany.

A suggested system for new accounts and order referral

(i)   A list of current export buyers should be maintained, containing information such as:

● Customers who have been invoiced during the last two years, other buyers being deleted from the Master File.
● Customers listed under the heading of the importing country.
● Where there is more than one delivery address within the same country, only the invoice address is shown.
● UK buying agents listed with a cross-reference to ultimate destinations.
● A separate order-referral list. All orders for customers on this list to be referred to Credit Department.

(ii)   The following controls must be observed:

● No orders accepted from unlisted buyers.
● Credit approval sought for unlisted buyers as early as possible – preferably at the enquiry stage.
● Orders from 'referral' customers referred to Credit Department for approval.
● Orders requesting different payment terms from those established referred to Credit Department.

Credit information should be regularly updated for large buyers plus reviews on any account where an increase in activity is identified.

Control procedures for letters of credit

Requested by Sales Offices from certain customers (as agreed with Credit Department) prior to order being placed on factory.

1st Check Point   –   Sales Office must ensure no order is placed until L/C arrives and is certified. If L/C is not confirmed by Uk bank, Credit Department must be told immediately to decide whether acceptable or to seek confirmation.

| 2nd Check Point | – | Sales Office must check the L/C very carefully per checklist. Copy of L/C sent to Credit Department who will also check for possible problems. |
| 3rd Check Point | – | Sales Office must check that shipping and other necessary documents are in complete conformity with the L/C before sending to Credit Department for presenting to bank. |

Letter of credit – points to note

(i)   To be of value a Letter of Credit must be IRREVOCABLE.

(ii)   A CONFIRMED Irrevocable Letter of Credit is preferable for the following reasons:

  (a)   Confirmation by a London bank removes any doubts about the originating or issuing bank. Confirmation is therefore unnecessary where the issuing bank is a branch of a reputable UK or US bank, advised through their London office.

  (b)   Confirmation removes the risks that for political or exchange reasons, funds cannot be transferred out of the importer's country.

(iii)   A customer may refuse to make an L/C Confirmed because of the cost. It is sometimes possible to obtain confirmation – after the L/C is issued and without involving the customer – at a nominal cost. All unconfirmed L/Cs must be referred to Credit Department immediately details are available (e.g. when customer cables advice of issue).

  There are a number of markets for which confirmation is unobtainable due to serious balance of trade or political problems.

(iv)   A Letter of Credit is of no value unless all its terms and specifications are complied with in every detail. Amendments can only be made on the instructions of the customer to the issuing bank.

(v)   A bank will only accept an indemnity if there is no possibility of the documents being amended. Indemnities should be avoided wherever possible since the bank's first obligation is to the issuing bank not the exporter.

3-stage checklist for letters of credit

(i)   Tell customers vital requirements before L/C is opened.

1   Allow sufficient time for possible production delays, e.g. request L/C to be valid one month beyond scheduled delivery date.

2   Ensure all particulars are complete and accurate.
3   State whether part-shipment and trans-shipment must be permitted.
4   For FOB contracts ask that payment be made against presentation of freight forwarder's receipt.
5   If goods are specially made to customer specifications, ask for the L/C to be opened and in your possession before you start manufacturing.

(ii)   Check on Receipt
1   Is the L/C IRREVOCABLE – it must be?
2   Is the L/C CONFIRMED BY A UK BANK or US BANK? It is infinitely preferable but not mandatory. Please contact Credit Department if it is not.
3   Is the name of the customer correct and spelled correctly?
4   Do validity, expiration and shipping dates give sufficient time to get documents together to assure payments? (Special attention to juxtaposition of these with shipping/airline schedules.)
5   Is the L/C amount enough to cover the quotation?

   (a)   Cost of goods plus profit.
   (b)   Inland transport to dock or airport, including wharfage and handling charges.
   (c)   Ocean/Airline transportation charges.
   (d)   Forwarding fees.
   (e)   Consular charges.
   (f)   Insurance costs.
   (g)   Miscellaneous charges.

6   Is description of goods correct? If errors are not amended the incorrect description must appear on ALL documents as well as correct description.
7   Is quantity of goods correct?
8   If required, is partial shipment permitted?
9   Is shipment required at a given rate or amount, if so, is this acceptable?
10   Is shipment permitted from any place in the United Kingdom or only from one named place?
11   Does named destination (Port of Discharge) in contract agree with L/C?
12   Export Licences required?
13   Is the Import Licence shown? (usually required on invoice).
14   Is L/C in a foreign currency? If so, please contact Credit Department.
15   Are guarantees of any sort required by buyer?
16   Can proper documents be obtained to conform with L/C (in the language of the buyer if required)?

Bill of Lading
Air Waybill

Parcel Post Receipt
Invoices – Commercial, Preferential, Consular, Legalized
Packing List
Certificate of Origin
Insurance Policy/Certificate
Certificate of Inspection
Certificate of Quality

17 Is any specified agency required to issue or authenticate any of these documents?
18 Can insurance risks required by L/C be covered? Does credit require policy or certificate?
19 Do the conditions of the contract of sale remain intact in view of the L/C?
20 Where is payment to be made? If not in the UK does the expiry date allow sufficient time for documents to be presented at the overseas bank?

If, after examining the L/C against this checklist and comparing the sales contract with the L/C, amendment or clarification of the L/C is needed, cable the customer requesting clarification or amendment, bearing in mind the risk of amendments not being received in time to honour shipping and validity dates.

(iii)   Check before claiming payment.
Because (a) documents are produced in different places, some of them outside the company, and (b) there is usually a last-minute rush to beat the L/C expiry, it is vital that a single person be responsible for assembling and checking the documents, prior to claiming payment from the advising or confirming bank.

The check follows most of the checks in stage (ii), but essentially checks that:

● Documents conform to the L/C specification.
● Documents conform with each other (shipping marks, etc.).
● Dates have been met.

Where there are discrepancies, the solutions are:

(a)   to correct documents in good time; or
(b)   where there is not enough time, or where documents cannot be changed (e.g. Airway Bill instead of Bill of Lading), telex the customer to instruct the bank to accept the discrepancies;
(c)   where there is not time for (b), offer the bank an indemnity so that payment is made under reserve.

Control procedures for bonds and guarantees

<table>
<tr><td colspan="1" align="center">Checklist: Bonds and Guarantees</td></tr>
</table>

Bonds and guarantees are required as payable 'on demand' or against evidence of non-performance. For the latter, it is normal to approach a Surety Company who only pay when default has been proved.

It is increasingly common for overseas buyers to require 'on demand' bonds which are provided by banks.

The following notes relate to bank bonds:

- There should be definite expiry dates both for liability and for submission of claims.
- There must be a specific maximum liability which should reduce pro-rata to contract performance.
- Since the bank cannot be asked to judge the performance of the seller, the conditions under which the bond may be called must be stated precisely and evidenced by specific documents.
- A form of guarantee frequently used by American banks is a 'Standby Letter of Credit' which guarantees immediate payment on production of specific documents. This offers more protection than an ordinary bank guarantee but the buyer has to be persuaded to accept it.
- Banks regard bonds as part of their customer's overall credit facilities. A bond will therefore absorb part of an overdraft facility.
- Protection against the 'unfair' calling of a bond can be obtained through a Lloyd's insurance policy (cost and availability depending on the market involved) or from ECGD provided the underlying contract is insured with ECGD.

1st Check Point – On receipt of an order requiring a bond or where this need is revealed during or prior to negotiations, credit approval must be obtained.

2nd Check Point – Credit Manager must be informed of full particulars to obtain availability, cost and risk exposure of a bond. He will recommend action and advise on all aspects.

3rd Check Point   –   Credit Manager must ensure that expiry performance dates are regularly checked against actual performance so that problems are foreseen in good time.

Foreign currency controls

(The purpose of quoting in foreign currency should be to obtain business, not to seek windfall exchange profits.)

(i)   If a decision is made to quote in currency, guidance on exchange rates must be obtained from the Credit Manager, as the use of currency can often affect the choice of payment terms. It is prudent to arrange currency and terms at the same time.

(ii)   When a currency order is received, details must be given to the Credit Manager so that forward contracts can be made to sell the expected receipts.

(iii)   When the forward contract is made, confirmation of the rate and Sterling proceeds is provided to the departments concerned.

Author's note:

The foregoing is a sample of the direct advice and encouragement given by the Institute of Credit Management to members and to companies engaged in the export trade. Readers are urged to ensure that their credit staff become professionally qualified via the examinations of the Institute.

Index